FEMINISM AND
THE FINAL FOUCAULT

FEMINISM AND THE
FINAL FOUCAULT

Edited by Dianna Taylor
and Karen Vintges

University of Illinois Press

Urbana and Chicago

♾ This book is printed on acid-free paper.

Library of Congress Cataloging-in-Publication Data
Feminism and the Final Foucault /
edited by Dianna Taylor and Karen Vintges.
p.   cm.
Includes bibliographical references and index.
ISBN 0-252-02927-5 (alk. paper)
ISBN 0-252-07182-4 (pbk. : alk. paper)
1. Feminist theory. 2. Foucault, Michel—Contributions in
feminist theory. 3. Feminist ethics. 4. Self. 5. Power (Social
sciences) 6. Postmodernism—Social aspects. I. Taylor, Dianna.
II. Vintges, Karen.
HQ1190.F4176   2004
305.42′01—dc22   2003023675

CONTENTS

Introduction: Engaging the Present   1
Dianna Taylor and Karen Vintges

Part 1:   Women's Self-practices as Ethos: Historical Perspectives

1.   The Shaping of a "Beautiful" Soul: The Critical Life of
     Anna Maria van Schurman   15
     Jeannette Bloem

2.   E.G.: Emma Goldman, for Example   28
     Kathy E. Ferguson

3.   Exit Woolf   41
     Stephen M. Barber

Part 2:   Feminism as Ethos

4.   Experience and Truth Telling in a Post-humanist World: A
     Foucauldian Contribution to Feminist Ethical Reflections   67
     Mariana Valverde

5.   An Ethics of the Self   91
     Helen O'Grady

6.   Inventing Images, Constructing Standpoints: Feminist Strategies
     of the Technology of the Self   118
     Sylvia Pritsch

7.   Practicing Practicing   143
     Ladelle McWhorter

8. Foucault's Pleasures: Desexualizing Queer Politics   163
   Jana Sawicki

9. Bodies and Power Revisited   183
   Judith Butler

Part 3: Feminist Ethos as Politics

10. Feminist Identity Politics: Transforming the Political   197
    Susan Hekman

11. Foucault and Feminism: Power, Resistance, Freedom   214
    Margaret A. McLaren

12. Foucault, Feminism, and the Self: The Politics of Personal
    Transformation   235
    Amy Allen

13. Foucault's Ethos: Guide(post) for Change   258
    Dianna Taylor

14. Endorsing Practices of Freedom: Feminism in a Global
    Perspective   275
    Karen Vintges

Contributors   301

Index   305

FEMINISM AND
THE FINAL FOUCAULT

INTRODUCTION: ENGAGING THE PRESENT

Dianna Taylor and Karen Vintges

> The fundamental moment is no longer the origin, and intelligibility's starting point is no longer the archaic element; it is, on the contrary, the present.
>
> —Michel Foucault

Reflecting upon the state of human existence in the wake of the political, moral, and metaphysical devastation wrought by totalitarian domination and the Second World War, Albert Camus writes, "Absurdism, like methodical doubt, has wiped the slate clean. It leaves us in a blind alley" (Camus 1991, 10). And Hannah Arendt observes that trying to make sense of and within a post-totalitarian world is like "trying to count without a notion of numbers," or "measure things without the use of a yardstick" (Arendt 1994, 313). For Camus and Arendt, the events of the war changed the face of the world so fundamentally that new ways of making sense were required not only to sort out what had happened but to go on living in the world at all. Traditional concepts, categories, and principles—modes of meaning-making—were considered unreliable and their uncritical application dangerous for two related reasons. First, totalitarianism was "unprecedented" and, as such, existing concepts could not grasp its "terrible newness." Second, traditional modes of meaning-making had been used in the service not of understanding but of domination and destruction. As Camus puts it, "slave camps" were erected "under the flag of freedom," and "massacres [were] justified by philanthropy" (1991, 4). Still, Arendt and Camus, like many other thinkers of their time, do not despair. From their perspectives, the apparent ruin of Western culture presented persons with a simultaneous opportunity and obligation: to develop new, emancipatory modes of existence through critical and creative engagement with and reflection upon their present, their reality.

The editors of this volume believe that the late work of Michel Foucault furthers and expands the efforts of thinkers such as Camus and Arendt to think and act critically, within a context of uncertainty and contingency, in ways that facilitate new, nonoppressive forms of commitment and responsibility. In other words, it is our common intuition that Foucault's late work realizes an opportunity and fulfills an obligation which, given the current state of the world, are no less compelling today than they were in 1945. As we see it, "the final Foucault" represents a voice that needs to be heard in our times: a post-postmodern voice that reconciles postmodernism's critique of universals with politics. The final Foucault fills the normative gap in postmodern thinking, but not, as some of his critics argue, by reasserting normativity as a necessary ground for ethics and politics (or, as other critics claim, by simply dispensing with the notion of norms altogether). Rather, by critically analyzing the function of norms and normativity and illustrating the potentially oppressive effects of their uncritical acceptance, Foucault facilitates their reconceptualization. Most relevant for us are the new formulations and enactments of commitment and responsibility that his work enables. Foucault's notion of "politics as ethics" emphasizes the practice of political commitment by way of a personal ethos. Personal and political identities, in other words, are conceived in terms of personal and political commitments. Approaching "ethics as politics" elucidates the need to rethink politics in the face of contingency. When politics is conceived in terms of ethos, political movements like feminism are seen as shared yet open practices or identities that critique reality and work on its limits without the aid of what Foucault himself refers to as "blueprints." Politics as ethics emphasizes commitment as a critique. From different sides of the Atlantic Ocean, we as editors accentuate different aspects of this complex thinking of the final Foucault: commitment without Truth (Vintges) and responsibility in the face of contingency (Taylor).

Foucault belongs to the generation of French intellectuals who experienced the Second World War and witnessed the deterioration of Soviet Communism into Stalinism. French existentialists responded to Nazism and the Second World War by unmasking humanist moral and political truths as fairy tales. For them, responsibility need not appeal to absolute truth or prefixed morality; rather, it pertains to everyday life and stems directly from our absolute freedom. French postmodern thinkers both radicalized Sartre's attack on humanism and went a step further by attacking the idea that humans are absolutely free. Doing so, they dispensed with any remaining essential foundation for meaning and sense, as well as with any remaining value, leaving merely the contingency of "floating signifiers." This radicalization was necessary in order to fulfill the "end of ideology" or, more specifically, the end of entrenched ideologies (not only socialism and communism but also liberalism) that made claims in the name of absolute truth. Postmodernism thus unmasked the interconnection of truth claims with pernicious and exclusionary relations of power.

Given that the catastrophes of the last century took place in the name of Truth, postmodernism rightly criticized that century's "grand narratives." But helpful as it was in making contingency more evident and present, postmodernism threatened to produce a kind of ethico-political vacuity. The final Foucault (who referred to himself as a modernist, not a postmodernist) responds to this threat by appealing once again to responsibility—but not to absolute freedom. For Foucault, responsibility stems from freedom that is discursively situated: it exists in discourses that offer tools and vocabularies that persons can utilize in creating themselves as responsible, ethical, and political—but always discursive—subjects. Foucault thus reintroduces ethical and political agency without falling back upon notions of human essence and Truth. He creates a theoretical framework within which to conceptualize ethics and politics in terms of a critical, creative ethos.

The final Foucault turns to the ancient Greeks for inspiration in this endeavor. Of particular interest to him are practices of ethical self-formation, a part of ancient philosophical life that he refers to as "aesthetics of existence," "practices" or "care" of the self, and "practices of freedom." Such practices figure prominently within the contours of the ethics and politics that Foucault posits for our own times because he sees them as key elements in a "counterattack" against modern (normalizing) forms of power. Introducing ancient practices within a contemporary context, he argues, produces something new in any case, but he explicitly reconceptualizes practices of the self in order to rid them of their elitist character. He retains the Greek notion that care of the self involves care for others: self-care and care for the polis were linked in antiquity, a relation that is significant for our own times. Foucault's ethics neither advocates living like a work of art for art's sake nor retreats into a world of inner contemplation. Rather, for Foucault, an ethos characterized by critical, creative engagement with one's present constitutes the work of freedom, where commitment and responsibility materialize from the bottom up instead of from the top down. Commitment and responsibility, in other words, emerge from and as practices, instead of deriving their function and meaning from universal models and blueprints. Granted, it is difficult to make, let alone sustain, an ethico-political commitment to the world in the face of its turmoil: war, genocide, terror, oppression, and mass displacement of persons appear to be permanent fixtures within the geopolitical landscape. But recognizing the interconnection between taking care of oneself and of the world in which one lives can function to at least reduce the perceived distance between individual and collective existence.

We believe that the salient characteristics of a Foucauldian ethos (engaging the present, taking responsibility for oneself and the world, furthering and expanding the work of freedom) are highly compatible with the aims and objectives of contemporary feminism. Feminist politics and theory are no longer oriented merely toward internal struggles to establish their identities but are actively concerned with and directed toward issues and struggles relevant for our time, including war, justice, emancipation, and polarization between cultures. At the same time that we support this confrontation with the present and enactment of responsibility, we also believe that this work must be undertaken in such a way as to strengthen the feminist movement in all of its diversity: confronting and striving to overcome worldwide problems challenges feminists once again to critically analyze the nature of our own endeavors. Feminism is strengthened not by the assertion of a single, homogeneous identity but rather through a dedicated, contextual, and critical engagement with itself and the world.

Feminism and the Final Foucault, we believe, reflects just this kind of engagement. While the volume in no way presents a unified voice (it is composed of essays written by feminists from Australia, Canada, Europe, and the United States, some of whom find Foucault's later work politically and ethically prescient, others of whom are more tentative or even critical), a common thread nonetheless runs through it: the belief that feminism and the final Foucault do have something to say to each other. The question of how this conversation will ultimately play itself out is left in abeyance, for although we clearly believe that the conversation is a productive one, unlike many previous works in which feminists have engaged the work of Foucault, our overarching objective is not merely to debate the merits or limitations of Foucault's later work vis-à-vis feminism. Rather, we aim to elucidate, put into practice, and experiment with the political "tools" that the final Foucault provides for feminists today.

Our volume is divided into the three sections described below.

WOMEN'S SELF-PRACTICES AS ETHOS: HISTORICAL PERSPECTIVES

The first section of the volume shows that women in both historical and contemporary contexts have developed ethical self-techniques and therefore suggests that it is possible to trace a line in history of women's "arts of existence." From a later Foucauldian perspective, each of the women considered here—Anna Maria van Schurman, Emma Goldman, and Virginia

Woolf—created a certain ethos that took the form of a free "critical life," pushing and transforming the limits of culture and of politics. The essays in this section illustrate how Foucault's own reconceptualization of the work/life split facilitates new perspectives on the relationship between everyday life and the life of the mind.

What is particularly significant in the case of Van Schurman and Goldman is the importance they place upon "the heart" in their works and lives. In "The Shaping of a 'Beautiful' Soul: The Critical Life of Anna Maria van Schurman," Jeannette Bloem demonstrates how the perspective of the later Foucault can shed new light on the lives and works of religious women. The work and life of seventeenth-century Dutch intellectual Anna Maria van Schurman are often seen as contradictory. Specifically, her self-created image of the emancipated woman and her belief in women's right to an education are said to conflict with her later life as a devotee. Construing van Schurman's life and work in terms of ethical self-practices, however, provides a new perspective on this apparent ambiguity. Van Schurman emerges as a woman who developed her own ethos within the frameworks of religion, an unequivocal woman who not only passionately took on the shaping of a beautiful soul but also wanted to transform the image of the Christian woman. Her example also illustrates that practices of freedom occur within religious as well as secular contexts.

Similarly, in "E.G.: Emma Goldman, for Example," Kathy Ferguson analyzes Emma Goldman's life and work from the perspective of the later Foucault. She shows that Goldman shaped her life into an ethical enterprise through extensive writing practices. Ferguson refutes the more standard approach to Goldman, which is to belittle her "theorizing" and praise her "activism," an approach that implicitly accepts a conventional theory/practice distinction that the later Foucault's ideas challenge. Foucault's genealogy of self-constitution offers a fruitful strategy for understanding E.G. not as a failed political philosopher but as a successful and exemplary political philosophy-in-action. Emma Goldman lived as an example of anarchism. She created herself, flamboyantly, persistently, often painfully, through long-lasting techniques of self-production. E.G. was a remarkable performance.

Stephen M. Barber's essay, "Exit Woolf," elucidates the critical or transgressive, as well as the creative, character of women's self-practices. Barber shows that, from 1932 until her death in 1941, Virginia Woolf elaborated a philosophy of freedom and an aesthetics of existence that in strikingly prescient ways exemplify Michel Foucault's final work on the ethics of the concern for self as the practice of freedom. During the final decade of their lives, both thinkers endeavored to fulfill a kind of responsibility that both recog-

nized, described by Foucault as "the permanent reactivation of an attitude—
that is, of a philosophical ethos that could be described as a permanent critique of our historical era." Woolf's great contribution to modern political
and ethical thought ("my debt to civilization," as she puts it in her antifascist essay and book of ethics, *Three Guineas*) proves to be a critical ontology that is also and at once an ethical self-fashioning, one that Foucault perceives as an "exit," or "way out." Woolf's invention of and invitation to a
new relationship to politics remain widely unrecognized or unanswered:
her exit beyond the form of suicide is rarely perceived.

FEMINISM AS ETHOS

The second section of the volume is devoted to identifying and analyzing
contemporary feminism in terms of an ethos characterized by self-practices. Feminism facilitates the production of female subjectivities and identities that are informed by, but nonetheless do not adhere to, traditional
notions of what it means to be a woman. Through this facilitative role, feminism functions as a kind of "umbrella" identity under which multiple individual and group identities, subjectivities, and modes of existence are
collected. While the identity "feminism" is often used in a normative sense,
a late Foucauldian-inspired feminism can resist performing the normalizing function of norms that Foucault as well as feminists today find so problematic. This section thus explores the production and various manifesta-
tions of feminist identities, subjectivities, and modes of existence.

The first four essays in the second section consider ways in which Foucault's later work might facilitate new, potentially emancipatory perspectives on particular dilemmas within feminism, some of which have threatened to become impasses. Mariana Valverde, in "Experience and Truth
Telling in a Post-humanist World: A Foucauldian Contribution to Feminist Ethical Reflections," draws upon Foucault's reflections on ethical practices in order to make a case for abandoning the either/or debate about
truth telling and the feminist experiential subject. Feminisms differ a great
deal, but they generally share a fundamental interest in providing a space
in which women can finally speak openly. The 1960s innovation of the
"consciousness-raising group" may have gone out of fashion, but many of
the speech practices associated with it have become ubiquitous in both feminist and nonfeminist contexts where various forms of "truth telling" are
practiced by women. Valverde argues that the diverse dialogic practices that
elicit and produce such gendered truth telling are frequently lumped together under a single banner with the result that they are either praised or
derided in toto. Foucault's recovery of Greek truth-telling practices, how-

by examining how Islamic mysticism, and Sufism in particular, can be conceptualized as "freedom practices" or "spiritual exercises" that implicate women as well as men. The concept of the free individual life for men and women exists in the heart of Islam. Vintges argues that freedom practices are to be recognized in many religious contexts. She conceives of a cross-cultural feminism as the (re)endorsing of freedom practices for all women throughout all cultures.

WORKS CITED

Arendt, Hannah. 1994. "Understanding and Politics." In *Essays in Understanding: 1930–1954.* Edited by Jerome Kohn. 307–27. New York: Harcourt Brace.

Camus, Albert. 1991. *The Rebel: An Essay on Man in Revolt.* Translated by Anthony Bower. New York: Vintage.

Part 1:
Women's Self-practices as Ethos:
Historical Perspectives

The Shaping of a "Beautiful" Soul: The Critical Life of Anna Maria van Schurman

Jeannette Bloem

Another kind of picture I guard in my soul. Through it I can depict . . . the divine virtues . . . in my soul in some manner. I see more and more that this art is long while life is short and circumstances difficult.

—Anna Maria van Schurman, *Eucleria*

In his *Renaissance Self-fashioning,* Stephen Greenblatt argues that in the early modern period there was an increased self-consciousness about the fashioning of human identity as a manipulable, artful process. "It was Christianity that made suspect the self-consciousness that had been widespread among the elite in the classical world. 'Hands off yourself,' Augustine declared. 'Try to build up yourself, and you build a ruin.' But from the sixteenth century onwards a powerful alternative began to be fully articulated: the alternative of self-fashioning," asserts Greenblatt. His subject is "self-fashioning from More to Shakespeare" (1980, 1–2).

What interests me, however, is the question as to what self-fashioning and identity meant to sixteenth- and seventeenth-century women who were faced with the stereotypical image of the silent, obedient, self-effacing woman. Feminist studies like those collected in *Women of the Golden Age* reveal how some seventeenth-century women dealt with this stereotype in their own work. The Englishwoman Margaret Cavendish wrote her autobiography (1656) and justified her decision to do so with a reference to "Caesar, Ovid and many more, both men and women and I know no reason I may not do it as well as they" (Wilcox 1994, 154). In her historical studies, Mirjam de Baar demonstrates that the mystic Antoinette Bourignon,[1] although kept in her place by religious conventions, was nevertheless able to establish spiritual leadership over a group of Christian men. She legitimated her position by using the metaphor of motherhood in her letters, while in her autobiographical work she used the image of the unlettered virgin who could establish her authority as the instrument of God (De Baar 1994, 151). In contrast, the Dutch scholar Anna Maria van Schurman (1607–78), author of the famous *Dissertatio* (1641) in which she defended a woman's right to learning, evidenced her intellectual authority and religious freedom when, at the age of sixty-two, she turned her back on the Reformed church and joined the separatist community of the minister Jean de Labadie. She made it clear in the *Eucleria* (1673)—a work in which she justifies her new Christian lifestyle with knowledge and vision—that this meant neither a radical break with her former life nor submissively following others.[2]

With a self-created image of the self, these seventeenth-century women broke through gender codes or distanced themselves from them, argues De Baar, referring for support to Greenblatt's concept of "self-fashioning" (ibid. 1994, 148). But the relationship between the self and the transgressing of the code of feminine normality can, in my view, be formulated even more penetratingly by taking an approach that draws on the concepts of "freedom practices," "aesthetics of existence," "askesis," and "care of the self" expressed by Michel Foucault in his later work. With these concepts, explained in such works as *The Use of Pleasure* (1986), *The Care of the Self* (1986), and later essays and interviews (Rabinow 1997), Foucault broke with his former idea that subject constructs are always the result of normalizing and disciplining. The construction of an identity may also be an effect of "self-techniques," forms of practical rationality, with which an ethical self is achieved.

I have studied the shaping of the identity of the learned and devout Van Schurman from the perspective of this ethical philosophy. By using the concept of self-care as a heuristic means, a more accurate image of Van Schurman emerges, as opposed to the more limiting, traditional psychological reading of her life. Psychological readings present Van Schurman as an essentially ambiguous woman, whose life and self-created image are said to conflict with reality, whereas reading Van Schurman's life in terms of self-techniques opens up space to examine how she consciously undertakes a relationship with herself and others. The ethical-political dimension of the self then takes center stage. I will point out that she challenged the seventeenth-century stereotype of the Christian woman on different levels such as subject identity, clerical institutions, and the dominant normative framework more generally.

Who was this extraordinarily learned and devout woman, this woman who—in the eyes of a male contemporary—was the "tenth Muse, one of the wonders of her century and her sex"? Anna Maria van Schurman was born in Cologne in 1607 to a wealthy Calvinist family of noble birth. Around 1610 the family moved from Catholic Cologne, first to Utrecht and ten years later to Franeker, where Anna Maria's father attended the lectures given by the theologian William Ames.[3] In 1623 they returned to Utrecht. Encouraged by her father, the young Van Schurman developed her artis-

16

tic,[4] literary, and scholarly talents. She rapidly mastered Latin and Greek, and from her mentor Gisbertus Voetius she learned Hebrew, Syrian, and other Oriental languages, which she used in her studies of the Bible. Her literary work brought her into contact with personages such as Queen Christina of Sweden and Dutch writers Jacob Cats and Constantijn Huygens, with whom she kept up a correspondence for many years. Her contacts with the Reformed theologians Voetius and André Rivet placed her at the center of the world of scholarship and the theological movement of the further (second) reformation.[5] Voetius arranged for her to attend lectures in Utrecht—the first Dutch woman to be allowed to do so, but only on condition that she sit behind a wooden screen so that her male fellow students could not see her. Her correspondence with Rivet, the professor of theology at Leiden, on the question of whether scholarship was a suitable pursuit for a "Christian" woman resulted in the publication of her *Dissertatio.*[6] The work was widely acclaimed and brought her great fame and standing at home and abroad.

As well as maintaining contacts with the cultural elite of Europe, she had domestic duties to occupy her. After the death of her mother, she assumed responsibility for caring for her aunts and sometime around 1653 went to Cologne to settle a matter of an inheritance. During her stay there and later in Lexmond, the practical exercise of her faith assumed an ever greater role in her life, and her interest in study and the arts receded into the background. In 1666, indirectly through her brother Johan Godschalk, she met the minister Jean de Labadie, whose preaching made a deep impression on her. When the former Jesuit was expelled from his ministry in 1669 as a result of a conflict with the Reformed church and established himself in Amsterdam with a few followers, Van Schurman took a radical decision. She sold her house in Utrecht and part of her library and moved to Amsterdam where she joined the sectarian group as a "convert." Thenceforth Van Schurman led a nomadic existence. The group was not tolerated for long in Amsterdam or in Herford where it subsequently moved, but eventually it found a settled home in Friesland.

When in her later life the unmarried Van Schurman lived under the same roof as men, she was subjected to severe criticism by the "great men" (De Baar 1987, 20–24). Friends in the church and literary contemporaries, including Huygens, believed her decision to have been unwise. Leading Reformed theologians and ministers went so far as to condemn her way of life and spiritual practices as unchristian, heretical, and immoral. She was tarnishing her fame and her lustre with her reprehensible doctrines, and the separation from the church was surely a cardinal sin (Graafland 1989, 325). For was it not evidence of spiritual egotism were someone to leave the church to provide for their own piety, wondered her contemporaries (ibid. 1989, 332).

These criticisms derived on the one hand from certain ideas about appropriate female conduct and on the other from theological controversies and religious conventions. Van Schurman was said to have thrown away her reputation, to have lost her wits, and to have flouted the stereotype of the virtuous woman, a passive believer who followed ecclesiastical authority.

Goaded by the constant stream of criticism and rumor, she decided to accept the confrontation with herself and others and wrote the *Eucleria* in Latin. In it she talks about her life, the reason for her conversion, and the vicissitudes of "the family" in order to "counter any lying impression with a truthful one" (Van Schurman 1684, 2–3). It is generally viewed as an apologetic work in which she underpins her religious choice and the spiritual practice of her faith with her views on theological, philosophical, and ethical questions (De Baar 1992, 106).

AN EXCEPTIONAL CASE OF SELF-CARE

Many people have devoted a great deal of time to studying the *Eucleria*. Ecclesiastical scholars regard it as confessional literature and refer to the sources of inspiration that Van Schurman herself mentions in her work: Augustine's *Confessions* and *Of the Imitation of Christ* by Thomas à Kempis (Van Schurman 1684, 14, 31). De Baar describes the work as a spiritual autobiography and views this genre—referring to Greenblatt—as "a particularly good example of the process of self-fashioning." In this context she talks about Van Schurman's work as a "self-created image of Self, one-sided as it was" (De Baar 1994, 148). The autobiographical genre thus becomes a constructive exposition that generates a fictitious subjectivity.

Subjectivity of this kind is precisely what Foucault does not have in mind with the concept of care for the self he puts forward in his later work. The care of the self, which occurs, for example, through writing techniques, means actually bringing about self-involvement—relating the self to itself. Bringing about this relationship is a creative activity that involves the person himself or herself. "Why should a painter work if he is not transformed by his own painting?" asks Foucault (1997a, 131). The construction of a self is thus primarily a process of shaping in which fiction certainly plays a role, but as the creator of a reality of the self. The fictitious moment covers the ontological and not the epistemological level. In my view this classification applies to Van Schurman's *Eucleria* because this work encompasses much more of a process of self-fashioning in the ethical Foucauldian sense.

In her essay "The *Eukleria* as Autobiography," De Baar makes an important but subtle distinction here. The classification as a spiritual autobiography might be legitimate on historical grounds,[7] but the work nonetheless occupied an exceptional position (1992, 98, 107). The reason, according to De Baar, is that Van Schurman presented herself as a learned woman, a theologian, who defended her religious choice and lifestyle on rational grounds by examining the theology on her own authority and writing about it (ibid. 1992, 106). Viewed thus, Van Schurman did not make a radical departure from her earlier life and from her scholarship, but she did abandon the "modesty topos" that characterized her earlier work (De Baar 1994, 150). She also distanced herself in her late work from medieval devotees and female contemporaries such as Eleonore Von Merlau in Germany and Jane Leade in England, who usually based their work on revelations or dreams (Scheenstra 1992, 130). Van Schurman thus broke not only gender codes but also religious codes when she dealt with theological questions for a learned audience. Scheenstra argues that in this respect Van Schurman, as a woman, was a pioneer (ibid. 1992, 130).[8]

We can thus say that the *Eucleria* is not straightforward confessional literature or an autobiography, because we know that Van Schurman was not striving for introspection or describing her perceptions of God at length. The rational tenor and theological dimension of the work make the model of self-fashioning with a view to ethical self-constitution very plausible. This is a constitution in which the relationship between how to live and who to be in the world is linked with the self-technique of writing. True, Van Schurman talks in terms of "God's workings" in her, but I would argue that the process of self-fashioning was dominated by rational and emotional desires to enter into a relationship with herself and others. She wanted, after all, to prove to her contemporaries, eminent men, in a "sincere manner" that the change in her way of life was an improvement (Van Schurman 1684, 2–3). Of course she praises God for this and makes herself very small, but not without presenting herself as a spiritual being and thus as an ethical self.

Van Schurman fearlessly develops her scholarly vision and love of God when, in the third chapter of the *Eucleria,* she formulates her views on metaphysics, physics, ethics, and theology. From these views we can derive an ethical and a theological-philosophical vision in which the significance of the heart receives due attention. But this attention in no way leads to a plea for a "pious anti-intellectualism," argues Angela Roothaan, because with her vision of human knowledge, ethics, and God, Van Schurman transforms philosophy into a Christian philosophy (Roothaan 1992, 119).

A striking aspect of this philosophy is the distance from scholastic learning, emerging rationalism, and the mechanistic view of nature, and also from the blurred Christian morality of the Reformation. Van Schurman values the human forms of knowing, when set against the verities of the Holy Scriptures, purely as artificial or representation, because this knowledge affords only indirect access to reality. In her view, natural wisdom is consequently overshadowed by true science (Van Schurman 1684, 56). True knowledge, she believes, provides immediate insight. This intuitive knowing and the inner experience become important as soon as she discovers that "knowledge without feeling is barren" (1684, 14; Roothaan 1991, 5).[9] Van Schurman therefore counters the mechanistic view with the idea that the physical reality is inspired and has a purpose. Nevertheless she distances herself from theological orthodoxy because, although she regards God as the prime mover, she stresses that God is "real" and "inwardly present." This view of the faculty of cognition and God, says Roothaan, is closely related to Spinoza's ideas—that only God is the substance and immanent cause of all things (Roothaan 1991, 6). This view was branded as heresy in the orthodox Christian faith because it appeared to imply the denial of a God who transcends existence (Roothaan 1992, 116).

On the basis of experience and theological insights, the emotional piety and spirituality therefore acquired an important place in Van Schurman's Christian philosophy, which was ultimately strongly inspired by the traditional form of the earliest Christian communities. In her own way, using the arguments of heart, mind, and soul, Van Schurman refutes church dogma and a theological morality in which spirit and life diverge (Scheenstra 1992, 124).[10] Spirituality and emotional piety are thus tools with which to oppose what is accepted and to make her own conscience, virtue, and spiritual welfare the central issue. Van Schurman's endeavor, after all, was "Through it (the divine image) I can depict . . . the divine virtues . . . in my soul in some manner. I see more and more that this art is long while life is short and circumstances difficult. . . . I wish to dedicate the rest of my life to this pursuit . . ." (Van Schurman 1684, 32; Irwin 1998, 86).

She thus dedicated her life to this art by constant practice. And here we come close to Foucault's concepts of the "aesthetics of existence" and "askesis," which are practiced in the context of an ethical "care for the self." And yet does the religious context of Van Schurman's ethical self-care allow itself to be identified so easily with the late Foucauldian approach? Can his concepts really be applied to her life and work?

The atheist Foucault took a critical view of the soul and the spiritual life. We know that "salvation and a beyond are seen by Foucault to be illusory" (Carrette 2000, 122) and that Foucault actually regards *Discipline and Punish* as "a correlated history of the modern soul" in which "the modern soul is related to the penal practice of the body . . . whereas the theological soul is built on sin and (theological) punishment," according to Jeremy Carrette (ibid. 2000, 123). Foucault also sees contemplation, a Christian self-technique, in a critical light because "acquiring ontological knowledge about the state of the soul is separate from the practice of self-involvement" (Foucault 1997b, 276). If the mode of being of the soul is conceived, then, according to Foucault, there is no need to ask yourself what you have done or what you think. The soul, after all, is not a synonym for conscience.

This Christian heritage has meant that we subject ourselves to external rules for moral action. Foucault argues that the classical personal ethic in the Christian era transmutes into a monastic morality in which subjection to God's will and the control of the Almighty are central (Foucault 1988). As this change takes place, so autonomous formation of a moral identity disappears and the care for others achieves absolute priority over care for the self. We are then dealing with a subject aspiring to self-denial and bound by a moral code.

Nevertheless Foucault qualifies the idea that the Christian heritage is monolithic and has implacably produced a subjugated subject. Carrette points out that Foucault's interest in the religious, spiritual transformation of subjectivity is evident in his journalistic reports on the Iranian Revolution in 1978 (Carrette 2000, 137).[11] Foucault explicitly readdresses the question of religion with his observation that there were religious groups in the Renaissance who lived according to rules they had drawn up for themselves: "According to these groups the individual should take care of his own salvation independently of the ecclesiastical institutions and of the ecclesiastical pastorate . . . we can see . . . a reaffirmation of its [the self] autonomy" (Foucault 1997b, 278). We really can thus link the constitution of a religious identity with freedom practices and autonomy—the ideal opportunity to consider Van Schurman as an exceptional case of self-care.

THE CRITICAL LIFE OF A CHRISTIAN WOMAN

What did autonomy and freedom practices encompass for a devout seventeenth-century woman? In the Renaissance and during the Reformation,[12] humanistic and Protestant values like authenticity and sincerity were developing apace, and this offered devout women the opportunity to demand their autonomy and construct an identity of their own. Demanding autonomy was linked to a crisis in the institutional system of faith, but the social and intellectual inequality between men and women was also exposed.

In the Dutch Reformed religious practice of the time, only men were permitted to hold public office or to speak about God, but there were groups, such as the Quakers, who did accept the equality of men and women and what was described as "women-speaking." Some Reformed ministers saw this speaking as an offense. In 1669, for instance, the church council wrote that there had been unseemly conduct during a conventicle held by the group surrounding De Labadie (De Baar 1987, 31). Van Schurman was not accused personally, but it is not inconceivable that she spoke on this occasion.

To Van Schurman, as a Dutch woman, the "further reformation" was an invitation to develop her own independent theological vision and to opt for a life of piety in which inner truth, spiritual welfare, and personal conscience were the guiding tenets. However, her decision to choose a spiritual movement has been received in a wide variety of ways. Feminist historians not unreasonably link her choice with an implicit longing for spiritual equality and intellectual freedom. De Baar argues convincingly that women were particularly attracted to spiritual sectarian movements because of the spiritual equality that existed between the members—an equality that was expressed in the acceptance of the idea that the Holy Spirit could also descend directly on women. In spiritual movements, moreover, differences in gender and class were usually irrelevant.[13] Believers could join the house community so long as there was a sincere desire for conversion. On the other hand, it is striking that the practice of the spiritual life by women is explained by some scholars and theologians then and now with descriptions in which "aversion to sectarianism and sexist prejudices" ring out.[14]

We overcome this aversion, these prejudices, when we consider Van Schurman's choice from the perspective of self-care. With her views about the virtuous life and God, Van Schurman took the bold step of moving outside the sphere of influence of her mentor, Voetius, and ignoring the dogmas of the church. By demanding this independent position, she naturally challenged the stereotypical image of the silent and obedient Christian woman.

In his later work, Foucault describes self-care as a freedom practice in which the individual draws up rules for his or her conduct with which he or she aims to achieve a transformation in ethical terms. Foucault points to self-techniques such as writing and corresponding with friends. These techniques allow the individual to change his or her ideas and views, and to achieve a certain state of wisdom or happiness.

When we look at the way of life of the reborn Christian Van Schurman, it is above all the unconventional rules and controversial standards that strike us. The group around De Labadie, for example, used a free liturgy and sang psalms by David but also by De Labadie (Graafland 1989, 322). In the *Eucleria*, Van Schurman even discusses the question of the Sabbath. For the church at that time, Sunday was a separate day of celebration and abstention, and this, in her view, showed that the church was under the yoke of the law. But it was the spirit of the law that had to be understood, and Van Schurman therefore observed the Sabbath every day (ibid. 1989, 319). In emulation of the first Christian community, the group pursued an austere lifestyle every day, in which earthly beauty was rejected. Jewelry was not worn, and occupations that had to do with beauty and luxury were prohibited (ibid. 1989, 330).

In Van Schurman's view, paralleling De Labadie's ideas, being a Christian was an occupation that had to be practiced. The techniques of faith encompassed active purification by means of mental prayer, fasting, and song during which, incidentally, the women were permitted to continue with their handwork. This purification was necessary to achieve mystical union with Christ. In an exchange of letters with Johann Jakob Schütz of the Frankfurt circle, with whom she corresponded from 1674 to 1678,[15] Van Schurman discussed the means by which the soul found union with God. Notwithstanding De Labadie's emphasis on self-denial, which Van Schurman certainly did not reject, she showed that "daily life can take its rightful place alongside the service of God" (Scheenstra 1992, 127).

Nevertheless some contemporaries branded De Labadie's "mystical" theology as unnatural and full of awful depths.[16] But in fact De Labadie radicalized the Reformed grace and election doctrine. According to cultural historian Leszek Kolakowski,[17] this radicalization went hand in hand with an anti-confessional spirituality. This view is supported by the fact that Van Schurman did not elaborate the confessional culture in any great detail. Nor in any real sense did she speak about the inner occurrence between her and God—this after all was not to be expressed in words but only felt, and that feeling required contemplation.

To Van Schurman, contemplation meant laying open the heart—an essential self-technique with which she shaped and deepened her spirituality and piety. This technique embraced not so much self-deciphering or the examination of conscience but continual reflection and practice to achieve union with God and to allow the Divine love to make itself felt in active life. She regarded this union as the highest form of ethics (Graafland 1989, 318).

The entirely subjectivistic character of contemplation gives some Reformed scholars grounds for rejecting this belief technique as a heathen heritage. It appears that, in contrast to the malleable conscience, the inner experience of faith and spirituality is a completely inaccessible and uncontrollable area for ecclesiastical authorities. We are thus touching here on the political dimensions of spirituality and piety. In my view, Van Schurman proved in her *Eucleria* that she had taken control of her own spiritual life and determined for herself "how to govern herself, how to be governed (by God) and how to govern others."[18] In so doing she consulted not only her inner experience and emotions but also her intellect. The way Van Schurman made her ethical care for the self into an inherent consequence of her spiritual religious practice can be seen from her views about ethics.

In the *Eucleria,* Van Schurman sets out her "unfeigned judgement" and her position on ethics. It is a criticism of the Platonists and the Aristotelian doctrine of virtue with which, as Roothaan demonstrates, she rejects anthropocentrism. The consequence of this rejection is that she denounces the accepted morality because, in her view, it is self-important (Roothaan 1991, 6).

Van Schurman believes that the Platonists, who stated that the highest good consists in becoming equal to God, are "mistaken" about God and have become mired in their own supposed perfection. Because, says Van Schurman, "they (human beings) do not exist through their own power, and if they have anything which is true and perfect, they derive it from God" (Van Schurman 1684, 58–59). For their blessedness, true Christians concern themselves solely with God and not with material things like riches, freedom, and health that are part of the Aristotelian virtue system (Roothaan 1992, 117). Van Schurman is convinced that true knowledge of virtue appears as soon as man has experienced the love of God in himself (ibid. 118). With these views she is opposing the Christian morality of her time, which she sees as conceited. In its place she puts forward her personal ethic, in which the care for the soul is the most rudimentary form of self-care.

The significance of her ideas about virtue and ethics may be contrasted with what Van Schurman says in the *Eucleria.* She mentions her restraint in respect of her involvement in the polemic between theology and philosophy, explaining it by saying that taking part would have offended against her "innate modesty" and the "sincere desire to remain concealed" (Van Schurman 1684, 37; Rang 1992, 41). Here Van Schurman appears to be advocating self-effacement. But we have to realize that she was listening, thinking, and corresponding with people of like mind about a God who, in the final analysis, could not exist without her scholarly and spiritual self. For her the self is part of God and God is in the self. Through this internal connection she establishes the self as a factor that cannot be erased and emerges as a perfectionist of the further reformation.

With her way of life and her views in the *Dissertatio* and the *Eucleria,* Van Schurman actually reforms the conventional image of the "Christian" woman in the practical sense. There can be no passivity without activity, no obedience without a reasoned choice while courage and pride certainly do not stand in the way of modesty. This image appears in her *Dissertatio* and, even more particularly, in the *Eucleria.* But from Van Schurman's experience we can also draw some conclusions. A "woman's self" needs not to be constrained by gender stereotypes or clerical institutions. Van Schurman reaches her ethical life-goal and changes from the inside out the dominant stereotype of the Christian woman. She shapes her own Christian identity and with this reformation she transforms her life into an "experiment of living,"[19] an intriguing example of a freedom practice in a religious context.

NOTES

I thank Karen Vintges for her suggestions and critical comments on this essay and Lynne Richards for her translation. Dianna Taylor developed the notion of a "critical life" in order to conceptualize the political character of Foucauldian self-techniques. See Taylor (2003).

1. Van Schurman met Bourignon in 1668. See De Baar (1994, 143–52).

2. The Latin edition was published in Altona in 1673. I have used the Dutch translation of 1684, a facsimile edition published in Leeuwarden in 1978. For the English translation of the first two chapters, see Irwin (1998).

3. On his deathbed, her father urged Anna Maria to eschew the earthly ties of marriage because they were pernicious.

4. An engraved self-portrait dating from 1640, which Van Schurman sent to close friends, demonstrates what she was capable of. She added a telling caption: "See my likeness depicted in this portrait; May your favour perfect the work where art has failed." See van der Stighelen (1992, 61). Van Schurman's work can be seen in Franeker.

5. Voetius was said to have corrupted Van Schurman. She was besotted with the theologian and was concerned only with theological controversies, according to Descartes's letter to Mersenne in 1640. See Rang (1992, 38).

6. An English edition of the *Dissertatio* entitled *The Learned Maid or Whether a Maid May Be a Scholar* appeared in 1659.

7. This genre was very much in vogue in German pietist circles and among radical religious groups in England at the end of the seventeenth century. See De Baar (1992, 96) and (1987, 20–24).

8. Scheenstra contends not only that Van Schurman abandoned the traditional Reformation position, but also that in terms of Van Schurman herself there is an old and a new identity. See Scheenstra (1992, 131).

9. Spinoza, contends Roothaan, identifies this knowing as imaginative knowledge, a knowledge that transcends the rational and is linked to an unquestionable knowledge that conveys moral certainty. See Roothaan (1992, 111–12).

10. Scheenstra notes that Van Schurman reduces the imparted righteousness of God's reconciliation with man through Christ to a sanctity that could be measured by man, and that it is very probable that Van Schurman considered herself to be one of the chosen. See Scheenstra (1992, 131–32).

11. For a more lengthy discussion of Foucault's view on religion, see the chapter by Vintges in this volume.

12. Carrette contends that Foucault saw the Reformation as the great crisis of Christianity. See Carrette (2000, 137, n.51).

13. De Baar makes a distinction between spiritually oriented and Bible-oriented sects. See De Baar (1987, 14–15).

14. De Baar (1987) refers to Max Weber, who suggests that women are pre-eminently receptive to religious movements with orgiastic, emotional, and hysterical aspects. Van Schurman's friend minister Koelman regards it as a consequence of female temperament and passion.

15. From the unpublished correspondence referred to by the church historian Wallman, Scheenstra deduces that Van Schurman was an authority for Schütz. See Scheenstra (1992, 126).

16. In the view of minister Koelman, Van Schurman's friend, De Labadie's mystical theology is really a monastic mystique about false delights, invented by monks and beguines. See Graafland (1989, 329).

17. See Graafland (1989, 337).

18. Carrette contends Foucault links the term "political spirituality" with "government and truth." See also Vintges in this volume.

19. As implied by Birch (3). Birch is a pseudonym of Constance Pope-Hennessy-Birch.

WORKS CITED

Baar, Mirjam de. 1987. "'En onder 't hennerot het haantje zoekt te blijven,' Vrouwenlevens 1500–1850." Edited by U. Jansz et al. 8ste jaarboek Vrouwengeschiedenis, Nijmegen.

———. 1992. "'Wat nu het kleine eergeruchtje van mijn naam betreft . . .' De Eucleria als autobiografie" ("The Eucleria as Autobiography"). In Anna Maria van Schurman, een uitzonderlijk geleerde vrouw. Edited by Mirjam de Baar and Agnes Sneller. Zutphen: Walburg Pers. 93–108. English translation: Choosing the Better Part: Anna Maria van Schurman (1607/1678). 1996. Edited by Mirjam de Baar et al. Dordrecht: Kluwer Academic Publishers.

———. 1994. "Transgressing Gender Codes." In Women of the Golden Age. Edited by Els Kloek, Nicole Teeuwen, and Marijke Huisman. 143–52. Hilversum: Verloren.

Birch, Una. 1909. Anna Maria van Schurman: Artist, Scholar, Saint. London: Longmans, Green.

Bouwman, J. 1996. Verhandeling over de aanleg van vrouwen voor wetenschap, Anna Maria van Schurman. Edited by J. Bouwman. Groningen: Xeno.

Carrette, Jeremy R. 2000. Foucault and Religion: Spiritual Corporality and Political Spirituality. New York: Routledge.

Eck, Caroline van. 1992. "Het eerste Nederlandse feministische traktaat." In Anna Maria van Schurman, een uitzonderlijk geleerde vrouw. Edited by Mirjam de Baar and Agnes Sneller. 49–60. Zutphen: Walburg Pers.

Foucault, Michel. 1986. The Use of Pleasure. Harmondsworth: Penguin.

———. 1986. The Care of the Self. Harmondsworth: Penguin.

———. 1988. "An Aesthetic of Existence." In Politics, Philosophy, Culture: Interviews and Other Writings 1977–1984. Edited by Lawrence D. Kritzman. 47–53. New York: Routledge.

———. 1997a. "An Interview by Stephen Riggins." In *Ethics: Subjectivity and Truth: Essential Works of Michel Foucault.* Volume 1. Edited by Paul Rabinow. 121–33. New York: New Press.

———. 1997b. "On the Genealogy of Ethics: An Overview of Work in Progress." In *Ethics: Subjectivity and Truth.* Edited by Paul Rabinow. 253–80. New York: New Press.

Graafland, C. 1989. "De Nadere Reformatie en het Labadisme." In *De Nadere Reformatie en het Gereformeerd Piëtisme.* Edited by C. Graafland and W. van 't Spijker. 275–346. The Hague: Boekencentrum.

Greenblatt, Stephen. 1980. *Renaissance Self-fashioning.* Chicago: University of Chicago Press.

Irwin, Joyce L. 1998. *Anna Maria van Schurman, Whether a Christian Woman Should Be Educated and Other Writings from Her Intellectual Circle.* Edited and translated by Joyce Irwin. Chicago: University of Chicago Press.

Rabinow, Paul, ed. 1997. *Ethics: Subjectivity and Truth: Essential Works of Michel Foucault.* Volume 1. New York: New Press.

Rang, Britta. 1992. "Een sonderlingen geest." In *Anna Maria van Schurman, een uitzonderlijk geleerde vrouw.* Edited by Mirjam de Baar and Agnes Sneller. 29–48. Zutphen: Walburg Pers.

Roothaan, Angela. 1991. "Kritiek op het antropocentrisme." In *Mededelingen vanwege het Spinozahuis.* Delft: Eburon.

———. 1992. "Anna Maria van Schurmans hervorming van de wijsbegeerte." In *Anna Maria van Schurman, een uitzonderlijk geleerde vrouw.* Edited by Mirjam de Baar and Agnes Sneller. 109–22. Zutphen: Walburg Pers.

Scheenstra, Erica. 1992. "Over de goede keuze." In *Anna Maria van Schurman, een uitzonderlijk geleerde vrouw.* Edited by Mirjam de Baar and Agnes Sneller. 123–38. Zutphen: Walburg Pers.

Schurman, Anna Maria van. 1641. *Nobiliss. Virginis Annae Mariae a Schurman Dissertatio De Ingenii Muliebris ad Doctrinam, & meliores Litteras aptitudine.* Elsevier. English translation: *The Learned Maid or Whether a Maid May Be a Scholar,* 1659.

———. 1684. *Eucleria of Uitkiezing van Het Beste Deel.* Amsterdam: Jacob vande Velde. Facsimile edition, 1978, Leeuwarden.

Stighelen, Katlijne van der. 1992. "Et ses artistes mains (. . .)." In *Anna Maria van Schurman, een uitzonderlijk geleerde vrouw.* Edited by Mirjam de Baar and Agnes Sneller. 61–74. Zutphen: Walburg Pers.

Taylor, Dianna. 2003. "Practicing Politics with Foucault and Kant: Toward a Critical Life." *Philosophy and Social Criticism* 29, no. 3: 259–80.

Wilcox, Helen. 1994. "A Monstrous Shape." In *Women of the Golden Age.* Edited by Els Kloek, Nicole Teeuwen, and Marijke Huisman. 153–58. Hilversum: Verloren.

2

E.G.:
Emma Goldman, for Example

Kathy E. Ferguson

Emma Goldman crafted herself as an example of anarchism in life. Her "beautiful ideal" of anarchism can be seen as the text she wrote on her body, on her life world. She exemplified her anarchism, living a life that produced the kinds of social relations she endorsed and the form of political space for which she worked. Her labor producing herself as an anarchist was not, toward the end of her life, inspired primarily by belief that others would follow her example: after many disappointments in "the movement," she concluded in a 1928 letter to her friend Alexander Berkman, "I no longer consider comrades capable of learning by good example" (Drinnon and Drinnon 1975, 96). Her anarchism is better thought of as an example for herself, a textual space within which she wrote meaning onto life, and perhaps as an example for the future. The textuality of Goldman's life, as I am interpreting it here, exceeds distinctions between written and spoken language, or between speaking and acting. Her "text"—in the sense of that which one must create and recreate, interpret and reinterpret—was her life in the anarchist movement, which she constituted daily through ongoing practices of words/deeds.

Like Socrates, E.G. was an irritating gadfly to the authorities, pushing a so-called democratic government to reveal its deadly hypocrisy. Like him, she preferred speech to writing, privileging face-to-face relations and engaged dialogue. Both radicals were primarily educators, speaking the forbidden words that provoked states to violence. Both were sentenced to exile: while Socrates killed himself rather than leave his city, E.G. took her city with her, made her city around herself through the network of communicative relations she generated. She produced herself in dialogic involvement with some of the practices of self-construction that Foucault marks as "technologies of the self," articulating her identity as both the source and the outcome of her politics.

The concept of *"epimeleia heautou,* which means taking care of one's self . . . describes a sort of work, an activity; it implies attention, knowledge, technique" (Foucault 1994, 269). In the essay "Technologies of the Self," Foucault sketches "four major types of these 'technologies,' each a matrix of practical reason" (Martin, Gutman, and Hutton 1988, 18). The first two, technologies of production and of sign systems, permit the making of things and the practices of signification. The third type is "technologies of power, which determine the conduct of individuals and submit them to certain ends or domination, an objectivizing of the subject" (ibid.). The fourth type, a central focus of Foucault's work at the end of his life, consists of "technologies of the self, which permit individuals to effect by their own means or with the help of others a certain number of operations on their own bodies and souls, thoughts, conduct, and way of being, so as to transform themselves in order to attain a certain state of happiness, purity, wisdom, perfection, or immortality" (ibid.).

Foucault articulated an uneven trajectory of practices by which human beings turn themselves into subjects. Beginning with Socrates' self-understanding as a condemned man in *The Apology*, to Socrates' engagement with Alcibiades over his preparation for public life in the dialogue of that name, to Greco-Roman philosophy in the first two centuries A.D., and finally to Christian spirituality and monasticism in the fourth and fifth centuries, Foucault traced the articulation of practices for "care of oneself" (ibid., 3–4). His sketch of this historical trajectory presents not a seamless unfolding of a nascent historical practice but an uneven production of strategies by which people act on their "bodies, souls, thoughts, conduct and way of being in order to transform themselves . . ." (ibid., 4). The Socratic version was perhaps the most highly politicized, caring for the self and the city simultaneously. It was also the most dialogical, seeking knowledge in a shared inquiry into the truth of the soul (ibid., 31). While the later Stoics moved away from public dialogue grounding knowledge in the *polis*, they moved toward self-constituting exercises "to get prepared": "In the philosophical tradition dominated by Stoicism, *askesis* means not renunciation but the progressive consideration of self, or mastery over oneself, obtained not through the renunciation of reality but through the acquisition and assimilation of truth. It has as its final aim not preparation for another reality but access to the reality of this world. The Greek word for this is *parakeuazo* ('to get prepared'). It is a set of practices by which one can acquire, assimilate, and transform truth into a permanent principle of action. *Alethia* becomes *ethos*. It is a process of becoming more subjective" (ibid., 35).

The "process of becoming more subjective" entailed a practical set of activities: "not abstract advice but a widespread activity, a network of obligations and services to the soul" (ibid., 27). This network, more explicitly public for Socrates and Plato, more rooted in personal communications for the later Stoics, was constitutive of a social self, a self-in-relation. While

Socrates advised Alcibiades that he must attend to himself when he was young, for "at the age of fifty, it would be too late" (Plato, in Foucault 1986, 44), for the Stoics it was "never too early or too late to care for the well-being of the soul" (Epicurus, in Foucault 1986, 46). Luther Martin echoes Foucault in finding, in both Greek traditions, "an epistemological technology of the self. This tradition emphasizes the activity of self-disclosure always in terms of an other. By disclosing oneself in dialogue self was constituted" (Martin, Gutman, and Hutton 1988, 60). One "occupied oneself with oneself" through types of activities (ibid., 20). Foucault describes three Stoic techniques of the self: writing letters to friends; examining oneself and one's conscience, reviewing one's actions; and testing oneself through imagination of possible situations and through training (ibid., 36).

Emma Goldman made vigorous use of some of the Socratic and the Stoic practices of self-care. She constituted herself in relation to her "beautiful ideal" and to the concrete others who shared her journey. Foucault's inquiry into the Greek practices of self-care provides a useful invitation (as opposed to a literal map) for interpreting Goldman's politics. Foucault's return to the Greeks did not produce, in his argument (or mine), a timeless blueprint for self-construction but rather an intriguing set of possibilities. Rather than rediscovering ancient truths, Foucault offered suggestive encounters between contemporary political problematics (either Goldman's or ours) and the ethos of ancient Greek culture.[1] Hubert Dreyfus comments that "Foucault undertook a restorative historical analysis . . . not to 'return' to some archaic mode of social order but, rather, to make visible a bygone way of approaching the self and others which might suggest possibilities for the present" (Dreyfus in Foucault 1994, xxvii). Foucault's invitation to engage the Greek problematic of self-formation offers intriguing points of entry into Goldman's political thinking by highlighting the political inspiration and consequences of her ways of inhabiting her world.

While Goldman may not have been consciously attentive to the provocative pun her initials suggest, she made full use of its possibilities of self-representation. She signed many of her letters as E.G. Her lifelong comrade Alexander Berkman referred to her as E.G. in his own letters. When she went underground, her alias was E.G. Smith. Emma Goldman was always "for example," creating and using concrete strategies and activities to relate herself to herself, her comrades, and the ideals for which she worked.

WRITING ONESELF IN POLITICAL SPACE

E.G.'s audience entails an intellectual and political community that extends from the late nineteenth century into the present. Her voice is central to the discursive trajectory of anarchism, formative of a line of connections represented through books, journals, libraries, archives, underground papers, strikes, student groups, protests, campaigns, collectives, unions, political organizations, and ways of being. From 1885, when she arrived in New York, a sixteen-year-old immigrant from Russia, until she died in 1940, her voice and her life were present in American and European radical politics. Labor organizing, birth control advocacy, free speech campaigns, antiwar struggles, activism on behalf of political prisoners, organizing alternative schools, fund-raising for the Spanish anarchists during the civil war, ceaseless "propaganda" on behalf of the oppressed—in all these contexts and more E.G. lived a life critically engaged.

Goldman has frequently been praised for her effective political organizing and her eloquent public speaking. Yet even Goldman's admirers have been dismissive of Goldman's theorizing about politics, claiming that her real contributions lay instead in the realm of activism. "She was an activist, not a theoretician," states Alex Kates Shulman in her introduction to *Red Emma Speaks*. "The libertarian vision she began with at twenty served for theory, and from it, together with her large emotional resources, flowed her commitment to action" (Goldman 1972, 21). David Porter offers a similar observation in his introduction to *Vision on Fire:* "Needless to say, her commentary as well as her commitment in these texts is as fully *emotional* as intellectual and as such needs no apology. She never posed herself as a deeply philosophical writer" (Porter 1983, 17). Such well-meaning apologies may obscure our ability to articulate E.G.'s particular way of doing political thinking, one that is located quite specifically in a radical political space, articulated passionately amid intense personal relationships in response to an immediate set of questions about oppression and possibility. There is an implicit and highly conventional gendering in the distinction between the emotional activist and the theoretically sophisticated intellectual, a recapitulation of patriarchal gender codes that inhibits both our reading of Goldman's political thinking and our ability to engage theories as kinds of practices. In some ways Shulman and Porter are correct—E.G. was not so much a theorist (if "theorist" is taken to mean the opposite of "activist") as a site of theory/practice, her life a space for writing meaning onto being. Distinctions between cognitive and emotional engagements, like distinctions between theory and action or between speech and writing, can be usefully blurred by examining Goldman's political thinking through her dense network of self-creating practices. Foucault's genealogy of self-constitution offers a fruitful strategy for apprehending E.G. not as a failed political philosopher but as a successful political philosophy-in-action.

E.G.'s production of herself shared Socrates' explicit politicization of the life of the individual within the life of the city. The Socratic art of life required no reward beyond its own intrinsic value, because the concern with self was at the same time a concern for the city. In *Alcibiades I* Plato develops the intersection of erotic and political knowledge that can enable the Platonic virtues of wisdom, courage, temperance, and justice.[2] E.G., too, integrated erotic, pedagogical, and political domains of knowing, caring for herself not as an object but as an activity, a *subject-en-process.* "The effort of the soul to know itself," remarked Foucault about Alcibiades, "is the principle on which just political action can be founded" (Martin, Gutman, and Hutton 1988, 25). The requisite knowledge is embedded in and produced by acting on oneself: "Concern for self always refers to an active political and erotic state. *Epimelesthai* expresses something much more serious than the simple fact of paying attention. It involves various things: taking pains with one's holdings and one's health. It is always a real activity and not just an attitude" (ibid., 24).

For E.G., the central political virtue binding care for herself with politics is the anarchist ideal of freedom within community more than the Platonic notion of justice as harmony. While Socrates prepared Alcibiades for a life participating in governance, E.G. chiseled her identity out of an unrelenting opposition to government. Yet her opposition to centralized authority propelled her into a variety of grassroots institutions, constituting alternative publics based on direct democratic action. Richard and Anna Maria Drinnon aptly characterize Goldman's and Berkman's anchor as "their refusal to be reconciled to the wretchedness and injustice in the world" (Drinnon and Drinnon 1975, 194). They chose to be flung into that wretchedness rather than to become complacent about it.

E.G. was more like Socrates than the Stoics in the importance she gave to emotion as a dimension of knowing. Unlike the Stoics, who thought that the passions and the sensuous world were disastrous for self-knowledge, E.G. linked Eros to knowledge. In a letter to Berkman's companion, Emmy Eckstein, Goldman observed that "if you do not feel a thing, you will never guess its meaning" (ibid., 164). Knowledge of others, she wrote to Berkman, required both careful observation and "the capacity for love" (ibid., 94). The anarchist "spirit" that she often invoked as both a cause and consequence of political change combined passion, commitment, creativity, and courage.

Yet she did not underestimate the corrosive power of oppressive social arrangements to generate other kinds of spirit, those accompanying the emotional frenzy of nationalism and militarism. At her deportation hearing in 1919, E.G. challenged the United States to live up to its guarantee of freedom of opinion. The virulent postwar Red Scare brought down the establishment's rage on her and Berkman as the anarchist Other. At the hearing she stated: "I protest against the whole spirit underlying it—the spirit of an irresponsible hysteria, the result of the terrible war, and of the evil tendencies of bigotry and persecution and violence which are the epilogue of five years of bloodshed . . ." (ibid., 11). Lucidly connecting the attacks on political speech with the bereft social capital circulated by war, she problematized the state's agitated production of otherness, an otherness she herself embodied.

Goldman's and Berkman's "beautiful ideal," plus their ties with cherished others, sustained them. In their letter from Ellis Island on December 18, 1919, as they awaited their deportation to the Soviet Union for their opposition to World War I, they wrote, "We have great faith in the American people" (ibid., 12). In 1919 they could still write confidently about the people rising up against the state. They could still see their own sacrifices as enabling revolution. "We go strengthened by our conviction that America will free herself not merely from the sham of paper guarantees, but in a fundamental sense, in her economic, social, and spiritual life" (ibid., 12). Fifteen years later, they could no longer see themselves as history's winners, yet their spirit of rebellion persisted. After leaving the fledgling U.S.S.R. in 1921, E.G.'s restless exile in England, France, and Canada was accompanied by increasing despair about the eroding interest in struggles for freedom, until the short-lived anarchist successes in the Spanish Civil War reenergized her for the last few years of her life.

The Drinnons estimate that E.G. wrote some two hundred thousand letters in her lifetime (ibid., xiv).[3] She based her autobiography on ten volumes of collected correspondence, "veritable mountains of letters" sent back to her by her friends (ibid., xv). To some extent this reflects the endemic circumstances of those in exile, yearning to hear from home. Yet not all exiles, in fact rather few exiles, produce the extraordinary network of communication that E.G. generated. She wrote to Berkman nearly every day, often pamphlet-sized epistles covering a range of topics: friends; acquaintances; their health; former, present, and future lovers; the destruction of the revolution in Russia; the place of violence in anarchist struggles; relations between women and men; the vagaries of "the masses"; articles and speeches they helped each other write; finances; books; government harassment of exiles; their own enduring friendship. Writing late in 1931, E.G. assured Berkman that she wrote often, and she described her weariness of life, her fatigue at the "useless labor" of writing hundreds of letters: "But it is the only link in my life, to keep in touch with our friends in America. And so I keep at it" (ibid., xiii). After a time she began to create a sort of impromptu newsletter by "broadcasting[ing] carbon copies to a wide circle of correspondents" (ibid., xv). Goldman claimed she did this because "I find much

typing sheer torture beside being a rotten typist!" (ibid., xv).[4] Yet the practice did not seem to lessen the amount of time she spent typing, only to am-
plify the number of people to whom she was connected.

Writing to British novelist Evelyn Scott, she noted, "I must say I find it
infinitely easier to express myself in letters than in books. My thoughts come
easier though not always worthwhile" (ibid., xv). The Drinnons speculate
that E.G.'s prodigious letter writing was the nearest substitute, under conditions of exile, for the speeches, lectures, and conversations that had been her
forte in the United States: "Letters became Emma Goldman's medium primarily because she was an exile and because in them the gap between the
written and the spoken word was at its narrowest. A short stride over the gap
enabled her to express her great strength as a speaker and conversationalist:
It was as though she were responding to an earnest questioner after a lecture
or having her say after a fine meal in someone's apartment" (ibid., xv).

Both kinds of activities were no doubt readily imaginable by most of her
correspondents, many of whom had seen her at work in both contexts,
holding crowds spellbound in lecture halls and holding forth to her friends.
She was a public intellectual in a unique sense, creating a public and herself within that public through a network of connecting.

The Drinnons continue: "This 'proclivity to spread myself in letters,' for
which she was chided by Berkman and others, meant that her distant friends
had access to her continuous present and to her self-revelation of different
aspects of character to different correspondents. Her letters gave them immediate data on how she was living her life and were in a sense invitations
to live as much of it as they could with her" (ibid., xv). At least one historian,
the anarchist Max Nettlau, appreciated her epistolary style. He wrote to her
in 1929 that, while "tiptop up to date otherwise," in her mode of communication "you are eighteenth century, doing honor to the good old art of letter
writing . . ." (ibid., xv–xvi). Nettlau contrasted the "rapid talk" of "the wire
and telephone" with E.G.'s "thoughtful way of communication by letter, a
practice more widely utilized two centuries earlier" (ibid., xvi). Following
Foucault's lead, we can connect Goldman's letter writing to the ancient practices of care for the self. She engaged in what Foucault called a continuous
"self-exercise": "Writing was also important [along with meditation] in the
culture of taking care of oneself. One of the main features of taking care involved taking notes on oneself to be reread, writing treatises and letters to
friend to help them, and keeping notebooks in order to reactivate for oneself the truths one needed" (Martin, Gutman, and Hutton 1988, 27).

Had exile not intervened, perhaps E.G. would have maintained the priority of the oral communications at which she excelled (although even before exile she frequently wrote several letters a day, usually to absent lovers,

distant friends, or comrades arranging her lectures in other cities). But exile forcibly relocated her, and her many thousands of letters after 1919 represented her determined effort to relocate herself once again, by sheer force of will and tenacity to maintain herself within her community, to take care of herself and her community. Her letters were a kind of self-craftsmanship, working on/with her interior resources and her circumstances to constitute herself as a political subject. Through what Nietzsche called "much obstinate, faithful repetition of the same labors, the same renunciations" she both marshaled the self that was there and articulated the self that could be there (Nietzsche quoted in Connolly 1988, 163). Her missives can be attended as a kind of body writing, always addressed to someone in particular, anchored in that relation, moving outward from that base while sustaining that concrete connection. Her letters were simultaneously rough drafts for articles, speeches, or other letters. Her letters were a critical vehicle of self she crafted. She wrote herself to others.

CONSTITUTING OR POLICING THE SELF?

The technologies of self-care, through which one *makes oneself into a subject,* bear an uneasy relation to the technologies of domination, through which one *is subjected* to the prevailing regimes of power/knowledge. Foucault pointed out that they "hardly ever function separately, although each one of them is associated with a certain type of domination . . . each implies certain modes of training and modification of individuals. . . . I wanted to show both their specific nature and their constant interaction" (Martin, Gutman, and Hutton 1988, 18). In the Hellenistic age, Foucault found "a relation developed between writing and vigilance. Attention was paid to nuances of life, mood and reading, and the experience of oneself was intensified and widened by virtue of this act of writing" (ibid., 28). The distinction here is not a clear-cut dyad between being a subject versus being an object, but rather a less clear contrast between writing oneself and being written as a self. Power, Foucault consistently maintained, does not just say "no." It does its work by saying "yes," by constituting identity and desire. Since technologies of domination do their work constitutively, not just prohibitively, the affirmations involved in crafting the self are intertwined uneasily with those involved in policing it.

The vigilance that E.G. exercised over herself can sometimes suggest that she fought off change by calling the anarchist police. There is a pervasive demand for consistency within herself: she routinely insists to her correspondents that she has *never changed her mind* on a variety of events and positions. Declarations that "I have always believed . . ." or "I have never

35

argued . . ." pepper her letters. Any accusation of ideological inconsistency from her correspondents provoked stinging rebukes in subsequent letters. The distinction between changing one's mind, which E.G. did with some regularity, and abandoning one's principles, which was anathema to her, was rather heavily policed.

One might understand this drive to self-discipline as marking the appearance of the second kind of self-technique that Foucault describes, that which appeared in fourth- and fifth-century Christianity as penitence: "the model of death, of torture, or of martyrdom. The theories and practices of penance were elaborated around the problem of the man who prefers to die rather than to compromise or abandon the faith" (ibid., 43). The "paradox in the care of the self in Christianity" is that "salvation is attained through the renunciation of self" (Foucault 1994, 285). This paradox of liberation through renunciation, which both awed and horrified Goldman in her early years in the movement (Goldman 1970, 76) was not unfamiliar to the persons in the anarchist movement in Goldman's time, not because they were simply recapitulating the early Christians' views but because their ideologies, strategies, and circumstances located them in a similar relation to their world. Following Foucault's analysis of fifth-century monasticism, William Pade offers a gloss of monastic leader John Cassian's "path of the soul's perfection" (Martin, Gutman, and Hutton 1988, 65) that sounds a lot like anarchism: "Cassian's vocabulary highlights the active, determinative character of this system. There is consistent use of terms for struggling, resisting, overcoming, fighting, prevailing. He relies on words for attaining, achieving, gaining, winning victory. His writings are saturated with the language of vigilance, discrimination, watching, weighing. Such a lexicon is possible only where there is a fixed discrimination of opposite realms" (ibid., 66). Much anarchist writing, including Goldman's, is similarly saturated with the language of struggle: the people versus the state; liberation versus oppression; the workers versus capital. The "fixed discrimination of opposite realms" invites a constant, sterile judging, a need to enforce consistency, to firmly establish the lines of demarcation between what one endorses and what one opposes. E.G. was drawn early in her life to the model of the anarchist martyr, the courageous individual who commits an *attentat,* an act of political violence rousing the masses to revolution. She and Berkman planned and carried out an assassination attempt on Henry Clay Frick, the man responsible for the killing of workers and their families at the Homestead Massacre. The attempt failed in all respects: Frick lived; Goldman and Berkman were not able to use the courtroom to explain their act and "awaken the masses" (many of whom were appalled by the act) to revolution; and Berkman spent fourteen horrendous years in prison. Goldman's reflections on this event, on the proper connections between means and ends in revolutionary action, became a persistent axis of her political thinking, the marker around which she recalibrated her understandings of politics. She outraged the nation in 1901 by defending the political sensibilities of Leon Czolgosz, the young man who assassinated President McKinley, while at the same time opposing his *attentat* and offering to apply her medical training in service as nurse to the dying president.

When E.G. was preparing to write her autobiography in 1928, attorney Arthur Leonard Ross advised her to exclude her role in Berkman's attempted assassination of Frick. She refused, calling that episode and her lifelong relation to Berkman "the leitmotif of my forty years of life [since]": "As a matter of fact it is the pivot around which my story is written. You are mistaken if you think that it was only 'the humane promptings of a girlish heart' which impelled my desperate act contained in the story. It was my religiously devout belief that the end justifies all means. The end, then, was my ideal of human brotherhood. If I have undergone any change it is not in my ideal. It is more in the realization that a great end does not justify *all* means" (Drinnon and Drinnon 1975, xx). The event and subsequent trajectory represented, she said, "the very essence of my book" (ibid., xx). While to the end she prided herself on being embroiled in political struggle, the "fixed discrimination of opposite realms" blurred into a more ambiguous, ironic tension, especially within the contradictory and tragic circumstances of the Spanish Civil War. "Life is stronger than theory," she wrote in 1937 to her friend Tom Bell (Porter 1983, 227). E.G.'s early inclinations toward martyrdom and the black-and-white world of subduing the self became overwritten by the complexities of self-construction and political struggle within a contradictory world. While E.G. often characterized herself as a believer, the arts of renunciation were never as attractive as the arts of exuberance.

LIVING THE REVOLUTION

E.G. and her colleagues spent a great deal of their time discussing how to "live the revolution." Ironically, her most revolutionary act can be seen as having little to do with bringing herself into ideological line, and everything to do with constituting herself as a revolutionary in exile. Those two hundred thousand letters she wrote created a network of critical thinking, a set of lives interconnected in resistance. As the Drinnons note, "She spoke [in her letters] with directness and intensity from the current edge of her thinking, feeling, experiencing—and not incidentally therewith effectively revoked the official edict of separation from all she held dear" (Drinnon and Drinnon 1975, xv). It was the ultimate act of anarchist creativity, of the sheer will to deny the state its victims, to find a way to maintain the self-creating connections at the heart of her technologies of the self. Her remarkable ability and willingness to carry on in the face of defeat, to find some satisfaction in the process of rebelling even if she never won: that indefatigability is in fact what allowed her to win. She beat the authorities in that she recreated the political space they tried to take away; she herself was that space, a space of anarchism.

Responding to Berkman's despair ("There really seems no such thing as progress," he grieved), E.G. replied in her letter of November 18, 1931, by locating herself in the energy created by the friction between a bitter sense of futility and an unreasoning determination to persevere:

> I too have come to the conclusion, bitter as it is, that hardly anything has come of our years of effort. And that the mass is really hopeless as far as real progress and freedom are concerned. The trouble is the recognition of a fact does not make it easier to reconcile oneself to it. For instance, I have come to see that nothing I can do in the way of bringing our ideas before the people will leave much trace or make a lasting impression. Yet I never was in greater revolt against my being gagged as I am now. What sense is there to continue living when I have no outlet of any sort? Even if I had material security, which of course I have not, nor do I expect to get it from *Living My Life*, it would still be inane to go on merely eating, drinking, and having a roof over my head. I can't stand the thought of it. So you see, my dear, though "Du has mir aus dem Herzen gesprochen" ["you have spoken my deepest belief"] as regards the masses, the inherent love of power to dominate others whoever wields that power, anarchists and syndicalists included, the still voice in me will not be silenced, the voice which wants to cry out against the wretchedness and injustice in the world. (Ibid., 50)

She compared her anarchist life to one withdrawn from public life ("merely eating, drinking, and having a roof over my head") and found the latter unthinkable. She heard "a voice within herself" that was detectable through the labor that it took to produce it.

E.G. continued: "I can compare my state with that of a being suffering from an incurable disease. He knows there is no remedy. Yet he goes on trying every doctor, and every kind of quack. I know there is no place where I can or will gain a footing and once more throw in my lot with our people who continue in the struggle of liberation. Yet I cling to the silly hope as a drowning man does to a straw" (ibid., 50). Yet she did find that place again, regained her footing, and threw in her lot with the Spanish anarchists in the civil war. Berkman did not. E.G. offered Berkman that same lifeline, that same self-constituting space in which political resistance continues *because* it continues, because it is a space of identity, of being, because that is where

E.G. *happens:* "Fact is, dear heart, you do the same. You say in yours of the 15th that if you have to get out of here, you'll go to Spain. You know as well as I that you could do nothing there. Yet you want to go because you want to be close to the activities of our comrades and if possible make yourself felt among them. It is no use, Sash, you and I have been in battle too long to content ourselves with a humdrum existence. And yet we both know how little we have achieved in the past and how little we will leave behind when we go . . ." (ibid., 50). She held up to her old comrade the twin opportunities of relationship and agency, "to be close to the activities of our comrades" and "make yourself felt among them." In Berkman's case, these strategies were, in the end, insufficient: suffering from ill health and political despair, he committed suicide on June 28, 1936. E.G. lived four more years, dying after a stroke on May 18, 1940, in Montreal, while campaigning to stop the deportation of some Italian activists.

Acting on yourself through yourself, articulating yourself in passionate connection with others, *doing* the things that create *being:* Emma Goldman lived as an example of anarchism. She created herself, flamboyantly, persistently, often painfully, through long-lasting techniques of self-production. Her self-in-relation was constituted through the intimate relations and political spaces she helped to create. Exile did not deprive her of that space or render her incapable of creating it. E.G. was a remarkable example.

NOTES

For an elaboration of this interpretation of Goldman, see my forthcoming book on Emma Goldman to be published by Rowman and Littlefield.

1. In a 1984 interview, in response to the question "Should the concept of the care of the self in the classical sense be updated to confront this modern thought [about the centrality of the knowing subject]?" Foucault replied: "Absolutely, but I would certainly not do so just to say 'We have unfortunately forgotten about the care of the self; so here, here it is, the key to everything.' Nothing is more foreign to me than the idea that, at a certain moment, philosophy went astray and forgot something, that somewhere in its history there is a principle, a foundation that must be rediscovered." Contact with the world of ancient self-care is useful, both to Foucault's analysis and to mine, because it produces "something new" (Foucault 1994, 294–95).

2. Foucault noted the controversy surrounding this dialogue; both the date and the authorship have been questioned. He nonetheless found it pivotal for later neo-Platonist expressions of Platonic philosophy. See Martin, Gutman, and Hutton (1988, 23).

3. Think what she could have done with e-mail! But we might not have the record of it.

4. My guess, based on comments by her editors as well as my own reading of her unedited letters, is that Goldman was dyslexic. While her editors have cleaned up her prose in publication, they all refer to her poor spelling. See Drinnon and Drinnon (1975, xviii) and Porter (1983, xii). Her troubles with written English were far greater than would be expected solely as a result of being a non-native speaker. She confused short vowels with one another, mixed *t* and *th*, confused different *r*-controlled syllables (*er, ar, ir, ur, or*), intermixed *cal* with *cle*, confused homonyms, and butchered idioms. About her own spelling she said, "I suppose there is no help for me on this or the other world" (Drinnon and Drinnon 1975, xviii). Perhaps her unique skills in spoken expression are also traceable to the creative and nonconventional relation to language that dyslexic learners frequently manifest.

WORKS CITED

Connolly, William E. 1988. *Political Theory and Modernity*. Oxford: Blackwell.

Drinnon, Richard, and Anna Maria Drinnon, eds. 1975. *Nowhere at Home: Letters from Exile of Emma Goldman and Alexander Berkman*. New York: Schocken.

Foucault, Michel. 1986. *The Care of the Self*. New York: Pantheon.

———. 1994. *Ethics: Subjectivity and Truth*. Edited by Paul Rabinow. Translated by Robert Hurley and others. New York: New Press.

Goldman, Emma. 1970. *Living My Life*. Volume 1. New York: Dover.

———. 1972. *Red Emma Speaks: Selected Writings and Speeches by Emma Goldman*. Edited by Alex Kates Shulman. New York: Random House.

Martin, Luther H., Huck Gutman, and Patrick H. Hutton, eds. 1988. *Technologies of the Self: A Seminar with Michel Foucault*. Amherst: University of Massachusetts Press.

Porter, David, ed. 1983. *Vision on Fire: Emma Goldman on the Spanish Revolution*. New Paltz, N.Y.: Common Ground.

3

Exit Woolf

Stephen M. Barber

And now I can put my philosophy of the free soul into operation.
—Virginia Woolf, *Diary*

Freedom is the ontological condition of ethics. But ethics is the considered form that freedom takes when it is informed by reflection.
—Michel Foucault, *Ethics*

From the early 1930s until her death in 1941, Virginia Woolf elaborated a philosophy of freedom and an aesthetics of existence that in strikingly prescient ways exemplify Michel Foucault's final work on the ethics of the concern for self as a practice of freedom. For all of its presaging force, though, Woolf's political philosophy is identified by contemporary readers with ideas immeasurably less original and radical than Foucault's, not to mention her own. Indeed, various commentators go so far as to connect Woolf with the very object of her critique, as testified for instance by a recent biography of her which reports that "in Britain there is still a version of Woolf as politically ineffectual or, even, a quasi-Fascist" (Lee 1996, 679).

Woolf certainly intuited as inevitable the charge of political ineffectuality or elitism, and her foreboding sense of indictment on the eve of the publication of her antiwar and antifascist essay *Three Guineas* (1938) correctly identifies the terms by which this derision was to be played out. "I can foretell," she prophesied, "that those who dislike [it] will sneer at me for a well to do aesthete" (Woolf 1984b, 145). After the first reviews, one of which criticized that Woolf "preach[ed] sitting still on a sofa" (Woolf 1984b, 145), Queenie Leavis publicly denounced *Three Guineas* by explicitly associating Woolf's aesthetics of existence with fascism. For Leavis, Woolf's essay read "like Nazi dialectic," and it offered, she derided, "the art of living as conceived by a social parasite" (quoted in Lee 1996, 692). Why, from its inception to today, is Woolf's "art of living" generally confronted with an epistemic block? In addition to her borne-out anticipation of acerbic reviews motivated by sex- and class-resentment, Woolf accurately assessed that the specific charge against her of fascist sympathy was a reaction to her epistemically disruptive conception of an inextricable relationship between politics and aesthetics. Throughout the 1930s these terms were, after all, predominantly conceived in Britain as properly separate if not opposed; concomitantly, fascism was prevalently understood by critical theorists as the aestheticization of politics. The attendant response by those who apprehend fascism thus is to invert that process: any artistic venture that sought to oppose fascism must redress it by politicizing aesthetics. Woolf not only distanced but removed herself from this arguably formalist paradigm (of which she has so long been held a champion) because she perceived its ideology as presupposing a separation between and reification of "art" and "politics."

The positive aspect of Woolf's epistemic self-removal—her establishment of an aesthetics of existence, or her novel conception and creation of an ethicized relationship between politics and aesthetics—links her to Foucault for whom philosophy is an "activity, . . . [a] movement by which, not without effort and uncertainty, dreams and illusions, one detaches oneself from what is accepted as true and seeks other rules." More, Foucault continues, philosophy is "the displacement and transformation of frameworks of thinking, the changing of received values and all the work that has been done to think otherwise, to do something else, to become other than what one is" (Foucault 1997, 327). Woolf's concept of the "free soul" or the "outsider" (developed respectively in her diary and *Three Guineas*) embodies this force, this activity, and her philosophy of freedom presages even as it is in turn retroactively intensified and enriched by Foucault's late work on ethics which stages anew, as it were, her dramatic exit from the British political terrain of the 1930s. If it is Foucault's final writings that are able to make salient for contemporary thinkers the radical aspects and implications of Woolf's thought, this undoubtedly is owing to his related escape from a persistent feature of contemporary politics identified and fought against by both, namely, that "contemporary political thought allows very little room for the question of the ethical subject" (Foucault 1997, 294). Woolf and Foucault pose the question of the ethical subject on the terrain of a philosophy that reconceives not only politics, aesthetics, responsibility, and thought as such, but also the precise political problem of fascism, *and* they each do so by means of an ethicization of aesthetics. This aesthetics, which comprises critique and asceticism ("not in the sense of a morality of renunciation but as an exercise of the self on the self by which one attempts to develop and transform oneself, and to attain to a certain mode of being" [282]), is portrayed by both thinkers as an *ethos* or an *attitude*.

During the final decade of their lives, Woolf and Foucault grasped as their responsibility "the permanent reactivation of an attitude—that is, of a philosophical ethos that could be described as a permanent critique of our historical era" (Foucault 1997, 312). This philosophical ethos involves an exploration of the ways in which human beings are transformed into subjects by different modes of objectification, a discursive procedure Foucault calls "subjectification." With the introduction of an unconventional understanding of aesthetics into the itinerary of his thought, Foucault turned his attention in his final phase from exclusive focus on the subject *of* history—that is to say the subject of discursive constraints—to the process of "subjectivization," by which is meant aesthetic procedures undertaken *by* the subject to constitute *for* itself an ethical subjectivity.[1] If for a long while he had understood the relationship between philosophy and politics to be "permanent and fundamental" (293), it was in his relatively late project to fashion the philosophical life itself as an escape from "those prisons of thought and action which shape our politics, our ethics, our relations to ourselves" (Bernauer 1992, 179) that he came to accord an equally fundamental status to aesthetics. "From the idea that the self is not given to us," he offers in one of his last interviews, "I think that there is only one possible consequence: we have to create ourselves as a work of art" (Foucault 1997, 262).

Woolf orchestrates a comparable if converse move. In the midst of perceived social and political intolerability she evolved, for the here and now (rather than for some future present), new possibilities of resistance, intervention, and life, an ethical elaboration she refers to as her philosophy of the free soul. Throughout the 1930s, Woolf attempted to address ethically thought and its encounter with history. After two decades of literary experimentation, she decisively turned to an unconventional form of philosophy that, like Foucault's, expresses "a mode of relating to contemporary reality; . . . a way of thinking and feeling; a way, too, of acting and behaving that at one and the same time marks a relation of belonging [to the contemporary world] and presents itself as a task [within it]" (309). Foucault names this ethos or mode of philosophical activity *critical ontology,* which he further and more precisely describes as "a philosophical life in which the critique of what we are is at one and the same time the historical analysis of the limits imposed on us and an experiment with the possibility of going beyond them" (319). Woolf's late writing shares with Foucault *this* conception of philosophy, although her attempt to articulate herself as an ethical thinker within its terms is conducted primarily not by means of "philosophy" (strictly speaking, as in Foucault's case) but rather by establishing a particular relation to her writing. Two statements from 1933 exemplify this resolve: "Where truth is important . . . I prefer to write fiction" (Woolf 1977, 9), and then, "I thought . . . something very profound about the synthesis of my being: how only writing composes it . . ." (Woolf 1984a, 161).

The degree to which Woolf identifies writing and the "true life," "mental fight" and joy (Woolf 1967b, 174), reaches unprecedented intensity during just those years when not only her own life (her name would appear on the Gestapo list) but also the social structure that had sustained it—"the whole liberal milieu from which she came"—were most threatened by fascism.[2] Yet she rejected the hegemonic view of Britain as merely threatened by fascism since the political terrain of her "civilized" country was, she maintained, itself already not only possibly subject to but also indeed constitutive of the very power it sought so ardently to characterize as "barbarous." The problem of fascism, Woolf was to argue, had been dangerously obscured by contemporary British political thought. Whether the latter's hegemonic conception of "freedom" had led to this obscurity, or whether the obfuscation of "fascism" was responsible for an inadequate problematization of freedom, Woolf viewed in any case the contemporary political terrain of Britain not in terms of its self-representation as a civilized force in opposition to the barbarism of Fascist Italy and Nazi Germany but rather as itself an imposition of limits on freedom. Her close observation of political culture throughout the decade led her to both a new conception of fascism and a novel sense of freedom. Confronted with hitherto unexamined and unnamed fascist forces, Woolf undertook in *Three Guineas* to describe and critique this form of fascism, and she refused to accept her situation as condemned merely to converse with its power. In her task to create an exit from its terms, she unfolds her critique and forges her ethics as a response to questions echoed thirty years later by Foucault and posed in rememoration by his friend Gilles Deleuze: "What are our ways of existing, our possibilities of life or our processes of subjectivization; are there ways for us to constitute ourselves as a 'self,' and (as Nietzsche would put it) sufficiently 'artistic' ways, beyond knowledge and power? And are we up to it, because in a way it's a matter of life and death?" (Deleuze 1995, 99).

THE TURN TO ETHICS: POLITICS AND THE PRACTICE OF FREEDOM

> The question now to settle is what "attitude" to adopt. . . . I want to forge ahead on my own lines.
> —Virginia Woolf, *Diary*

The story of Woolf's turn to ethics, which she describes as her "spiritual conversion" (Woolf 1984b, 141), begins early in the 1930s. During those years she refers several times across her writings to a philosophical ethos born of "revelation," the key terms of which are "freedom" and "attitude." Writing in her diary of the autumn of 1932, for example, she recalls her "great sea-

son of liberation [when] everything appeared very distinct, amazingly ex-
citing. I had no restrictions whatever, & was thus free to define my attitude
with vigor and certainty [such as] I have never known before" (Woolf 1984a,
134–35). Despite the confidence and sense of possibility bequeathed her by
this "tremendous revelation," Woolf cautiously acknowledges that "it is always doubtful how far one human being can be free"; still, she had "said I
will no longer be fettered by any artificial tie" and "therefore spoke out in
my own voice" (1984a, 135). The exact year of Woolf's foray into subjectivization is, of course, impossible to determine with any certainty not only
because her many references to it yield different dates (all of which point to
the years between 1932 and 1935) but also because it is doubtful that one
could assign with any chronological precision the time of ethical revelation,
notwithstanding Woolf's own attempts. In her 1937 memoir of her nephew
Julian Bell who was killed that year in the Spanish Civil War, she dates, for
example, her philosophical position ("a complex state which I would one
day have discussed with him" [Woolf 1987, 257]) to 1935, and in 1938 she con-
jectures in her diary yet another date: "I must cling to my 'freedom'—that
mysterious hand that was reached out to me about 4 years ago" (Woolf
1984b, 137). In any event, certainly by 1938 she could write with confidence,
"I possess my soul—now that's a thing one can do" (1984b, 147).

Many accounts, both philosophical and biographical, have been offered
to explain Foucault's turn from analyses of knowledge formations and apparatuses of power to his work on ethics, but the novel terms of Woolf's
own conversion to a philosophy of freedom remain largely unexamined,
perhaps exactly because of their subtle, difficult, and radical originality.[3]
That Woolf uses the phrase *spiritual conversion* to indicate her turn to the
development of a political ontology seems, for example, precisely at odds
with a *critical* itinerary until one accesses Foucault's own idiomatic sense of
spirituality.

Before broaching that precise understanding, though, it is helpful to note
that for his part, Foucault acknowledges a certain change early in the 1960s
within his own life resulting from "the fact that there has been political innovation, political creation, and political experimentation outside the great
political parties, and outside the normal or ordinary program" (Foucault 1997,
172). Foucault's involvement with political experimentation led directly to his
account of ethics and to his analyses of "governmentality" (which implies
the relationship of the self to the self). "Let's escape as much as possible from
the types of relations that society proposes for us and try," he suggests, "to
create in the empty space where we are new relational possibilities" (160).

Woolf's problematization of freedom in the 1930s likewise began with a
perceived necessity for political experimentation. "[H]ow widely I feel out-

side it all," she affirms of her experience with political programs: "un-trapped by [not only] the Morgan [Forster] communist group," but by its liberal alternatives, as well (Woolf 1984b, 189). Before an array of political positions staged by the Labor Party and numerous antifascist organiza-tions, she felt she had no choice but to forge an exit from "the immersion in all that energy & all that striving that is quite oblivious of me; making me feel that I am oblivious of it" (Woolf 1984a, 345).

Woolf's antifascist critique is elaborated, as she notes, "against the [polit-ical] current," against a backdrop, in other words, of what Foucault refers to as "the normal and old traditional political organizations" (which, "since the nineteenth-century . . . have confiscated the process of political creation in order to take over power") and in opposition to what she dismisses as a per-vasively cultural and merely "touching belief in English intellectuals" to counter the growing phenomenon of fascism (Foucault 1997, 172, 173; Woolf 1984b, 17). If both Foucault and Woolf establish their respective and resonant conceptions of critique and ethics in opposition to what they discerned as a politically dominant inability to identify new forms of fascism, these forms could be articulated, according to both, only within the political experi-mentation of a philosophy of nominalism where even and especially "poli-tics" is itself, in turn, reconceptualized.[4] "I am not a politician, obviously," Woolf claims of her own responses to fascism. "I can only rethink politics very slowly into my own tongue" (Woolf 1984b, 114). For the new forms of fascism that she sought to make visible and intolerable correspond neither to the state formations represented by Mussolini's Fascism and Hitler's Nazism nor to the political programs of Oswald Mosley's British Union of Fascists and its rival, Arnold Leese's Imperial Fascist League. In her diagno-sis of current British society, Woolf finds that she must forge in *Three Guineas* the concept of "infantile fixation" (or, in the shorthand of Deleuze and Félix Guattari, "microfascism") in order to articulate her discernment of an "em-bryo . . . in the heart of England, the creature, Dictator as we call him when he is Italian or German, who believes that he has the right, whether given by God, Nature, sex or race is immaterial, to dictate to other human beings how they shall live; what they shall do" (Woolf 1966, 53).

The radical difference between Woolf's conception of fascist power and that held by British political and social thought may be gleaned in her pro-ductive interest, shared by Foucault, in the "puzzling" nature of the political similarities between fascist and liberal states. For all of the "historical unique-ness" of fascism, Foucault contends, it is "not quite original." What he means by this is comparable to Woolf's response to British liberal newspapers and speeches that represent women in ways not dissimilar to their representation by official Fascist and Nazi ideology. Comparing two speech extracts—one

British, the other German—Woolf asks, "Where is the difference? Are they not both saying the same thing? Are they not both the voices of Dictators, whether they speak English or German?" (Woolf 1966, 53). Like Woolf, Foucault claims of fascism that it "used and extended mechanisms already present in most other societies. More than that, in spite of [its] own internal madness, [it] used to a large extent the ideas and the devices of our own political rationality" (Foucault 2000, 328). Woolf's discernment of an underlying ideational symmetry between "civilization" and "barbarism," as her consequent analysis of political rationality evinces, left her with little patience for the manner in which the question of political responsibility was broached by British antifascists, as in the debates between the great parties or between the various pacifist and nonpacifist organizations. Hence, when Woolf refers to herself in 1936 as "a pacifist" (Woolf 1984b, 17), she decisively has in mind both a new sense of that term and a new sense of its target. An "outsider," her pacifism is directed not only at the grand narrative of war in the frame of international state politics but also at the form of war that masks itself as peace and at the form of barbarism that masks itself as civilization.

The question, then, to which Woolf seeks to respond in *Three Guineas*, "How can we prevent war?" (Woolf 1966, 3), combines with Foucault's, "How can we practice freedom?" (Foucault 1997, 296) to disclose a yet more radical and ethically prior question, "*We who are free, are we free?*"[5] These questions emerged to interview both Foucault and Woolf in their respective confrontations with fascism. The analyses of fascism that Foucault, along with Deleuze and Guattari, developed during the 1960s and 1970s resonate deeply with Woolf's critical and creative account. "I think that what has happened since 1960," Foucault speculates, "is the simultaneous appearance of new forms of fascism, new forms of consciousness of fascism, new forms of description of fascism, and new struggles against fascism." In profound if unwitting accord with Woolf's antifascist work, Foucault goes on to say that "the role of the intellectual is to situate oneself according to one's experiences, one's skills, one's personal choices, one's desire—to situate oneself at a certain point that will be such that one can simultaneously make visible forms of fascism that unfortunately are not seen or are too easily tolerated, describe these forms of fascism, try to make them intolerable, and define what specific form of struggle can be undertaken against fascism" (quoted in Eribon 1991, 312). Then in 1972 Foucault introduced the first volume of Deleuze and Guattari's *Anti-Oedipus: Capitalism and Schizophrenia* as a "book of ethics" that took fascism as its "major enemy," its "strategic adversary." The work's enemy, Foucault discerns, is "not only historical [or macro]fascism, the fascism of Hitler and Mussolini—which was able to mobilize and use the desire of the masses so effectively—but also the [micro]fascism in us all, in our heads and in our everyday behavior, the fascism that causes us to love power, to desire the very thing that dominates and exploits us" (Deleuze and Guattari 1983, xiii). It is this double form of fascism that Woolf takes as the strategic enemy of *Three Guineas,* and, as we shall see, she foreshadows Foucault in her invitation to readers to undertake a re-cognition of the fascist figure as not only embodied in the Führer and Il Duce but also in our present selves.

A PHILOSOPHY OF THE OUTSIDE: *THREE GUINEAS* AS CRITICAL ONTOLOGY

> My mind is made up. . . . I am an outsider. I can take my way: experiment with my own imagination in my own way. The pack may howl, but it shall never catch me. And even if the pack—reviewers, friends, enemies—pays no attention or sneers, still I'm free. This is the actual result of that spiritual conversion (I can't bother to get the words right) in the autumn of 1933—or 4—when I rushed through London, buying, I remember, a great magnifying glass from sheer ecstasy.
> —Virginia Woolf, *Diary*

Woolf's great contribution to modern political and ethical thought—"my debt to civilization," she muses somewhat ironically of *Three Guineas*— proves to be a critical ontology that, as Foucault specifies, is also and at once an ethical self-fashioning, "a vitalism rooted in aesthetics" (Woolf 1984b, 170; Deleuze 1995, 96). For, as her example testifies, the philosophical life that Foucault perceives as "an 'exit,' a 'way out,'" is not simply "a form of relationship to the present; it is also a mode of relationship with oneself," a "mode of being to which philosophy gives access," "an indispensable asceticism" that "takes oneself as object of a complex and difficult elaboration" (Foucault 1997, 294, 305, 311). Foucault identifies four major aspects of this activity of self-formation: ethical substance, mode of subjectivization, asceticism, and telos. These aspects, present throughout Woolf's final writings, are nowhere more explicit than in *Three Guineas*. The ethical substance Woolf investigates there is *being* itself. She at once invites and incites her readers to pursue a mode of subjectivization—the recognition of our ethical obligations—in the form of rational rule. The asceticism or self-forming activity advanced by *Three Guineas* involves a three-fold process: the first, *depersonalization,* is the means by which Woolf as writer *accesses* critical ontology; the second, *de-individualization,* is the means by which Woolf *activates* critical ontology; like the first, it suggests an apparent paradox, for self-mastery obliges the dispossession by the self of the self; and the third is the development of a series of rules to be followed by "outsiders" in order to access and activate "the true life." Finally (and each of these aspects involves the others), the kind of being to which Woolf would have us aspire—her telos—in her account of ethical behavior is *the free soul* or *the outsider:* the joyful if reviled philosopher, of whom she instances herself as an example. (There is no difference between the concept and life.)

Woolf's apparently counterintuitive attribution of her critical ontology to a spiritual conversion—which she intimates is but a proximate naming (in the diary entry that serves as epigraph to this section)—finds an echo and an explanation in the thought of Foucault, who understands philosophy and spirituality to be not only closely associated but also at times identical. "By spirituality I mean," he specifies, "the subject's attainment of a certain mode of being and the transformations that the subject must carry out on itself to attain this mode of being" (Foucault 1997, 294). In the same breath Foucault stresses the critical aspect of this philosophy whose task it is to "call into question domination at every level and in every form in which it exists, whether political, economic, sexual, institutional, or what have you." This critical inquiry, according to Foucault, is inextricably linked to ethics and is present at the dawn of Western philosophy. For, he claims, "this critical function derives from the Socratic injunction 'Take care of yourself,' in other words, 'Make freedom your foundation, through the mastery of the self'" (300–301).

The critical function of Woolf's spiritual conversion announces itself in the epigraphic allusion to her accompanying act of the acquisition of "a great magnifying glass," an image that powerfully conveys the turn that saw her through to becoming, in Brenda Silver's phrase, a "systematic read[er] of her culture," a kind of physician of her own life and civilization (Silver 1983a, 22). For *Three Guineas* functions as that magnifying glass: an optical instrument through which phenomena, like British clothes, ceremonies, and "reason" itself, appear as signs or symptoms that reflect a state of microfascist forces.[6] This clinical and ethical treatise offers at once a symptomatological diagnosis of present power and its treatment: *Three Guineas* diagnoses a disease (infantile fixation) by isolating its symptoms (the passive state of human bondage, fear, resentment, intellectual slavery, and cultural prostitution), by tracing its etiology to a certain state of forces (the genealogical method that traces to the nineteenth century the rise of new forms of power, to which Foucault would give the overall name "bio-power"), and by setting forth a prognosis (infantile fixation culminating in war) as well as a treatment for becoming active (the ethical task: severing oneself, by means of de-individualization, from a science of life and its processes of subjectification, and creating in its stead an attitude, an aesthetics of existence).

Woolf mounts in *Three Guineas* an extraordinary critique of modern power relations by using her text as this magnifying glass to reveal religion, patriotism, nationalism, fascism, and individualism as causal and optical *effects:* effects whose processes of production she seeks to disclose by connecting them to their rational causes as they affect persons who do not understand them.[7] That this critique is inextricable from the ethics advanced by *Three Guineas* becomes evident as Woolf simultaneously composes a self-relation—the aforementioned ethics which takes the form of critical ontology and consequent facilitative or optional rules—that allows her, and that invites us, to resist, to elude fascism, and to turn life against a certain inherited relation to power. If *Three Guineas* closes with this invitation, from its beginning it has itself also and already sought to undermine our inherited relation to politics by undoing the political separation between private and public spheres; not only does each sphere bleed into the other at all times, Woolf argues, but each is also the other's condition of determination. Studying a photograph of dead bodies and ruined houses sent from Spain during the civil war (but not actually reproduced in *Three Guineas*), Woolf perceives the public and private worlds as inseparable: "the tyrannies and servilities of the one are the tyrannies and servilities of the other" (Woolf 1966, 142). To drive this point home, Woolf includes in *Three Guineas* a series of five photographs representing the customs of British civilized life that betray as suspect and ultimately untenable yet another politically maintained truism: the opposition of British "civilized" life to the "barbarity" of fascism and Nazism. Woolf frames these photographs with a detailed analysis of the aesthetic element in the conduct of life, but rather than unfolding a critique that exclusively identifies fascism as the aestheticization of politics, she appropriates the aesthetic element for (1) an ethics that effectively challenges the "post-enlightenment conception of the ethical person as merely public"[8] and for (2) a critique that departs from the apprehension of fascism as a uniquely German and Italian problem against which Britain's liberal individualism is self-represented as civilized.

Three Guineas takes the form of a letter addressed by the text's narrator to a British barrister who has written to ask, "How in your opinion are we to prevent war?" (1966, 3). Within this letter Woolf includes other letters and drafts of letters to women correspondents who, like the barrister, have written to request of the narrator financial assistance for, respectively, a women's college and an organization that helps women find work. The first chapter analyzes the relationship between education and war; the second analyzes the relationship between the professions and war; and the third examines notions of culture and intellectual liberty. The unity of the parts of *Three Guineas* derives from the narrator's continuous recourse throughout her letters to that photograph of dead bodies and ruined houses, a photograph that Woolf treats as a sign to be read symptomatologically. To begin with, the photograph in question represents, as we have noted, a civilization in ruin. By the third chapter and in the closing pages another figure appears at the forefront of the photograph: "It is the figure of a man; some say, others deny, that he is Man himself, the quintessence of virility, the perfect type of which all the others are imperfect adumbrations. He is a man certainly. His eyes are glazed; his eyes glare. His body, which is braced in an unnatural position, is tightly cased in a uniform. Upon the breast of that uniform are sewn several medals and other mystic symbols. His hand is upon a sword. He is called in German and Italian Führer or Duce; in our own language Tyrant or Dictator" (142).

Woolf's critique to this point has been tracing several startling associations: between British sartorial customs and war, between education and war, between ceremonies and war, and even between British rights and microfascist power; now Woolf traces a penultimate connection between the ruined houses, dead bodies, and a masculinism that affects fascist and liberal nationalisms alike. But Woolf does not halt at this analysis since yet another and final figure appears in the foreground of the palimpsest photograph. The human figure that Woolf has traced there—the figure that has emerged as "a man certainly"—suggests "other and more complex emotions," the discovery of which obliges her to renounce a critique whose end would be merely to identify masculinism and war. For as she continues reading the image a final and still more disconcerting portrait emerges: a portrait whose subject is *ourselves:* "we cannot dissociate ourselves from that figure," Woolf concludes, "but are ourselves that figure" (142).

Woolf's recognition of ourselves as inscribed in the figure with which *Three Guineas* closes is the climactic discovery of her critical philosophy: it arises out of her sustained symptomatological analysis and opens onto the work's ultimate and affirmative revelation. This critical apprehension in turn leads to the text's ethical opening: the fact of seeing ourselves in the fascist figure suggests to Woolf that "we are not passive spectators doomed to unresisting obedience but *by our thoughts and actions can ourselves change that figure*" (142; emphasis added). There are, in effect, two orders of response to the text's opening question: first, if war is to be prevented we must apprehend our being as written into a force field of a hitherto unacknowledged form of fascism; second, in order to prevent war *here and now,* we must devise and follow a series of ascetic practices and rules that will enable us to break with the reproduction of fascist modes of life.[9]

Reopening the text, one sees that *Three Guineas* involves a second reading: from the start ethics is at work rather than reached; it is not only that

Woolf's critique moves to a culminating ethics, but ethics is also the condition for the critique in the first place. We move, in a systematic reading, from Woolf's initial problematization of sexual differentiation in productions of knowledge and their relations to power to an account of ethics that serves as an antifascist guide to life. We move, in other words, from "the attempt—even if it is doomed to failure"—of Woolf to answer "a letter perhaps unique in the history of human correspondence, since when before has an educated man asked a woman how in her opinion war can be prevented?" (3) to the text's earned claim that "by our thoughts and actions [we] can ourselves change [the fascist] figure" in and by whom we are inscribed. Woolf sustains a critical position of sexual differentiation throughout *Three Guineas* and refuses to the end to merge an outsider's ethos with an insider's identity, and the collectivity of outsiders with the political organization of insiders. But she also closes her argument with the claim that the individualization of men and women alike is operated by un-apprehended fascist forces, the recognition of which can lead to processes of de-individualization in the formation of an antifascist life. And Woolf's argument is the effect of her own practice of de-individualization.

Although the antifascist analyses of Woolf and Foucault address totalitarianism, their critiques more precisely and seriously problematize and target what Deleuze and Guattari were to name collectively microfascist forces. Like Woolf, who asks "What right have we . . . to trumpet our ideals of freedom and justice to other countries" when microfascist forces are constitutive not only of our present selves but also of our notions of liberty and justice, Deleuze and Guattari confer considerable critical power to the analysis of microfascism when it is detached from a logic that theorizes it merely as chronologically prior or geopolitically confined to macrofascism: "We would even say that fascism implies a molecular [or individualizing] regime that is distinct from molar [or state] segments and their centralization. . . . Only microfascism," they claim, "provides an answer to the global question: Why does desire desire its own repression, how can it desire its own repression? . . . It's too easy to be antifascist on the molar level, and not even see the fascist inside you, the fascist you yourself sustain and nourish and cherish with molecules both personal and collective" (Deleuze and Guattari 1987, 214–15). Woolf's antifascist thought adumbrates this concern and participates in Deleuze and Guattari's apprehension of desire as critique's necessary object. "Let us drag up into consciousness the subconscious Hitlerism that holds us down," she urges in an essay of 1940. "It is the desire for aggression; the desire to dominate and enslave. . . . If we could free ourselves from slavery we should free men from tyranny. Hitlers are bred by slaves" (Woolf 1967b, 174).

Woolf's "freedom" here is "a complex state" (which nevertheless requires permanent reactivation) as well as a practice ("a thing one can do"), an attitude as well as a relation to contemporary reality ("And now I can put my philosophy of the free soul into operation"). Precisely because of this relational aspect, which requires of its subject persistent attention to the historicity of the present in all its contingent forms, the concept of "freedom" must be a nominalist one; that is, Woolf's concept of freedom, like Foucault's, does not refer to a transcendental "truth" but rather is defined by and forged in specific historical contexts. Woolf underscores her nominalism by frequently placing her concept within quotation marks, as when she writes: "I must cling to my 'freedom.'" Ironically, the resonance between the nominalist philosophies of Woolf and Foucault sounds in the symmetrically *discordant* objections to freedom thus conceived that arise in critical commentary. With respect to Woolf's "obsession" with freedom, for instance, Nigel Nicolson expresses bafflement before the "strength of her feeling": "nothing in her own life, nor in the lives of her close friends quite explains it. . . . In the 1930s, [after all,] when her anger boiled over, she was in every sense one of the most liberated women in England, and had been so for twenty years" (Nicolson 1979, xv).

It is this sense of liberation (however putatively multilayered) that both Woolf and Foucault so object to in their respective political critiques. The latter considers liberation to be an idea that "should not be accepted without scrutiny," and he, too, was often confronted with the mistranslation of "freedom" as "liberation." With respect to the equation of "a work of the self on the self" and "a process of liberation," Foucault objects:

> I would be more careful on that score. I have always been somewhat suspicious of the notion of liberation, because if it is not treated with precautions and within certain limits, one runs the risk of falling back on the idea that there exists a human nature or base that, as a consequence of certain historical, economic, and social processes, has been concealed, alienated, or imprisoned in and by mechanisms of repression. According to this hypothesis, all that is required is to break these repressive deadlocks and man will be reconciled with himself, rediscover his nature or regain contact with his origin, and reestablish a full and positive relationship with himself. (Foucault 1997, 282)

For Woolf, "freedom, which is the essence of our being, has to be controlled" (Woolf 1967a, 22). This sense of freedom links to Foucault's definition of it as "inherently political . . . insofar as being free means not being a slave to oneself and one's appetites, which means that with respect to oneself one establishes a certain relationship of domination, of mastery, which was called [in ancient Greek culture] *arkhe,* or power, command" (Foucault

1997, 286–87). Like Foucault, who distinguishes the practice of freedom from a process of liberation (the latter, he writes, "is not in itself sufficient to define the practices of freedom that will still be needed if . . . society . . . and individuals are to be able to define admissible and acceptable forms of existence or political society" [282–83]), Woolf must reject a series of meanings that attach to "freedom" in order to have it signify anew in her philosophy. "The old word 'freedom' does not serve," she cautions, for example, in *Three Guineas*, "for it is not freedom in the sense of license that we want; [we] want . . . not to break the laws, but to find the law" (Woolf 1966, 138). Ethics entails neither the liberation of "self-discovery" nor simply liberation in the conventionally political sense of license or infraction; it involves, rather, the work of self-formation in and as a practice of freedom following the acknowledgment of the *contingency* of what otherwise appears as epistemic "necessities." Thus, when Woolf remarks to her diary in 1935 that "Happily, uneducated & voteless, I am not responsible for the state of society" (Woolf 1984a, 345–46), she writes with neither simple disapproval nor conclusive defeat but rather with an astonishingly original sense of *representational responsibility*. Since as a woman writing in the 1930s Woolf had been without access to the political sphere, she is, she avers, strictly speaking not responsible for its present state. But she concedes—implicitly here, and explicitly in *Three Guineas*—that if her history as a woman had exiled her from the political terrain, she is nevertheless socially and politically represented *by* that terrain, and it is this representation or portraiture that she transgressively occupies in order to ethicize representativeness or exemplarity. This she does in *Three Guineas* by examining subjectification, or her history of "womaning," and she wrests from that history a precise procedure for subjectivization. By means of the ascetic work of "de-individualization," Woolf stages her critical affirmation of an outsider status. The practice of subjectivization that she develops in the 1930s in order to forge an antifascist life comprises a strategic renegotiation with and manipulation of the "special knowledge and power" or "unpaid for education" incurred in and by subjectification (Woolf 1966, 72).

It is for this reason that Woolf describes *Three Guineas* as "autobiography in public" (Woolf 1984b, 141). An autobiographical account of a de-individualizing "I," *Three Guineas* is mobilized by "an awareness that what is one's own, one's identity, [that which] is proper to one, is also a biography, and has a history" (Spivak 1993, 6).

Woolf claims as the outsider's "only qualification" for countering war the use of her "psychological insight" (Woolf 1966, 58). This unpaid-for education neither derives from a science of life nor defers to a juridical conception of the subject but evolves instead an art of living. It is this critical ontology that both mobilizes and is the condition of *Three Guineas'* critique, just as it mobilizes and is the condition for the outsider's deliberate and difficult practice of freedom. The practice is difficult because its "freedom" adheres to "the unwritten law," that is to say, to "the private laws that should regulate certain instincts, passions, mental and physical desires." These ethical "laws" refer neither to a transcendental moral order ("God is now generally held to be a conception of patriarchal origin") nor to "nature" but have instead "to be discovered afresh by successive generations, largely by their own efforts of reason and imagination" (1966, 184–85, n.42).

The ethics of *Three Guineas* explicitly opposes morality or "an absolute point of view" (9). To the question "Can we not find somewhere written up in letters of fire and gold, 'This is right. This wrong?'—a moral judgment which we must all, whatever our differences, accept?" (9), Woolf unambiguously replies by fashioning a certain way of acting that is ethically responsive to her *historicity.* In *Three Guineas* Woolf gives outsiders four rules or ways of acting that, if adopted, can open existence onto "the good and true life": a life in opposition to the subjectifying force field that leads inevitably to war. These rules, to which, again as a nominalist, she gives a novel sense, are *poverty* (by which is meant making enough money to live upon but "not a penny more"); *chastity* (refusing to sell one's intellectual labor); *derision* (refusing fame and praise—"ridicule, obscurity and censure are preferable, for psychological reasons, to fame and praise"); and *freedom from unreal loyalties* (pride of nationality, family, religion, and sex) (80).

These optional rules that read as ascetic virtues "are not," Woolf wryly offers, "for the most part as things are at present very difficult of fulfillment. With the exception of the first—that we must have enough money to live upon—they are largely ensured us by the law of England. The law of England sees to it that we do not inherit great possessions; the law of England denies us, and let us hope will long continue to deny us, the full stigma of nationality" (82). Here is the double movement of subjectification/subjectivization that characterizes the practice of freedom in critical ontology. As effects of subjectification, the "virtues" of poverty, derision, and chastity imposed on women are but components of a "slavish mentality"; they are constitutive of what Woolf calls the womanhood emotion that must be overcome if women are to move from subjectification to subjectivization. Such an overcoming is effected in critical ontology exactly by virtue of their transformation into optional rules, and these ascetic principles that Woolf devises for the outsider's existence indeed cannot be extracted from the philosophical project of which they are a necessary but component part.

This outsider's philosophy, as elaborated by *Three Guineas,* extends a line that runs underneath traditional philosophy, a line occupied by the

Cynics, Spinoza, Nietzsche, Deleuze, and Foucault. Indeed, Foucault identifies the ascetic virtues of humility, poverty, and chastity as constitutive of
the exemplary ethical *parrhesia* (or truth telling) undertaken by those ancient outsiders, the Cynics, for whom the philosophical or good life was
the true life—public, scandalous, and provocative. The Cynic way of life
forged a truth inextricable from ethics. This truth telling was transmitted
by word and example (the renunciation of luxuries, for instance) and involved the critique of political institutions and moral codes. It implied the
inversion of roles (the powerless tells the truth to the powerful) and the
risk of being despised (*On Being Despised:* this is Woolf's rejected title for
Three Guineas); moreover, it carried with it the obligation of telling the
truth to everyone, not only to the elite—an obligation that was new to classical philosophy.[10] *Three Guineas* revitalizes this tradition by introducing
parrhesia and askesis into modern political discourse.

THE ESCAPE ARTIST; OR, "AN INDISPENSABLE ASCETICISM"

> Literature begins only when a third person is born in us that strips
> us of the power to say "I."
>
> —Deleuze, *Negotiations*

Three Guineas requires as its condition for truth telling the enterprise of de-
individualization, but for Woolf a prior activity is necessary: depersonalization by means of writing. She associates her six-year (1932–38) composi-
tion of *Here and Now*—her radically experimental "novel-essay" which was
to combine "vision" and "fact"—with the inception of her newly evolved
attitude. "I must be bold and adventurous," she writes in 1933 about this
project. "I want to give the whole of present society—nothing less: facts, as
well as the vision. And to combine them both" (Woolf 1984a, 151–52). Ultimately *Here and Now* took the form of two distinct works, although Woolf
would continue to regard them as "one book": her "so-called novel" (Woolf
1985, 70), *The Years*, and her antiwar essay *Three Guineas*. "[T]hat's the end
of six years of floundering, striving, much agony, some ecstasy: lumping the
Years and 3Gs together as one book—as indeed they are," Woolf attests in
1938 (Woolf 1984b, 148). Scholars of Woolf tend to emphasize the agony of
those six years, as the above diary entry recommends, but the "ecstasy"
linked to her discovery of subjectivization is a no less resounding note and
accounts for the remarkable accomplishments secured by her during these
years of intensifying political and cultural crisis.[11] For *Here and Now* marks
the introduction into her writing of an ethics as a form to be given one's

life, and this ethics is not only addressed in the work but is also a consequence for Woolf *of* its writing. In 1937 she refers to this process in the following terms: "& then I am so composed that nothing is real unless I write
it" (Woolf 1987, 255). Woolf's claim is echoed by Deleuze, who asserts that
"style in a great writer is always a style of life too, not anything personal, but
inventing a possibility of life, a way of existing" (Deleuze 1995, 100).

That the writing of *Here and Now* acted for Woolf as the invention of a
possibility of life is evident across many diary entries. Woolf indeed judged
this work finally as having authored *her* since by means of its writing she
had procured a conclusive and affirmative sense of being an outsider. In
1937, then, anticipating reviews of *The Years* and in the midst of a "good
gallop" with *Three Guineas,* she reflects: "I . . . know that I have reached
my point of view, as writer, as being" (Woolf 1984b, 65). This seems the natural outcome of her claim in 1933, with but one year of work behind her
on *Here and Now,* that "I have at last laid my hands upon my philosophy
of anonymity. How odd last winter's revelation was! Freedom. . . . The
thing is to free one's self" (Woolf 1984a, 186–87).

Since for Woolf, as for Foucault, "the individual is the product of power,"
depersonalization and de-individualization—or, in Woolf's shorthand,
anonymity—operate as the ethical move from subjectification to subjectivization (Foucault 1983, xi–xiv). The concept of anonymity developed by
Woolf in the 1930s refers, in other words, not to a modernist aesthetic of
impersonality but to these two essential components of her problematization of freedom: depersonalization and de-individualization. Woolf accomplishes depersonalization by addressing herself to "that good friend
who has never deserted me" (Woolf 1985, 155), that is to say, by addressing
herself to *writing.* Foucault too conceives of his writing in these terms: "I
am," he comments, "no doubt not the only one who writes in order to have
no face" (quoted in Bernauer 1992, 180). This work he perceives as fundamentally ethical in its resistance to a form of power that "categorizes the
individual, marks him by his own individuality, attaches him to his own
identity, [and] imposes a law of truth on him which he must recognize"
(Foucault 2000, 331). And so, Foucault determines, "What can be the ethic
of an intellectual . . . if not that: to render oneself permanently capable of
getting free of oneself?" (quoted in Bernauer 1992, 179).

To render oneself anonymous or free of one's subjectified self by means
of perpetual askesis requires, according to Woolf and Foucault, the production of a subjectivized self. Deleuze correctly notes that Foucault's subjectivization is without identity. "It's a strange business," he muses, "speaking for yourself, in your own name, because it doesn't at all come with seeing
yourself as an ego or a person or a subject. Individuals find a real name for

themselves . . . only through the harshest exercise in depersonalization. . . .
History is not experimentation. . . . Experimentation on [ourselves] is our
only identity" (1995, 6, 106). For Woolf, this critical experimentation is the
predicating feature of her self-ascribed ethos as outsider, as writer. She assumes subjectivization as the condition for the artist to carry out a will to
truth on the terrain of critical ontology (and indeed *defines* as "the artist"
the one who undertakes this task: "Isn't the great artist the only person to
tell the truth?" [Woolf 1980, 453]) and consequently evaluates as inartistic
those autobiographical projects that stage a mimesis of presumed psychic
truth and coherent individuality. "My own longing in reading your [auto-
biographical] article," she discloses to her esteemed feminist friend Ethel
Smyth, "is to escape the individual."

In writing *Here and Now* Woolf felt she was able to "reach her point of
view, as writer, as being," as truth teller, and she connects this to her development in that work of an ethos that is diacritically *queer.* "[I] have a feeling that I've reached the no man's land that I'm after," she says suggestively
of this labor of depersonalization. "A queer very happy free feeling, such as
I've not had at the finish of any other book" (Woolf 1984a, 355). Foucault
stresses that the ethics of concern for the self as a practice of freedom obliges
recourse to "a guide, a counselor, a friend, someone who will be truthful
with you" (1997, 287). "I recall," Woolf notes about a difficult time, "that the
good friend," that is to say, *writing,* "who is with me still, upheld me" (Woolf
1985, 70). In her elaboration of *Here and Now,* Woolf devised and thereafter
in her task of truth telling took recourse to another great and related friend:
her queer fictional character, Nicholas Pomjalovsky. For Woolf creates by
means of her "third person," Deleuze's "third 'I'/eye," a great concept in the
figure of the philosopher-as-outsider who functions as the magnifying glass
that Woolf associates with her turn to subjectivization. Here, character-
creating and concept-creating constitute somewhat the same enterprise; specifically, this fictional character, Nicholas Pomjalovsky, takes on the dimensions of Foucault's concept of ethics, and the concept is the character: a
conceptual persona figured as the outsider.

It is a curious coincidence that during the final decade of their lives both
Foucault and Woolf conceived of askesis in terms of queer (self-) relations.
The example par excellence that Foucault so frequently draws upon in his
accounts of self-stylization is (a nominalist account of) homosexuality.[12]
"The problem is not to discover in oneself the truth of one's sex," he proposes, for example, "but, rather, to use one's homosexuality henceforth to
arrive at a multiplicity of relationships. And, no doubt, that's the real reason why homosexuality is not a form of desire but something desirable"
(Foucault 1997, 135–36). Or, again, "To be 'gay,' I think, is not to identify

with the psychological traits and the visible masks of the homosexual but to try to define and develop a way of life" (138). Eve Kosofsky Sedgwick names as "queer" this development of a way of life and, like Foucault, she distinguishes this from imposed categorizations: "'gay' and 'lesbian' still present themselves (however delusively) as objective, empirical categories governed by empirical rules of evidence (however contested). 'Queer' seems to hinge much more radically and explicitly on a person's undertaking particular, performative acts of experimental self-perception and filiation" (Sedgwick 1993, 9). If for Foucault the personal foray into an aesthetics of existence marks the advent of "queer" into, and as, his ethical thought, no less is this the case for Woolf, whose antifascist critique and ethics in *Here and Now* and *Three Guineas* are articulated by and in her inscription of the queer Nicholas Pomjalovsky.

A HYPER- AND PESSIMISTIC ACTIVISM

> The critical ontology of ourselves must be considered not, certainly, as a theory, as a doctrine, nor even as a permanent body of knowledge that is accumulating; it must be considered as an attitude.
>
> —Foucault 1997

Three Guineas not only gives a philosophy to its readers for practicing the good or true life—"the life of natural happiness" (Woolf 1980, 380)—it also *is* philosophy. It involves the introduction of a new word (the outsider) and gives an unusual sense to ordinary words (pacifism, obscurity, chastity, poverty, derision); it makes visible a force field of microfascism that Woolf seeks to make intolerable to her readers; and it stages a war of joys pitted against sadness or misery.

Woolf's invention of and invitation to a new relationship to politics remain widely unrecognized or unanswered: her exit beyond the form of her suicide is rarely perceived. Since the publication six decades ago of *Three Guineas,* it has, with notable exceptions, met with silence, misunderstanding, or fierce objection.[13] That this book of ethics recovers a practice of truth telling (*parrhesia*) associated with the Cynics, that it poses questions and conducts analyses in a manner reminiscent of the thought of Spinoza, Nietzsche, Deleuze, and Foucault, with which it forms a subterranean and prestigious lineage, are events in the history of thought that, perhaps not surprisingly, but nonetheless scandalously, have not been given their due. This is scandalous not so much in terms of intellectual history, but rather in terms of a politics of ourselves, because our political terrain continues to be dictated by options that Woolf sought assiduously to undermine half a century ago.

No less than Foucault, Woolf belongs to that line of "private thinkers" who overturn values and construct their philosophy with hammer blows; she is not one of the "public professors" whom it afforded her such mirth to criticize, but rather an *outsider.* "For having spat it out," she records in her diary upon the completion of *Three Guineas,* "my mind is made up. I need never recur or repeat. I am an outsider" (1984b, 141). For all of the book's pacifism, there is (as the hammer blows suggest) a violence in Woolf, a violence that resonates with that ascribed by Deleuze to Foucault: "an intense violence, mastered, controlled, and turned into courage" (1995, 103). "I shall never forget this book completely," she reflects shortly after completing it. "I never wrote a book with greater fervor; under such a lash of compulsion" (1984b, 137). "I wanted," she also observes, "—how violently, pressingly compulsorily I can't say—to write the book; & have a quiet composed feeling; as if I had my say" (1984b, 133). And while writing it: "Oh how violently I have been galloping through these mornings! It has pressed & sizzled out of me, if that's proof of virtue, like a physical volcano I've had sizzling now since [1932]" (1984b, 112). The book left her feeling "philosophic, fundamentally," and in possession of "immense relief & peace" (1984b, 139, 141). "I now feel entirely free. Why? Have committed myself, am afraid of nothing. Can do anything I like. No longer famous, no longer on a pedestal; no longer hawked in by societies: on my own, for ever. That's my feeling; a sense of expansion" (1984b, 136–37). Woolf projected that the essay would "excite nothing but mild sneers: & [reviews noting] how very inconsequent and egotistical V.W. is," but she also felt that "I said what I wanted in 3Gs & am not to care if its . . . made my own friends hostile; laid me open to abuse & ridicule" (1984b, 136, 170). Ultimately she held to the hope that "the honesty of my intention in 3Gs is bound to see me through," but its publication met immediately with silence on the part of her intimates ("Not one of my friends has mentioned it"; "Not a word said of it by any of my family" [1984b, 193, 156]) even when discussion of that work was on the agenda for a planned encounter. But an explosive book always keeps its explosive charge (the image is Woolf's—"I have collected enough powder to blow up St Paul's" [1984a, 77]): one still cannot read *Three Guineas* without discovering in it philosophy's function as a radical enterprise of demystification and exit-making—the thought of the outside.

The specific mission of *Three Guineas* is to awaken others to be concerned with themselves and with their truth. If Woolf sometimes felt that her effort had been "futile," that her "book may be like a moth dancing over a bonfire—consumed in less than one second," both her effort and her work nevertheless remain vitally with us (1984b, 130, 142). Although in 1938 the *London Times* represented *Three Guineas* as "a serious challenge that must be answered by all thinkers" and the *TLS* suggested "this book may mark an epoch if taken seriously," *Three Guineas* has not emerged as a player in the contemporary political scene of ideas (1984b, 149, 148). Since, to re-cite Foucault, "contemporary political thought allows very little room for the question of the ethical subject," the history of Woolf's reception is hardly surprising. And yet both Woolf and Foucault, in their uniqueness and activism, do play a role in the ethics of our contemporary world. "Am I a failure?" Woolf asks. "Not a question I intend to ask: since clearly one must act" (Woolf 1984b, 108). Woolf's statement fore-echoes Foucault's account of "a hyper- and pessimistic activism": "My point," he concludes, "is not that everything is bad, but that everything is dangerous, which is not exactly the same as bad. If everything is dangerous, then we always have something to do. So my position leads not to apathy but to a hyper- and pessimistic activism" (Foucault 1997, 256). And Woolf has the last word: "This may be the last day of peace; so why not record it? Why record this? But this why has to be battened down" (Woolf 1984b, 174).

NOTES

1. Foucault is careful to stress that subjectification and subjectivization are not to be distinguished in terms of unfreedom and freedom: the "passive" subject of subjectification is not, he claims, "unfree," but is "constituted as a subject in relation to and over against" discursive procedures of normalization and individualization; similarly, the "active" subject of subjectivization, who "constitutes itself . . . through practices of the self," is beholden to "practices [that] are nevertheless not something invented by the individual himself. They are models he finds in his culture and are proposed, suggested, imposed upon him by his culture, his society, and his social group" (Foucault 1997, 291).

2. Zwerdling (305). Zwerdling alludes to the appearance of Woolf's name on the Gestapo arrest list for the planned German attack (289).

3. On Foucault's turn, two texts are notable for their singularly philosophical *and* biographical accounts. These are, respectively, Deleuze (1988) and Eribon (1991). Acknowledgments of Woolf's turn may be found in Hussey (1986) and Mepham (1991). Zwerdling's first chapter of *Virginia Woolf and the Real World*, "The Enormous Eye," quietly but masterfully notes and accounts for Woolf's turn. "By that point in her career," he says of her final writings, "the stream of history, the stream of consciousness, and the flow of her artistic imagination had become a single current. . . . [T]he realization that public and private are really inseparable was not a sudden revelation; it was an insight Woolf gradually won over the course of her career" (Zwerdling 1986, 25).

4. "One needs to be nominalistic, no doubt," Foucault writes in *The History of Sexuality*, volume 1: *An Introduction*, while explaining his recourse to the name "power" to describe a phenomenon for which that name (or, for that matter, any

other) does not conventionally apply (Foucault 1980). The full passage runs as follows: "One needs to be nominalistic, no doubt: power is not an institution, and not a structure; neither is it a certain strength we are endowed with; it is the name that one attributes to a complex strategical situation in a particular society" (1980, 93). "Power" conventionally refers, of course, to the very phenomena about which Foucault claims "Power is not . . ." He knows that "power" refers to these phenomena; yet he also knows that these phenomena do not comprise in their totality the phenomenon of "power" he is describing in this work. He needs a word for the latter, and "power" must do, but only after he has wrenched it away from the usual significations that nevertheless still cling to that word. For an incisive analysis of Foucault's nominalism, see Spivak (1993, 25–51).

5. The formulation of the final question belongs to Cixous (1993, 201–19).

6. *Three Guineas* traces a connection between "the sartorial splendors of the educated man and the photograph of ruined houses and dead bodies" (Woolf 1966, 21). "Even stranger," Woolf writes, "than the symbolic splendor of your clothes [she is addressing an educated man] are the ceremonies that take place when you wear them" (1966, 20).

7. For Woolf the optical is literal: she reproduces in *Three Guineas* alongside her symptomatic reading of British sartorial customs five photographs that feature, respectively, a British General, British heralds, a British university procession, a British judge, and a British Archbishop in order to set into relief the "barbarism" that underwrites Britain's self-perceived "civilized" institutions.

8. This is Spivak's phrase to describe Foucault's ethics, which she characterizes as anti-post-Enlightenment. See Spivak (1993, 30).

9. An inability to grasp Woolf's ethical temporality burdens the current critical possibility for her philosophy to be understood beyond the claim that its "positive suggestions" are appropriate only to liberal democracies. John Mepham asserts, for instance, that "Woolf's prescriptions [to prevent war] was that women should remain outside the system of social rewards and privileges which encourage the dictatorial psychology, while cultivating their own civilization. By the time the book was published, Hitler had invaded Austria and the threat of war was very real. Her argument for resistance by a Society of Outsiders who would practice experiments in civilized living takes it for granted that the social space, of financial independence and cultural freedom that women win when they earn their own living, would survive fascism. But the social space occupied by active, independent citizens, 'civil society' as it is called, is the first thing that totalitarian regimes abolish" (Mepham, 171). My argument here is that *Three Guineas* exemplifies a politics that seeks to undermine just this political distinction between private and public spheres, and in that undoing to prevent a political teleology whose end is fascism. It is not that Woolf "takes for granted" a private sphere that would survive fascism; rather, Woolf's ethics are meant to *prevent* fascism here and now in her creation of new forms of life.

10. For a detailed description of Foucault's engagement with *parrhesia,* see Flynn (1994, 102–18).

11. Lee, for example, writes that "this novel nearly kill[ed] her. . . . The 'dark'

connection between her 'drudgery' and the world's 'crisis' is like the relation which the novel is precariously trying to maintain between inner and outer. It is the painfulness and perilousness of that balance which made it difficult to write and led her to think of it as an inevitable failure" (Woolf 1992, xvii).

12. See Halperin (1995) for a superb account of Foucault's queer ethics.

13. For an excellent survey of these responses, see Silver (1983b, 254–76). See also Snaith (2000), who further discusses these letters from correspondents in the context of Woolf's role as a public intellectual.

WORKS CITED

Bell, Quentin. 1987. *Virginia Woolf: A Biography*. London: Triad Paladin Grafton Books.

Bernauer, James W. 1992. *Michel Foucault's Force of Flight: Toward an Ethics for Thought*. New Jersey: Humanities Press.

Cixous, Hélène. 1993. "We Who Are Free, Are We Free?" *Critical Inquiry* 19 (Winter 1993): 201–19.

Deleuze, Gilles. 1988. *Foucault*. Minneapolis: University of Minnesota Press.

———. 1995. *Negotiations: 1972–1990*. Columbia University Press.

Deleuze, Gilles, and Félix Guattari. 1983. *Anti-Oedipus: Capitalism and Schizophrenia*. Preface by Michel Foucault. Translated by Robert Hurley et al. Minneapolis: University of Minnesota Press.

———. 1987. *A Thousand Plateaus: Capitalism and Schizophrenia*. Translated by Brian Massumi. Minneapolis: University of Minnesota Press.

Eribon, Didier. 1991. *Michel Foucault*. Cambridge: Harvard University Press.

Flynn, Thomas. 1994. "Foucault as Parrhesiast: His Last Course at the College de France (1984)." In *The Final Foucault*. Edited by James Bernauer and David Rasmussen. 102–18. Cambridge, Mass.: MIT Press.

Foucault, Michel. 1980. *The History of Sexuality*. Volume 1. *An Introduction*. New York: Vintage.

Foucault, Michel. 1983. "Preface," In *Anti-Oedipus: Capitalism and Schizophrenia*. By Gilles Deleuze and Félix Guattari. xi–xiv. Minneapolis: University of Minnesota Press.

———. 1997. *Ethics: Subjectivity and Truth: Essential Works of Michel Foucault*. Volume 1. Edited by Paul Rabinow. New York: New Press.

———. 2000. *Power: Essential Works of Michel Foucault*. Volume 3. Edited by James D. Faubion. New York: New Press.

Halperin, David. 1995. *Saint Foucault: Towards a Gay Historiography*. Oxford: Oxford University Press.

Hussey, Mark. 1986. *The Singing of the Real World: The Philosophy of Virginia Woolf's Fiction*. Columbus: Ohio State University Press.

Lee, Hermione. 1996. *Virginia Woolf*. London: Chatto & Windus.

Mepham, John. 1991. *Virginia Woolf: A Literary Life*. New York: St. Martin's Press.

Nicolson, Nigel. 1979. "Introduction." In *The Sickle Side of the Moon: The Letters of*

Virginia Woolf. Volume 5. Edited by Nigel Nicolson and Joanne Trautmann. London: Hogarth Press.

Sedgwick, Eve Kosofsky. 1993. *Tendencies.* Durham: Duke University Press, Series Q.

Silver, Brenda, ed. 1983a. *Virginia Woolf's Reading Notebooks.* Princeton: Princeton University Press.

————. 1983b. *"Three Guineas* Before and After: Further Answers to Correspondents." In *Virginia Woolf: A Feminist Slant.* Edited by Jane Marcus. 254–76. Lincoln: University of Nebraska Press.

Snaith, Anna. 2000. *Virginia Woolf: Public and Private Negotiations.* New York: St. Martin's Press.

Spivak, Gayatri Chakravorty. 1993. *Outside in the Teaching Machine.* New York: Routledge.

Woolf, Virginia. 1966. *Three Guineas.* New York: Harcourt Brace.

————. 1967a. *Collected Essays.* Volume 3. London: Hogarth Press.

————. 1967b. *Collected Essays.* Volume 4. London: Hogarth Press.

————. 1977. *The Pargiters: The Essay-Novel Portion of* The Years. Edited by Mitchell Leaska. New York: Readex Books.

————. 1979. *The Sickle Side of the Moon: The Letters of Virginia Woolf.* Volume 5. Edited by Nigel Nicolson and Joanne Trautmann. London: Hogarth Press.

————. 1980. *Leave the Letters Till We're Dead: The Letters of Virginia Woolf.* Volume 6. *1936–1941.* Edited by Nigel Nicolson and Joanne Trautmann. London: Hogarth Press.

————. 1984a. *The Diary of Virginia Woolf.* Volume 4. *1932–1936.* Edited by Anne Olivier Bell, assisted by Andrew McNeillie. New York: Harcourt Brace Jovanovich.

————. 1984b. *The Diary of Virginia Woolf.* Volume 5. *1936–1941.* Edited by Anne Olivier Bell, assisted by Andrew McNeillie. New York: Harcourt Brace Jovanovich.

————. 1985. *Moments of Being.* Edited by Jeanne Schulkind. 2nd edition. New York: Harcourt Brace.

————. 1987. "Appendix C: Virginia Woolf and Julian Bell." In *Virginia Woolf: A Biography.* By Quentin Bell. London: Triad Paladin Grafton Books.

————. 1992. *The Years.* Oxford: Oxford University Press.

Zwerdling, Alex. 1986. "The Enormous Eye." In *Virginia Woolf and the Real World.* Berkeley: University of California Press.

Part 2:
Feminism as Ethos

Experience and Truth Telling in a Post-humanist World: A Foucauldian Contribution to Feminist Ethical Reflections

Mariana Valverde

Feminisms differ a great deal, but they generally share a fundamental interest in recovering women's experiences of oppression by providing a space in which women can finally speak openly. The 1960s consciousness-raising group may have gone out of fashion, but many of the speech practices associated with it have become ubiquitous in both feminist and nonfeminist sites. Support groups, political gatherings, self-help meetings, informal conversations, and radio and television call-in programs are just some of the arenas in which various forms and styles of "truth telling" are practiced by women. The description of experiences construed by the speaker as gendered and hence as relevant to the particular "women's" speech act at hand is generally taken (by feminists) to lead to the discovery of a hitherto hidden experiential truth, a truth that has value not only for the speaker or her immediate audience but also for the movement as a whole.

The diverse dialogic processes that elicit and produce such practices of gendered truth telling have all too often been lumped together under a single banner and either praised or derided *in toto*. Some feminists, in the academy and outside, sing the praises of any and all autobiographical accounts—whereas the skeptics, often gathered under the misleading banner of "postmodernism," tend to see the quest for authenticity as deluded, and the construction of a unified humanist feminist subject as an ideological and political trap. The purpose of this chapter is to cut through this rather stale debate. Using the reflections on ethical practices generated by Foucault in the last few years of his life, I will here argue that there are good grounds for abandoning the either/or debate about truth telling and the feminist experiential subject, with its programmatic pretensions, and turning instead to a more modest pursuit, namely, the documentation of the rich variety of gendered dialogic practices.

Some practices of personal truth telling, I shall argue here, have social and ethical effects that clearly differentiate them from the classic "confes-

sional" genre critically analyzed by Foucault and often derided by postmodern feminist theory (Foucault 1980). Reflecting upon one's experience
and engaging in truth telling is not necessarily tied to the perpetuation of
humanist assumptions about the deep self. This chapter uses some ethnographic work but stops short of actually documenting the different effects
of various dialogic practices; given the tenor of the collection as a whole,
the task here is simply to try to clear the theoretical ground and enable future, more empirical, studies of truth-telling practices. Such studies could
serve as material for the elaboration of future theoretical work beyond the
dichotomy of humanism versus postmodernism.

FEMALE AGENCY, FOR OR AGAINST

Truth-telling practices, by all accounts crucial to the historical development
of second-wave feminism, have in recent years been criticized as theoretically naive, politically dangerous, or both. What started out as a minor revolt among postmodern literary critics, philosophers, and artists has grown
into a more generally felt skepticism. Isn't experience always linguistically
and culturally constructed? Don't we always resort to stereotyped narrative forms in telling our story, so that a transgressive tale of coming out as
a lesbian ends up sounding remarkably like an evangelical conversion experience, and is to that extent hardly authentic? Isn't "the subject" dead?
If Man is dead, does that mean that Woman is equally defunct? If we are
not autonomous subjects who create meanings, as eighteenth-century European intellectuals believed, but rather mere effects of discursive and cultural practices, then what is the status of the tales we tell? Can honesty and
sincerity be a sound basis for knowledge as well as ethics, if, as Jacques
Lacan tells us, not only is self-knowledge impossible but, more disturbingly,
self-identity is but a perpetual illusion? Young undergraduates with minimal training in philosophy and cultural studies are often heard giving voice
to this sort of concern; and books relating personal struggles with oppression and misfortune, while still wildly popular on the bestseller list, tend
to be met with a certain skepticism in university circles and in the art world.
Experience just isn't what it used to be.

   And yet what would seem to follow logically from this new skepticism,
namely, a decision to consign authenticity and all other quests for truth to
the garbage bin of history, and to be content with reveling in postmodern
fragmentation, is a move that only some feminist intellectuals are willing to
make. Even those of us who can deconstruct a humanist subject at twenty
paces often feel nostalgia for "experience," for the humanist subject and for
her ethics of personal authenticity. We might be well read in deconstruction

and/or postcolonial studies and be very skilled at taking apart other people's naive realist assumptions about "the inner self"; and we might scoff at slogans that seemed very good only ten years ago—"breaking the silence," "hearing new voices," and so forth. But we also know that "breaking the silence," however trite as a book title, and however problematic as a theoretical project in the post-Foucauldian age, remains a real, meaningful imperative for many ordinary women facing up to the old problems of oppression, violence, sexual shame, and so on. After all, most women who become feminists do so not by reading postmodern theory but by participating in some kind of truth-telling activity, such as coming out as a lesbian or going to a support group in which one learns that one's own experience of rape or incest is part of a large collective problem.

There is thus a contradiction between the emotional and interpersonal dimension of becoming and remaining a feminist, on the one hand, and on the other hand the theoretical tools that deconstruct binary opposites and interrogate the cultural assumptions of narrative forms used to tell one's tale. Contradictions are of course the stuff of life; but these particular contradictions, instead of being accepted and acknowledged, were quickly turned into an either/or "debate." One well-known version of the humanism versus postmodernism debate was that counterposing Judith Butler and Drucilla Cornell on one side against Seyla Benhabib and Nancy Fraser on the other. This was originally published in a journal in 1991 and reprinted in a much-read 1995 book, *Feminist Contentions.*[1] Like other similar debates, this text lumped together a whole series of already complex discussions, thus producing an indigestible mass. Questions about the status of truth and the possibilities for knowledge were mixed in with discussions of identity politics, the status of historical narrative, and a number of other equally large and not necessarily linked issues. Because the text, as well as the larger discussion it represented, was from the outset constructed as a "debate," its necessary effect was to constitute a single postmodern view of texts and of subjects—as if Foucauldian approaches were compatible with Derridean discourse analysis or with Lacanian analytic methods, and as if a common skepticism about traditional philosophical tools sufficed to constitute a new unified theory of everything.

Sticking for a moment to only one of the many themes lumped together in this debate, namely, the question of personal agency and ethical authenticity, the polarization of feminist thought effected through the debate format made it seem as if all feminists needed to take sides either "for" or "against" something that came to be called "the humanist subject." In the subsequent controversies, the best-known antihumanist iconoclast was—and still is—Judith Butler. Butler made her considerable reputation with the

1990 theory bestseller *Gender Trouble,* which argued that subjectivity, including gendered subjectivity, is an effect of various performances—not only of our own personal performance but also of the combined effects of the culturally available performances that we all reiterate. As if that were not sufficiently upsetting for believers in authenticity, she went on to argue that in performance there is no such thing as either faithful reproduction or original invention. Performances necessarily fail to reproduce "the original," for the very good reason that there is no original, no one true essence, of gender or of anything else. Combining Jacques Derrida's notion of "iteration" with Foucault's critique of liberation discourse, she argued that subversive gender performances are extremely important as political tools but are less original than they claim, since they are nothing but creative combinations of available tropes and gestures. There is therefore no such thing as originality or authenticity in the classic Rousseauian sense. Authenticity, however passionately desired and sincerely sought, is nothing but a culturally specific effect of particular material and discursive practices.

Given the polarized context within which Butler's work was read, her position was—inevitably, one is tempted to say—reduced to something like: "there is no subject, and hence agency is impossible, and women do not even exist!" The patently ridiculous claim "there are no subjects," although constantly disavowed by Butler herself (Butler 1987 and 1997) was then endlessly refuted by humanist feminists who proceeded to denounce postmodern feminism in prophetic tones because it denies ethical agency. These refutations have not been confined to academic publications. Martha Nussbaum's vicious attack on Judith Butler in the progressive American magazine the *New Republic* stands out as a particularly nasty example of what happens when one assumes that humanist ethics is the only possible ethics, and it is worth noting here because of the way Nussbaum caricatures Foucault to trash Butler: "Butler, like Foucault, is adamantly opposed to normative notions such as human dignity, or treating humanity as an end, on the grounds that they are inherently dictatorial" (Nussbaum 1999).

As one might have predicted, the liberal humanist polemic in defense of human dignity (identified with European humanist philosophy of the subject!) in turn generated more or less polemical criticisms. Those polemical debates have by now largely exhausted themselves, having produced much heat and little light. And yet, the issues around which they swirled have hardly gone away.

The first step toward getting beyond or at least outside of the humanist versus postmodern polemics is to question the either/or *format* of the "debate"—not to find a "happy medium," I hasten to add, but to question an assumption, shared by both sides, that in retrospect can be seen to have enabled the whole "debate": the assumption that engaging in the dialogic exercise of personal truth telling is always and everywhere linked to a specific form of subjectivity—the humanist "inner self."[2] Personal truth telling need not be "confessional," or even at all psychological, I will show: autobiographical dialogical speech is not always constitutive of the psychic self associated both with contemporary mainstream feminism and with older European traditions, such as Romanticism. The activity of dialoguing (even with oneself) to probe our actions and to account for them by sharing personal stories, self-criticisms, longings, and hopes is not the monopoly of that long confessional tradition that goes from Jean-Jacques Rousseau through 1960s pop psychology to Oprah Winfrey. Truth telling, I will argue here, also takes place in situations that promote a less "deep" and serious sense of self, a more pragmatist, flexible, de-centered, less territorialized ethical self.

NONCONFESSIONAL TRUTH TELLING

In the course of the lectures on truth telling given at Berkeley shortly before his death, Foucault noted that Stoic practices of *parrhesia* or truth telling did not amount to confession: they did not involve "the disclosure of a secret that has to be excavated from out of the depths of the soul" (Foucault 2001, 165). Reading the texts of Seneca, Epicurus, Serenus, Galen, and other thinkers, Foucault came to the conclusion that not all personal truth telling assumes or produces the mythical humanist subject and its naive theory of meaning as generated by the individual mind. There are in fact modes of truth telling that work at a level that one could call Deleuzian— the level of de-centered ethical assemblages. Gilles Deleuze thought that the unified, territorialized, psychological self characteristic of the "disciplinary" society whose emergence Foucault had carefully traced was already on the wane even in the 1970s, and he tried to analyze the fragmented and fluid "selves" emerging in post-disciplinary societies with purely philosophical (rather than genealogical) tools. While Deleuze and postmodern theorists such as Jean-François Lyotard and Jean Baudrillard tried to discern the shape of our immediate present and imagine the near future, in order to question the suitability of inherited categories, Foucault, never a postmodern, took a different tack.[3] Avoiding general pronouncements about "our present," and resolutely refusing to engage in debates about whether we live in "postmodernity," he looked through ancient sources in order to find inspiration and resources for his desire to develop a post-psychological, post-disciplinary, post-Romantic ethics.

Foucault's education and friendship networks facilitated his search for classical sources of ethical practices and insights that might be redeployed in the present in order to go beyond the "self" of the psy disciplines. Without explicitly discussing his method, Foucault showed in his commentaries on Greco-Roman ethical practices that the ethical resources of a *pre*-psychological age could be mined with a view to equipping us to come to grips with what Deleuze would call our *post*-disciplinary lives. Foucault, more of a historian than Deleuze, would not have made the claim that our lives are already in fact post-disciplinary, since he was well aware of the persistence of both disciplinary and biopolitical programs for managing problem populations. But in struggling with the question of where to find resources for post-psychological ethical self-creation and ethical reflection, Foucault's work is in deep sympathy with Deleuze's experiments with "assemblages" and other nonterritorializing ways of thinking about selves, bodies, desires, and ethics.

Feminists in less elitist educational institutions than those attended by Foucault and his peers, and whose cultural background and gender make it difficult to identify with Greco-Roman gentlemen's dilemmas,[4] can still find useful insights in Foucault's reading of Greco-Roman writers. To do this, however, it is necessary to question more than the masculinism of Foucault's personal and intellectual networks: it is equally necessary to critique the privileging of "high culture" sources. Some of the themes and insights found by Foucault in his favorite authors can be more easily discerned in contemporary lowbrow genres of ethical reflection than in tomes on "virtue ethics." Pursuing questions similar to Foucault's, but into fields of experience and thought quite alien to his Parisian philosophical existence, I have argued elsewhere that Alcoholics Anonymous groups work for many people partly because they don't force people to probe the inner soul as psychoanalysis does—an analysis in keeping with Foucault's comments on nonconfessional truth telling in the classical world, but using research at the opposite end of the high-low cultural spectrum. AA meetings, my ethnographic research showed, allow people to work on themselves by taking up a position anywhere between the deep level of "conversion" to a new master identity, on the one hand, and on the other hand, the practical level of "handy tips for staying sober." Importantly, the latter stance is not derided as inauthentic or superficial, as it would be in the Rousseauian humanist tradition (see Valverde 1998, chapter 5). Going to AA meetings rather than to the bar is for some people just a practical harm reduction measure, not a sign or cause of inner truth. AA does not force its members to undergo any particular spiritual process, and it demands no deeply personal confession beyond the simple declaration "I am an alcoholic," whose reach into the soul is something that only the speaker is allowed to define. Or in other words, AA as an organization allows many kinds of selves and many approaches to ethical self-formation, without insisting on authenticity and depth. "It's bullshit but it works" is not only a commonly voiced view among those who attend AA groups but a view that is not discouraged by the organization. Such an inbuilt skepticism encourages idiosyncratic, pragmatic uses of ideas and techniques picked up at meetings or while reading AA texts and discourages the cult-like pursuit of theoretical or even psychic coherence. Anyone who reads Foucault's sympathetic commentary on Greco-Roman handy tips for staying honest (in the Berkeley lectures published as *Fearless Speech* [2001]) cannot but be struck by the parallel.

Taking this exploration of nonpsychological, nonunifying practices of self out of the context of addiction and recovery, I will argue here that Foucault's reading of Greco-Roman practices of self-formation can be used by feminist thinkers and feminist activists to get us past the impasse created by the misleading debate that counterposed humanism to postmodernism. We can use Foucault's thoughts to become more aware of the fact that women— and men—can and do much ethical work, and much truth-telling work, that does not fit the Rousseauian paradigm of authenticity and truth telling. In doing so, we do not have to denounce authenticity, personal autonomy, and sincere truth telling in the name of postmodern parody—a move that would simply reinscribe the old debate that bored us so thoroughly in the early 1990s. We can instead consider the possibility that there are many different practices of truth telling and, therefore, many different kinds of selves, and that these can easily coexist, even in the same person. Or to put it differently: if we take the death of God seriously, as an event that, as Nietzsche showed, necessarily involves the death of the Kantian unified subject, a key ethical problematic for our time is the fact that there are different, heterogeneous ethical demands to which we have to respond, not necessarily with the same tools or the same aims. Political pluralism has become so dominant as to have turned into a somewhat trite ideology, but ethical heterogeneity remains largely unexplored: the same people who admit that heterogeneous political projects can coexist in the same state or even in the same citizen will find it difficult to admit that the ethical self, as Luce Irigaray might put it, is not one.

In his thoughts on the relation between ethics and history, Jacques Derrida invokes Paul Klee's powerful painting *Angelus Novus,* which portrays a ghostly figure that allows us to both feel a common past and hope for a better future—a figure that looks backward and forward at the same time and forces us to respond not to an abstract moral law but rather to a specific, historically grounded, demand: the demand to do justice to those who have gone before us (us as a specific group, not just as humans in general) and to those who will come afterward.[5] This image, whose theoretical articulation, Derrida convincingly argues, is to be found in Walter Benjamin's powerful call for a justice that is political, historical, embodied, and utterly non-Kantian, has features that make it suitable for feminist use. Feminist truth telling, I would argue, can help to construct a community united both through shared memory and through common hopes. Or to put it in less poetic, more Foucauldian language: the effectivity of the angel that incites us to remember the past and to hope for the future does not depend on its ontological status. Just as we can be inspired by Klee's angel even if we are not religious, so too we can acknowledge the need to continue to engage in truth-telling exercises even if we no longer believe in absolute truth.

Benjamin and Derrida, however, tend to think of ethical duty—the call of justice—as singular. What justice demands varies historically and culturally; the angel of justice calls a particular people at a particular time, but each historical situation is envisaged as having basically one privileged ethical problematic. Hence the apocalyptic tone of both Benjamin and Derrida's writings on politics and justice.

But if we in the twenty-first century no longer think of ourselves as engaged in "the struggle," as Benjamin and others who lived in the 1930s did, but rather as having to juggle ethical responsibilities that emanate from diverse sources and elicit heterogeneous responses, since for us now struggles around sexism, for instance, are not experienced as automatically included under some mega-struggle by a unified "people," then we will have to go further than Derrida and think about the possibility that there are, at the same time, several "angels" calling on us, and that we have no master plan with which to prioritize and hierarchize their diverse demands. The process of coming to grips with the complexities of ethical pluralism could begin, I suggest, by being attentive to and respectful of a variety of problematics articulated in a variety of genres. Earnest accounts of one's experience of victimization do not have to be dismissed as naive by those of us who feel more comfortable with cosmopolitan irony: it is possible to respect both. If ethical truth is plural, then it makes sense that a variety of formats and genres can be used for different instances of ethical reflection.

FOUCAULT ON TRUTH TELLING IN A PRE-PSYCHOLOGICAL AGE

In the reflections upon Greco-Roman ethics developed in the last volumes of *The History of Sexuality*, in the articles and interviews collected in the anthology *Ethics, Subjectivity, and Truth*, edited by Paul Rabinow, and in the lectures given at Berkeley in 1983–84 on *parrhesia* in Greco-Roman ethics (recently edited by Joseph Pearson as *Fearless Speech*), Foucault developed some unsystematic thoughts that help us to think about personal truth telling without assuming or constructing a "deep inner self" (Foucault 1980, 1994, 1998, and 2001). Many feminist writers have used Foucault's critical account of "the confession" as a mode of governance, as developed in volume 1 of *The History of Sexuality*, to analyze popular and highbrow writing practices described, often pejoratively, as "confessional"; but few have explored the resources that the later writings offer to those thinking about truth telling and ethics after the death of God. I will here show that some current practices of ethical reflection—within feminism but also in other grassroots movements, such as twelve-step recovery groups—can be understood critically but sympathetically with these Foucauldian resources. This sympathetic understanding does not have to lead us into giving up on postmodern critique in favor of "authentic" first-person storytelling; different ethical needs and demands can coexist in the same site, and it makes sense that each ethical need or value will be best furthered by a particular kind of writing style or knowledge format.

Since Foucault's late writings on ethics are fragmented, unfinished, and reticent about their own context and theoretical implications, it may be useful to provide a brief account that contextualizes them. In the late 1970s and early 1980s, Foucault's work consisted mainly of analyses of mechanisms and diagrams of governance developed in the context of modern European "human sciences." Unlike intellectual historians and deconstructive literary critics, he was not interested in "discourses" for their own sake, and indeed he preferred reading manuals and reports by obscure physicians or social engineers to engaging with "the greats." And when reading such low-status texts, his interest was not in the internal textual constitution of the discourse but rather in its effects—especially when texts by hygienic reformers or sex experts or prison designers appeared to "problematize" social relations in new ways.[6] Foucault's focus on practical projects for governing poverty, madness, sexuality, and crime was not, it needs to be stressed, the same as that of social historians who otherwise shared his research interests. If Foucault's work is not intellectual history insofar as it focuses on problematizations, wherever those occur, rather than in major texts, it is nevertheless not social history insofar as he is not interested in narrating, say, the actual development of prisons or of asylums in this or that place. Institutions are not studied for their own sake. Rather, the development of various institutions is studied for what it can tell us about the technologies of governance that have come to shape not only our world but our hopes and dreams about our world, particularly our sense of personal autonomy. And among the many techniques for inscribing what Mary Poovey has called "the modern fact" and elaborating new identities, Foucault selects those that were most influential because they were not limited to a single institution or profession.

One could argue that Foucault's brilliance lay not in any one idea but in this unusual focal length. By focusing on generalized techniques for governing spaces, activities, and persons, the attention of historians and theorists alike was drawn away from *both* institutions and discourses. This opened the way for studies of techniques of governance (hierarchical observation, normalizing judgment, the examination, pastoral confession, etc.) that have proliferated throughout both state and nonstate institutions of all kinds and have to a large extent made us the sort of individualized human beings that we expect ourselves to be. He made us see that the striking similarities in how monks in monasteries, soldiers in armies, and children in old-fashioned schools are governed lies not in a hegemonic "ruling ideology" but rather in the fact that a number of handy techniques to arrange people, activities, and spaces had been in circulation across spheres. Techniques such as the Panopticon did not, however, spring out of nowhere: particular innovations in how to observe and manage people and things are always connected to specific ways of "problematizing" the world, specific projects or crises of governance. Always putting questions of causality to one side, Foucault did not spend any time discussing whether technologies of governance brought problematizations into being or vice versa—he would not have wanted to engage in the old historians' debate about whether the printing press brought about literacy or whether it was the other way around. For him, the point is simply that problematizing the world in a new way makes certain techniques appear as more useful than others.

The analyses of the techniques of governance associated with "modernization" in Europe that was carried out by Foucault deconstructed—although he would have hated to hear this word being applied to his work—the opposition between structure and agency, determinism and agency, that is so dear to sociologists, historians, and feminist political theorists. How? By showing that the very same techniques that produce mass conformity—examinations, case files, psychoanalytic confession, medical observation—also produce individualization. To give but a simple example: we all take the same exam, and after we get our grades we know what our individual place is on the normal curve and derive an inner sense of individual identity from knowing that we are smart enough for law school, poor at math, or whatever. Personal autonomy, as Nikolas Rose has influentially argued, is these days not the opposite of expert governance, but its very tool (Rose 1989, 1996, 1999).

Some people have read this way of using Foucault as a Frankfurt School lament gone paranoid: even our freedom and our hopes are governed, woe is me. But this is precisely to miss the point made particularly strongly in Foucault's later work, namely, that modern programs for managing people, populations, and desires do not generally work against individual freedom. There are of course biopolitical programs, many of them coercive, for managing populations; but, especially in urban settings in rich countries, there are also vast arrays of programs—medical, commercial, and philanthropic—providing us with tools for governing our selves through, not against, our wish for freedom. All of us living in relative wealth are in the habit of using any number of techniques available in our culture originally developed by commercial enterprises or by authoritarian experts, in order to work on and maximize our ethical freedom.

Many strains of feminism, particularly in the academy, are concerned about the purity of our tools. One might admit to learning tips for everyday life from an aboriginal group; but, as a feminist, one constantly worries about resorting to what Audre Lorde famously called "the master's tools." In sharp contrast to this feminist concern about contaminated analytical tools, Foucault harbored a deep suspicion of all attempts to be original and to cleanse one's mind or one's book of corrupting influences. While eclecticism is not explicitly embraced, Foucault's work uses tools from a number of otherwise incompatible sources and traditions—Nietzsche, Marx, Kant, the history of scientific knowledge, and so forth. Creative combinations of tools of diverse origins are, in keeping with Nietzsche's spirit, valued rather than dismissed as inconsistent. And this mixing and matching is not accompanied by long explanations and tight definitions. Foucault just gets on with using the tools, keeping discussions of "method" to a minimum (and often relegating such discussions to interviews). Like an AA group leader, he seems to be saying to us: "use what you like, leave the rest, don't waste your time interpreting and criticizing." Everything is corrupt, but by the same token, everything is available and usable and transformable.

When writing about ethics—defined as the reflexive government of the self by the self, in contrast to morality, which Foucault defined as the use of standard codes to govern others—Foucault's focus on practices and his avoidance of theoretical discussions meant that he stayed away from the traditional debates. For Foucault as for pragmatist thinkers like William James, ethics was a matter of practice—reflexive and reflective practice, admittedly, but practice nevertheless, and this practice was envisaged as necessarily unfinished. James would have approved of Foucault's quasi-pragmatist description (not "definition") of thought: "Thought is freedom in relation to what one does" (Foucault 1994, 117). And, in keeping with the pragmatist debunking of high culture, Foucault also looked outside of the canon for ethical inspiration. Although his lack of training in social sciences meant

that his ability to study everyday ethical practices was limited, when comb-
ing libraries for appropriate source material, his attention was more often
drawn to "secondary" or "minor" writers than to the canon. And when reading their works, he was more concerned to see how they came up with what
we would now call "tips" for ethical reflection and ethical monitoring than
to discuss the grand established categories of stoicism, epicureanism, and
so on. In keeping with this antiphilosophical reading, when he does cite
Plato or Aristotle, it is often against the philosophical grain. Without pub-
licizing his subversion, he will cite some comment made by Aristotle on the
importance of regulating one's diet, for example, and not bother to discuss
what philosophy curricula would consider the key ideas.

Foucault's subversive project to prioritize practices of self-reflection and
self-governance rather than theories does not, then, have much relation to
the history of ethics as developed by professional philosophers. It does, however, have some affinity with concerns that would in philosophy curricula
be classified as "aesthetic" rather than as "ethical." As Alexander Nehamas
has argued in relation to both Foucault and Nietzsche, Foucault's ethical
project was not "ideas-driven": it was an effort to return to the approach
and the spirit of people such as Galen and Seneca, men who defined themselves in relation to everyday practices of self-governance and not in relation to the academic philosophy (Nehamas 1996 and 1998). Pierre Hadot's
Philosophy as a Way of Life, which recovers this pre-academic sense of the
close relationship between everyday life and critical thought, shows that
Foucault had some encouragement from classical scholars—Hadot himself
(1995, 1996), along with Paul Veyne and Peter Brown—to deploy at least
some Greco-Roman traditions as a "machine of war," as Deleuze would say,
against academic philosophy.

Greco-Roman reflections on ethical self-governance became, in Foucault's hands, a tool to encourage integrated, embodied, and practice-based
reflections that do not separate thought from life. Feminist philosophers
have for some time now argued that we need ways of thinking that do not
separate life from theory, the body from the mind, and so on. In some cases
the content of feminist writing on ethics has been reflected in innovative—
usually, somewhat personal—formats; but at the level of "serious" theory,
feminist texts are too often thoroughly academic treatises that theorize the
relation between body and mind but in traditional formats and writing
style. However radical the content, then, the format is still that of the academic treatise, in sharp contrast to the kind of low-level, practice-driven
reflections upon everyday life that Foucault favored in his later years. What
is at stake in the writings on ethics of the later Foucault, then, is not so
much a different "theory" but a different way of doing thinking. In a sense

78

addressing Heidegger's famous question "Was heisst denken?" (What is called thinking?) from a standpoint that Heidegger would regard as hopelessly caught up in the lowly ontic, Foucault refused the temptations and the consolations of philosophy and cultivated instead a more modest, socially embedded, and consciously passionate stance: what he would not call philosophy but rather "thought" became for him a way of (thoughtful) life—or everyday life as a process of reflection.

ETHICS AFTER THE DEATH OF THE AUTHOR

In some of his comments on Greco-Roman ethical exercises, Foucault noted that a very popular format was the *hypomnemata,* collections of little sayings and quotes, often anonymous, that could be reread and reused in various ways. The *hypomnemata* format constituted not a "text" in the literary or Derridean meaning, but on the contrary, "a material memory of things read, heard, or thought. . . ." These memory books were *not* intimate, confessional diaries; they did not seek to "reveal the hidden, to say the unsaid" but rather to "collect the already said" (Foucault 1994, 273). Such a format undermines the pretensions of literary authorship and the related ideals about individual creativity that have been absorbed by Western feminism and reproduced as distinctly feminist quests for originality and authenticity. Foucault went on to explain that this format (one that challenges not only our conventions about academic genre but also our laws of intellectual property) has many useful functions.

What he did not add, however, is that the *hypomnemata* genre is indeed ubiquitous, but strictly as a lowbrow technology for ethical self-governance. My local popular bookstore always has several such collections near the cash register. Some are 365-page collections of spiritual sayings for every day of the year—a format that evokes the Christian practice of recalling the life of one saint each day through the technique of the calendar. Some are specifically geared to "busy women," whose busyness is always regarded as ethically problematic and hence as in need of techniques of self-care. Some are for lovers of nature, who can reexperience past nature walks and fantasize future ones even as they do their urban morning routine and get ready to drive to work. And some are subversive of the genre, in that they are resolutely anti-spiritual, providing a joke for each day of the year rather than an uplifting thought.

Some of these contemporary *hypomnemata* are authored—*The Prophet* by Kahlil Gibran is the all-time favorite, according to my local bookseller. But, in keeping with the Greek format, many do not purport to represent the original thought of any one author, producing instead a collective, collage-like ethical knowledge. It is perhaps worth asking why such collections are more likely to be found in the kitchens of university secretaries than in the studies of feminist faculty. Thinking back to my very limited ethnography of AA, my guess would be that for ordinary people in North America, ethics is to a large extent a matter of "handy tips" and little sayings rather than a matter for systematic philosophy. Many peasant peoples, when commenting upon ethical issues, routinely resort to "folk sayings" rather than to abstractly rational rules; but urban people too live by analogies and folk sayings more than anthropologists perhaps realize, even if some of these are derived from Hollywood movies or pop songs rather than from "tradition." Foucault's reclaiming of Greco-Roman handmade collections of quotes and sayings suggests that today's feminists might profit from reflecting on our elitist prejudices about the *form* of ethical reflections. If there is no Truth and no Author, why are we still reading "Great Books" and footnoting them carefully in our own work? Why not just borrow interesting passages from here and there, pasting them into a workbook?

Of course, Foucault was not the first philosopher to rebel against the traditional criteria for what counts as philosophy. Nietzsche put his whole life, all his vital energy, into the task of using the resources of Greek and Roman culture as hammers with which to break all the shibboleths of modernity—artistic, political, and philosophical, putting the philosopher's own self at risk. And yet, for all his iconoclasm, Nietzsche remained committed to the European ideal of the isolated genius. He believed in the individual prophetic truth teller. By contrast, Foucault was able to draw on the ethical, political, and intellectual resources of several overlapping movements and friendship networks that shaped his particular present (including the time he spent outside of France): the artistic avant-garde of 1960s Paris; May '68; antipsychiatry; gay male personal politics of the late 1970s and early 1980s; the democracy movements of Eastern Europe in the 1970s; North African anti-imperialist politics; and others to a lesser extent. These resources were not merely political: they were also ethical. As ethical resources, they in turn shaped his theoretical development.

The movements within which Foucault's political interests developed all emphasize "truth telling" in ways that are similar to those found in feminist networks—which is hardly coincidental, since contemporary Euro-American feminism is itself one of the most successful of these post-1968 movements. As his biographers have noted, Foucault was heavily influenced in his youth by writers such as Maurice Blanchot and Georges Bataille, who pursued projects of personal truth telling that, in keeping with the Greek tradition of courageously facing up to established power with one's truth, ran counter to the demands of academic career building and institutional development.[7] Although his later work on ethics is much less naively anarchist than that developed both by his early literary friends and by his own early writings on "transgression," nevertheless there is some continuity in Foucault's thinking about ethics. That continuity is perhaps captured (with inevitable oversimplification) by the term "aesthetics of self."

The idea of an aesthetics of the self, the self as a work of art, has often been dismissed by both mainstream and feminist ethical thinkers as masculinist dandyism, Romantic egoism, and so on. One could comb feminist critiques of Foucault—not to mention the critiques produced by rationalists such as Jürgen Habermas and Charles Taylor—and come up with dozens of citations in which Foucault's individualist anarchism and hedonism are denounced. Instead of reproducing these critiques here and commenting on them from a feminist perspective, I think it is more useful to put to one side our established positions about "postmodernity" and about aesthetics and simply try to see what can be gained for feminists if we engage in the "spiritual exercise" of following Foucault as he reads the Greeks and Romans. This does not suggest, of course, that Foucault has all the answers; it is merely to note that since feminists have already incorporated into feminist ethical projects a number of key stances and analytic tools from various modernist traditions (Kantian ethics, Marxist collectivism, etc.), it is perhaps time to look more closely at the resources recalled and deployed by Foucault in his last writings. In borrowing Foucault's borrowing of Greco-Roman practices for feminism, the first thing to note is that the key term "aesthetics of self" is sometimes replaced, in the Berkeley lectures and elsewhere, by the perhaps more feminist-friendly term "askesis."

ASKESIS

That all ethics is practical, embodied, and unfinished is an insight often associated with the misleading phrase "the aesthetics of existence," a phrase that, as Nehamas has so ably shown, has been reduced to a stereotyped image of hedonism. When earnest feminists dismiss others for being overly concerned with "the aesthetics of existence," this reenacts the Christian assumption that aesthetics works against ethics rather than with it—the assumption, repeated in countless popular as well as highbrow texts (Henry James's *Portrait of a Lady* being one of the best known) that those who are fastidious about aesthetic matters are automatically, necessarily, ethically suspect. Perhaps to counter this assumption about the supposed contradiction between ethical and aesthetic concerns, in his last years Foucault talked less about aesthetics of life and more about askesis.[8]

Askesis bridges the gap between ethics and aesthetics, reminding us of their common origin. Greek askesis was not, Foucault tells us, asceticism in the Max Weber–Protestant ethic sense. It was "the work that one performs on oneself in order to transform or make the self appear" (Foucault 1994, 137); it is, therefore, a "cultivation of self" (1994, 99), not a denial of self. Elsewhere, Foucault tells us that each kind of ethical practice has its own distinct askesis—just as it has its peculiar telos and its peculiar ontology (1994, 265). Thus, there is no such thing as askesis in general; there are only different ways of working upon the self in order to transform the self or make the self appear. In the Berkeley lectures this is elaborated upon:

> Although our word "asceticism" derives from the Greek word "askesis" . . . for the Greeks the word does not mean "ascetic," but has a very broad sense denoting any kind of practical training or exercise. For example, it was a commonplace to say that any kind of art or technique had to be learned by mathesis and askesis—by theoretical knowledge and practical training. And for instance, when Musonius Rufus says that the art of living, *techne tou biou,* is like the other arts, i.e. an art which one could not learn only through theoretical teachings, he is repeating a traditional doctrine. This *techne tou biou,* this art of living, demands practice and training: askesis. But the Greek conception of askesis differs from Christian ascetic practices [because] Christian asceticism has as its ultimate target the renunciation of the self, whereas the moral askesis of the Greco Roman philosophies has as its goal the establishment of a specific relation to oneself: a relationship of self-possession and self-sovereignty. (Foucault 2001, 143–44)

Consciousness-raising in the broadest sense—that is, dialogical practices involving peer support, including support groups for women not run on a feminist basis—constitutes a site for askesis, or, to put it in Foucauldian terms, a venue for developing and using certain technologies of the self. A wealth of research into the development of women's organizations, in the Third World as well as in wealthy societies, has shown that consciousness-raising has indeed proved useful as a way to develop, and to practice, what one might call "the feminist art of living." Why has it worked? Its success—and this is hardly an original observation—is probably due to the fact that it has a double effect: First, the dialogic practices developed in peer-support groups and feminist consciousness-raising create a strong link between individual stories and collective issues and political demands. Second, the same practices also have effects that go in the opposite direction: they inscribe larger political analyses into one's own biography and even one's very body. "Wife assault" or "gendered violence" as a major worldwide issue can be embodied, made real, through individual storytelling; and by the same token, an individual who has gone through years of abuse can begin to see herself as part of a large collective rather than as an isolated, dysfunctional individual.

At some level, every feminist knows this. But I am using this perhaps trite wisdom to argue that what people say in such support groups need not be automatically read as "confession." When a woman says "The worst thing he ever did to me was to . . . ," this does not necessarily produce, either in her or in her audience, the same effects accomplished through classic confessional narratives. In the case of an ordinary woman speaking to other women, especially women who also share her experience and are thus neither classic confessors nor voyeurs, her tale does not have to be experienced as a tale about the "inner self." Truth telling becomes confessional only under certain circumstances, in situations in which the institutional and cultural context and the speaker's own analytic tools favor such a move.

A woman telling her story might be psychologizing herself; she might speculate about having a self-defeating personality or being deficient in self-esteem. But a woman can also proceed to unburdening herself in ways that construct a sociological or economic cause of the violent situation rather than one rooted in some deep psychological truth. Perhaps even more radically subversive of the scientific allegiances of Western feminism is the simple refusal to even investigate causality, the refusal to take sides either with liberal psychology or with leftwing sociologism. Some of the women sensitively interviewed by feminist criminologist Beth Richie about their experiences of both abuse and crime, for example, offer no causal explanations, psychological or economic or historical, for their situation, saying only "I had terrible luck with men" or "My first husband was a creep" or "the stars were against me" (Richie 1996). Describing one's situation through the discourse of fate is very different from the psychological account that always looks for "deep" causes within one's own self and is equally distant from the structural causal accounts favored by most academic feminists.

Each of these three modes of truth telling—psychological, sociological, antiscientific—engages with the self or the person at a different level and in a different way. And there is no reason why they cannot coexist in the same person. One can explain one's fondness for parties by reference to a psychological notion of extroversion and simultaneously explain one's poverty through sociological determinism, while at the same time resorting to the astrological chart in the newspaper for a bit of advice on erotic interests. The rich diversity of selves and of ethical knowledges mobilized by or constituted through differing dialogical/ethical practices has rarely been acknowledged in the overly abstract debates about "confession."

The epistemological hybridity that is the necessary complement of ethical pluralism may not be conducive to building up what is grandiosely called "feminist methodology," but is very useful in everyday life. Women's descriptions of sexual abuse, for instance, often combine feminist insights about masculinity with moralistic ideas about what is sexually disgusting: this kind of piling up of incompatible rationalities seems to have the effect of strengthening a resolve to avoid that situation in a way that single, coherent, "pure" feminist analyses could not hope to match. Eclecticism may itself be a very useful *techne tou biou.*

Analytically, then, we need to understand the difference between seeing oneself as a random victim of fate, seeing oneself as a normal person engaging in less than healthy practices because of economic or other social forces, or labeling oneself as a particular kind of person with a certain inner essence. But having noted these (and other, hitherto unmentioned) genres for telling the truth about oneself, it may be wise to resist the temptation to then call for greater clarity and consistency in autobiographical speech. Achieving theoretical consistency is not necessarily a goal that will further ethical objectives, for those of us who do not see the Kantian unification of the "person" as either necessary or desirable.

Being attentive to the conflicting ways in which people can tell tales about themselves—the different kinds of selves that are given voice in and through such tales—is, it seems to me, more useful for feminist thought than making overall judgments about any one mode or vehicle for truth telling. One of the lessons we can learn from AA—an organization that has survived for six decades and flourished around the world precisely through its tolerance of diverse epistemologies—is that people don't have to be at the same meeting with the same attitude or for the same purpose in order to benefit from it. Some people in AA believe that they have "an addictive personality"; others—older working-class men, generally—stay away from such psychological paradigms and say "the bottle made me do it." The ethical and epistemological effects of a flexible dialogical format encouraging people to explore "the same" issue but in a variety of ways cannot be predicted in advance.

FRIENDSHIP AND TRUTH TELLING

Greco-Roman writers, including those in the Stoic tradition, pioneered some of the techniques of self later taken up by Christians and eventually inherited by Western feminism—diary writing, for example, a technique for scrutinizing the self, recording its vagaries and its doubts, and enabling an internal dialogue that has been thought to be useful for resolving or at least clarifying ethical dilemmas. Some writers, however, emphasized that diary writing and other purely individual practices for monitoring the self and evaluating one's ethical development were subject to the fallacy of grandiosity, the tendency of human beings to generate flattering explanations of our own conduct. Foucault reminds us that Plutarch wrote at length about self-delusion and recommended that we seek out a good friend who will act as "truth teller" (Foucault 2001, 134–36).

But why should we believe what someone else says about us? Plutarch and Galen, Foucault tells us in the section of the Berkeley lectures on truth telling in personal relations, spent some time thinking about the steps to take to ensure that the person being appointed, as it were, as truth teller, is right for the onerous job. The friendly truth teller must, in Plutarch's view, be courageous, so that he won't be tempted to flatter us or to lie in order to use us to advance his own interests. He must also be steadfast and stable. Commenting on a text by Galen with the interesting title of "The diagnosis and cure of the passions," Foucault tells us that Galen too was very worried about the negative ethical implications of flattery among friends (2001, 135). Feminists have rarely worried about flattery, perhaps because up until recently few if any feminists had sufficient power and influence to provoke flattery among either friends or strangers; but Galen's "tips" may be relevant in a present in which feminism, while still subversive, is nevertheless in some quarters a form of cultural capital.

> When a man does not greet the powerful and wealthy by name, when he does not visit them, when he does not dine with them, when he lives a disciplined life, expect that man to speak the truth; try too, to come to a deeper knowledge of what kind of man he is (and that comes about through long association). If you find such a man, summon him and talk with him one day in private; ask him to reveal straightaway whatever of the above mentioned passions [anger, lust, wrath, fear] he may see in you. Tell him you will be most grateful for this service and that you will look on him as your deliverer more than if he had saved you from an illness of the body. Have him promise to reveal it whenever he sees you affected by any of the passions I have mentioned. (2001, 140)

Foucault goes on to explain that, for Galen, the truth teller need not be a close friend—indeed, close friends might experience greater difficulties in telling each other the truth. Looking away from close friends might involve, especially for a physician such as Galen, turning to experts, professionals of the soul and its passions. But Foucault notes that Galen does not put any particular value on medical or any other training when discussing how to find an ethical truth teller. Neither intimacy nor expertise are thus required for truth telling; only the kind of insight that usually goes under the name of "wisdom" (as opposed to knowledge).

Women's groups and networks run on a feminist or quasi-feminist basis often use or create the sort of peer-counseling relations that one could trace back to Greek truth telling among friends. Female networks and friendships, however, tend to focus more on "support" and on "validation," and less on ethical criticism. Much has been written on the need to provide women—especially victimized and abused women—with support and reassurance. As it is generally understood, support is indeed a basic precondition of feminist activity, in that women whose self-image and self-esteem have been stomped into the ground are barely able to act for themselves, never mind for the collectivity. But while this is of course true, it may nevertheless be the case that today's feminists could find it useful to consider whether the simple affirmation of women's selfhood—you're okay, you can do it, you know best what's good for you—is all that there is to feminist ethical truth telling. Some biographies of influential women, and some reflections on the perils of mentoring that can be found circulating (verbally) among younger feminists, suggest that ethical problems can develop when women who have gone through hardship but have then "risen" persist in seeing themselves exclusively as victims in need of support. Their outdated self-image blinds them to the ways in which they misuse the power they have recently acquired—they/we don't even think of them/ourselves as having power and are hence unable to internally monitor the use of it.

What Foucault did not say in the Berkeley lectures, but which is a key theme in all his work, is that all forms of knowledge, including individuals' personal knowledge of the ambitions, hopes, and foibles of their friends, is immediately a form of power. Galen and Plutarch worried about how their own clearly evident power, power which they by no means wanted to give up, might make it difficult for their friends to speak honestly. By contrast, feminists, caught up as we have been in a decades-long crusade to "empower" ourselves and other women, have not thought a great deal about the problems of having too much power. In this way, we have been paralyzed by situations in which feminist leaders assumed a confessor role and proceeded, in the name of telling the truth, to abuse power (the case of the Parisian "Psych et Po" group is the most famous).

Any tenured professor who has experienced flattery by current or prospective graduate students, for instance, could benefit from considering alternative ways in which women can pursue practices of personal truth telling. Feminist reflections on "support," friendship, and the quest for "agency" and "autonomy" tend to assume that equality is the goal if not the reality; it seems to me that we have not developed practices of truth telling that acknowledge power differences.

Feminist ethics, at least in contemporary North America, offers very few resources to those women—white tenured professors, for instance—who are unhappy with a liberal moralistic response to power (Shame on you! Apologize for your privilege!) and who are looking for ways to acknowledge power, without engaging in the confessional self-absorbed breast-beating that women of color have repeatedly said is not particularly helpful to them. Given the impasse of contemporary feminism in regard to the ethical dilemmas of structural inequalities among women, reading what the Greeks had to say about flattery is more than an intellectual exercise. There is more to the ethical practices of friendship than simply support; and there is more to keeping an ethical eye on structural inequalities among coworkers and friends than the "bad dialectic," as Hegel would say, of guilt and shame.

TRUTH TELLING AND THE POLITICAL

Much ink has been spilled in recent years discussing whether the replacement of the old politics of interests and ideologies by the new politics of identity is a good thing. As in the confused debate about "postmodernism" discussed above, the debate about identity politics has produced more heat than light precisely because it was posed, in television talk-show fashion, as "a debate." People participating in the discussions have thus tended to assume that we all know what identity politics is and how it works, and that what needs to be done is to evaluate it and take a position either for or against or, perhaps, somewhere "in the middle."

But if telling personal stories, to oneself or to others, is not one thing with a single meaning—if autobiographies are not always confessional and if ethical reflection can proceed by way of using folk sayings to change one's habits rather than by way of deep psychological transformation—then it follows that telling one's story for a political purpose cannot be regarded as a distinct act with a single, predictable effect. Acknowledging that "identity" (personal history, antecedents, biography) matters, and matters politically, does not have to mean accepting all the baggage of "identity politics."

Foucault's recovery of Greek truth-telling practices helps us to think beyond the dichotomy of "old politics" versus "identity politics." For Foucault's Greeks, telling the truth about the self was an integral part of being in the polis, of being political, partly because this elaboration of the truth about oneself could be done only through dialogue and through friendship. The truth about the self was not perceived as lying inside oneself from the beginning; it was not something "deep" to be excavated with psychological tools. The ethical truth about persons lay in the evolving interactions between people—pedagogic interactions, friendship interactions, kin interactions, polis-based interactions. To be ethical was to cultivate a certain critical attitude with which to live and to keep questioning the world and oneself while living—not to follow a particular rule or to be in possession of any particular knowledge.

To put it another way, in many truth-telling practices, we don't actually ever seek to tell "The Truth." The truth, as Nietzsche told us, does not exist somewhere waiting to be discovered and told. And the identity that identity politics claims to speak from and about does not exist in that naive-ontological sense: gays, lesbians, "women of color," all get constituted in the process of truth telling. There is no rock-solid truth, then: but there is still the activity, the process of truth telling. And while the activity of monitoring oneself and speaking about oneself is of course constitutive of "the self," this is by no means a unitary or univocal process: there are as many different kinds of selves as there are ways of embarking upon and continually practicing truth telling. If feminists were to spend less time taking sides for or against confession, for or against identity, and more time documenting the myriad ways in which people speak about their ethical dilemmas, wishes, and fears, we might find that although there is no longer any Truth, nevertheless truth telling remains an integral part of ethical reflection, among ordinary people who read *The Prophet* as well as among feminist philosophers.

NOTES

1. See Benhabib et al. (1995). Among feminist historians, the key debate was that between Linda Gordon (against postmodernism) and Joan Scott (in favor). See Scott (1990) for a review of Gordon, and see Gordon (1990) for a review of Scott.

2. In part because feminism is to a great extent an oral rather than a written tradition, and in part because feminism is interactional and hence sociopolitical, not merely textual, the Bakhtinian prism of "dialogue" is a better framework than the Derridean tools of textual deconstruction for the analyses of women's truth-telling practices. I thus treat truth telling as a form of dialogue, whether the truth telling takes textual form (e.g., autobiographical writing) or oral form.

3. In the polemical booklet *Forget Foucault,* Baudrillard accused Foucault of failing to discern the outlines of contemporary postmodernity (Baudrillard 1987). This critique, while correct in pointing out that Foucault's work has a certain "owl of Minerva" quality, since the "Man" for whom he provides a partial genealogy was, admittedly, beginning to fray at the edges as Foucault was writing about him, fails to acknowledge that Foucault did not simply neglect to pronounce on the present. Rather, he had a strong theoretical and political distaste for the ways in which philosophers—particularly in Paris—have acted as self-appointed political gurus and prophets of the near future.

4. Into our own present, philosophical reflections on the ethical value of friendship tend to draw on a highly masculinist tradition that goes from Aristotle and other Greek gentlemen through Montaigne. While Derrida's own contribution to these reflections (Derrida 1997) acknowledges that European philosophical ethics are essentially, not just contingently, based on practices of brotherhood, he does not explore any alternative potential sources for a non- or post-masculinist ethics. See Valverde (1999) for a review essay of *The Politics of Friendship.*

5. As interpreted by Walter Benjamin, Klee's painting portrays the angel of historical responsibility, the ghost that forces us who are in the present to look back upon our past and act accordingly. This Benjamin figure of the Klee angel of history is linked by Derrida to the ghost of Hamlet's father, also a figure inciting us to ethical action, throughout the text of Derrida's *Spectres of Marx* (1994). See also Derrida (1992).

6. For some reason, many feminist scholars identify Foucault with "discourse analysis," which is a woeful misunderstanding, rather than paying attention to what he himself suggested was his major contribution to historical research, namely, the notion of problematization. For an explanation, see Castel (1994).

7. "The sovereign himself is not a parrhesiastes, but a touchstone of the good ruler is his ability to play the parrhesiastic game. Thus, a good king accepts everything that a genuine parrhesiastes tells him, even if it turns out to be unpleasant for him to hear criticisms of his decisions" (Foucault 2001, 22–23). While Antigone's truth telling is probably the best known example of such political *parrhesia*, it is significant that throughout the Berkeley lectures, Foucault himself limits his detailed commentary to male-on-male interactions, in keeping with his privileging of masculine ethical practices.

8. See Foucault (1994) for various essays and interviews, specifically pages 99, 137, and 265.

WORKS CITED

Baudrillard, Jean. 1987. *Forget Foucault.* New York: Semiotext(e).

Benhabib, Seyla, Judith Butler, Nancy Fraser, and Drucilla Cornell. 1995. *Feminist Contentions: A Philosophical Exchange.* New York: Routledge.

Butler, Judith. 1987. *Subjects of Desire: Hegelian Reflections in Twentieth-century France.* New York: Columbia University Press.

———. 1990. *Gender Trouble.* London: Routledge.

———. 1997. *The Psychic Life of Power.* Stanford: Stanford University Press.

Castel, Robert. 1994. "Problematization as a Mode of Reading History." In *Foucault and the Writing of History.* Edited by Jan Goldstein. Oxford: Blackwell.

Derrida, Jacques. 1992. "The Force of Law: The Mystical Foundation of Authority." In *Deconstruction and the Possibility of Justice.* Edited by D. Cornell, M. Rosenfeld, and D. Carlson. New York: Routledge.

———. 1994. *Spectres of Marx.* London: Routledge.

———. 1997. *The Politics of Friendship.* London: Verso.

Foucault, Michel. 1980. *The History of Sexuality.* Volume 1. *An Introduction.* New York: Vintage.

———. 1994. *Ethics: Subjectivity, and Truth.* Edited by Paul Rabinow. New York: New Press.

———. 1998. *Aesthetics, Method, and Epistemology.* Edited by James Faubion. New York: New Press.

———. 2001. *Fearless Speech.* Edited by Joseph Pearson. New York: Semiotext(e).

Gibran, Kahlil. 1923. *The Prophet.* New York: Knopf.

Gordon, Linda. 1990. "Review of Joan Scott." *Signs* 15, no. 4 (Summer 1990): 848–60.

Hadot, Pierre. 1995. *Philosophy as a Way of Life: Spiritual Exercises from Socrates to Foucault.* Translated by Michael Chase. Oxford: Blackwell.

———. 1997. "Forms of Life and Forms of Discourse in Ancient Philosophy." In *Foucault and His Interlocutors.* Edited by Arnold Davidson. Chicago: University of Chicago Press.

James, Henry. 1963. *Portrait of a Lady.* New York: Penguin; originally published in 1881.

Nehamas, Alexander. 1996. "Nietzsche, Modernity, Aestheticism." In *The Cambridge Companion to Nietzsche.* Edited by B. Magnus and K. M. Higgins. Cambridge: Cambridge University Press.

———. 1998. *The Art of Living: Socratic Reflections from Plato to Foucault.* Berkeley: University of California Press.

Nussbaum, Martha. 1999. "The Professor of Parody." *New Republic.* February 22, 1999, vol. 220, no. 8: 37–45.

Richie, Beth. 1996. *Compelled to Crime.* New York: Routledge.

Rose, Nikolas. 1989. *Governing the Soul.* London: Routledge.

———. 1996. *Inventing Ourselves: Psychology, Power, and Personhood.* Cambridge: Cambridge University Press.

———. 1999. *Powers of Freedom: Reframing Political Thought.* Cambridge: Cambridge University Press.

Scott, Joan. 1990. "Review of Linda Gordon." *Signs* 15, no. 4 (Summer 1990): 848–60.

Valverde, Mariana. 1998. *Diseases of the Will: Alcohol and the Dilemmas of Freedom.* Cambridge: Cambridge University Press.

———. 1999. "The Personal Is the Political: Justice and Gender in Deconstruction." *Economy and Society* 28, no. 2 (May 1999): 300–311.

An Ethics of the Self

Helen O'Grady

This chapter explores aspects of the relationship between gendered processes of identity formation and self-policing in women's lives.[1] Identified by Michel Foucault as a key mechanism of modern Western social control, self-policing frequently entails harsh and debilitating ways of relating to the self and keeps individuals tied to prescribed identities.[2] It effectively means that individuals live their lives as though under constant observation. I single out two factors typical of many women's experience—the cultural legacy of subordinate status and an imbalance between care for others and care for the self—that are likely to enhance the power of self-policing. Such forces encourage women to live according to the expectations of others, which both reflects and heightens vulnerability to practices of self-surveillance and self-evaluation. In this context, and against the background of a pervasive ethos of self-responsibility and the measuring of worth according to established categories of normality, failure to conform to common standards is frequently privatized and met with acts of self-recrimination. Pathologizing failure tends to preclude a contextualization of experience and to isolate individuals from one another. To speak generally of self-policing in women's lives, however, is not to imply a uniformity of experience. While the category of gender can illuminate certain common themes, clearly a multiplicity of factors intersect with gender to render identity processes a different experience for diverse groups of women. It is claimed that the intensity of self-policing is likely to vary according to social location and certain types of personal experience.

However, just as Foucault's work allows for the identification of this sort of mechanism in identity formation, so his work also points to possible ways of overcoming self-policing, or at least mitigating its harmful effects. I argue that the therapeutic environment (and other possible environments) makes it possible to destabilize the common assumption that self-policing technologies form an inevitable part of identity and to critically examine the cultural context in which they prosper. This opens up space for the exploration and performance of preferred ways of relating to the self. This does not entail the uncovering of natural, pre-social attributes but rather the constitution of a self-relationship always relative to a culture's ideas, practices, time, and context. At first blush, the linking of Foucault's thought to the therapeutic domain may appear paradoxical given his challenge to forms of knowledge that have constructed categories of illness, pathology, and so on. Nonetheless, in undermining the power of therapeutic discourse to impose an essential identity, the approach outlined is able to subvert rather than perpetuate taken-for-granted realities of its discipline. In a parallel move to Foucault, the problematizing of this and other key therapeutic "truths" makes it more difficult for those authorized by professional discourses to continue to speak and act in characteristic ways.

In thinking about ways to facilitate this type of self-making, I propose the usefulness of aspects of Foucault's later notion of care for the self. His emphasis on the ethical relationship we can have with ourselves offers a framework for redressing the imbalance in many women's lives between care for others and care for the self which contributes to the power of self-policing. This means that just as Foucault suggests that freedom comes from the ways in which individuals negotiate power relations, rather than evading them altogether, so he suggests that while some practices of the self are disciplinary and constraining, others are more autonomous. The sort of activities and dispositions involved in care of the self provide a way of using disciplinary practices in emancipatory ways: they facilitate the negotiation of power relations.[3] Yet while Foucault's later work provides useful avenues for reflecting on ways to diminish self-policing, it also poses problems for feminists who would adopt his idea of care for the self. Some of these worries have been forcefully expressed in the work of Lois McNay. Following an outline of some of McNay's concerns, I suggest certain ways of redressing these in efforts to undermine the power of self-policing. These are articulated more fully in the section on women's friendship with the self.

My interest in this area derives from working as a counselor in the area of women's health.[4] Before turning to the issue of self-policing, I will outline briefly Foucault's views on power and freedom that inform my own discussion of disciplinary and more autonomous practices. Toward the end of the 1970s, Foucault developed the notion of power-in-relation-to-freedom, which allowed him to retain his key insight that subjects always act within power relations in the same way that thinking always takes place within structures of knowledge (Tully 1998, 133, 136–37). For Foucault, the idea that power relations are inherent in every social relationship is not a recipe for despair (Foucault 1983, 223). Rather, acknowledging power's inevitable presence opens up space for thinking about the ways in which its effects can be minimized. Thus, while relationships of power clearly can be oppressive, this is not necessarily the case. For example, the teacher-student relationship becomes so only when arbitrary and unnecessary authority is exercised by the teacher (Foucault 1988d, 18). When power relations are oppressive, Foucault claims that the possibility of resisting them at varying intensity at different times and places is "a permanent condition of their existence . . ." (Foucault 1983, 225). It is therefore always possible to " . . . modify [power's] grip in determinate conditions and according to a precise strategy" (Foucault 1988c, 123). This reflects his view that the social sphere comprises a multiplicity of unstable and diverse relations of power that contain possibilities for both domination and resistance (Sawicki 1991, 25, 56). In this light, given power relations also may provide the means through which subjects move toward a creative expression of themselves (McNay 1994, 106).

Foucault's belief in the indissociability of power and freedom contrasts with the dominant Western tendency to view these as mutually exclusive and zero sum. Within such a view, increased freedom requires decreased power and vice versa. Conversely, for Foucault freedom must exist for power to be exercised: "Power is exercised only over free subjects, and only insofar as they are free" (Foucault 1983, 221), that is, insofar as they are able to choose from a range of possible ways of acting. In this way, he distinguishes between power relationships which always hold the possibility of reversal and relationships of domination which, because of the extent and immutability of asymmetry between parties, do not. Within relations of power, freedom for Foucault is not some kind of final, eternal state wrested from power's influence. It is rather an ongoing relationship of "agonism," of strategic contestation and renegotiation with power's limits whereby the rules of the game can be either modified or challenged (Foucault 1983, 221–22).

THE "INNER GAZE"

The relationship women have with themselves is one level at which the struggle to move beyond prescribed identities takes place. To focus on this relationship is not to imply that other levels of women's struggle for greater self-definition are less important. Indeed given the relationship between cultural ideas/practices/structures and identity formation, macro-level social change is crucial. Nonetheless, even in the face of such change internal struggles may continue. Moreover, the relative invisibility of such struggles means they are less likely to be articulated. Self-policing tends to be experienced as an automatic part of thinking and thus as reality. This makes it a particularly insidious form of oppression. In thinking about women's intra-subjective relations, I have found it useful to draw on Foucault's depiction of panoptical power. While criticisms of his portrayal of an all-encompassing dominatory power are important,[5] his use of the Panopticon as a metaphor for the modern condition is insightful. Within the ideal panoptical design, compliance with institutional/organizational norms is ensured ultimately through the inculcation of self-policing as individuals come to interiorize the external gaze of authority (Foucault 1980, 155).

The effectiveness of this type of power seems to lie in its ability "to grasp the individual at the level of its . . . very identity and the norms that govern its practices of self-constitution" (Sawicki 1998, 94–95). The power of self-policing can be understood, in part, in terms of the pervasive Western ethos of individual responsibility and autonomy. The internalizing impulse of such an ethos discourages the contextualization of experience. In addition, self-policing works in the service of what Foucault describes as the modern imperative toward sameness and the pathologizing of difference. This is characteristic of societies in which human worth has come to be measured primarily by the scientific categories of the "normal" and "abnormal" (Foucault 1979, 184).

In line with his general inattention to issues of sexual difference, Foucault does not investigate the relationship between gender and self-policing. Yet given the gendered process of identity formation this would seem important. Sandra Lee Bartky notes that while many of the disciplinary practices analyzed by Foucault are inscribed on both female and male bodies, he ignores those disciplines producing a peculiarly feminine mode of embodiment. Clearly this is problematic from a feminist perspective as it takes no account of the inscription of an inferior status on the female body/self (Bartky 1990, 65, 71). If self-policing ties individuals to given norms and practices, it is likely to play a key role in maintaining aspects of women's subordination. At the same time, factors such as the legacy of subordinate status can enhance the power of self-policing.[6]

HISTORICAL LEGACY

While factors other than gender may contribute to an inferior status, in the historical context of subordination it is not surprising that many women find themselves captured by an apologetic mode of being and a general sense of being "less than": "it is not by chance or as a result of some personal inadequacy that many women find self-doubt an unwanted part of our lives. . . . [T]his is understood to be a direct consequence of the ways patriarchy operates in women's lives to undermine our sense of self and thus, through self-surveillance, maintain particular relations of power" (Swan 1999, 104–5).

Bartky's critique of conventional understandings of shame and guilt sheds light on this type of disempowerment. She claims that within conventional moral psychology, emotions such as shame and guilt are conceived as playing the important role of reaffirming a person's moral commitments and, in this sense, are "a disruption in an otherwise undisturbed life" (Bartky 1990, 97). In examining the type of shame commonly experienced by women—that which manifests in "a pervasive sense of personal inadequacy" (Bartky 1990, 85)—she argues "there is no such equilibrium to which to return" (Bartky 1990, 97); a person's whole emotional existence may be imbued with a sense of inadequacy. This is understood in light of women's systematic subjection to demeaning treatment in a wide variety of arenas in sexist societies. This means that, in addition to more visible structures of disadvantage, shame and guilt can constitute aspects of gender oppression. She claims that such a notion is missing from conventional moral psychology whose explanation of these emotions lies "almost entirely in its relationship to individual failure and wrongdoing, never in its relationship to oppression" (Bartky 1990, 97). Such an explanation is made possible by positing as universal a specific privileged subject "whose social location is such that he has the capacity not only to be judged but to judge, not only to be defined by others but to define them as well" (Bartky 1990, 97). As Bartky notes, such an agent is free from the characteristic types of psychological oppression on which modern class, race, and gender hierarchies are so dependent (Bartky 1990, 90, 96–97).

Gender subordination is further reflected in the imbalance in many women's training between care for others and care for the self. Women traditionally have been assigned a disproportionate responsibility for the care of others. Generally this has not been accompanied by a corresponding emphasis on care of the self (Strickling 1988, 197).[7] The social expectation to care for others tends to be internalized as an ethic of responsibility. Jean Grimshaw points to the complex nature of such an ethic. She argues that the emphasis in women's lives on "emotional maintenance" and preserving relationships has not only engendered a common belief in women that they must maintain relationships, but that they must bear the full responsibility for this. Such a belief renders them particularly vulnerable to guilt and to a concern with "not upsetting people" or ever acting so as to fracture a relationship. Women are also vulnerable to the feeling that their own needs or desires should never come before those of others (Grimshaw 1986,

195–96). It is not hard to see how this type of training renders women vulnerable to heightened experiences of self-policing.

TECHNOLOGIES OF THE SELF

In the context of cultural inferiorization and predominantly other-oriented training, there are many incitements for women to monitor rigorously their thoughts, feelings, speech, and actions to ensure conformity to accepted rules or the approval of others. This can result in a strict overseer type of relation to the self that precludes spontaneity and diminishes possibilities for self-fashioning. When individuals perceive themselves as having failed to meet accepted norms, this can be experienced not just as a slipup or error but as a transgression against the self. Such a notion is captured in Bartky's description of the type of shame commonly felt by women: "Shame is the distressed apprehension of the self as inadequate or diminished: it requires if not an actual audience before whom my deficiencies are paraded, then an internalized audience with the capacity to judge me, hence internalized standards of judgment. Further, shame requires the recognition that I *am*, in some important sense, as I am seen to be" (Bartky 1990, 86).

Failure to measure up to accepted standards also can induce self-punishment. One example of this is self-criticism.[8] This type of criticism usually takes the form of derogatory thoughts about the self that tend to invoke a range of disempowering feelings. These can include feelings of depression, worthlessness, inadequacy, insecurity, hopelessness, anxiety, and so on. Moreover, the power of such criticism frequently is reinforced within the broader culture as, for example, through media representations of a uniform and unrealistic standard for women's bodies, abuse or harassment of girls and women, and a general attitude of criticism and perfectionism in the school system (Dickerson 1998, 43). Like all self-policing technologies, critical voices tend to appear as an automatic, natural part of thinking that makes it difficult to recognize their effects. As clinical psychologist Marie-Nathalie Beaudoin notes: "It is always incredible to discover how harsh these voices can be and how conditioned and accustomed we are at listening to them and believing them. Most of us would never even consider saying such . . . things to any enemy, yet we accept their daily torture on ourselves" (Beaudoin in Dickerson 1998, 43–44).

Both inside and outside the therapeutic context, women often reveal harsh practices of self-recrimination when judging themselves to have failed to meet certain prescribed norms. Just one example is the imposition of punishing forms of exercise or food deprivation if body weight is perceived to exceed mainstream culture's relentless expectation for slim girls and women. Self-recrimination also can take the form of insidious comparisons with others, which inevitably confirm one's worst fears and suspicions. For example, a university student who perceives herself to have performed inadequately may perceive others, including other women, as competent and "normal" in this regard. This can intensify her own sense of incompetency, which is frequently interpreted as personal deficiency. Such pathologizing leaves little room for an understanding of competency in terms of experience and tends to obscure memories of past competence. It also tends to preclude a consideration of cultural factors such as the structuring of academic institutions in what are characteristically male ways of thinking and behaving. Furthermore for certain groups, simply being in a university can generate self-doubt. This may be the case for mature students who have spent time outside the education system, and whose sense of intellectual ability has been structured, in part at least, by the general devaluing of women. It also may be the case for working-class women stepping into a domain traditionally reserved for the middle class. Indigenous, black, and some immigrant women are confronted further by an institution wholly defined and structured by white standards. In a study of American college life, Bartky also refers to the confusing effects of a contradiction between a professed commitment to gender equality at institutional and individual levels and "its actual though covert and unacknowledged absence" (Bartky 1990, 94). She claims that this type of ambiguity, whereby women are in some ways affirmed and in others diminished, tends to create a sense of inadequacy in many women despite any concrete evidence of failure (Bartky 1990, 94).[9] Finally, the possibility of contextualizing one's experience is diminished further by the isolating effects of insidious comparisons with others. By reinforcing a belief in personal deficiency, such comparisons render a sense of solidarity with others less likely. This type of personal exile reflects the starkest aspect of panoptical power (Foucault 1979, 200–201). For Bartky, it is characteristic of the secrecy requirements associated with many women's experience of a pervasive sense of inadequacy (Bartky 1990, 97).[10]

MULTIPLE SITES OF SUBJECTIVITY

I have pointed to certain common features of women's general training likely to enhance the power of self-policing. Once factors other than gender are considered, a multiplicity of intersecting influences can be seen to affect the intensity of that power. If self-policing ensures the measuring of worth in terms of conformity to accepted modes of identity, the intensity of the "inner gaze" is likely to vary according to social location and life circumstances. When individuals are positioned beyond "the norm," commonly accepted ways of being frequently clash with experiences of the self—for example as black; as indigenous; as non-Anglo; as working class; as lesbian, gay, bi- or transsexual; as single parent; as ill; and so forth. Moreover, in the case of a constantly visible difference such as skin color or physical disability, daily exposure to the discriminating gaze of white or able-bodied culture can be unrelenting.[11] Although marginalized groups can and do develop critiques of the dominant culture and construct alternative identity practices, it is important not to underestimate the myriad ways in which mainstream culture continues to discriminate against those who do not fit its norms and the ceaseless invitations to internalize this oppression.[12] In addition to the broad categories of race, class, sexuality, health, and so on, experiences of violence and abuse also may intensify self-policing.[13] Such experiences can generate negative identity narratives that are frequently informed and reinforced by broader cultural beliefs.

CHALLENGING TECHNOLOGIES OF THE SELF

The entrenched nature of self-policing can result in its ongoing presence despite the existence of various institutional and attitudinal improvements in the social position of women.[14] Foucault's insistence on the need to study the constitutive effects of power at the "microphysical" level of bodies, thoughts, wills, conduct, and everyday lives of individuals is apposite here (Foucault 1979, 27). If the microlevel of life is ignored in the push for progressive social change, a range of power relations will remain intact. This points to the importance of addressing power's hold at the intra-subjective level. One strategy for achieving this is to destabilize the idea that self-policing technologies form an inevitable part of identity.

In the therapeutic context, this can be achieved through relational externalizing conversations. The notion of externalization is a key aspect of narrative therapy (see note 4 for a brief elaboration of this approach). Based on the idea that the problem is separate from the person, externalizing conversations create space to explore the type of relationship people have to problematic experience and the ways in which they may be both participating in and resisting it. Out of this process a revised relationship with the problem becomes possible (White and Epston 1990, 38–76). While advocating a similar ethical and political framework to narrative therapy, Johnella Bird is concerned about the extent to which an emphasis on the problem as separate from the person linguistically reinforces the conventional notion of an autonomous self. She posits an alternative notion of relational externalization that provides a way of *performing*, as opposed to simply valuing, the idea of a self always in relationship to a set of sociohistorical language practices.

Rather than encouraging a person to define her/himself in opposition to the problem, relational externalizing emphasizes the relational connection between the person and problematic experience. In addition to challenging the idea that disabling practices of the self are internal to a person, relational externalizing questions encourage contextualization of such practices (Bird 2000, xi, 7–9, 15, 47, 82, 89, 128–29). In this way women can gain a clearer sense of the cultural structures of inequity relating to gender, race, class, sexuality, and so forth that have provided the context for many of their struggles in life. This helps diminish immobilizing feelings of self-blame and creates space for a revision of the relationship with self-policing technologies. In this revision, the relational aspects of preferred practices continue to be emphasized. Thus, women can work toward strengthening their relationships with confidence, trust, playfulness, spontaneity, and so forth. In this way the agency required to bring these into one's life is not diminished (Stacey 1997, 36). Emphasizing one's relationship to preferred practices also diminishes the power of self-policing technologies when such practices are less present in people's lives. Thus, a focus on one's relationship to, say, confidence at such times is more enabling than the idea of one no longer being a confident person. It also allows for the possibility of degrees of confidence. Moreover, a relational focus encourages reflection on the context within which preferred attributes tend to be more present or absent. This precludes any attribute acquiring a status of neutrality, highlighting instead the notion that all attributes, all ideas, are sustained by forces greater than "I" (Bird 2000, xi, 8, 20–25, 47, 82, 128).

The process of revising the relationship with self-policing technologies can be aided by charting personal histories of resistance to these and the unwanted identities they support. This helps strengthen belief in one's ability to perform preferred practices of the self (White and Epston 1990, 15–17, 55–65). It also can be helpful to identify and strengthen links to histories of resistance to patriarchal norms by various family members or others across generations. This provides an audience of support and legitimation for revised relations with the self (see White 1997, 22–24). Charting histories of resistance enables the realization of the feminist project, at an individual level, of rediscovering and revaluing women's experiences (McNay 1992, 12). It, moreover, reflects the notion that subjects are simultaneously produced by and resist patriarchal power. It thus cuts across any idea of women as passive receptors of such power.

It is difficult to convey the sense of empowerment expressed by women when, against years of training and habit, the shackles of self-policing begin to loosen. Although I do not want to downplay the frequent complexity of this process, it entails a growing sense of acceptance, belief, love of the self, qualities difficult to achieve within patriarchal prescriptions of womanhood. Thus, a student may find herself checking out the experiences of peers instead of automatically pathologizing and isolating herself. A young woman whose life has been dominated by anorexia nervosa may begin to hear herself say "nobody's perfect" rather than automatically subjecting herself to grueling physical and emotional punishments for failing to meet its perfectionist demands. A mother may find herself noticing positive aspects of her parenting. A survivor of child sexual abuse may begin to experience a move toward self-belief or self-love. These are powerful experiential moments of resistance to oppressive practices of power, which give rise to the possibility of preferred constructions of self and relationship with profound consequences for enhanced quality of life.[15]

The significance of such transformative moments lies in their demonstration of the illusory nature of taken-for-granted, seemingly fixed notions of identity. Once this has been experienced, a more fluid notion of identity becomes possible. Discovering that aspects of the self can be superseded through active intervention in one's own life gives rise at least to the possibility of ongoing destabilization of fixed categories of identity. This is not, therefore, an argument for advancing any particular notion of what it means to be a woman, or indeed the idea that there is any natural or inevitable female identity. Such an argument would entail the substitution of one regime of truth for another as opposed to "increasing the sites of resistance" to privileged knowledges (Law and Madigan 1994, 5). As Vanessa Swan argues, the latter rather than the former should be the aim of a progressive feminist therapy (Swan 1999, 106).

As suggested above, the creation of a space that problematizes privileged knowledges opens up possibilities for agency that are precluded when identity categories are seen as fixed or foundational. In this way "the proliferation of gender style and identity" (Butler 1990a, 339) can be fostered. This implicitly challenges what Judith Butler calls "the regulatory fiction of heterosexual coherence" (Butler 1990a, 338) which stabilizes and unifies the category of woman (Butler 1990a, 338–39). Butler points out that gender requires continual performance, which means that representations other than those that have taken on the appearance of the natural are possible (Butler 1990b, 141, 145–46, 148). In this light the task is "to redescribe those possibilities that *already* exist, but which exist within cultural domains designated as culturally unintelligible and impossible" (Butler 1990b, 148–49).

AN ETHICS OF CARE FOR THE SELF

I have argued that Foucault's depiction of the central role of self-policing in maintaining dominant identity practices illuminates an important aspect of women's struggle toward greater self-definition. Interestingly, this insight about the modern system of social control seems to be absent from the later work on ethics. This may be due, in part, to his continued inattention to issues of gender. Lois McNay points to his blurring of distinctions between those practices of the self that are more readily accessible to self-fashioning and those that are less so because of their deep inscription upon the body and the psyche, for example those relating to gender and sexuality (McNay 1994, 155). Despite these lacunae, aspects of the later work may provide a useful framework for countering self-policing technologies and the given identities they support. In his work on ethics, Foucault singles out the relation to the self as a discrete component of morality: "there is another side to the moral prescriptions, which most of the time is not isolated as such but is, I think, very important: the kind of relationship you ought to have with yourself, *rapport à soi*, which I call ethics, and which determines how the individual is supposed to constitute himself as a moral subject of his own actions" (Foucault 1984a, 352).

The significance for women of Foucault's emphasis on the intra-subjective relationship lies in its implicit challenge to the dichotomizing of self- and other-directed care. In women's training, the establishment of ethical relations with others has frequently entailed forsaking oneself as a person meriting equal consideration. Conversely in Foucault's account of antiquity, relations of integrity with others require active participation in the fashioning of one's own ethical subjectivity. This entailed practices of care for the self through which free men were able to establish a relationship of self-mastery over the passions and basic appetites. Such practices were oriented toward achieving a full enjoyment of oneself, setting an example for future generations, and establishing the basis for ethical relations with others. This ethics does not take the form of a universal law but is rather a personal choice for those motivated toward an aesthetic lifestyle. It involves a particular art of life requiring the development of practical wisdom about the appropriate ways to behave in variable circumstances (Foucault 1986, 21, 30–31, 53–62, 73, 75–76, 78, 80–81, 89–91, 93, 250–53). What Foucault admires in classical ethics is the scope afforded individual creativity in relation to general social and moral rules (McNay 1992, 85). While this is missing from Christian and modern secular ethics, he believes the contemporary climate is ripe for a return to a more individual-based ethics (Foucault 1988a, 49). In his view, this type of personal aesthetics has the potential to counter the normalizing and homogenizing tendencies of modern society (McNay 1992, 86). The type of creative self-making envisaged by Foucault does not presuppose the uncovering of a natural subjectivity (Foucault 1988a, 50–51). Rather, he sees the notion of historically contingent subjectivity as offering greater scope for the development and expression of human creative powers. This is reflected in his advocacy of an ethos of ongoing reflection on, and transformation of, ourselves (Foucault 1984b, 43, 45–47).

Such an ethos has the potential to encourage an attentiveness to the self so often missing from women's lives. This lack of attentiveness, rather than increasing the likelihood of women exploiting or dominating others as in Foucault's account of ancient ethics, holds the reverse danger. A lack of attention to the self can render women vulnerable to exploitation or abuse. It also has the potential to deprive women of satisfying relations with the self or in ancient terms a full enjoyment of oneself. When care for others is the primary focus, knowledge about one's own desires, needs, values, tastes, beliefs, and so forth can be patchy or even nonexistent. This is not surprising, as women's caretaking role frequently entails a forsaking of their own knowledges in order to please and accommodate others (Dickerson et al. 1994, 9). Conversely, when the relationship one has with oneself is conceived as an important component of ethics, a space is created for the generation of one's own knowledges and skills. This requires creative interaction with given identity practices, standards and norms through which a reshaping of one's relationship with the self/others/life begins to take form. As in Foucault's work, this does not entail the discovery of intrinsic qualities but is, rather, a remaking of the self in accordance with preferred discursive practices, including, as Butler contends, those yet to be articulated (Butler 1990b, 148–49).

THE POLITICS OF SELF-MASTERY

Although Foucault's later work on ethics provides some useful avenues for thinking about ways in which the harmful effects of self-policing on women's sense of self can be lessened, his conception of care of the self also is limited in a number of important ways. These have been usefully highlighted by McNay. The following sections summarize some of her concerns. They also gesture toward some alternative attitudes to the self. These attitudes are articulated more fully in the section proposing that women become friends to themselves. All of these alternative approaches to the self's relationship to itself help redress some of the difficulties in Foucault's ethic of care for the self.

While Foucault distanced himself from the sexist (and elitist) dimension of ancient ethics (Foucault 1984a, 344, 346), McNay points to his failure to critique the privileging of a masculine self in the Greek theme of self-mastery from which he derives the notion of an ethics of the self. In ancient practices the "virile" character of self-mastery entailed a battle against the excessive and feminine aspects of one's character. This inferiorizing of the womanly is echoed at the social level through the performance of mastery over others. Thus, despite Foucault's assertion that one cannot draw uncritically on practices from another era, McNay argues that he appears to do just that in relation to the theme of self-mastery which privileges an implicitly masculine self. She sees the notion of "virile self-mastery" as enhanced through his depiction of Charles Baudelaire the dandy as the paradigmatic self-inventing individual of modernity. From a feminist perspective this is problematic, not simply because of the well-known misogyny characterizing Baudelaire's work, but because it illuminates Foucault's relatively uncritical celebration of "a certain tradition which normalizes as *the* experience of modernity a *particular* and gendered set of practices" (McNay 1994, 149). This is incompatible with his insistence on a rigorous, detailed self-critique as the initial task of an ethics of the self. McNay argues that he assumes, rather than critically investigates, the radical force of the male avant-garde tradition of literature embodied in Baudelaire's work. Moreover, he does not take into account the problem of "a contemporary morality that addresses itself to women as ethical subjects but draws, nevertheless, on a tradition in which woman has historically been positioned as the 'beautiful object'" (McNay 1994, 151). Thus, while Foucauldian ethics purport to begin from embedded practices, they actually ignore the possible implications of structures of gender on an aesthetics of the self (McNay 1994, 134, 149–54).[16]

McNay's critique brings to light certain similarities between the ancient practices of caring for the self favored by Foucault and those that characterize self-policing. In Foucault's account, relations with the self in antiquity are characterized by masculine notions of control, battle, conquest, and hierarchy (Foucault 1986, 66–70, 82–83, 91). This type of orientation to the self mirrors structures of domination and subordination integral to the strict overseer type of intra-subjective relationship imposed by self-policing. Thus, while Foucault's emphasis on the relationship we have with ourselves offers a useful framework for redressing the imbalance between self- and other-oriented care in many women's lives, the notion of self-mastery he draws on is unlikely to achieve this. In thinking about a more appropriate orientation to the self, bell hooks's call for relationships to be structured around the organizing principle of love rather than patriarchal, authoritarian models suggests an alternative approach: "Recognising love as the effort we make to create a context of growth, emotional, spiritual, and intellectual, families would emphasize mutual cooperation, the value of negotiation, processing, and the sharing of resources. Embracing a feminist standpoint can serve as an inspiration for transforming the family as we now know it" (hooks 1996, 73).

Although hooks is specifically referring to the organization of black families in the United States, embracing such a feminist standpoint also could inspire a more enabling relationship with the self than that historically encouraged. This type of orientation encourages an exploration of the types of practices, attitudes, and relationships that support love, respect, and equality. Moreover, in seeking to replace a patriarchal orientation to the self, women can draw on aspects of their caring relations for others. Thus, an alternative to conquering, mastering, or controlling unwanted thoughts, desires, feelings, or acts can emerge through the reflexive application of practices associated with robust friendship. These practices include wanting the best for the other, enjoying their company, honesty, acceptance, tolerance, compassion, forgiveness, and so forth. Developing a loving attitude to the self provides a context in which the self is no longer in battle with itself and which, as hooks claims, is conducive to a flourishing of the emotions, spirit, and intellect.

Maria Lugones's notion of playfulness also may be useful here. She describes playfulness as the loving attitude required for the development of nonimperialistic relations between white/Anglo women and women of color. This type of attitude fosters the requisite willingness of white women to visit the very different worlds inhabited by other women. Playfulness for Lugones involves "openness to surprise, . . . to being a fool, . . . to self-construction or reconstruction. . . . [It] is characterized by uncertainty, lack of self-importance, absence of rules or a not taking rules as sacred, a not worrying about competence and a lack of . . . resignation to a particular construction of oneself, others, and one's relation to them" (Lugones 1990, 401). She contrasts this conception of play with the agonistic notions proposed by Johan Huizinga and Hans-Georg Gadamer, which ultimately involve contestation, battle, winning, and losing and for which the only possible playful attitude is combative and competitive. For Lugones such a conception of play is inimical to the development of nonimperialistic relations (Lugones 1990, 390, 393, 396, 399–400). For the present purposes, the agonistic notion of play Lugones challenges parallels the type of intrasubjective relation characteristic of self-policing. Conversely, the sense of creative curiosity, flexibility, generosity, and willingness to experiment that characterizes her preferred conception of playfulness provides a way of thinking about a nonimperialistic approach to relations with the self. The development of such an approach has the potential to generate much kinder, more flexible, and enjoyable relations with the self. In turn, this increases possibilities for a creative interaction with given identity practices, standards, and norms through which a reshaping of self-interpretations begins to take form. In this way a more loving/playful orientation toward the self can play a crucial role in the type of ethics advocated by Foucault. At the same time it provides a safeguard against care of the self turning back into another form of self-policing; qualities of generosity, acceptance, and appreciation toward the self are antithetical to the type of self-relations required for the effective operation of self-policing technologies.

CARE FOR THE OTHER

A further concern expressed by McNay is the inadequacy of a notion of care for others in Foucault's work. Foucault claims that in ancient ethics the possibility of dominating others can derive only from a *lack of* care of one's self involving enslavement to one's desires (Foucault 1988d, 8). As McNay notes, however, in contemporary Western societies the hierarchical structure of relations means that taking care of oneself inevitably entails attempts to dominate or silence (or perhaps just neglect) others whose inferiorization has been culturally predetermined (McNay 1992, 172).[17] While Foucault's response may be that the privileged subject is not caring for him/herself properly, McNay argues that his refusal to lay down even the most general guidelines about what does and does not constitute a legitimate use of power renders his conviction about the self-limiting nature of care for the self problematic. Although he claims that a safeguard against care of the self turning into the domination of others is the coexistence of power relations and the capacity to resist them (Foucault 1988d, 12), in her view the generalized category of resistance does not adequately take into account broad structures of inequality and discrimination that ensure that the possibilities for resistance are frequently limited for some groups (McNay 1992, 172–74).

McNay's concerns make sense against the backdrop of individualistic Western cultures in which the notion of caring for the self is unlikely to incite people to investigate the ways in which their positions of privilege are maintained by the subordination of others. In this sense, against his own intention, Foucault seems to be transplanting the ancient notion of care for the self onto modern society. Although in his account of ancient ethics proper care of the self ensured the nonabuse of others, care for others nonetheless remained within the constraints of strict hierarchical relations. While he clearly envisioned a modern pluralistic structure of values and identities in which all individuals have the opportunity for self-experimentation, he does not explain how practices of care for the self will disrupt entrenched structures of domination to guarantee such an opportunity. Indeed it is possible to imagine people today practicing the ancient notion of self-mastery without challenging or even recognizing the ways in which their privilege depends on the subordination of others. This is reflected in the views of paternalistic men and white women and men who are often perplexed by accusations of sexism/racism. It also is evident in views that claim that black people/women/non-heterosexuals simply need to take up the equality available to all citizens and to stop complaining about marginalization. The extent to which, for example, the problem of entrenched structural racism remains invisible to those in positions of privilege is reflected in the difficulty many white people have in even acknowledging their whiteness: "When have you heard of a white person referring to him or herself as 'non-black'? We do not even think of ourselves as 'white.' Taking ourselves and our whiteness for granted, we do not consider our skin as a colour, we are 'just people'" (MacKinnon 1993, 118).

While not wanting to downplay the importance of McNay's concerns, in light of women's practice in caring for others these could be seen as more relevant to men than to women. The first point to make, however, is that women's caring does not necessarily include all others, not even all other women, as evidenced by histories of the relationship between black and white women, heterosexual and lesbian women, and upper- and working-class women. Elizabeth Spelman argues that an emphasis on the notion of women as caring tends to obscure the often exploitative and demeaning relationships between women in positions of privilege and those deemed socially inferior (Spelman 1991, 213–14, 216–20). It is important to remain aware of the way in which women's traditional role as carers itself has been mediated by categories of race, class, and sexuality, but the general point remains that gendered processes of identity formation commonly orient women more toward the care of others (even if only select others) than of the self. Conversely such processes, again in a general sense and mediated by factors other than gender, have historically oriented men more toward an emphasis on the self, often with the expectation that others, primarily girls and women, will actively support its development and consolidation. From this perspective, it is argued that the absence in Foucault's work on ethics of an adequate way of ensuring that care for the self does not lead to the domination or abuse of others is likely to be more problematic in relation to men than it is to women. This is reflected in the level of men's violence toward women, children, and other men.[18] The problem for women, and some women more than others, is the expansion of other-oriented training to include those women and men socially constructed as inferior in terms of race, ethnicity, class, sexuality, and so forth.[19] Nonetheless, the general other-orientation of women's training provides the groundwork for a greater inclusion. Moreover, it is precisely an imbalance between training in care for others and care for the self that can render women vulnerable to abuse and exploitation or to a sense of self characterized by doubt and criticism. Finding ways to assist women to increase the focus on their selves is the challenge often faced by those consulted by women in the therapeutic context. Furthermore, when women have been subject to abuse, the fragmentation of self can be such that the forms of protest individuals participate in may be those that further impoverish the self, as for example in the case of self-mutilation, the misuse of alcohol or drugs, or eating disorders (Sawicki 1991, 106). For many women, caring for the self is likely to be a crucial aspect in the destabilization and transformation of disabling identity practices. This is not to understate the equal importance of care for others. Rather, it is to underscore Foucault's point that a crucial dimension of ethical relations with others is the development of a caring relationship with the self. Because the imbalance between self- and other-oriented care tends to work in the opposite direction in the general training of boys and men, McNay's concern about the primacy of care for the self in Foucault's work on ethics may be more relevant generally to the experience of males.

FRIENDSHIP WITH THE SELF

In thinking about the implementation of greater care in women's lives, I suggest the value of friendship as an organizing principle in relations with the self. For Janice Raymond the notion of women's friendship with the self represents an act of personal and political defiance against women's training in male-defined societies to take care of the needs of others often at the cost of being absent to a knowledge and appreciation of one's own needs, values, interests, and beliefs. In a similar vein to Foucault, she depicts friendship with the self as a crucial aspect of satisfying relations with others (Raymond 1986, 8–10, 220–21, 222, 230–32).

In the therapeutic context, one technique for developing this type of self-value is to encourage women to relate to themselves as they would to a friend. Such a practice undermines the common existence in women's lives of one set of rules for others and another, less generous, set for the self. Illuminating this disparity provides a yardstick by which women can begin to move toward a relationship with the self that embodies the level of care and compassion so often extended to others. The notion of friendship with the self can be explored by checking out with women what their attitude would be toward a friend struggling with similar issues. What might they say about her feelings of self-blame in relation to such issues, about the pressure she puts on herself to be a certain sort of person/partner/mother, about her tendency to "beat herself up" for falling short of this expectation? So often women reveal qualities of acceptance, tolerance, patience, compassion, and support toward others that are absent in relations with the self.

This frequently includes a readiness to take into account various external factors contributing to the difficulties of others. When this type of orientation toward others is identified, it can be useful to ask: What would it be like to imagine extending the same level of compassion, support, tolerance, acceptance, and so on to yourself? Even to try to imagine this can engender feelings of discomfort, so unfamiliar is such a notion to many women. A further question might be: What difference, if any, do you think it might make to your current situation if you *were* able to be more caring and supportive toward yourself? This type of question can assist women to gain a sense of what it might be like to become less beholden to harsh and punitive technologies of the self. Reference to friendship foregrounds the possibility of an alternative orientation to the self.

Once the taken-for-granted nature of self-policing technologies has been disturbed through an exposé of their purposes and tactics, women can begin to experiment with becoming their own friend in day-to-day life. This process draws again on asking a woman to imagine how she would react to a friend in the same situation she finds herself in. She can be invited to observe the type of feelings, thoughts, and actions characteristic of self-policing at any given time and to consider how she might respond if that were the experience of a friend. At such times she might ask herself: What's the difference between how I'm feeling/thinking/acting toward myself and how I would react to —— in this situation? This type of reflection also can lead to a consideration of various personal/family/social contexts that may be contributing to her own problematic experience. This, in turn, can foster a more accepting attitude toward the self; for example, she might find herself thinking: Given what I'm up against (social attitudes toward single or lesbian mothers/lack of community or family support/financial struggle, etc.), I'm actually not doing too badly as a parent. It is not meant to imply that this type of negotiation with given power relations is easy or straightforward. The entrenched nature of such relations makes this unlikely. Nonetheless, the space created by undermining the idea that self-policing technologies are a fixed aspect of identity and experimentation with the alternative mode of friendship with the self can yield gradual change. Over time, women may notice themselves resisting punitive attitudes toward the self that previously would have been automatic. Interestingly, the greater level of self-acceptance characteristic of practices of friendship with the self does not mean that current limitations will always remain. To the contrary, an acceptance of who one is in the present seems to increase possibilities for change. Conversely, when the self is divided against, or in battle with, itself such possibilities often diminish. Developing qualities of friendship with the self challenges the power of self-policing to dominate intra-subjective relations, and this, in turn, increases possibilities for active participation in the creative process of self-making.

TOWARD A HOLISTIC NOTION OF CARE

A gender-related imbalance between care for the self and care for others reflects the way in which the concept of care has been dichotomized into two distinct types of activity. This can be understood in light of the cultural primacy of notions of autonomous and separate selves and the dualism that characterizes much of Western thought. The latter embodies a series of mutually reinforcing binaries—mind/body, reason/emotion, subject/object—in which the first term is both privileged and associated with the masculine and the latter is associated with the feminine. In a similar fashion, care for the self has tended to be a male preserve, while caring for others has been assigned to women and attributed the customary devaluation. Indeed the qualities of interconnectedness and particularity required for the provision of emotional nurturance are diametrically opposite to those traditionally associated with the privileged masculine self, that is, autonomy and a capacity for objective generalized reasoning.[20] The effects for women of the sexual division of caring can include a lack of adequate care from others, the normalizing of uncaring relations, and a lack of ease in receiving care from others and/or the self. Conversely, if a dichotomous notion of care were replaced by a holistic conception in which there is an inextricable link between giving and receiving, women would be more likely to feel uneasy if they were *not* the recipients of care. Conceived thus, care of the self becomes an integral aspect of the general notion of care. Moreover, within such a notion, caring for others becomes an activity for which we are all responsible. This cuts across the sexual division of caring and creates a space for the acknowledgment of care as a crucial and desirable aspect of human existence. When caring ceases to play a role in women's (or anyone's) subordination, the full vitality of its creative capacity to structure human relations can flourish.

CONCLUSION

This essay has focused on women's intra-subjective relations as one level at which the struggle for greater self-definition takes place. It draws on Foucault's notion of panoptical power in which self-policing is portrayed as a key mechanism in the maintenance and reinforcement of dominant identity prescriptions. While Foucault does not investigate the relationship between gender and self-policing, I have argued that factors such as the legacy of subordinate status and a frequent imbalance between care for others and care for the self render women especially vulnerable to debilitating practices of self-surveillance, evaluation, recrimination, and isolation. It is claimed that the intensity of self-policing is likely to vary according to women's relationship to broad social categories of race, class, sexuality, health, and so forth, and experiences of violence and abuse.

Because self-policing has become such a commonplace part of the psychic makeup of individuals, it remains invisible to conscious awareness most of the time. This makes it difficult to subject it to critical scrutiny. I outlined a therapeutic approach capable of destabilizing the idea that disabling technologies of the self are an inevitable part of identity and of exploring the social context in which they prosper. This creates space for the development and performance of preferred ways of living with the self. Just as relations characteristic of self-policing and the identities it maintains are exposed as cultural constructions, preferred practices of the self also are depicted as nonessential. This enables a sense of agency in the enactment of such practices and diminishes the potential for pathologizing failure when these are underperformed. It also provides greater scope for creativity in the open-ended revision of identity formation. Given the power of self-policing to dominate intra-subjective relations and maintain prescribed identities, this type of self-remaking can be seen as an important part of women's struggle toward self-understandings over which they have a greater say. In this light, it constitutes political activity at the local microlevel that would seem to correspond with McNay's emphasis on the importance of a feminist politics grounded in the "idea of woman as an active social agent capable of instituting radical change at the micro-political level . . ." (McNay 1992, 115).

In thinking about the facilitation of this type of political activity, I have drawn on aspects of Foucault's later work on ethics. I argued that his emphasis on the type of ethical relationship we have with ourselves provides a way of redressing an imbalance in many women's lives between care for others and care for self that contributes to the power of self-policing. The type of care of the self advocated by Foucault involves creative interaction with given relations of power in order to participate actively in fashioning different (nonessential) subjectivities. In this way, care of the self provides a way of using disciplinary practices in emancipatory ways. Yet while Foucault's work on ethics provides useful avenues for thinking about ways to subvert the harmful effects of self-policing, McNay highlights some key problems with his conception of care for the self. Following an outline of some of these concerns, I suggested certain ways of redressing these in efforts to undermine the power of self-policing. A fuller articulation of this was developed in the section on friendship with the self. Finally, I signaled the need for a less dichotomous conception of care that cuts across the sexual division of caring and encompasses the notion of both giving and receiving.

An emphasis on greater care for the self in women's lives is not to ignore the continuing presence of broader social structures and practices that perpetuate subordination and call for political resistance and change at the macrolevel. Rather, it is argued that care for the self provides a way of resisting and transforming the intra-subjective effects of given identities and the self-policing technologies that support and maintain them. Again, in this light greater care for the self can be seen as constituting political activity at the "microphysical" level.

NOTES

I would like to thank Karen Vintges, Dianna Taylor, the reviewers, and Ruth Abbey for their helpful suggestions on this essay. The original version was presented at the "Gendering Ethics/The Ethics of Gender" conference, Leeds University, June 23–25, 2000. It was written during my postgraduate studies at Flinders University of South Australia; final revisions were completed at the Centre for Interdisciplinary Gender Studies, Leeds University, during a postdoctoral year courtesy of a fellowship from the American Association of University Women.

1. Although aware of both advantages and disadvantages of referring to women in either the first or third person, I have elected to use the latter to correspond with a nonuniversalizing concept of gender.

2. Clearly there are numerous self-policing practices that do not fall into the first category—e.g., the routine ordering of daily existence, taking care of one's health to ensure quality of life, or behaving in ways that make it possible to live in relative harmony with others.

3. Thanks to Dianna Taylor for suggesting I foreground this reading of Foucault. As is evident in the text, my use of the term "emancipatory" does not connote any notion of freedom as separate from relations of power or the arrival at some final state or telos.

4. A key influence informing my work is narrative therapy. Central to this approach pioneered by Michael White and David Epston is the idea that identity and experience are constituted historically and linguistically through culturally dominant narratives. Narrative therapy assists people to deconstruct narratives that have come to dominate and oppress them. This opens space for the development and performance of preferred constructions of self/relationship/life. See White and Epston (1990). The type of therapeutic relationship characteristic of this approach is a collaboration in which those seeking consultation are seen as best placed through their direct experience to be an authority on the effects of problems and

the content of preferred ways of being (Freeman and Combs 1996, 282). This contrasts with a more conventional "expert" stance in which the therapist is seen as the dispenser of therapy and those seeking assistance as the recipients (White 1997, 120, 127–28). As such, it attempts to address the problem identified by Foucault of how to provide crucial services without establishing "a type of authoritarianism— *a system of obedience*" (Foucault 1988b, 195).

5. This is addressed in Foucault's later work through the introduction of a notion of power as a subjectivizing, rather than merely objectivizing, force. This provides the basis for articulating the possibility of resistance to given power relations (McNay 1994, 122–23). Some commentators claim that while Foucault's use of holistic rhetoric leads to a common reading of his work on the Panopticon as portraying modern society as totally disciplined, it is intended to represent only a slice of modern reality. For example, see Sawicki (1988, 169).

6. This is not to imply that males are not subject to disempowering forms of self-policing. Nonetheless, the gendered nature of identity formation ensures that the sexes interiorize different and unequal self-understandings. Moreover, dominant male identity practices are implicated in the perpetuation of female subordination (McLean 1996, 11, 24–25). Acknowledging this important difference does not preclude the possibility of some overlap between the sexes in relation to self-policing. This may be the case for women and men occupying marginalized social locations by virtue of race, sexuality, class, and so forth.

7. This does not imply the impossibility of some women being generally uncaring toward others or being primarily absorbed with the self. Neither is it the case that men always are more oriented toward the self than others. (See note 20 for an elaboration of this point.) Rather, this is a general claim about the common effects of gender socialization processes.

8. I am not referring here to the type of reflective critique to which one might subject one's relationship to certain values, ethics, attitudes, desires, and so on in order to consider their impact and create possibilities for change. Rather, self-criticism in this context refers to a debilitating, and often immobilizing, type of self-castigation that gives rise to feelings of personal failure and tends to close down options for change.

9. While I have focused primarily on the example of women in an educational setting, self-policing can pervade a wide range of areas including mothering, intimate and other relations, sexuality, self and body image, workplace relations, and so on.

10. Recognition of the political significance of this type of isolation is central to the work of some of the early second-wave feminists. For example, Catharine MacKinnon describes how in consciousness-raising the shared nature of various oppressions was revealed. It was out of this process that women's feelings of discontent came to be redefined as indigenous to their social situation rather than to personal deficiencies, and it came to be seen that collective action could be taken to alter given relations between the sexes (MacKinnon 1989, 95, 100).

11. Generally I argue that when factors other than gender are considered, self-policing is likely to intensify for those in marginalized social categories. Nonethe-

less, difference can at times provide an exit point to the self-policing of dominant identity prescriptions. For instance, bell hooks identifies self-love as a key strategy of the black liberation struggle of the 1960s (hooks 1996, 119). A more recent example is reflected in a study that demonstrates the diminished influence of dominant notions of beauty, body image, and weight among African-American adolescent girls compared to their white counterparts. See Parker et al. (1995, 103–14). (Thanks to Diana Tietjens Meyers for pointing me to this study.) Moreover, for women in nonprivileged social locations, for example in relation to race or sexuality, concern about the judgments or reactions of others can entail a self-protective function in terms of helping to detect or predict potentially denigrating or dangerous situations. In this sense, self-policing can be experienced as empowering. (Thanks to Sharon Gollan for this point.)

12. In relation to race, Lugones describes the way in which white/Anglo women's behavior toward women of color in the United States (neglect, ostracizing, stereotyping, labeling as crazy, rendering invisible) results in a lack of recognition that robs women of color of their solidity (Lugones 1990, 393–94). Hooks also has written about the impact of internalized racism on African Americans, which can include self-hatred (hooks 1996, 32). In the Australian context, Aboriginal magistrate Pat O'Shane points to the ongoing crisis characterizing the lives of many indigenous families and communities as a direct result of colonization. One of the aspects of this legacy has been the internalization of negative characteristics attributed to indigenous people as a standard part of the colonizing process (O'Shane 1993, 197–98).

13. This also can occur through certain types of religious training that entail the ongoing monitoring of one's thoughts, desires, and actions in order to root out sin or immorality. In relation to situations of domestic violence, many women are forced to intensify surveillance of their behavior in order to try to minimize the amount of violence against them and their children. A similar link between self-surveillance and safety is made in note 11 in relation to those marginalized by the dominant culture.

14. A similar point is made by Naomi Wolf in relation to many contemporary Western women's concerns about their failure to measure up to prescribed notions of beauty, as reflected in the widespread incidence of eating disorders and use of cosmetic surgery. In Wolf's view, these concerns can be understood in terms of a concerted backlash against feminism (Wolf 1992, 9–12).

15. Clear parallels exist between the type of therapeutic approach outlined and the feminist practice of consciousness-raising. Most obvious is the contextualization of individual women's lives within a sociopolitical framework. This assists the move away from a sense of personal deficit or inadequacy and undermines the common experience of isolation. The therapeutic environment outlined offers specific strategies for diminishing or overturning entrenched aspects of self-policing and associated identity prescriptions and for the performance of preferred identities. Finally, this type of therapy has the potential to facilitate the politicization of many women whom feminism may not otherwise reach. On this final point, see Swan (1999, 111, 113–14).

16. McNay's critique also points to Foucault's uncritical stance toward the historical sources used in the later genealogies in relation to the issue of gender. See McNay (1992, 76–79). Her critique of these (and other) aspects of Foucault's later work has been contested by some feminists. For example, see Lloyd (1996, 241–64) and Sawicki (1998, 93–107). In relation to debate about whether Foucault's notion of care for the self is derived from the "virile mastery" model of the ancient Greeks, see Vintges in this volume.

17. For a more positive interpretation of the critical power of Foucault's thought in this regard, see Hoy (1998, 29–30).

18. This is not to deny that some women engage in violent behavior toward others including children.

19. Lugones's notion of "loving" rather than "arrogant perception" offers a way of developing nonimperialistic relations among women. See Lugones (1990).

20. This is not to deny the reality of men's care for others, which has included, for example, financial provision for, and protection of, families. Nonetheless, many working-class (and increasingly middle-class) women have participated in financial responsibility while continuing to carry the full burden of physical and emotional nurturance. The male protector role also has diminished with the increase in female-headed households and the greater independence of many women. Increasing awareness of the unequal distribution of women's caring responsibilities has given rise to greater involvement by some men in emotional nurturance. While this is encouraging both on egalitarian grounds and because it provides greater opportunities for the expansion of men's emotional capacities and greater care for women, it is still common to hear women describe an imbalance in the emotional energy invested in family relationships despite the fact that their male partners are generally caring. This may, in part, be because men commonly associate care with problem solving rather than emotional support and availability (see Tannen 1991, 49–53).

WORKS CITED

Bartky, Sandra Lee. 1990. *Femininity and Domination: Studies in the Phenomenology of Oppression.* New York: Routledge.

Bird, Johnella. 2000. *The Heart's Narrative: Therapy and Navigating Life's Contradictions.* Auckland, New Zealand: Edge Press.

Butler, Judith. 1990a. "Gender Trouble, Feminist Theory, and Psychoanalytic Discourse." In *Feminism/Postmodernism.* Edited by Linda J. Nicholson. 324–40. New York: Routledge.

———. 1990b. *Gender Trouble: Feminism and the Subversion of Identity.* New York: Routledge.

Dickerson, Vicki. 1998. "Silencing Critical Voices: An Interview with Marie-Nathalie Beaudoin." *Gecko: A Journal of Deconstruction and Narrative Ideas in Therapeutic Practice* 2: 29–45.

Dickerson, Vicki, J. Zimmerman, and L. Berndt. 1994. "Challenging Developmental Truths—Separating from Separation." *Dulwich Centre Newsletter,* no. 4: 2–12.

Foucault, Michel. 1979. *Discipline and Punish: The Birth of the Prison.* Middlesex, England: Penguin.

———. 1980. "The Eye of Power." In *Power/Knowledge: Selected Interviews and Other Writings. 1972–1977.* Edited by Colin Gordon. 146–65. Brighton: Harvester.

———. 1983. "The Subject and Power." In *Michel Foucault: Beyond Structuralism and Hermeneutics.* Afterword. By Hubert L. Dreyfus and Paul Rabinow. 208–26. Chicago: University of Chicago Press.

———. 1984a. "On the Genealogy of Ethics: An Overview of Work in Progress." In *The Foucault Reader.* Edited by Paul Rabinow. 340–72. London: Penguin.

———. 1984b. "What Is Enlightenment?" In *The Foucault Reader.* Edited by Paul Rabinow. 32–50. London: Penguin.

———. 1986. *The Use of Pleasure.* Volume 2. *The History of Sexuality.* New York: Vintage.

———. 1988a. "An Aesthetics of Existence." In *Politics, Philosophy, Culture: Interviews and Other Writings, 1977–1984.* Edited by Lawrence D. Kritzman. 47–53. New York: Routledge.

———. 1988b. "Confinement, Psychiatry, Prison." In *Politics, Philosophy, Culture: Interviews and Other Writings, 1977–1984.* Edited by Lawrence D. Kritzman. 178–210. New York: Routledge.

———. 1988c. "Power and Sex." In *Politics, Philosophy, Culture: Interviews and Other Writings, 1977–1984.* Edited by Lawrence D. Kritzman. 110–24. New York: Routledge.

———. 1988d. "The Ethic of Care for the Self as a Practice of Freedom: An Interview with Michel Foucault on January 20, 1984." In *The Final Foucault.* Edited by James Bernauer and David Rasmussen. 1–20. Massachusetts: MIT Press.

Freedman, Jill, and Gene Combs. 1996. *Narrative Therapy: The Social Construction of Preferred Realities.* New York: Norton.

Grimshaw, Jean. 1986. *Philosophy and Feminist Thinking.* Minneapolis: University of Minnesota Press.

hooks, bell. 1996. *Killing Rage: Ending Racism.* London: Penguin.

Hoy, David C. 1998. "Foucault and Critical Theory." In *The Later Foucault: Politics and Philosophy.* Edited by Jeremy Moss. 18–32. London: Sage.

Law, Ian, and Stephen Madigan. 1994. "Introduction: Power and Politics in Practice." *Dulwich Centre Newsletter,* no. 1, 3–6.

Lloyd, Moya. 1996. "A Feminist Mapping of Foucauldian Politics." In *Feminist Interpretations of Michel Foucault.* Edited by Susan J. Hekman. 241–64. University Park: Pennsylvania State University Press.

Lugones, Maria. 1990. "Playfulness, 'World'-Travelling, and Loving Perception." In *Making Face, Making Soul = Haciendo Caras: Creative and Critical Perspectives by Women of Color.* Edited by Gloria Anzaldua. 390–402. San Francisco: Aunt Lute Foundation Books.

MacKinnon, Catharine. 1989. *Toward a Feminist Theory of the State.* Cambridge: Harvard University Press.

MacKinnon, Laurie. 1993. "Systems in Settings: The Therapist as Power Broker." 117–22. *Australian and New Zealand Journal of Family Therapy* 14, no. 3.

McLean, Christopher. 1996. "The Politics of Men's Pain." In *Men's Ways of Being.* Edited by Christopher McLean, Maggie Carey, and Cheryl White. 11–28. Boulder: Westview Press.

McNay, Lois. 1992. *Foucault and Feminism: Power, Gender, and the Self.* Cambridge: Polity Press.

———. 1994. *Foucault: A Critical Introduction.* Cambridge: Polity Press.

O'Shane, Pat. 1993. "Assimilation or Acculturation: Problems of Aboriginal Families." 196–98. *Australian and New Zealand Journal of Family Therapy* 14, no. 4.

Parker, Sheila, Mimi Nichter, Mark Nichter, Nancy Vuckovic, Colette Sims, and Cheryl Ritenbaugh. 1995. "Body Image and Weight Concerns among African-American and White Adolescent Females: Differences that Make a Difference." 103–14. *Human Organisation: Journal of the Society for Applied Anthropology* 54, no. 2 (Summer).

Raymond, Janice. 1986. *A Passion for Friends: Toward a Philosophy of Female Affection.* London: Women's Press.

Sawicki, Jana. 1988. "Feminism and the Power of Foucauldian Discourse." In *After Foucault: Humanistic Knowledge: Postmodern Challenges.* Edited by Jonathan Arac. 161–78. New Brunswick: Rutgers University Press.

———. 1991. *Disciplining Foucault: Feminism, Power, and the Body.* New York: Routledge.

———. 1998. "Feminism, Foucault, and 'Subjects' of Power and Freedom." In *The Later Foucault: Politics and Philosophy.* Edited by Jeremy Moss. 93–107. London: Sage.

Spelman, Elizabeth V. 1991. "The Virtue of Feeling and the Feeling of Virtue." In *Feminist Ethics.* Edited by Claudia Card. 213–32. Lawrence: University of Kansas Press.

Stacey, Kathleen. 1997. "Alternative Metaphors for Externalizing Conversations." *Gecko: A Journal of Deconstruction and Narrative Ideas in Therapeutic Practice* 1: 29–51.

Strickling, Bonnelle L. 1988. "Self-Abnegation." In *Feminist Perspectives: Philosophical Essays on Method and Morals.* Edited by Lorraine Code, Sheila Mullett, and Christine Overall. 190–201. Toronto: University of Toronto Press.

Swan, Vanessa. 1999. "Narrative, Foucault and Feminism: Implications for Therapeutic Practice." In *Deconstructing Psychotherapy.* Edited by Ian Parker. 103–14. London: Sage.

Tannen, Deborah. 1991. *You Just Don't Understand: Women and Men in Conversation.* Milson's Point, New South Wales: Random House.

Tully, James. 1998. "To Think and Act Differently: Foucault's Four Reciprocal Objections to Habermas' Theory." In *Foucault Contra Habermas: Recasting the Dialogue between Genealogy and Critical Theory.* Edited by Samantha Ashenden and David Owen. 90–142. Thousand Oaks, Calif.: Sage.

White, Michael. 1997. *Narratives of Therapists' Lives*. Adelaide, South Australia: Dulwich Centre Publications.

White, Michael, and David Epston. 1990. *Narrative Means to Therapeutic Ends*. New York: Norton.

Wolf, Naomi. 1992. *The Beauty Myth: How Images of Beauty Are Used against Women*. New York: Doubleday (Anchor Books).

❧ 6

Inventing Images, Constructing Standpoints: Feminist Strategies of the Technology of the Self

Sylvia Pritsch

> Roughly speaking, the problem is how to get to the self without
> going through the individual.
> —Elspeth Probyn

FOUCAULT AND FEMINISM: DIS-AS-SOCIATION

The work of Michel Foucault figured prominently in feminist debates during the 1990s about the issue of subjectivity. His notion of disciplinary
power and its subjecting forces helped to elucidate the socially constructed
nature of gender and subjectivity, but it did so in such a way as to facilitate
a reconsideration of self and subjectivity under changed conditions. It was
not until the discursive, constructed nature of the subject had been widely
accepted that pragmatic feminist approaches could undertake a reconstruction of self and subjectivity that aimed to take into consideration both
the subjective point of view and personal agency. It is within this context
that Teresa de Lauretis, Elspeth Probyn, and Donna Haraway—three feminist theorists discussed in this chapter—reevaluate the self as both a strategic, discursive topos that provides speaking positions on the basis of social
experiences of gender, and a "lived" reality. The crucial point here is how
to acknowledge gendered experience without unifying and naturalizing
something like "female experience" as an unquestionable basis for truth
claims—the dead end of identity politics. Hence the general question concerning a self beyond identity politics: how can the self be used to enable
speaking positions that allow for interpretations of the world that could
change meaning patterns and gender arrangements without reifying the
subject? Or, how does one move from the self to the world?

Foucault's aesthetics of the self—that is, the set of practices described as
technologies of the self through which a form of a self-understanding and
a self-problematizing is created—seems promising in this regard. Insofar
as his starting point is the individual's existence embedded in an existential ethic, Foucault's aesthetics of the self seems compatible with feminist

views. For Lois McNay, Foucault's nonfoundationalism provides a fruitful alternative to feminist theories of "feminine" or "mothering" ethics, which, by legitimatizing the vantage points of women through use of anthropological foundations, played an important role in the standpoint theories of the 1980s (McNay 1992, 4). Older standpoint theories became problematic not only because of their truth claims but also, as Susan Hekman points out, because they entailed a self-deconstructing mechanism: the privileged perspective on the social situation—be it legitimized by social status ("the oppressed") or by nature ("the female")—was opposed to the hegemonic ("male") perspective that is characterized as partial and contingent. The two understandings of reality therefore contest each other: one in assuming the socially constructed character of reality, and the other in claiming to perceive the real situation "behind" the ideology. Given these preconditions, feminists had difficulty explaining why their own point of view should *not* be a contingent, social construct (Hekman, 1999, 33).

While Foucault's understanding of pluralism and openness is highlighted as an important contribution of his work, pragmatic feminist strategies maintain the necessity of having a clear standpoint: in the interest of changing actual hegemonic discourses, an appeal to basic norms seemed unavoidable. McNay argues that norms provide a "safeguard" against the abuse of power and domination and also criticizes what she sees as the underlying rationality of the ethics of the self: an "isolated aesthetic autonomy" that appears too atomized to be able to explain how the actions of individuals may contribute to a radical reworking of the practices of the social or public (McNay 1992, 8, 180). Other feminists, such as de Lauretis, also believe that a lack of clear normative foundations at least weakens and at worst destroys the emancipatory potential of Foucault's ethics. The efficacy of "practices of freedom" and "self-styling"—at least for feminist identity politics, however revisited—may therefore be called into question.

In what follows, I consider the work of feminists (de Lauretis, Probyn, and Haraway) whose work highlights the ambivalent character of the relationship between Foucault and feminism with respect to the kinds of issues I have raised above. These feminists' search for a way to combine the pragmatic demand for a clear standpoint with the ethical demand for discursive plurality and nonfoundationalism leads them to develop a notion of *constructed standpoints*. Although their strategies differ considerably due to varying interpretations and usages of aesthetics (only Probyn takes the concept of the aesthetics of the self as her point of departure), all of the projects come close to the ethos that Foucault describes in his later texts. My reading will follow the question of how visual images are proposed to be "positive" technologies of the self in the sense of a collective practice that is able to challenge hegemonic gender discourses. I will identify three ways in which images of the self are put into the emancipatory service of self-determination and social change: first, as forms for collective speaking (expressed by de Lauretis's *feminist subject*); second, as strategies for speaking that subvert the discourses of cultural studies from within (outlined in Probyn's *sexed self*); and last, as a witness to technoscientific developments (enacted by Haraway's *feminist cyborg*). The next section of the chapter calls for conceptions of power and possibilities for change that are equally articulated by images. Here, the limits of positive and instrumental aesthetic strategies become visible. Finally, I briefly outline how, despite internal tensions and contradictions, these feminist approaches provide a new theoretical background on the basis of Foucault's concept of the *technology of signification*. What kind of power and agency is provided through narrative/imaginative technologies of the self? How do they help to get from self to world? And do they overcome the contested limits of Foucault's framework, or do they ignore the incalculability of discursive power while trying to master it? In order to provide a background for these questions, I discuss why Foucault's concept of the aesthetic self and his notion of power are not as easy to adopt as they may appear to be.

TECHNOLOGIES OF THE SELF AND THE FREEDOM OF THE AESTHETICAL SELF

Feminist theorists identified a positive notion of self and subjectivity in Foucault's later work that they understood in terms of a "turn" from the passive subject of *Discipline and Punish*, toward a concept of the subject as a self-determining agent. McNay, for example, revisits the concept of autonomy which she seeks to ground within the technologies of the self. By her reading, the Foucauldian concept of the self converges with feminist interests by positing subjects "who are capable of challenging and resisting the structures of domination in modern society" (McNay 1992, 4). In contrast, Probyn believes that Foucault's concept of the self provides an alternative to autonomy and individuality. She argues that it provides the basis for a radically reformulated, nonindividualistic and multilayered subjectivity that avoids the misleading alternative between the *subject*, that is, in an Althusserian sense, subjugated under the ideological apparatus and its interpellations, and the return to an "authentic" *individual*, whose resistant agency is guaranteed through its truth (Probyn 1993, 134f.). When we look at these diverging interpretations, questions arise regarding how Foucault's concept of the self, as it is outlined in the last two volumes of the *History of Sexuality*, can be judged as a reaffirmation of the (rational) subject and how it is located in relation to power: is it autonomous enough to "resist" normalizing power relations?

Foucault provides an ambivalent picture of the self. At first glance, he seems to support those interpretations that highlight the process of self-fashioning as an act of (relative) freedom as well as resistance. For example, he presents technologies of the self as a set of practices an individual performs upon him or herself, which "permit individuals to affect, by their own means, a certain number of operations on their own bodies, their own souls, their own thoughts, their own conduct, and this in a manner so as to transform themselves, modify themselves" (Foucault 1988, 18). But technologies of the self must also be understood as offering a critique of modern instrumental rationality, as articulated within and supported by modern legal, scientific, and religious discourse. Foucault identifies the legitimization of modern rationality within "code-oriented" morals that ground those universal laws to which the knowing subject has to subject itself in order to produce itself as a subject at all (Foucault 1984b, 37). Whereas these types of morals are linked to Christianity in general, it was Kant who provided the modern model of regulative rationality with its normalizing and dividing effects. Foucault describes this process of self-subjugation, which at the same time enables or produces the subject, in his work on *biopower*. According to Foucault, the modern subject is produced by certain scientific practices of knowledge, by techniques of classification, and especially by acts of confession coerced onto the subject and its desires. Moreover, *sex* becomes the privileged key to self-recognition through which the individual self is produced. While the individual imagined itself to be in possession of the (its own) truth, according to Foucault it was in fact captured in the dividing practices of biopower, where "the subject is either divided inside himself or divided from others" (Foucault 1982, 208). And it is because of its totalizing and individualizing effects that this model of the individual self must clearly be avoided.

Foucault therefore looked for a type of ethos where questions of morals (such as how to lead a good life) and aesthetic techniques for organizing one's life were not based on universal codes or on the divided individual. In *The Use of Pleasure,* he describes a model of alternative rationality found in the ancient world. In these "ethic-oriented" morals, the emphasis lies not on the symbolic code and the question of truth and desire but on the practices of self-care organized around pleasures. The guiding question is how to lead a good life under aesthetic criteria. This implies the task of *producing* oneself in contrast to the demand of *finding* a hidden, authentic self, as was the guideline for the modern subject of knowledge. The focus thus shifts from a mode of self-care, which implied the care of the city and others and was understood to be a precondition of knowledge about the world, to a problematization of the self itself respective to the evident truth of the world. Foucault thus posits a completely different model of knowledge in which the self is not the aim but rather the starting point of knowledge production.

The role of the other within self-care further illustrates the distinction between technologies of the self and traditional forms of subjectivity. The other is not merely, in a negative sense, a limit to subjective agency but is rather a constitutive force: s/he takes the role of a mediator between the "I" and the rules and practices that relate a self to the external world while simultaneously producing it. The relationship between self and other can be described as a "mutual, decentralizing transformation" (Hebel 1990, 237; my translation). Constituted by an interiorization of elements of the external world, the self is not based on a strict split between subject and object, inside and outside, but appears as a permeable form, or to put it differently, as a continuous activity of styling that constitutes new forms by restructuring previous ones. Instead of autonomy—which would still imply subjugation under a law, even if it is one's own—a restricted sovereignty of the self can be located within this activity.[1]

According to this model, Foucault proposes a completely revised understanding of the self: it is neither an identity based on a substantial core nor a self-determining agent but rather a space of styling, "une forme de vie," which enables for the alteration of self-relations and the invention of new forms. Practices of self-care thus appear as aesthetic. The aim is not for the fixed form of an "emancipatory subject" but for the never-ending movement of the transgression of the form.

AMBIGUOUS POWER PLAY: BETWEEN SILENCE
AND DISCURSIVE PLURALIZATION

Looking at aesthetic practices of the self, their relation to power appears rather contradictory: Although these practices must be located clearly within relations of power, they appear as a transgressive force that subverts disciplining and normalizing power. This apparent contradiction can be attributed to the fact that power manifests itself in different ways. Power can first be understood as a constitutive, omnipresent force that is built from "below" in each social relation. The popular image used by Foucault is that of a net of power relations, which build a kind of backdrop for society, institutions, and actors, and one that produces its own points of resistance. As such, there is no outside. Rather, every constellation of power can be countered by another one. In contrast to the dialectical understanding of counter-discourses as an antagonistic force, in this context the aesthetic practices of the self can be understood as a competing kind of power.[2] Second, power can be un-

derstood as a specific historical form called disciplinary power, normalizing power, or bio-power. Such power is intimately linked to the instrumental rationality criticized so sharply by Foucault. The aesthetic practices of
the self appear in this context as a historical alternative, but one which still
rests inside the conditions of power.[3] Consequently, Foucault speaks of processes of self-domination and thus denies any possibility of an "innocent"
self-relation apart from or in opposition to power.

Both versions of power have their problems. Through offering an unstable structure that does not allow for the normative criteria necessary to
distinguish affirmative practices from subversive ones, the status of the self
is necessarily restricted to a microstructural context. This problem leads to
feminist concerns about formulating a clear, oppositional standpoint (cf.
McNay 1992, 8). A second problem, identified by Hubert Dreyfus and Paul
Rabinow, concerns the fact that normalizing power can seemingly appropriate every discursive practice—even genealogical ones that reveal the constructed nature of the subject and other leading concepts (Dreyfus and Rabinow, Afterword). Hekman echoes this concern when she states, "Foucault
is at best vague on an issue that must be at the forefront of the feminist critique: change" (Hekman 1999, 135).

In fact, Foucault does not provide clear counter-strategies. But he does
offer two different responses to the problem of power and discursive appropriation. On the one hand, he attempts to interrupt the function of modern
power structures. His objections against both a fixed ethics and his attempt
to counter disciplinary norms with different ones can be read as a move to
avoid normalization—one that relates to a political strategy of refusal: "Maybe the target nowadays is not to discover what we are, but to refuse what we
are. We have to imagine and to build up what we could be to get rid of this
kind of political 'double bind,' which is the simultaneous individualization
and totalization of modern power structures" (Foucault 1982, 216). On an
epistemological level, a rupture with discourse itself appears necessary, which
can seemingly be provoked by practices of silence—but even these may be
part of a process of normalization.[4] The most reliable stance seems to be offered by negative strategies, which lead to an "empty" program in an "empty
space" instead of a law: "But the idea of a program of proposals is dangerous. As soon as a program is presented, it becomes a law, and there's a prohibition against inventing. . . . The program must be wide open. We have to
dig deeply to show how things have been historically contingent, for such
and such reason intelligible but not necessary. We must make the intelligible
appear against a background of emptiness and deny its necessity. We must
think that what exists is far from filling all possible spaces. To make a truly
unavoidable challenge of the question: What can be played?" (Foucault 1997,

139–40). The self as such may now be understood as a fictive vacuum-space within power relations that, by interrupting prevailing discourses, allows for possibilities to think differently.

On the other hand, Foucault argues in favor of a pluralization of discourses that could multiply the points of resistance within the field of power. Against the dividing practices of modern power, he sets aesthetic practices and a corresponding philosophical ethos that link the self, the other, and the world together in common nets of knowledge production. This ethos entails some formal guidelines for ensuring responsible dealings with the self and the world that do not fall back upon misleading questions about universal or personal truth. In "What Is Enlightenment?" Foucault defends a certain notion of the modern attitude of Enlightenment as a starting point for reflecting upon the present. He describes such an attitude as a philosophical ethos, an activity guided by a "limit attitude." By "ethos" or "attitude" he refers to a "mode of relating to contemporary reality" that should take shape in "a permanent critique of our historical era" and that occurs "through a historical ontology of ourselves. "The critical ontology of ourselves has to be considered not, certainly, as a theory, a doctrine, nor even as a permanent body of knowledge that is accumulating; it has to be conceived of as an attitude, an ethos, a philosophical life in which the critique of what we are is at one and the same time the historical analysis of the limits that are imposed on us and an experiment with the possibility of going beyond them" (Foucault 1984c, 40, 41, 45). Philosophical activity consists of deferring the limits of the discursive framework through critical questioning or, more exactly, through a practical critique that takes the form of a possible transgression.[5] This can also be read as a projection or translation of the ancient concept of self-care: the emphasis still lies on social practices that are the condition of opening up the subject disciplined by symbolic codes.

To sum up, Foucault offers some formal guidelines of a critical, relational, contextualized, and plural understanding of the self that gains shape through its historical framework, which, at the same time, is the key to deferring its own conditions. The self is rooted within an aesthetic rationality that emphasizes the styling and restyling of existence as a value in itself—apart from external demands. The aesthetic strategies he proposes lead to a tension between being inside power structures and the possibilities of transgressing them, a tension that is maintained by the overlapping of two different strategic aims. While this overlapping itself may subvert the borderlines between inside and outside, it provokes discomfort because of its opacity. Difficulties in adopting Foucault's strategies may also be attributed to his avoidance of programmatic texts.

FEMINIST TECHNOLOGIES OF THE SELF:
IMAGERY AND REPRESENTATION

Feminist politics of representation are centered on mechanisms of "sexing" (Probyn's term) which gender self and subject(ivity). The crucial issue here is how to bring together the social experience of sex and gender and its representation or, more precisely, how to acknowledge the facticity of gender constructions without reaffirming them. In their refusal of dominant representations of identity, feminist politics approach Foucault's own gestures of refusal. But in contrast to Foucault, the approaches of de Lauretis, Probyn, and Haraway search for a positive use of representations, which they find in the reconstruction of given images. In order to demonstrate the subjectivating work of gender representations, de Lauretis takes up Foucault's concept of the discursive and practical fabrication of the self through a historical power constellation. As an analogy to the *technology of sex*, she coined the term "technology of gender," similarly thought of as "the product and the process of both representation and self-representation" (de Lauretis 1987, 9). De Lauretis identifies various "technologies" that produce gender images, including both the cinema and academic as well as subcultural discourses. Representations play an important role as they interpellate the individual *as* female or male: "The sex-gender system, in short, is both a sociocultural construct and a semiotic apparatus, a system of representation which assigns meaning (identity, value, prestige, location in kinship, status in the social hierarchy, etc.) to individuals within the society. If gender representations are social positions which carry differential meanings, then for someone to be represented and to represent oneself as male or female implies the assumption of the whole of those meaning effects" (ibid., 5). By conceptualizing gender as an ideological apparatus, de Lauretis shifts the theoretical framework toward a structural-psychoanalytic one. Louis Althusser's assumption that ideology operates by means of its engagement of subjectivity serves as a starting point to question the processes of gendering and the constitution of sexually differentiated subjectivities.[6] The intimate link between the self and gender representation is made through the use of psychoanalytic concepts of unconscious identification that offer an explanation for how imaginary representations become a central part of subjectivity and hence are taken for reality.

In this psychoanalytic context, subjectivation is defined as the gaining of a sexually differentiated self-identity which basically works through images. As these images are culturally bound, self representations cannot be thought of apart from sexual difference or gender hierarchy.[7] According to the psychoanalytically inspired theoretical framework developed in the feminist film theory of the 1980s, sexual difference and heteronormativity form the underlying (subconscious) structure that works as sociosymbolic law.

Through this perspective, gender hierarchy takes the form of a constantly working asymmetry that informs social relations by linking representations to individuals through processes of identification. This function of gender is clearly left out by Foucault, who cannot explain the workings of representation because of his refusal of psychoanalysis.

The power of images to define identities provides a basis for feminist counter-practice. In the program of de Lauretis, they consist, first, in a critical reflection on representations and their exclusions—the well-established feminist *reading against the grain*—and, second, in the construction of counter-images. Such feminist practices can be described as technologies of the gendered self: On an individual level, the analytical and critical practices could lead, as de Lauretis describes, to a special experience, one that provides patterns of meaning for self-understanding. What it means "to live as a woman" is given a social and political framework. On a collective level, feminist practices lead to the construction of a collective self-image, the "subject of feminism." De Lauretis is not referring to a representation but to a mode of articulation; a concept to refer to "female experience" that now is a product of gender constructions.[8] In psychoanalytic terms, the subject of feminism functions as a collective *imago* that constructs links between the subjective imaginary, the sociosymbolic, and the real. Thus, feminist practice in the model of de Lauretis can be understood as technologies of consciousness and experience. These technologies function to create both a subject of knowledge and critical action in the figure of both a strong collective and individualist feminist subjectivity organized around a gender identity to which agency is linked: one that includes the creation of a critical epistemological *ethos* in the shape of a "gender consciousness" as a basis for a critical standpoint. In contrast to some former standpoint theorists, de Lauretis takes seriously the constructed character of such a standpoint: It is not legitimated automatically by being or living as a woman but by collective negotiations about what it means to "be" or "live" "as a woman." Yet while de Lauretis denounces as a social construct the gender hierarchy legitimized by naturalizing sexual difference, she retains sexual difference as the ultimate reference point, thus positioning gender in precisely the way that Foucault positions *sex* in his description of biopower: that of an imaginary point which promises truthful access to self-knowledge, body, and identity. Consequently, sexual difference as an agent of power relations *within* the subject of feminism—the widely known critique by Judith Butler—remains unresolved.

De Lauretis's precondition of sexual differentiated subjectivities provides the focus for Probyn's inquiry into possibilities for producing a sexed self. Probyn seeks to avoid the misleading distinction—partially retained by de Lauretis—between the Althusserian subject, subjugated under the ideological apparatus and its interpellations, and the return to an "authentic" *individual* whose resistant agency is guaranteed through its truth (Probyn 1993, 134f.). But concerning the representation of experience, Probyn's self is constructed in ways analogous to that of de Lauretis's feminist subject. Its task is to articulate and reflect female experience and, by doing so, to foster relations between women. The self here is explicitly founded on Foucault's concept of self-care and, consequently, is thought of as a practice, a theoretical articulation or an analytic tool "to cut into that real" (ibid., 135). The construction of the self is designed as a collective process but not as a collective subject on the basis of identification: "the self," Probyn states, "does not have to stand in for all other blacks, Jews or Indians" (ibid., 31). But similar to de Lauretis's approach, image production is also thought to be a privileged strategy for articulating new positions. Instead of processes of identification (or interpellation), Probyn stresses the cognitive and the imaginary force of images. As a mode of cognition, images link different and arbitrary elements. In addition to their constructive abilities, images become important because they are self-reflexive: "images are not . . . 'what I think,' but rather 'what I think with' or, again, 'that by which what I think is able to define itself'" (ibid., 91).[9]

In this social-constructionist frame, the image does not provide a direct representation of reality. Nevertheless, it provides a link from the discursive to a social that is left to be reconstructed. The point of Probyn's model is to think of the self as such an image, one that produces its frame of reflection by mapping points of view onto reality: "Re-figuring the self as an image, we can begin to locate feminist speaking positions within a tactical use of images as points of view. In this way, the self works at a discursive level, operating epistemologically within various systems of thought. The self is made to designate and allow for certain configurations of knowledge to proceed, and concurrently to function at (but not necessarily indicating a correspondence to) an ontological level" (ibid., 92). At the same time, the self is still considered a social reality that may act to counter discursive structures. *Self* thus designates both "the activity of theory and of being." It is "a mode of holding together the epistemological and the ontological" (ibid., 169, 4). What "sex" means, apart from a "felt facticity," remains open (ibid., 168). Instead of defining the concept, Probyn emphasizes the imaginary force of representations, which should both highlight differences of experiences of gender and provide an (empathetic) bridge toward the other (which is thought of as the other woman). On a formal level, the sexed self, or, more precisely, the image of a sexed self, also describes limits as the possibility of transgressing oneself qua projection: "This imagined and imaged self serves to figure a point where we could talk about 'she and me'" (ibid., 171).

Like de Lauretis, Probyn thinks of the self both in the Foucauldian sense as a practice *and* as a representation. In contrast to Foucault, who emphasizes the effects of subjugation by representations of self and subjectivity, both feminist authors locate in images important empowering effects that lead to collective practice. While de Lauretis stresses the close link between representation and existence, Probyn keeps a distance between the "me" and the represented self. She therefore comes closer to Foucault's idea of the self as an "empty space." However neither she nor de Lauretis aim to disrupt or finish the discourses of knowledge as such. To the contrary, they seek to enable reconstructions and transformations through the construction of standpoints or speaking positions within. Given that no outside to gender representation exists, images *must* be used as a starting point from which to speak. Only if the prevailing discursive power constellations provide the conditions for such technologies of the self can questions arise regarding how to mark a difference between feminist and nonfeminist imaginations.

PRACTICES OF REPRESENTATION: FIGURING AND WITNESSING

In the mid-1980s, historian of science Donna Haraway developed the figure of the mythological (feminist) *cyborg*. It appeared as the embodiment of a feminist normative program and can also be seen as a practical realization of the formal guidelines outlined by Probyn. On an ontological level, the cyborg is an articulation of existence under postmodern conditions: "By the late twentieth century, our time, a mythic time, we are all chimeras, theorized and fabricated hybrids of machine and organism; in short, we are cyborgs" (Haraway 1991, 150). With this (at the time) provocative statement in her "Cyborg Manifesto" (Haraway 1991, 149–82), Haraway marked a fundamental breach created by the melting of science and technology under late-capitalist conditions. Haraway's story of *technoscience* can be read as a postmodern continuation of Foucault's history of the modern episteme. Technoscience is characterized by a new quality of power called *technobiopower* that works through a rationalized mode of production under the auspices of cybernetics (Haraway 1997, 12). Haraway asks for the construction of reality through the logic of technobiopower—applied and distributed by biotechnology and technologies of information—and for new regulations of identities through technoscientific practices. She identifies the underlying logic as an instrumental one that seeks to combine heterogeneous living and nonliving elements, regardless of ethical or other reservations. Haraway supposes the effect to be an "implosion" of dichotomies of order, mainly those of nature/culture, human/animal, organism/machine that would lead to new *hybrid* entities such as the cyborg (Haraway 1991, 151f.). Cyborgs would appear not only in the biotechnological laboratory but also in everyday life.[10] In sum, the cyborg is an embodied artifact as well as a metaphorical figure that would demonstrate the contemporary conditions of existence and thus work as a basis for the construction of feminist selves. Haraway proposes "the cyborg is a kind of disassembled and reassembled, postmodern collective and personal self. This is the self feminists must code" (ibid., 163).

Instead of a return to a stable subjectivity, Haraway proposes to use the possibilities produced by the contestation of identity categories through the notion of hybridity.[11] Referring to a "feminist-socialist antiracist cyborg," Haraway describes a self characterized by differences, by the overlapping of multiple relations within and between dominant forms of gender, sex, ethnicity, class, culture, and other identities, which add to, substitute for, or contradict each other. Insofar as gender identity is not privileged but simply comes into play as one social location among others, it is expected to "implode" in the play of construction and reconstruction. Multiplied into a "universe," the figure of the cyborg constitutes, on an epistemological level, an analytical and critical stance in relation to developments within science and technologized society. Thus, the cyborg can be construed in terms of a Foucauldian ethos as a practice and an attitude of a self that is directed toward the production of knowledge about the world. The main function of the cyborg is witnessing: "Witnessing is seeing; attesting, standing publicly accountable for, and psychically vulnerable to, one's visions and representations. Witnessing is a collective, limited practice that depends on the constructed and never finished credibility of those who do it, all of whom are mortal, fallible, and fraught with the consequences of unconscious and disowned desires and fears" (Haraway 1997, 267). The ethical basis of the cyborg consists in the acknowledgment of the constructed character of reality as the product of common social practices, and in taking responsibility for the products of these constructions—including those of the subjects of knowledge.

In contrast to dominant practices of narration and visualization in modern science, which represents itself as an objective reflection of the world, Haraway proposes a social-constructivist approach in which the social and political impacts of the production of knowledge are made visible. Figuration and narration play an important role here, as they guide practices as well as worldviews: "Figurations are performative images that can be inhabited. Verbal or visual, figurations are condensed maps of whole worlds. In art, literature, and science, my subject is the technology that turns body into story, and vice versa, producing both what can count as real and the witness to that reality" (ibid., 179). Figuration can thus be understood as a technology of the self in two senses: it produces the subject-object by subjection (here Haraway joins de Lauretis and the Althusserian concept of interpellation), and it provides self-identities on the basis of hybridity and construction attributed with self-reflection. Beyond single figurations or "performative images," available attitudes depend on a frame for narration: "I consider figures to be potent, embodied—incarnated, if you will—fictions that collect up the people in a story that tends to fulfillment, to an ending that redeems and restores meaning in a salvation history. After the wounding, after the disaster, comes the fulfillment, at least for the elect. God's scapegoat has promised as much. . . . In that sense, the 'human genome' in current biotechnical narratives regularly functions as a figure in a salvation drama that promises the fulfillment and restoration of human nature" (ibid., 44).[12]

The effects of knowledge and power working as "figural realism" are coercive: "there is little choice: we inhabit these narratives, and they inhabit us" (ibid., 172). As the power of figuration determines what counts as reality, there seems to be no way out. But Haraway also defines power according to *which* metaphors link worlds together. Therefore, she claims a subversion of technoscientific salvation stories by inventing her own feminist stories and figures designed to counter technoscientific interpellation. Finally, the feminist cyborg does not stand isolated but is part of a "political myth" that Haraway first formulated to be "faithful to feminism, socialism, and materialism" (Haraway 1991, 147). Thus, Haraway not only proclaims formal criteria for the cyborg ethos, but she combines it explicitly with norms for a political practice that will take place within pre-given relations of power.

All three feminist authors, then, come close to (or, like Probyn, explicitly relate their program to) the Foucauldian idea of a philosophical ethos that responsibly constructs knowledge about the self and the world which is inseparably linked to the self's own existence. Their work may thus be understood as a feminist realization of a "critical ontology of ourselves." At the same time, their methods reflect the idea of a clear standpoint, legitimated through values and norms, from which to speak within prevailing discourses. Thus, the necessity of having a standpoint is not given up; rather, it is modified into a *constructed standpoint* led by images that are open to further reconstructions to be undertaken in collective practice. In contrast to Foucault, their autonomous subject is not transformed into a self-shaping, permeable form but, most clearly in the texts of de Lauretis and Haraway, is turned into a platform for collectivity. The constructed collective subject—and the collectively constructed subject—is the agent of social change that comes into play as an antidote to totalizing and individualizing power effects. A transgressive force is linked to a presupposed polyvalence and ambiguity of images that may enable plural interpretations that are able to work against a fixed coding. In contrast to aestheticism, the poetic character of images is not opposed to rationality but rather demonstrative of their constitutive and underlying mechanism, as Haraway made clear for the logics of science. Thus, on the level of representation, the foremost role of the constructed collective subject is contesting, subverting, and reconstructing meaning that is enabled by its consistent speaking position.

IMAGES OF POWER

While the ethical aspects of the work of de Lauretis, Probyn, and Haraway converge, the aesthetics aspects do not. As discussed above, Foucault emphasizes aesthetic freedom as a moment of release that enables lives via disruption of instrumental rationality. His position can thus be understood only in terms of *negative* aesthetics: a process that interrupts the automatic application of meaning by focusing attention on the question of what can and cannot count as "meaningful." Within this process, the *materiality* of an object—in this case, the form of the self—comes into the foreground, while its *understanding* is turned into an infinite movement of self-subversion.[13] The feminist aesthetic practices point in the direction of a positive aesthetics: images explicitly function in the emancipatory service of self-determination and social change under the aspects of self-constitution (images as a technology of the self), of cognition and knowledge (images as figurated perspectives on the world), and of building collective relations (images as objects of identification). Seen from a Foucauldian perspective, the question arises of whether this feminist strategy will give way to disciplining or prescriptive mechanisms. Problems do arise within the feminist models regarding the images they invent to demonstrate the work of power as well as for possibilities for invention and, consequently, for positive social change.

The crucial question here is how to get from image to social reality. De Lauretis attempts to link the construction of counter-images to a certain sociosymbolic power. To do this, she posits an "other" space of feminist subculture: "those other spaces both discursive and social that exist, since feminist practices have (re)constructed them, in the margins (or 'between the lines,' or 'against the grain') of hegemonic discourses and in the interstices of institutions, in counter-practices and new forms of community. These two kinds of spaces are neither in opposition to one another nor strung along a chain of signification, but they coexist concurrently and in contradiction" (de Lauretis 1987, 26). De Lauretis borrows the model for this sociosemiotic interstice from film theory, the *space off:* "the space not visible in the frame but inferable from what the frame makes visible" (ibid.). The movement in and out of ideological gender representation, of what can and cannot be represented, designates for de Lauretis the feminist critical practice. Her construction of feminist standpoints and practices in between dominant discourses reflects Foucault's concept of multiple forms of power. At the same time, the "juridical model," the idea of a determining symbolic law on the basis of sexual difference, is still maintained. Through this perspective, the position of the female/feminist subject turns out to be a doubled one: existing both within and in opposition to the power discourse of gender in its unrepresented "elsewhere." Contrary to de Lauretis's own intentions, in the end her approach comes close to the antagonistic model of older standpoint theories in which only two kinds of gender images seem to exist: oppressive ones produced by the patriarchal discourse, and empowering ones produced by feminists. Thus, the understanding of multiple power, discourses, and counteracting images is contradicted by a model of two spheres that keep sexual difference as their key determinant. Foucault's objections against the model of juridical power seem to be confirmed here:[14] Instead of countering a binary structure, de Lauretis's model stays inside, thus risking to continue the endless repetition of the same. More problematic appears to be her gesture to take the image not only as a theoretical orientation to make visible exclusions but literally as the social place where positions of women or feminist speaking are rooted: in the *space off.* Due to a confusion between constructionist and realist assumptions, a discursive and symbolically defined place seems to be the unmediated condition of social existence.

In contrast to de Lauretis, Probyn not only constructs a paradoxical position with respect to the inside/outside of power but also seeks a theoretical model or image that could handle it. To this end she appropriates the image of the *pli* from Gilles Deleuze's reading of Foucault. The self is pictured as the effect of a doubling-up that creates an inside as the "folding" of the outside. While this image illustrates the topological character of different modes of being within the thinking of Foucault, Probyn uses it in a strictly social context to relate the self to itself and its surroundings: "Thus the line of the outside is folded, and refolded against the inside along a series of 'optional' practices involved in the relation of self to self and to selves. As Deleuze argues, 'this is subjectification: to bend the line so that it comes back upon oneself.' . . . The production of subjectification then allows us to envisage ways of living with ourselves and with others" (Probyn 1993, 129; quoted in Deleuze 1990, 154). As it "scrambles any dichotomy of interior self and exterior social," this concept of the self not only offers "a model of individuation without an individual" but should contribute to social transformation by showing new ways of experiencing oneself in relation to others (Probyn 1993, 128).

Compared to de Lauretis's image of the *space off*, which describes the outside of the inside, the image of the *pli*—the inside of the outside—is not only envisaged from an oppositional angle but seems to be more dynamic, insofar as it entails a movement of folding and unfolding internal and external elements instead of locating them in separate spheres. Probyn's crucial aim is to overcome the dichotomy of a speaking from the inside versus from the outside of hegemonic discourses, and by implication the dichotomy between the self and the social, the epistemological and the ontological. But this movement of subverting the borderlines conflicts with the clear division *within* the self. Through her distinction of the epistemological and the ontological, Probyn systematizes the functions assigned to the self in quasi-Kantian terms and thus diverges from Foucault's effort to dissolve the separation between the spheres of knowledge production and existence.[15] This distinction makes sense in a feminist context, however, in which it can be read as a strategy of avoiding the risk of hypostasizing one level over the other; concretely, to subordinate either the actual, experiential moment of sexed and gendered lives under reflection and its discursive forms, or to privilege a moment construed as "authentical" without reflecting its reification. Probyn's demand for self-reflection as a (formal) norm appears much more voluntaristic than Foucault would have intended, as collective self-reflections not only provide reliable statements about reality but offer practical guidelines for transgression through "folding of the lines." Here again, the image of a theoretical concept is read literally with the effect being that the abstract image of the *pli*—originally used to describe structural processes—is thought of as an individual act of subject production.

Haraway solves the problem of being inside or outside of (discursive) power relations by a model of a pure inside. In her 1997 publication *Modest Witness*, she adopts the image of the net to figure agency, cognition, and experience as a collective practice of creating relations in which meanings emerge. Instead of the traditional entities of "subject," "object," or "society," we now find structural networks of "knots"—figured as "cyborgs"—which can be reworked over and over again by linking their elements to different nets.[16] In an earlier text, Haraway outlined the net in the image of cat's cradle, a game that involves the fabrication of string figures. This metaphor is used to emphasize the agency and relatedness of each player, regardless of its organic or personal properties (Haraway 1994). Through use of this model of networking, which approaches Foucault's practices of knowledge, Haraway avoids the assumption of an outside or of determining hierarchical organizations. At the same time, the differences between semiotic and material elements, between reality and discourse, seem to be eliminated too as all elements are equally qualified as "actors" in the common process of meaning-production.

In order to decide about differences and what counts as difference, however, Haraway finally returns to normative principles. Formally, the net is judged only by its possibilities for enabling or disabling connections, meaning that plurality becomes a value in itself. In contrast, the implantation of cyborg figures leads to a content-bound, ethical program in the form of an underlying narrative. But Haraway's narrative, the "political myth, faithful to feminism, socialism, and materialism," risks becoming as teleological as the modern salvation history it is intended to counter (Haraway 1991, 147). Later, Haraway modifies her story toward a more open and liberal version that seeks freedom, "rooted in the reinvented desire for justice and democratically crafted and lived well-being" (Haraway 1997, 267). Doing so, she insists on the necessity of general principles in order to indicate the difference between stories that enable or disable not only plurality, that easily could be appropriated by technobiopower, but also "lived well-being." Here, we find an ethical frame that differs significantly from Foucault's. Foucault posited aesthetic means within ethical practices in order to reach freedom of existence through the transgression of every form. Haraway, in contrast, adopts the utilitarian ethic that determines a good life by luck and benefit. Therefore, she needs norms to decide upon the right way to live. Consequently, Haraway claims a privileged perspective based on the "vantage point of nonstandard positions" that refer to the marginalized positions "that don't fit but within which one must live" (ibid., 269). The danger of defining a privileged standpoint soon became obvious in the "Cyborg Manifesto," where women of color function as the personification of marginalization such that they function as the reference point for the cyborg figure. Well aware that linking real persons to images raises the problem of reification, Haraway defines the "vantage point" only in terms of principles (of responsibility, situatedness, embodiment, and relatedness) (ibid., 35f.). Nevertheless, the problem of conferring a programmatic image onto social reality remains unresolved.

All of the power models presented start from the concept of multiple forms of power elaborated by Foucault. But the instrumental use of images is directed toward strengthening subjective agency, may it be conceptualized as the feminist subject, located at the excluded *space off* (de Lauretis), as the feminist self as an image of "folding" power relations toward each other (Probyn), or as the cyborg-figured "knot" in the net that enables "worlds worth to live in" (Haraway). Possibilities for transgression that appeared as a "passive" or undirected structural movement within the model of Foucault are now understood as the effect of an intentional acting, guided by programmatic images. And what was meant to describe abstract power structures is transferred directly onto the social: de Lauretis equates the *space off* with feminist subculture; Probyn and Haraway see the "folding of the self" and the establishment of the right net, respectively, as controlled social activities.

All three approaches thus work according to what Probyn describes as a special feminist use of theoretical constructs: a projection onto the real. Probyn offers it as a methodological way of opening hegemonic discourses by the "transposition" of theoretical concepts "from the status of a system to that of a *point of view* oriented to a theoretical intent" (Probyn 1993, 89).[17] Most significant is not the question of a "correct" appropriation of theory, but how this appropriation reflects back upon the social context. Simone De Beauvoir's views on the practice of writing are instructive on this point: "The trick is to articulate 'an involvement in the real' with the reference-point of a certain philosophical project. Thus, one can argue that de Beauvoir viewed existentialism from a very localized point and that this point of view changed the parameters of what she saw. The image is bent, or refracted, by being tied to the primacy of an involvement in the real. The discursive image is thus 'worked over' by the very materiality it describes" (ibid.). This "trick" appears rather magical: what does it mean that the discursive image is "worked over by the materiality it describes"? At first glance, one could think of the same effects described above as "negative aesthetics," the rupture of unquestioned meaning through foregrounding of an object's material aspects. However, it becomes clear that the subversion of meaning itself is not the chosen aim. On the contrary, the "materiality" now acquires the force of an unquestionable, evident facticity with the effect that the image regains its realist function of representation. In Probyn's own model, this contradiction is brought under control in the image of the *pli* in which both levels can coexist and problematic impacts are bypassed. I therefore consider Probyn's reading of Foucault to be similar strategically as it uses the image of the *pli* to demonstrate a practical holding-together not only of the ontological and the epistemological but even of the social and the discursive. This leads to problematic consequences as the gap between levels of reality and its representation become filled in by the image of the folding self. Risks of conflation are present as well in the images produced by de Lauretis and Haraway, as images might appear as unmediated social reality itself. The refiguring of images suggests that they could be taken for the transformation of reality. Here we meet the flip side of the social-constructivist frame chosen by the feminist authors: While the instrumental use of images allows us to use their prescriptive function for our own purposes, the concept of an unmediated reality is reinstalled within this frame and serves to legitimate the standpoint. At the same time, it is suggested that this reality willingly could be changed by self-invented images.

THE POWER OF IMAGES: TECHNOLOGIES OF SIGNIFICATION

In the feminist perspectives I have presented here, images, representation, and signifying processes become important technologies of the self and technologies of power. The relationship between the self to the world runs along images such that imagery and representation can be considered as a feminist response to the three questions formulated by Foucault regarding the main dimensions of subjectivation: "how are we constituted as subjects of our knowledge? How are we constituted as subjects who exercise or submit to power relations? And how are we constituted as moral subjects of our own actions?" (Foucault 1984c, 49). The conclusion one might draw is something like this: we are constituted as subjects (and objects) of knowledge, power, and morals by (our own) images.

The work of images can be summarized as a "technology" that links the self, the world, and collective practices through subjectivation, empowerment, and constructing knowledge. The production of images may be considered a collective practice through which the feminist, sexed, and gendered self gains shape. This focus on images offers explanations for the effects and the power of representation, both on a cognitive and a sociopractical level: On the cognitive level, images produce meaning as they offer perspectives onto the world. In doing so, they not only determine cultural meaning-patterns and thus what counts as reality, but they also offer possibilities for refiguring. On a social level, processes of common practices of image construction and imaginary processes of interpellation and identification produce social links.

These conceptions of self and power in the frame of representation and imagery explicitly or implicitly use concepts developed by Foucault at the same time that they modify such concepts by combining and adding other theoretical elements. Working as a *technology of the self*, the power of images is described in a social-constructivist frame as the productive power of creating worldviews and of interpellating subjects into being. De Lauretis's and Haraway's references to Althusser underline the subjugating force of discursive structures that is comparable to Foucault's disciplined subject. In contrast to Foucault, the process of subjectivation finds a plausible explanation in the concept of imaginary force. In addition, Foucault's *critical ontology of ourselves* becomes the programmatic basis for reflection and resignification of the subjugated subject toward a "hybrid" (Haraway), "sexed" (Probyn), or "multiple" (de Lauretis) self that turns its own conditions of existence into a transgression of the assigned position. In contrast to Foucault's aesthetics of existence, possible existences are not searched for outside of the structures determined by instrumental power— put in the concrete form of technobiopower by Haraway—but from within, in interstices and breaches. The freedom of creation here is not merely formal but, rather, relates to the content of pre-given forms or images, be they referred to as "subject," "self," or "cyborg." Accordingly, feminist selves do not exist in a formless form but instead become social beings structured on the basis of sex and gender. While all three authors risk overestimating personal agency, they show that subjective autonomy, in the sense of pure self-determination, is not necessary in order to change existing structures. The way out of individualism lies in collective practices. The strengthening of the collective marks their most important difference from Foucault's aesthetics of existence and is thus far from an "isolated aesthetic autonomy" (McNay 1992, 8). De Lauretis, Probyn, and Haraway demonstrate that discursive space can be created from within by reinventing the self as a speaking position that is directed by norms, not "empty." Their perspectives thus appear more compelling than Foucault's; politically it seems to be easier to bring people together under certain ideas than under pure refusal; logically, even a formal definition of the self under the guiding line of pluralism or "freedom" relies on a norm that assures its validity.[18]

While these feminist models tend to dissolve ambiguities in order to gain clear standpoints from which to decide what should count as real, they risk closing the gap between social and discursive reality by reestablishing truth claims that cannot be legitimized apart from "the real itself" and thus supporting the problematic, normalizing function of self-produced images of selves and experiences of "women" or "gendered selves." This risk is even more problematic considering what Haraway has identified as the key mechanism of technobiopower, namely, the naturalizing of metaphors in technoscientific constructions. For example, the gene becomes the signifier of "life itself" by denying its constructed nature, thus attaining the unquestionable status of "a thing-in-itself where no trope can be admitted" (Haraway 1997, 11). That they are constructed alongside a metaphorical image—and this is the metaphor of the "text" (or "code-writing")—remains invisible. Nevertheless, they were treated—and "called into being"—as if they worked like a text. Haraway describes such mechanisms as a typical aspect of techno-biopower that works on the basis of signification and communication: "The world-building alliances of humans and nonhumans in technoscience shape subjects and objects, subjectivity and objectivity, action and passion, inside and outside in ways that enfeeble other modes of speaking about science and technology. In short, *technoscience is about worldly, materialized, signifying and significant power*" (ibid., 51; emphasis added).

This point also sheds new light on Foucault's systematics. In *Technologies of the Self*, Foucault distinguishes four modes of technology: technologies of power, technologies of the self, technologies of signification/communication, and technologies of production. The first two are directed toward the self and install relations between self and self/selves, whereas the latter two are considered to be "political technologies" that install relations between the self and sociopolitical institutions. Though discursive modes of representation and their productive force play an important role throughout his work, the concrete relation between processes of signification such as writing technologies and imagery, on the one hand, and power and self-constructions, on the other, nearly recede from sight.[19]

In contrast, the feminist approaches presented emphasized the constitutive relation between self, signification processes, and power. All consider the effects of gender as a dominant technology of both self and social relations inside and outside of cultural and scientific institutions. In these frameworks, normalization and the basic constitution of the social come together in a mode of *construction power*, which can be thought of as simultaneously oppressive (insofar as it provokes exclusions) and productive. Thus, the concepts of Foucault are consequently utilized while his consequence is refused: Neither de Lauretis, Probyn, nor Haraway support the political necessity of separating the ethos of the self as an aesthetic affair of the sociopolitical structures as their determining condition of existence (cf. Foucault 1984d, 350). Instead of focusing on a distinct aesthetic sphere, the feminist authors stress the cognitive aspects of images that shed light on social reality; a reality which itself consists of imaginary and narrative processes. Whether they take the form of Haraway's program of witnessing naturalizing processes, Probyn's epistemological questioning of the self, de Lauretis's awareness of social constructions, or Foucault's limit attitude, what seems most important is to use the program of the ethos for every kind of construction, including feminists ones, in order not to repeat precisely those mechanisms that need to be unmasked. The focus on witnessing may also mediate against normalizing effects of an unquestioned identification of feminist selves and subjects—if cyborgs are our ontology, as Haraway writes, they are clearly not a mirror-image.

NOTES

I am indebted to Dianna Taylor for her excellent editing of the English text. Many thanks also to Rosalie Donaldson for her careful reading and transformation of my language monsters. This essay is part of my dissertation project and was funded by the University of Bremen.

1. In this context, Kirsten Hebel puts the emphasis on the notion of "freedom *to*" ("Freiheit zu etwas"). This refers to a form in which the self could manifest itself and differs from "freedom *from*" ("Freiheit von") power (Hebel 1990, 233).

2. For this power model and the idea of "agonism" (instead of "antagonism"), see Foucault (1982, 222, 225).

3. At the same time, Foucault (1984a) describes processes of overlapping and integration of Greek elements of self-care in the Christian mode of normalizing power; thus one cannot accurately speak of an opposition.

4. Foucault (1981, 133) showed this with the power of the secret. Finally, both discourse and silence are ambivalent.

5. The emphasis still lies on the historical practical approach, which should not be confounded with transcendental grounding. In this context, McNay's observation of a "transcendent" force seems to be misleading, as the concept of the self is explicitly not linked to an ideal that has to be reached. See McNay (1992, 99).

6. By "ideology," de Lauretis refers to Althusser's definition: "Ideology represents not the system of the real relations . . . but the imaginary relation of those individuals to the real relations in which they 'live' and which govern their existence" (de Lauretis 1987, 6).

7. Lacan (1977) outlined the concept of the ideal image of the self (*imago*) as the imaginary body-self to which the individual submits itself in order to gain a stable identity. The concept of the *imago* has been of great influence within feminist theories of representation.

8. De Lauretis 1987, 9f. De Lauretis understands experience not as pre-given but as "a complex of meaning effects, habits, dispositions, associations, and perceptions resulting from the semiotic interaction of self and outer world (in C. S. Peirce's words)" (ibid., 18).

9. Probyn (1993) refers to the concept of image developed by Michèle Le Doeuff. This concept remains rather open, as no distinction is made between "concept," "sign," or "metaphor." In my understanding, it could be read as the latter, in the cognitive sense of a linguistic image that structures recognition and knowledge.

10. The first cyborg was constructed in the United States as part of a military space research program in the early 1960s. It was a rat with an implanted pump that would enable the control of its body system through an external access of chemicals. The

whole program was intended to explore the possibilities for organic beings to adapt to conditions of life in space. See Clynes and Kline (1995). Other examples of transgressions of borderlines between nature and culture, the organic and the artificial discussed by Haraway, include the implantation of pacemakers, working at a computer terminal, and pop-cultural icons such as "the Terminator."

11. Haraway borrowed the concept of the hybrid as a political strategy from postcolonial theorists, especially Chela Sandoval. For parallels, see Sandoval (1995).

12. Haraway borrows the term "salvation history" from Erich Auerbach's concept of *mimesis* that describes the work of "figural realism." Auerbach uses this term to refer to a style of images preferred in the Christian era. The power of such images rests in their promise of fulfillment or damnation and leads to a suggestive style that forces a certain perspective oriented toward the object to be interpreted. On the side of the subject, the suggestion encourages that "we insert our whole life into the world of the narrator" (Auerbach 1982, 18; my translation).

13. For a definition of negative aesthetics, see Menke, *Souveränität der Kunst* (1991), especially p. 43ff.

14. Foucault outlined the consequences of a dualistic understanding of power that he named "juridical power." He rejected this understanding explicitly in favor of multiple, productive power in his *History of Sexuality,* volume 1.

15. Foucault's concept of a "critical" or "historical ontology" of the self includes both the question of social practices and of reflection as outlined in the shape of the philosophical ethos. See Foucault (1984c, 47). Yet Foucault (1982) defines knowledge as well as power and the self as "different modes of being." Therefore, the epistemological, the question of discursive knowledge production, the question of being, and the ontological cannot be separated from this framework. Rather, the modern split between the universal subject of cognition and the world against which Foucault is arguing is vehemently perpetuated.

16. Haraway (1997, 272). Such cyborgs are the transgendered, "self-aware, accountable, anti-racist" *FemaleMan,* a metaphorical substitute of the pseudo-neutral, self-invisible, male subject of knowledge that is borrowed from a feminist science fiction novel (ibid., 35); or the *OncoMouse,* a patented mouse with an implanted cancer gene used in breast cancer research, thus a transgenic organism that replaces the (passive) object of knowledge (ibid., chapter 2).

17. The term "transposition" originally appears in Kristeva's model of intertextuality and refers to a rearticulation of meaning in the process of transgression from one semiotic system to another, and finally to the polyvalence of meaning due to belonging to different systems. See Kristeva (1974, 60).

18. For a discussion of this point in relation to Lyotard and Foucault, see Nagl-Docekal (1988). In his "What Is Enlightenment?" Foucault apparently had recognized this point.

19. The distinction between technologies of power and technologies of signification is attributable to Foucault's special concern over the concept of power that should be understood as its own mode of "being," and apart from domination. In order not to melt together power and the domination of communication and

signification—that is, to differentiate himself from Habermas—Foucault prefers a clear distinction on the analytical level. See Foucault (1982, 217f.).

WORKS CITED

Auerbach, Erich. 1982. *Mimesis. Dargestellte Wirklichkeit in der abendländischen Literatur.* Bern: Francke.

Clynes, Manfred E., and Nathan S. Kline. 1995. "Cyborgs and Space." In *The Cyborg Handbook.* Edited by Chris Hables Gray. 29–34. New York: Routledge.

Deleuze, Gilles. 1990. *Pourparlers.* Paris: éditions de Minuit.

Dreyfus, Hubert L., and Paul Rabinow. 1982. *Michel Foucault: Beyond Structuralism and Hermeneutics.* Brighton: Harvester.

Foucault, Michel. 1979. *Discipline and Punish: The Birth of the Prison.* New York: Vintage.

———. 1981. *The History of Sexuality.* Volume 1. Harmondsworth: Penguin.

———. 1982. "The Subject and Power." In *Michel Foucault: Beyond Structuralism and Hermeneutics.* By Hubert L. Dreyfus and Paul Rabinow. 208–26. Brighton: Harvester.

———. 1984a. "On the Genealogy of Ethics: An Overview of Work in Progress." In *The Foucault Reader.* Edited by Paul Rabinow. 340–72. New York: Pantheon.

———. 1984b. *L'Usage des plaisirs. Histoire de la sexualité.* Volume 2. Paris: Gallimard.

———. 1984c. "What Is Enlightenment?" In *The Foucault Reader.* Edited by Paul Rabinow. 32–49. New York: Pantheon.

———. 1988. "Technologies of the Self." In *Technologies of the Self.* Edited by H. Martin Luther, Huck Gutman, and Patrick H. Hutton. Amherst: University of Massachusetts Press.

———. 1997. "Friendship as a Way of Life." In *Ethics: Subjectivity and Truth.* Edited by Paul Rabinow. 135–40. New York: Pantheon.

Haraway, Donna. 1991. *Simians, Cyborgs, and Women: The Reinvention of Nature.* New York: Routledge.

———. 1994. "A Game of Cat's Cradle: Science Studies, Feminist Theory, Cultural Studies." *Configurations: A Journal of Literature and Science,* no. 1: 59–71.

———. 1997. *Modest_Witness@Second_Millennium. FemaleMan©_Meets_Onco-Mouse.* New York: Routledge.

Hartsock, Nancy. 1983. "The Feminist Standpoint: Developing the Ground for a Specifically Feminist Historical Materialism." In *Discovering Reality: Feminist Perspectives on Epistemology, Metaphysics, Methodology, and the Philosophy of Science.* Edited by Sandra Harding, and Merrill Hintikka. 283–310. Dordrecht: Reidel.

Hebel, Kirsten. 1990. "Dezentrierung des Subjekts in der Selbstsorge. Zum ästhetischen Aspekt einer nicht-normativen Ethik bei Foucault." In *Ethik und Ästhetik.* Edited by Gerhard Gamm and Gerd Kimmerle. 226–41. Tübingen: Edition diskord.

Hekman, Susan. 1999. *The Future of Differences: Truth and Method in Feminist Theory.* Cambridge: Polity Press.

Kristeva, Julia. 1974. *La révolution du langage poétique. L'avant-garde à la fin du XIXe siècle: Lautréamont et Mallarmé.* Paris: éditions du Seuil.

Lacan, Jacques. 1977. "The Mirror Stage." In *Écrits: A Selection.* 1–26. New York: Hogarth Press.

Lauretis, Teresa de. 1987. *Technologies of Gender: Essays on Theory, Film, and Fiction.* Hampshire/London: Macmillan.

McNay, Lois. 1992. *Foucault and Feminism: Power, Gender, and the Self.* Cambridge: Polity Press.

Menke, Christoph. 1991. *Die Souveränität der Kunst: Ästhethische Erfahrung nach Adorno und Derrida.* Frankfurt/M.: Suhrkamp.

Nagl-Docekal, Herta. 1988. "Das heimliche Subjekt Lyotards." In *Die Frage nach dem Subjekt.* Edited by Manfred Frank. 230–46. Frankfurt/M.: Suhrkamp.

Probyn, Elspeth. 1993. *Sexing the Self: Gendered Positions in Cultural Studies.* London: Routledge.

Rabinow, Paul. 1984. "Introduction." In *The Foucault Reader.* Edited by Paul Rabinow. 3–30. New York: Pantheon.

Sandoval, Chela. 1995. "New Sciences: Cyborg Feminism and the Methodology of the Oppressed." In *The Cyborg Handbook.* Edited by Chris Hables Gray. 407–22. New York: Routledge.

Practicing Practicing

Ladelle McWhorter

"There is something ludicrous in philosophical discourse," Michel Foucault writes, "when it tries, from the outside, to dictate to others, to tell them where their truth is and how to find it . . ." (Foucault 1985, 9). In our age of moral relativism and multiculturalism, it is easy to hear in this sentence a simple condemnation of intellectuals who pose as authorities on questions of belief, and it is all too easy to agree; yes, of course, we ought not tell other people what to think. But given the issues, directions, and investments of Foucault's work, especially in *The Use of Pleasure* where this passage is to be found, I think this sort of soft relativistic reading of him is a great oversimplification, if not a total error. As I see it, Foucault's statement is not so much a disparagement of authority and authoritative pronouncement as it is a gesture toward a philosophical reorientation; Foucault is developing an alternative conception of what philosophical work might be. Within this reorienting movement, authority ceases to be of very much concern, not because one comes to the realization that there are no authorities (there may well be) but because one ceases to be primarily concerned with *pronouncement;* that is, the formulation of true propositions is no longer one's primary philosophical goal. And once one ceases to focus one's energy on establishing the truth of propositions, one is no longer likely to spend much time dictating to others which propositions they should hold true.

In his last years Foucault became very interested in the Hellenistic period, a time when philosophy was less concerned with doctrine and more concerned with developing, as Pierre Hadot has put it, "a way of life." Hadot, whose work was extremely important to Foucault,[1] offers Stoicism as an example of this widespread Hellenistic view: "The Stoics, for instance, declared explicitly that philosophy, for them, was an 'exercise.' In their view, philosophy did not consist in teaching an abstract theory—much less in the exegesis of texts—but rather in the art of living. It is a concrete attitude and a determinate lifestyle, which engages the whole of existence. The philosophical act is not situated merely on the cognitive level, but on that of the self and of being. It is a progress which causes us to *be* more fully, and makes us better" (Hadot 1995, 82–83).[2] To illustrate this point, Hadot cites Seneca ("Philosophy teaches us how to act, not how to talk"), Epictetus ("spiritual progress does not consist in learning to explain Chrysippus better, but in transforming one's own freedom"; "the subject-matter of the art of living [i.e., philosophy] is the life of every individual"), and Plutarch ("since philosophy is the art of living, it should not be kept apart from any pastime") (1995, 110; notes 9, 10, and 11). It is from these texts and others from the Hellenistic period that Foucault takes his notion that lives can be works of art and that philosophical practice can be part of an *ethos,* a way of living.

Like Foucault, although without benefit of Hadot's work until recently, I have come increasingly over the years to view and to experience philosophy as a kind of self-forming activity. The point of philosophical endeavor is not to establish a body of cosmological or moral propositions that we might believe in or adhere to and that we might reasonably expect others to believe in or adhere to as well. Philosophy is not pursuit of truth. Philosophy is pursuit of wisdom. Truth, as Agent Mulder often claims, may well be out there, awaiting us like an as yet unidentified object just over the horizon. But wisdom's residence is never out *there;* if wisdom comes into view at all, its site of emergence will be *here*—with, through, and as the unfolding of my life, or your life, or the life of someone else. Whereas truth may occur as the timeless relationship between a proposition and a state of affairs, wisdom occurs as the temporal unfolding of human thought in practice. This is what Hellenistic philosophers such as the Stoics and Epicureans and Cynics seem to have believed. This is what I think Foucault came to believe. At any rate, it is what *I* believe.

But, if I am to be a philosopher, this presents me with a problem. The principal activity of philosophers in our time is the production of essays, like the one I am writing now. And essays—as fostered, encouraged, or even demanded by academic institutions—are usually construed as tools of transmission, a kind of intellectual transportation; essays are the vehicles in which our truths ride from one mind to another. Thus, philosophical practice in the present day is reduced to truth-acquisition followed by report-writing. The process by which one acquires the truths to be inserted into the vehicle is not at issue (unless one is accused of plagiarism); the point is to get into possession of some truths and to construct a vehicle adequate to bear them to their destination, "the audience." But what does any of that have to do with cultivating oneself as a site for the emergence of wisdom?

I'm not terribly sure. So the temptation, which I'm certain is not peculiar to me, is to set that question aside and just get on with the business of constructing intellectual vehicles for the small stock of ideas that one has already managed to amass,[3] or to undertake a frantic search for a new idea, a new truth that can be manufactured, packaged, and launched into the world by the editor's deadline, without regard to what effect that frantic process might have on the writer. It is very easy to succumb to this temptation without even realizing it, especially when living at the hectic pace that most of us maintain during the academic year. I have to admit that it is exactly what I did when I started working on this essay.

From the beginning of the project, I knew what I wanted to write about: the differences between feminist practices of woman-affirmation and Foucauldian care of the self, which might be construed as practices of self-affirmation. I wanted to say that even for someone who is a woman and comfortably identifies that way, woman-affirming practices may be positively antithetical to caring for one's self. (This is because feminist practices of woman-affirmation often make assumptions about the nature of selfhood that I believe are both mistaken and dangerous, especially for people who are oppressed. Foucault's conception of selfhood and descriptions of self-cultivating practices are less likely to support patterns of oppression that currently exist. But more about this later.) I also had what I thought were some pretty good ideas about how to illustrate those differences. Nevertheless, I seemed unable to settle into a consistent tone or style of writing, no matter how hard I worked at it. The essay just never sounded right to my ear.

At first it seemed that my problem was that I didn't know who I was writing for. Who was my audience for this explanatory exercise? Was it feminists interested in but not knowledgeable about Foucault, feminists hostile to Foucault, feminists already convinced by Foucault, nonfeminist Foucauldians? Who? How I styled the essay depended on which of these groups I wanted my message to reach. After all, essays are means of transmission. How I built my verbal vehicle depended on which audience I wanted my little truth transported to. But after weeks of struggle over the question of audience identity, I finally recognized that my problem was not in fact the lack of a clear sense of audience to which to present my thesis; it was the pernicious presence of a need to designate an audience for what supposedly was a philosophical exercise of *self*-transformation. I was focused on others when I should have been focused on myself. Furthermore, I had to ask myself, why did I want to explore the differences between feminist woman-affirming practices and Foucauldian care of the self? So that I could tell those feminists what they were doing wrong? So that I could enlighten some Foucault scholars about feminist practice? So that I could presume to tell those other people what to think? What would be the value in that, in relation to wisdom, even if I were in possession of some extraordinary truth? I began to worry that I didn't have a message after all. No message, no audience. Ultimately that seemed to equal no essay.

But, I realized, what I did have was a very real (in fact a fast-growing) concern. Something was gnawing at me. And that was a place to start. For the sake of the essay, if for no other reason, I needed to pay close attention to the nature and context of my own concern; I needed to take care of my self.

So I started all over again. The important thing to focus on, I decided, was the tension I feel between feminist practices of woman-affirmation and practices associated with a Foucauldian conception of care of the self. I'm attracted to practices of woman-affirmation, especially to those that involve revaluation of natural cycles, carnality, and the earth. Something important offers itself in those movements, and yet I feel that they endanger me in ways that Foucault's work warns me about and makes me sensitive to. I decided that if I paid attention to the uneasiness I feel when I try to situate myself in relation to both of these discursive practices simultaneously (which was the theme of the anthology, anyway, right?), maybe something unforeseen would happen. Who knows? Maybe I could even find a way to practice philosophy while still fulfilling the requirements of my academic job. Imagine that! So I turned my attention to feminist practices that have spoken most meaningfully to me over the last twenty-five years, namely, those that involve how I live with, through, and as my body.

Feminists nowadays write a lot about "the body," thereby acknowledging the importance of corporeal issues in our intellectual pursuits, but we don't often acknowledge straightforwardly how difficult it was to live life as a female body before our encounters with early radical feminist reinterpretations of female bodily existence. Simone de Beauvoir's inventory of masculine supremacist invective against female bodies in *The Second Sex* accurately portrays what many of us lived with—ubiquitous images of our bodies (which *were already* ourselves) as obtrusive, ugly, filthy, stinking, irrational, and inherently diseased. Beauvoir herself suggests that this construction of the female body is historical and therefore optional. The radical feminists of the late 1960s and early 1970s took her suggestion very seriously and began to critique the construct of femininity that produced and reinforced such degraded bodily existences. Alice Embree's analysis of Madison Avenue strategies to create and sustain feminine consumers and Naomi Weisstein's critique of contemporary psychological theories, both of which appeared in the 1970 publication *Sisterhood Is Powerful,* are cases in point, and they are only two of scores of articles that appeared around the same time.[4] Women believed we were stinking and filthy because profit-makers told us so through every medium available. We believed we were irrational and incompetent because professionals told us through every social institution in existence. Feminists told and *showed* us, however, that these messages were motivated politically and economically. They were not truths to be accepted despite humiliation and pain; they were propaganda to be resisted and opposed.

Feminist exposés and reinterpretations made it possible to imagine a culture in which female bodies would be celebrated and valued rather than denigrated, because they made it possible to believe that the denigration of *our* female bodies in *this* culture was a political rather than a biological fact, a matter of power arrangements rather than nature. As I read the words of feminist anthropologists, historians, poets, cultural critics, theologians, and others, I began to look at my body differently, to see potentials not seen before, and to feel different inside (and as) my skin. The practice of reading, discussing what I read with friends, and seeking out more feminist writings to read, was positively life-transforming for me and for many other women my age and older. It helped me realize that the body my culture had handed me was not the only one I might have and that with time and effort my corporeal existence could be otherwise, even radically otherwise.

This move toward the otherwise was no mere intellectual leap, no simple rational rejection of a false ideology soon replaced by the truth. This transformation was not something that took place just inside my head. Feminist writing that critiqued and reinterpreted bodily existence invited me and summoned me to conduct myself, as a bodily being, differently. As I saw new conceptual possibilities, I enacted new behavioral possibilities and then saw new conceptual possibilities in turn. Not just my thinking, but my whole comportmental ensemble changed.

And it didn't stop there. Through the 1980s feminists made connections between the denigration of female bodies that is still rife in our culture and the misuse and abuse of other beings. It became clear that our culture's disgust with and exploitation of female bodies is just one part of a much larger picture that includes refusal of human mortality and denial of our dependence upon nature. Along with writers such as Susan Griffin, Vandana Shiva, Ynestra King, and Starhawk, I too found that as my ways of thinking about and of *being* a female body began to shift away from the dualistic, quasi-Cartesian, masculine supremacist ways I had thought and lived before, I needed and wanted to develop and engage in new practices regarding aging, mortality, and ecological cycles. I couldn't just be a feminist. I had to be something like an eco-feminist. And this shift involved much more than just adoption of a new set of doctrines; it involved—it primarily consisted of—the practice of a new set of actions. I didn't just read Starhawk; I gardened and composted and contributed money to environmental lobby groups and educated myself about environmental issues and policies and drove a pick-up route for a recycling co-op. And I saw these things as directly and intimately related to my feminist practices. Once again, I was rethinking bodily existence—*with and through my body.*

Maybe that was how I started rethinking philosophy as a way of life. I'm not sure, but it was during that same period of time that I came to be consciously open to the import of Plutarch's words: "since philosophy is the art of living, it should not be kept apart from any pastime." It was about this time in my life that I became deeply aware of the need to think of philosophy not as mere intellectual exercise, as a mind/body dualist might have it, but as physical, material practice. With my changing, materially, ecologically thoughtful comportment, I was becoming a living critique of (albeit still a site of ongoing struggle with) Western metaphysical dualism. If one of the major philosophical issues of the twentieth century was the attempt to dismantle and move beyond metaphysics in general and dualism in particular, then I was twentieth-century Western philosophy incarnate. I think many of us feminists, particularly eco-feminists, were.

Throughout that long period in my life, then, feminist practices were very important for me. They focused and helped me focus on overcoming traditional—crippling—conceptions of female bodies and restructuring my bodily comportment; in doing so they helped me connect myself in new and positive ways with the other living beings and systems on our living planet; and all of this involved extensive engagement with other feminists in bodily practices such that I could not forget that even the seemingly most otherworldly, most abstract of intellectual pursuits is truly corporeal, material, and dependent upon the organic interconnections that make up our earth. Over the past twenty years, feminist practices have made me who I am; they have given me my self. And it is a much better, healthier, more beautiful self than it would have been had feminism never come to exist. Yet I am deeply suspicious of many feminist woman-affirming practices, even while I am so attracted (and so indebted) to them. My suspicions are painful to me; I want to avoid them. But as a philosopher, I find I just can't.

The effort to rid ourselves of the oppressive bodily comportments and self-images that patriarchal society constructed for us was in many respects a necessarily creative enterprise. In the process of rejecting that femininity, we had to imagine and build new ways to act, to see ourselves, and to relate to others and the world around us. We had to become other than what we had been; we had to invent ourselves. Had we just done that—had we just opened ourselves to possibility and experimentation—who knows what might have happened? What would women have become if we had simply dismantled 1960s-style femininity and female sex roles and embraced the unknown? But we didn't. Historian Alice Echols says that by

1975—and in some groups such as Boston's Cell 16 as early as 1970—radical feminism was in decline and was being replaced on the narrowly defined political front by liberal feminism and on every other front by cultural feminism.[5] For a variety of reasons, some of the same feminists who had been trying to destroy static images of femaleness began trying to construct an alternative image—an image they claimed did what the patriarchal images had failed to do: It captured the truth of womanhood.

Since that door began to open just before 1970—that door that was an exit from a patriarchically constructed female essence—feminists have agonized over the question of the truth of womanhood. Radical feminism's own analyses seemed to point to an absence of such a truth outside patriarchy (as well as, of course, an absence of actual *truth* within it). But if absence there were, then to step through that door would be to step out of womanhood altogether and, hence, to run the risk of scattering, of becoming so other that unity would be impossible and newfound feminist solidarity and support would be jeopardized and quite possibly lost. If feminism as an organized movement was to continue to exist, the door could not be merely an exit. It had to be a portal to something real and substantial enough to hold together, to hold *us* together, and to give us something to affirm.

This concern about the loss of unity and the belief it gave rise to—that there is a nonpatriarchal truth of womanhood—was subterranean in some of the work of the early cultural feminist and eco-feminist movements. And so it was possible, especially for those of us who still desperately needed the communities and practices that would help us resist the ever-evolving patriarchal images of femaleness that assailed and pervaded us, to ignore the danger that such a belief entails. We needed a community and a language to support our own creative ventures, so we were willing to overlook the denial of creativity that was taking the form of cries of discovery.

But it *was* a denial of creativity. As an illustration, consider the contributions of Judy Grahn. Like all good feminist work, Grahn's scholarly activity was not merely cognitive; it was a corporeal practice intended to change her own ways of living as a female body, and was offered to her readers as an aid in our own woman-affirming practices. In "From Sacred Blood to the Curse and Beyond," Grahn explores the importance of menstruation for the prehistory of human society, a task she undertakes in part as a way to come to terms with her own femaleness and female bodily functions. Since there is hardly any aspect of female embodiment that is more stigmatized in our culture than menstruation, as Beauvoir among others points out (Beauvoir 1989, especially 149–50), Grahn's choice of subject matter is extremely apt. Male commentators on the subject have typically found it to be filthy and disgusting. In the not-so-distant past, women's descriptions were filled with comments resembling those typical masculine judgments. Most girls—myself included—were taught to be ashamed of the function, to view it as compromising their standing as rational creatures and competent citizens, and to hide it at least from males if not from everyone.[6] No more than a generation or two ago, women regularly referred to it as "the curse." But far from being a painful curse, Grahn argues, menstruation was originally the very wellspring of culture. It was because of menstruation that human beings "saw and learned to capture the concept of time" (Grahn 1982, 268). Further, "[b]y carving the moon cycles onto bone, by putting counting sticks into a basket, by tying knots in string, and by stringing beads in a particular manner to account for their own periods and the moon's, women created counting—and accounting" (Grahn 1982, 268). She continues: "Without menstruation and the sciences of measurement women developed from watching first the moon and then the stars, there would be no clocks or watches, no astronomers, no mathematicians or physicists, no astronauts, none of the architecture and engineering which have been born from exact measurement and proportion. We could build a nest, like a bird, but not a pyramid, not a square or rectangle or round or any other regular geometric shape. Geometry was a gift of menstruation" (Grahn 1982, 269). Indeed, Grahn implies, without this now degraded and hidden mammalian function, we would hardly be human at all.

The thrust of Grahn's essay is not just that we need to find new ways to live and to value ourselves but that we need to recover the lost value of menstruation as a way of recovering the true value of womanhood. By doing that, we will discover ways to live menstruation (and our lives as women) differently. Grahn relates in some detail the new knowledge of her own body that she acquired and the practices that she engaged in after she began to learn about the ancient meaning and importance of menstruation. The process of learning about that prehistorical world where women's bodies were valued was life-transforming for her, as for other women she knows, and she hopes it will be life-transforming for her readers. She offers her scholarship as material for woman-affirming educational practices and suggests that women follow her lead in developing feminist rituals that celebrate womanhood by celebrating menstruation.

Kay Turner, who has studied feminist rituals (including rites of passage like the ones Grahn mentions), maintains, "Feminist ritual offers an imagistic revitalization for women and participation in the concrete, bodily expressive creation of new images of the feminine . . ." (Turner 1982, 220). Not just menstruation rituals but also cleansing rituals, equinox rituals, dream-sharing rituals, bonding rituals, and so on are important means, Turner argues, of "connect[ing] the individual with the group—dramatically, indissolubly" (Turner 1982, 226). Rituals are practices that produce a sense of group identity and cohesiveness. But they are just as important for the health of individuals as they are for the health of the groups to which those individuals belong. Through ritual, according to Turner, "A lost self is recovered, nurtured and allowed to emerge fully named" (Turner 1982, 231).

Grahn and Turner both assume that part of what happens in feminist consciousness-raising, feminist scholarship, and feminist ritual—in all practices that are woman-affirming—is that women find their true identities, their true selves. Woman-affirmation involves not so much self-creation or self-formation as the recovery of a self that is already formed. This recovery, or uncovering, can happen, they maintain, because through feminist activity women open spaces outside of patriarchal power, beyond the reach of the networks of power that define femaleness as inferior to maleness and impose hardship and shame upon women. This is why Turner asserts that feminist ritual in particular is a form of radical politics (Turner 1982, 222).

Grahn and Turner and their compatriots such as Kathleen Barry and Mary Daly might be viewed as extreme essentialists quite unlike a good many of their contemporaries and certainly unlike the anti-essentialist postmodern feminists of the turn of this century.[7] But I don't think we can dismiss them that easily. The turn away from radical creativity and toward discovery that we see full scale in their work haunts all of feminism, I think, including postmodern theory. And I fear it will continue to haunt us as long as feminists yearn to affirm ourselves as an "us," as members of an identifiable class of people called "women."

Yet what else are we to do? What is feminism about if it is not about people identifiable as women? What is it, if it is not a way of discovering commonalities and gathering women together to achieve certain goals? If we embrace the unknown and experiment with creating forms of existence beyond the category of womanhood, in what sense is what we are doing "feminism" anymore?

At this point I become extremely uneasy. What initially attracted me to feminism was its emphasis on moving beyond the present and the past— including any kind of mythical past. The old Women's Liberation Movement seemed to me to be about changing rules, loosening restrictions, opening doors, challenging traditions, and experimenting with personal styles and interpersonal relationships. It was a vigorous push outward, a breaking of bonds, a headlong rush out of confinement and into the world. It was not an inward-turning thing. It was leonine—ferociously destructive—and childlike—playful and creative. But of course, at the same time, it was also a product of its culture, a culture that resists with all its might any turn away from the stasis of traditional identity, any move into the unknown. Somehow that culturally pervasive resistance overcame iconoclastic feminist momentum. Feminism gradually began to have an identifiable center: Woman—woman the victim of oppression, woman the subject and object of efforts to emancipate, woman the site of downtrodden virtue and righteous social change. Feminism came to be about recognizing that Woman and nurturing her as she recovered herself and took her destined place as the catalyst for a general, culturewide moral revolution. What had perhaps started out as a courageous journey into the unknown somehow got recast as a kind of enlightened return to origins. What I fear is that within feminism, such a turn is in some sense inevitable.

I sincerely hope not, for I feel endangered in the movement of that return. In spite of all I may have gained through woman-affirming practices, I fear that in this re-centering movement I am being pulled back toward a way of thinking and living that I wanted to interrupt and re-form, back into a way of experiencing selfhood (and the world) that places stability over becoming and change, into a way of thinking that places knowledge over openness toward otherness and difference, toward that which eludes categorization. And this feeling doesn't dissipate completely when I read or work with anti-essentialist feminists. Underneath or alongside their ubiquitous critiques of essentialism I still detect a hint of the assumption that, despite it all and whatever happens, we are still women, and we can rest assured that nothing in feminism will compromise *that.*

Through personal experience and through my study of Foucault's work, I am deeply aware of how dis-affirming such assumptions and insistences ultimately are for the kind of self that I am. And that brings me to Foucault and self- (as opposed to woman-) affirming practices.

It has often been asserted that Foucault's early and middle works embody attempts to analyze political and social forces in the absence of subjectivity, which would seem to mean that any kind of self-affirmative gesture is impossible for Foucault. The first part of that assertion is true; Foucault did in fact say once in an interview that he wanted to develop a mode of analysis that did not rely upon a subject outside of history.[8] But he never maintained that there is no such thing, at any given point in history, as human subjectivity of one sort or another. In Foucault's view, whether there is or is not some form of subjectivity at a given place and time is an empirical matter. In the periods Foucault studied, there were various kinds of subjectivity. In fact, it is these variations, together with the possibility of variation itself, that Foucault is most concerned with through much of his career.[9] Foucault merely refuses to assume that subjectivity, selfhood, is foundational or ahistorical. Selves are historical creations, constituted within networks of power/knowledge relations; different networks of power/knowledge yield different types of self. Self-affirmation, then, is perfectly possible, but what sorts of practices are self-affirming depends upon what type of self one is.

Foucault gives the name "normalization" to the power/knowledge network that he believes is most prevalent in our society today. The selves that emerge within that network, various though they may be, are all normalized selves. This does not mean that all selves are normal—far from it!—or that all selves not deemed normal are constantly being subjected to treatments to make them normal. In the most general terms, what it does mean is, simply, that who one is can be fully characterized (insofar as it can be characterized at all) in terms of norms and deviations from norms. In other words, in every aspect of my being—physical, intellectual, moral, you name it—I am a being in process, proceeding through stages of existence and functions of daily life at a rate and along a vector that can be measured and plotted against a norm. My individuality, insofar as it can be an object of knowledge (mine or others'), just amounts to the totality of my deviations from established norms.

Normalization is what Foucault at an early stage in his career might have called a grid of intelligibility. It is a conceptual framework through which we view ourselves and others (both human others and nonhuman beings such as animals, plants, ecosystems, and human cultures). Since the beginning of the nineteenth century, Foucault tells us, we Westerners have learned to see all the world in terms of the category of development; all things develop, and their more or less natural patterns and forces of development can be studied, normed, and to a great extent harnessed and directed by scientific means. This way of seeing has institutionalized itself in disciplines such as psychology, criminology, sexology, biology, anthropology, pedagogy, and many other fields; as it has done so, it has permeated and to some extent reshaped the institutional settings where those disciplines are practiced: schools, hospitals, prisons, corporations, mental institutions, and social welfare bureaus. Thus, it is not simply a grid of intelligibility, a network of knowledge; it is also a network of institutional practices, public policies, and in general the routine exercise of social and political power. It is a network of power/knowledge.

On first hearing, many readers simply reject the idea that who an individual is can be characterized and known entirely within the terms of normalization. But in fact it is extremely hard to give any information about any person at all—oneself included—without referring to sets of norms. There is hardly any intelligible way to talk about our bodies without referring to norms; how tall a person is, how fit, how healthy—virtually any assertion you can make will refer to functional norms and established patterns of human physiological development and decline. Further, most of us reflect upon and present our personal histories in terms of developmental norms. We employ the language of developmental psychology to account for our behavior, our feelings, our inclinations, our talents, and our preferences in terms of developmental norms together with influences on our development that may have produced deviations from norms. In truth, most of us are quite comfortable with self-descriptions that rely upon established norms as reference points and may even feel slighted if our specific deviations go unrecognized. We know and experience ourselves as normalized selves. And this is understandable, because within the power/knowledge networks that shape our social world, the only kind of self that is intelligible at all is a normalized self. There is no outside to normalization, Foucault says, meaning that normalizing power/knowledge networks are so pervasive that beyond them nothing is knowable.

Many of Foucault's readers take these conclusions as cause for despair, for two reasons. First, if Foucault is right, our identities are all reifications of norms and/or deviations from norms and, as such, tie us to networks of power that use those norms to exploit and oppress us, as Foucault makes clear in detail. This is especially obvious with identities such as "the delinquent," "the homosexual," or "the at-risk schoolchild," but even the apparently natural category "woman" is an identity founded upon a set of developmental norms stretching from fetal sex differentiation through childhood gender acquisition through adolescent self-image formation.[10] To be a woman is to have passed through numerous stages of normed development and hence to display the physical and psychic marks of that developmental process. To bear the identity "woman" is thus to be available to the institutions and disciplines that seek to direct and manage our developmental trajectories. A second reason many readers despair is that Foucault seems to be telling us that, since we are normalized selves through and through with no residual essence, to attempt to dismantle the power/knowledge networks that hold us in bondage in oppressive institutions and practices is self-defeating; dismantling normalization would amount to dismantling our own conditions of possibility. What, then, is to be done? Aren't all our avenues for taking control of our lives and resisting oppressive institutions effectively blocked? How can we possibly care for ourselves under these circumstances?

Foucault certainly does not minimize the dangers that we face. Anything we do will be risky. We cannot withdraw from a corrupt society into the apolitical security of ahistorical identities; that is an illusion, as separatist movements of the 1970s demonstrated. By the same token, we cannot simply set our historically produced identities aside, for we *are* the developmentally emergent beings that society takes us to be. We cannot attack the very basis upon which our being is constituted and expect to be unshaken in the process. We risk ourselves, in our very being, no matter what we decide to do.

Foucault, then, speaks of ubiquitous danger. Yet his analysis does not make me feel endangered in the way that feminist woman-affirming practices do. I am much less frightened by Foucault's harsh picture of the current world than by Judy Grahn's or Kathleen Barry's optimistic exhortations to celebrate the recovery of a world and of selves we've supposedly lost. I don't recognize myself in their idyllic portrait of prehistorical womanhood, or any other portrait of womanhood for that matter. I don't feel comfortable figuring positive changes in my self-understanding and material comportment as a return to a reality obscured or lost. I can only think that positing a true or original womanhood to which we might return (to which we ought to be faithful?) will ultimately lead to (or at least play into) a defensive conservatism that fears creativity, difference, and change. Creative movements, differings, openness toward unmastered becoming will be suppressed, and those who embody and enact such movements will be oppressed within the same discourses and institutions that once held so much promise for freeing them. Within the terms of Foucault's analysis of normalization, however, I do recognize myself. I recognize myself as a self who, as "essentially" developmental, is "essentially" a phenomenon of becoming rather than of being. I recognize myself as a self who will always surpass what I have been, who will never be identical with myself from moment to moment. I recognize myself as a being who will always exceed the boundaries of any identity. If I can find ways to affirm and care for *that* self, that developmental self who "by nature" defies final categorization, I can resist the oppressive aspects of normalizing networks of power (without positing a place beyond normalization). Normalization gives us ourselves as perpetually developing. Technologies of normalization then attempt to control the direction and rate of that developmental energy. We cannot defy normalization insofar as it gives us ourselves entirely, but we can resist and gradually perhaps dismantle normalizing technologies and disciplines. We can affirm ourselves as developing beings, ever-changing beings, while at the same time adopting disciplinary practices—techniques of caring for ourselves—that affirm the movement of our own becoming at the expense of predetermined vectors and norms. In other words, we can affirm our developmental freedom without affirming the existing technologies that would harness that self-differing energy. And then perhaps perpetual self-differing will become self-overcoming and will allow something new to emerge beyond oppressive normalization.

A primary danger that Foucault sees is the almost irresistible temptation to affirm not my *self* as developmental becoming but my *identity* as some reified stage of that developmental process. The danger is that we will refuse our selves in our movements of becoming by embracing static identities. When feminists call upon me to affirm my identity as a woman, beneath this joyful affirmation of carnal and specifically sexual existence I also hear a demand that I abandon my developmental self, call a halt to becoming other, deny my potential for change and hence for self-formation, and thus abandon both the care of myself and the practice of philosophy.

What, by contrast, do I hear Foucault calling me to do? To affirm myself as a process of becoming, of becoming always other to what I have been, to find and cultivate practices that will militate against reification and thus place in question any identity's claim to timelessness. To take care of myself, in Foucauldian terms, is to foster an awareness of becoming, of otherness, to hold myself open to an open future, to give myself over to what is not and cannot yet be known.[11] This, for a developmental self, *is* self-affirmation; it requires the perpetual overcoming of identificatory categories. Care of the self, therefore, stands opposed to practices that affirm my identity as a woman. Practices of woman-affirmation stand opposed to affirmation of the free play of becoming, differing, and otherness.

This brings me, rather abruptly, into the full scope of the terrible tension I feel when I try to situate myself in relation to my philosophical work and my feminist work simultaneously. If philosophy is a lifelong activity of self-formation, which implies that the self is not a static entity awaiting recovery, can I be both a philosopher and a feminist?

I don't know. I want to say yes, because I know the creative power of the feminist practices that over the last twenty-five years produced *me*. But in all honesty, I'm not sure. That the way to an answer involves resolute living through the tension, though, I have no doubt. It is through attempts at philosophical, ethical *practice* of feminism that an answer will constitute itself for each of us.

This much is clear to me: If I am to continue to be a feminist, I have to find ways to rethink, but even more importantly to re-create, materially and bodily, both the concept and the experience of womanhood. One way to do that might be to learn to think woman not as a category of human being, not as an identity, but as the name for a locus of creative formation.[12] This would require first of all engagement in practices that would destabilize the category. If this were his project, Foucault would engage in genealogical scholarship, which is also an option for me. Reading (and teaching) the works of scholars who have produced partial genealogies of certain aspects of womanhood would surely be helpful—works like Elizabeth Badinter's

Mother Love and Thomas Laqueur's *Making Sex* come to mind. I might also focus my attention on womanhood as a visual phenomenon and try to destabilize categorical thinking by challenging visual expectations. I can place myself in situations where my visual images of womanhood are disrupted. These can be queer places—like bars that cater to mixed sex and transgender groups—or they can be all-female places—like gym locker rooms. In the former kind of place, obviously, it's hard to tell who is female (whatever that starts out meaning) and who is not, and after awhile I find I get numbed to the question and just put it aside. In the latter kind of place, femaleness ceases to be a distinguishing feature of anybody, so the huge variety of what gets called female embodiment and comportment comes into full view.[13] Maybe if the category woman is sufficiently destabilized and decentered, I could start working on ways to think woman as something other than a category, something more like a site of volatility. Affirmations of womanhood could then become not affirmations of a static presence or truth but rather affirmations of something precisely not fully present and not fully envisioned.[14]

I have to acknowledge that for all its postmodern rhetorical correctness, I'm a little wary of this path—not the practices of category destabilization, which I engage in regularly, but the redefinition of womanhood beyond categorization.[15] Although I believe such a thing is logically possible and even over time almost inevitable, such "solutions" offered hastily never sound like much more than some kind of verbal trick—like I could rectify all sorts of sexual injustices by just defining women as we know them/us out of existence. If women didn't exist, all kinds of important political issues (abortion, job discrimination, rape) wouldn't exist either. But those issues do exist, and no mere verbal contortion is going to set them aside. Although I see the philosophical value of this approach and I know its goal is the very opposite of the kind of loss I fear, I still worry that without a lot of careful work it could reduce my feminist practice to some kind of esoteric exercise in theory production, to something that won't have much impact on most people's lives, including my own. And what's the point of that? After all, if feminism is important at all, it is because it is first of all about securing justice, recognition, protection, and material well-being for people who currently fit rather static definitions of femaleness taken as a natural kind.[16] To do nothing more than just redefine feminism so as to leave out that kind of tough work is to skirt the most important issues. So one important question I have to ask is: Is it possible to engage in that more traditional kind of feminist political practice (the nitty-gritty equal rights and equal protections kind) while embracing a de-categorized conception of woman as a locus of becoming?

Although such engagement would require reorientation in our political thinking and extensive reworking of our liberal rhetoric, I believe it is possible. I think I can embrace the idea that "woman" (whatever else it may be) is the name for an important site for the emergence of a future and argue effectively that those whose lives unfold at such sites must be protected, physically and legally, and their free becoming fostered. What is important is not the preservation of whatever "woman" *is*,[17] but the openness to the becoming that occurs as what woman is overcomes itself and surpasses itself toward an open future. I think political action could be grounded in something no more doctrinal and definite than that. I think I could do significant political work on the strength of a belief in the importance of resisting governmental, legal, economic, and cultural foreclosure of creative possibility. That path might be a very hard one to negotiate, but that is no reason to avoid taking it.

Furthermore, some of the resources for developing such political strategies already exist in some of the feminist practices I've already encountered and cultivated for many years. When I (along with so many other feminists in the 1980s) was rethinking female bodies, was I not by so doing actually creating a new body for myself, a body that I now inhabit and enact? I think so, even if I and the feminists around me did not always recognize or acknowledge the creative dimensions of what we were doing. And when we challenged masculine supremacy and authority, did we do so always in the name of some older truth that had a prior claim? I don't think so; I think we often did so in the name of difference and futurity rather than in the language of return. Sometimes we made assertions; we made truth-claims, and truth-claims almost always at least implicitly ally themselves with timelessness, sameness, a present that does not change. But no matter what assertions we might have made, insofar as our feminism was embodied in practices rather than in doctrines and propositions, it allied itself with history, contingency, and difference. Even Judy Grahn's practices affirm difference and change, despite the fact that the conclusions she draws from them deny contingency. We, I, need to acknowledge that implicit alliance between history, difference, and practice and make it explicit in all our political acts.

Still, it remains to be seen whether the work we would undertake once these transformations had occurred would constitute something we would want to call "feminist." That work would certainly have feminism in its lineage; it would certainly have been conditioned by a feminist past. But would it be feminist? If we truly do embrace the future as open and ourselves as women as historical existences, I don't think that question is answerable in advance.

To conclude: I've said here that I believe, with Foucault, that philosophy is not a body of doctrine or even a set of analytical techniques. It is a way of living, a pursuit that informs all our activities and is informed by all our activities. It has been called pursuit of wisdom—which means that it is a kind of creative self-shaping, a kind of self-transformation that opens toward differing, toward the unmastered and the unknown. We normalized selves, fundamentally developmental and therefore perpetually transformative "in essence," are particularly well suited to take up philosophy and even to do so both as a means of resisting oppressive normalizing technologies and as a means of caring for and affirming ourselves. Construed in this way, as Foucauldian care of the self, can philosophy be feminist? Can feminism be philosophical? I hope so. But, in the end, whether feminism can be philosophical or philosophy can be feminist are not issues that can ever be settled on paper. They can be resolved only in practice, by being enacted and incorporated. Therefore I must leave the question open here. It stands as a challenge to me and to all feminists and philosophers to make it so. That is, to live it so.

NOTES

1. See, for example, the introduction to *The Use of Pleasure* where Foucault writes, "I have benefited greatly from the works of Peter Brown and those of Pierre Hadot, and I have been helped more than once by the conversations we have had and the views they have expressed" (1985, 8).

2. Hadot was Foucault's colleague for one year at the College de France, having taken the chair in the History of Hellenistic and Roman Thought in 1983.

3. This is a temptation that a lot of good thinkers succumb to; they write an extremely influential book or set of articles, and then they spend the rest of their lives repackaging the same ideas in better and better ways. Not that there isn't value in doing that, but it is primarily a literary, not a philosophical, activity.

4. See Embree (1970, 194–212) and Weisstein (1970, 228–45).

5. Echols (1989, 5). Echols maintains that there is a distinction of note between radical feminism and cultural feminism, even though some of the same thinkers are prominent in both. I'm less sure of her distinction, but whether it is conceptually sound or not, the point remains that the work of the 1960s and early 1970s has a different thrust or at least is open to a different interpretation than the work that came after it.

6. Beauvoir quotes several women's descriptions of their own extremely negative attitudes toward menstruation (1989, 310–14).

7. See, for example, Barry: "We must look to our matriarchal past for guidance in defining a culture that is a logical extension of nature. With the essence of motherhood and a sense of the preservation of life imprinted in our genes, matrilineal descent will naturally become the organization of the society we envision" (1973, 25). See also, for example, Daly (1984).

8. Foucault (1980, 117): "I don't believe the problem can be solved by historicizing the subject as posited by the phenomenologists, fabricating a subject that evolves through the course of history. One has to dispense with the constituent subject, to get rid of the subject itself, that's to say, to arrive at an analysis which can account for the constitution of the subject within a historical framework. And this is what I would call genealogy, that is, a form of history which can account for the constitution of knowledges, discourses, domains of object etc., without having to make reference to a subject which is either transcendental in relation to the field of events runs in its empty sameness throughout the course of history."

9. See, for example, Foucault's claim: "My objective, instead, has been to create a history of the different modes by which, in our culture, human beings are made subjects" (1983, 208).

10. I have an unpublished paper on this subject entitled "Of or Pertaining to a Female," which I presented as a keynote address at Vanderbilt University's Philosophy and Feminism conference in January 1999.

11. For a great deal more detail about this notion of a self-overcoming selfhood, see McWhorter (1999, especially chapter 7).

12. Much as we might think of the space formed by the interplay of Dionysus and Apollo in Nietzsche's *Birth of Tragedy*.

13. This doesn't work in same-sex spaces where people are particularly insistent upon a single image of their sex—like traditional baby showers or gyms where everyone is young and beautiful. The gym at my university is a good place to go because there are beautiful, slim, young women but also, since any employee can use the facility for free, there are older women with weight problems, women with injuries and disabilities, bull dykes with big muscles, and of course a number of anorexics. To categorize all these bodies and comportments as one type of human being, a type that overrides all other differences, seems ridiculous in that context. The more time I spend in that context, the less overriding the category "woman" comes to seem. I think Honi Haber is suggesting something like this tactic. See Haber (1996, 137–56).

14. I take this path to be the one advocated by Judith Butler: "Identity categories are never merely descriptive, but always normative, and as such, exclusionary. This is not to say that the term 'woman' ought not to be used, or that we ought to announce the death of the category. On the contrary, if feminism presupposes that 'women' designates an undesignatable field of differences, one that cannot be totalized or summarized by a descriptive identity category, then the very term becomes a site of permanent openness and resignifiability. . . . To deconstruct the subject of feminism is not, then, to censure its usage, but, on the contrary, to release the term into a future of multiple significations, to emancipate it from the maternal or racialist ontologies to which it has been restricted, and to give it play as a site where unanticipated meanings might come to bear" (1992, 15–16).

15. As Foucault says, everything is dangerous, and postmodernism is no exception.

16. Even the personal changes I've described above required social and legal

change. It really wasn't enough for me to rethink my female embodiedness. Laws had to change to allow women to engage in activities previously unavailable or off-limits to us. Attitudes of people around me had to change to accommodate my changes. There were communal forces at work in my feminist self-transformations, and those must not be overlooked or minimized.

17. It is important, though, to acknowledge and contend with the various things that woman *is*, to work through them and possibly at times to redeploy them strategically. We can't ignore the category. It does exist and have a very real place and impact.

WORKS CITED

Barry, Kathleen. 1973. "West Coast Conference: Not Purely Academic." *Off Our Backs* 3 (10) (September): 24.

Beauvoir, Simone de. 1989. *The Second Sex.* Translated by H. M. Parshley. New York: Vintage.

Butler, Judith. 1992. "Contingent Foundations: Feminism and the Question of 'Postmodernism.'" In *Feminists Theorize the Political.* Edited by Judith Butler and Joan W. Scott. 3–21. New York: Routledge.

Daly, Mary, 1984. *Pure Lust.* Boston: Beacon.

Echols, Alice. 1989. *Daring to Be Bad: Radical Feminism in America, 1967–1975.* Minneapolis: University of Minnesota Press.

Embree, Alice. 1970. "Media Images 1: Madison Avenue Brainwashing—The Facts." In *Sisterhood Is Powerful: An Anthology of Writings from the Women's Liberation Movement.* Edited by Robin Morgan. 194–212. New York: Vintage.

Foucault, Michel. 1980. "Truth and Power." In *Power/Knowledge: Selected Interviews and Other Writings, 1972–1977.* Edited by Colin Gordon. 109–33. New York: Pantheon.

———. 1983. "The Subject and Power." In *Michel Foucault: Beyond Structuralism and Hermeneutics.* Edited by Hubert Dreyfus and Paul Rabinow. 208–26. Chicago: University of Chicago Press.

———. 1985. *The Use of Pleasure.* Translated by Robert Hurley. New York: Pantheon.

Grahn, Judy. 1982. "From Sacred Blood to the Curse and Beyond." In *The Politics of Women's Spirituality: Essays on the Rise of Spiritual Power within the Feminist Movement.* Edited by Charlene Spretnak. 265–79. Garden City, N.Y.: Anchor Press.

Haber, Honi. 1996. "Foucault Pumped: Body Politics and the Muscled Woman." In *Feminist Interpretations of Foucault.* Edited by Susan Hekman. 137–56. University Park: Pennsylvania State University Press.

Hadot, Pierre. 1995. "Spiritual Exercises." In *Philosophy as a Way of Life: Spiritual Exercises from Socrates to Foucault.* Edited by Arnold I. Davidson. Translated by Michael Chase. 81–125. Oxford: Blackwell.

McWhorter, Ladelle. 1999. *Bodies and Pleasures: Foucault and the Politics of Sexual Normalization.* Bloomington: Indiana University Press.

Turner, Kay. 1982. "Contemporary Feminist Rituals." In *The Politics of Women's Spirituality: Essays on the Rise of Spiritual Power within the Feminist Movement.* Edited by Charlene Spretnak. 219–33. Garden City, N.Y.: Anchor Press.

Weisstein, Naomi. 1970. "'Kinde, Kuche, Kirche' as Scientific Law: Psychology Constructs the Female." In *Sisterhood Is Powerful: An Anthology of Writings from the Women's Liberation Movement.* Edited by Robin Morgan. 228–45. New York: Vintage.

❦ 8

Foucault's Pleasures:
Desexualizing Queer Politics

Jana Sawicki

At the conclusion of *The Interpretation of Dreams,* Freud imagines being asked the following:

> But what of the practical value of this study . . . as a means toward an un-
> derstanding of the mind, towards a revelation of the hidden characteristics
> of individual men? Have not the unconscious impulses brought out by
> dreams the importance of real forces in mental life? Is the ethical significance
> of suppressed wishes to be made light of—wishes which, just as they lead to
> dreams, may some day lead to other things?
>
> I do not feel justified in answering these questions. . . . I think, however,
> that the Roman emperor was in the wrong when he had one of his subjects
> executed because he had dreamt of murdering the emperor. (1978, 658)

Freud's response is significant, for in this seminal psychoanalytic text he positions the psychoanalyst as a mediator between the individual and the
state—an expert with authoritative insight into the political implications of
our deepest desires. The emperor should not kill the subject, Freud suggests,
because the manifest and deep meanings of the dream are often worlds
apart. Furthermore, even if the subject did entertain fantasies of regicide,
Freud continues: "Would it not be right to bear in mind Plato's dictum that
the virtuous man is content to dream what a wicked man really does?" (1978,
658). Freud was keen to emphasize the normality of wicked and perverse
fantasies. What makes individuals truly dangerous to themselves and others, he suggested, is their inability to own their fantasies and to rechannel
them in socially acceptable forms. We suffer from the repression of natural
impulses that may be recognized, but not directly satisfied, if we are to live
cooperatively in society with others. Indeed, repression and sublimation of
such impulses are essential for civilized life.

As a science of sexuality, *par excellence,* psychoanalysis represented a key
player in the regime of sexuality that Foucault identified in the first volume
of *The History of Sexuality.* One of the most provocative features of his mid-

dle writings was his claim that the ideology of individual autonomy, which modern liberalism promises to secure insofar as it limits state regulation of our private lives, veils another form of power, namely, biopower. Operating as it does outside the boundaries of political power in forms of knowledge, techniques, and institutions associated with the human sciences, biopower is charged with the task of administering life. With its panoply of disciplinary techniques and normalizing human sciences it governs both individual bodies and the social body more generally. Because it provided access both to individual bodies and to the population, "sex" played a central role in the rise of biopower. For the first time in our history we became a society of individuals endowed with a "sexuality"—a "sexuality" with deep significance for the fate of civilization.

By loading sexuality with profound significance, psychoanalysis provided fertile ground for a myriad of legitimate incursions into the private lives of individuals. It isolated numerous ways in which desire might go astray. It established developmental norms, isolated multiple abnormal sexual personages—the fetishist, the homosexual invert, and the hysteric, to name only a few—and devised therapeutic means of curing them. Yet its explanatory power was not restricted to uncovering the dynamics of the individual psyche. It also provided theoretical support for the view that heterosexual marriage constitutes a bedrock for civilized society—a prepolitical foundation for social life. Moreover, following Freud's example in *Civilization and Its Discontents,* Freudo-Marxists in the Frankfurt School suggested that the vicissitudes of our sexual desires might even explain the social and cultural dynamics involved in the rise of fascism.

To be sure, psychoanalytic theory offered tactical possibilities for political critique as well. Indeed, it inspired a discourse of sexual revolution. Thus, in Herbert Marcuse's synthesis of Freud and Marx, he suggested that insofar as capitalism relied on sexual repression to ensure the productivity of its labor force, lifting repressions on sexual life could be one means of undermining it. Of course, as we all know, the grand political promise of the sexual revolution was never realized. Capital was clearly flexible enough not only to accommodate a little desublimation but also to profit from it.[1]

While Foucault did not deny the importance of the loosening of sexual mores associated with the sexual revolution, he claimed that in the end, it was "nothing more . . . than a tactical shift and reversal in the great deployment [*dispositif*] of sexuality" (Foucault 1978, 131). In a similar vein, he suggested that although movements for homosexual liberation may have succeeded in freeing more individuals to express their sexual desires and assume their stigmatized identities, they did not liberate us from the new regime of sexuality itself. Within this regime, homosexuals embraced the sexologist's and psychoanalyst's understanding of sexuality as a natural, fixed and constitutive feature of persons—a move that Foucault regarded as the linchpin of the modern regime of sexuality.[2] Although homosexuals' strategic reversal of the meaning of homosexuality may have been a necessary political move—Foucault was by no means condemning it as insignificant—it remained caught in the regime of sexuality it was resisting. Foucault's "nothing more" suggests that there might be "something else" we could do to resist the insidious forms of power that he identified. Indeed, his prognosis was neither as grim nor as a normatively vacuous as many of his detractors have suggested.

In Foucault's later writings and interviews, one can tease out the outlines of a more positive account of sexual freedom. He consistently refused to offer solutions throughout his intellectual life, preferring instead to "problematize." Yet he did hope that his work would be useful. And I believe that his later work was designed to be especially useful to those of us interested in advancing gay and lesbian struggles against subordination.[3] In particular, as I read it, Foucault's later work suggests strategies for enhancing sexual freedom that desexualize our struggles and challenge cultural representations and self-understandings that characterize us as principally sexual beings.

Foucault described the final two volumes of his *History of Sexuality* as a "genealogy of desiring man." He asked: How is it that we, whether queer or not queer, have come to see the truth of ourselves as something that resides in our sexuality? Or, as John Rajchman aptly expresses it: "When did people start to assume that what is most questionable, and potentially most glorious or heroic about themselves as erotic beings, were not the occasions and distinctive pleasures of their activities, [as they had in ancient Greece], but the 'truth' of the fantasies, wishes and thoughts locked deep within the recesses of their minds or souls?" (Rajchman 1991, 89). Through genealogical inquiry, Foucault hoped to loosen the grip of the discourses of desire and repression that have governed thinking about sexuality throughout the twentieth century. He encouraged us to imagine a world in which we no longer felt compelled to decipher the deep meaning of our sexual desires, feelings, and practices. He regarded efforts to justify movements of sexual liberation through appeals to psychoanalysis and theories of desire as elaborate rationalizations that played into the hands of the regime of sexuality. By revealing the contingency of such self-understanding, he hoped to free the intellectual space necessary for creating others. What many sex radicals fail to notice is that Foucault may also have been urging us to move beyond the tendency to regard our sexual transgressions as the most heroic gestures in our struggles for sexual liberation—and to move beyond legal strategies focused simply on demanding the right to our sexuality.

❧

Each of my works is part of my own biography.
—Michel Foucault, "Technologies of the Self"

In a 1983 interview published as the "Postscript" to Foucault's study of the work of the homosexual writer Raymond Roussel, Foucault remarked: "The private life of an individual, his sexual preference, and his work are interrelated not because his work translates his sexual life, but because the work includes the whole life as well as the text. The work is more than the work: the subject who is writing is part of the work" (Foucault 1986, 184). The author who had once expressed the desire to disappear into discourse appears here to be inviting attention to his personal life.

Yet Foucault's own interest in the self—and in the relationship between an author's life and work—was not a reversal of his earlier proclamations about the death of the author. It certainly was not an invitation to biographers to psychoanalyze him. Instead, it was a reversal of the century-long habit of reducing an author's work (however one construes the term) to a sublimated expression of the truth about his or her desires. Rather than see the work as an expression of a "life," Foucault suggested that we treat the life and textual work on the same level. The individual's life—not only the writings but also the deeds, habits, and pleasures—might all be treated as works of art. He remarks: "[I]n our society, art has become something which is related only to objects and not to individuals, or to life. . . . But couldn't everyone's life become a work of art? Why should the lamp or the house be an art object, but not life? . . . [W]e should not have to refer the creative activity of somebody to the kind of relation he has to himself, but should relate the kind of relation one has to oneself to a creative activity" (Foucault 1984a, 351–52). In other words, Foucault asked, why can't we see our erotic practices as works of art? Must sexual desire be expressed in higher cultural forms for it to be considered creative, beautiful, or socially acceptable?[4]

❧

For centuries we have been convinced that between our ethics, our personal ethics, our everyday life, and the great political and social and economic structures, there were analytical relations—and that we couldn't change anything, for instance in our sex life or our family life, without ruining our economy, our democracy, and so on. I

think we have to get rid of this idea of an analytical or necessary
link between ethics and other . . . structures.

—Michel Foucault, "On the Genealogy of Ethics"

Foucault's turn to ancient Greek ethics might be understood as a revitalization of the Nietzschean project of transforming creativity into an ethical category—into a matter of the individual's work on the self. (To be sure,
Foucault's impulses were more democratic than Nietzsche's were. In Foucault's view, the project of making oneself might be taken up by anyone.
Indeed, it might even be taken up in the gay bathhouses!) Even more importantly, in his later work Foucault suggests that we refuse the temptation
to read our sexual desires for evidence of their complicity with pernicious
power relations. He introduced the idea of an "aesthetics of existence" in
order to displace the primacy of psychological understandings of sexuality. Correlatively, he implied that there may be very little sex involved in
the ethical work required to advance the freedom of sexual deviants.

For example, Foucault strenuously resisted the impulse to read his own involvement in S/M as a symptom of pathology—either individual or cultural.
In an interview with the gay press, he commented: "I don't think that this
movement of sexual practices has anything to do with the disclosure or the
uncovering of S/M tendencies deep within our unconscious. . . . I think S/M
is much more than that; it's the real creation of new possibilities of pleasure,
which people had no idea about previously. The idea that S/M is related to a
deep violence, that S/M practice is a way of liberating this violence, this aggression, is stupid" (Foucault 1994, 165). Why is it stupid? Because it is infected
with what Nietzsche referred to as the spirit of gravity. Exhibiting, as it does,
the will to discover the truth about our desires, and to assume their centrality to the fate of society, it takes the trope of "desiring man" too seriously.

One might read the final two volumes of *The History of Sexuality* as Foucault's response to this seriousness. In his effort to open up the conceptual
space for new ways of thinking about our relationship to self, Foucault did
not plumb the depths of his own past. Instead, he engaged in historical inquiry. His last two books, *The Use of Pleasure* and *The Care of the Self*, represent an ingenious use of genealogy to excavate the history of the idea of
"desiring man" from ancient Greece to the present. He approached the past
with questions such as the following: What are the different ways in which
individuals have constituted themselves as sexual subjects? When did we
begin to load sexuality with so much political and moral significance—to
install it at the center of our thinking about the foundations of social life
or at the center of our emancipatory strategies? Are there elements of Greek
ethics that might be useful for analyzing the present?

Foucault distinguished three different possible objects of historical investigation: (1) the record of people's actual behaviors; (2) moral codes, or laws; and (3) ethics, which he defined as the study of the self's relation to itself. Unlike most philosophers, who take moral codes and questions concerning their origins and justifications as principal themes of study, he focused on the domain of ethics. This shift of attention opened up a terrain of historical change not visible if we were to look merely at the history of moral codes, since the latter, he argued, have remained relatively constant. In *The Use of Pleasure*, Foucault highlighted the austerity found in ancient Greek attitudes toward the regulation of sexual pleasures. He was not arguing, as some have suggested, that ancient Greece represented a "Golden Age" of sexual freedom but simply describing the ways in which its regulation of pleasures were part of a radically different experience than our own. Although sexual activity and pleasure constituted an ethical problem for them, they did not base their ethics on a hermeneutics of desire. Thus, he implied, we might learn something from them insofar as we share a similar problem, namely, the need for an ethics—technology of self—that does not appeal to the regime of sexuality. Foucault stated: "Recent liberation movements suffer from the fact that they cannot find any principle on which to base the elaboration of a new ethics. They need an ethics, but cannot find any other ethics than an ethics founded on so-called scientific knowledge of what the self is, what desire is, what the unconscious is, and so on" (Foucault 1984a, 343).

Following Nietzsche's practice of distinguishing the relatively fixed and the fluid elements in our moral past, Foucault isolated four elements that structure an ethics: (1) ethical substance, the prime material of moral experience; (2) mode of subjection, the source of moral authority; (3) technology of self, the specific discipline by which one can change oneself to become an ethical subject; and (4) the telos or goal of self-formation, that is, the type of being to which one aspires. Using this grid of analysis, Foucault was able to identify important changes in the self's relationship to its own sexual pleasures and conduct that have been unnoticed by historians who have focused solely on laws and codes. Although it is true that in ancient Greece, male homosexuality constituted an ethical problem, the problem was not the same as that faced by early Christians or by us "moderns." The principal ethical aim of a Greek citizen (circa fourth century B.C.) was to exhibit the self-mastery expected of a proud ruler—to sculpt a beautiful and self-sufficient self. His principal ethical question was: How can I engage in pleasurable activities without being excessive, and without jeopardizing my status as a citizen and ruler of others? What work on my self must I perform to ensure that I am not enslaved by myself? Note that here "freedom" is not opposed to submission to an external authority, or to natural determination, but self-enslavement. It is not the pure freedom associated with a "free will." It is instead the freedom to use materials made available in the culture, materials found in a plurality of ethical schools, to shape and distinguish oneself. Moreover, although the political implications of one's sexual acts, and one's ability to moderate pleasure, are significant within this ethical structure, the nature of the desire itself, the choice of its object, was much less important for determining its ethical or political status.

Attention to the diverse and complex ways in which individuals have understood themselves as sexual subjects suggests that modern understandings of sexuality have naturalized structures of being that might be contingent. Here, what is instructive about ancient Greek ethics is that they offer normative practices of self-formation that are dissociated from more recent ethical, religious, legal, and scientific preoccupations with the truth about one's desire. (Is one a homosexual invert, a fetishist, a voyeur, and so on?) We could infer from Foucault's genealogy that social order and cultural achievement are not premised on ideas and practices associated with a social and cultural imperative to repress deviant desire and codify sexual morality in law. Indeed, civilizations have thrived without such measures. In ancient Greece, Foucault discovered a "strong structure of existence without any relation to the juridical per se, [yet] with an authoritarian system, [and] . . . a disciplinary structure" (Foucault 1984a, 348).

Thus, the last two volumes of The History of Sexuality represent Foucault's work to free himself, and us, from thinking that we *must* understand ourselves as subjects of desire. In his research into past understandings of homosexuality, Foucault did not find himself, but something other than himself, namely, the historical conditions and limits of his own self-understanding as a homosexual. This historico-ontological inquiry into the limits of possible experience is Kantian in form but not in content. Foucault described it thus: "It will not deduce from the form of what we are what it is impossible for us to do and to know; but it will separate out, from the contingency that has made us what we are, the possibility of no longer being, doing, thinking what we are, do or think. . . . [I]t thereby seeks to give new impetus to . . . the undefined work of freedom" (Foucault 1984b, 46).

Of course, genealogy is only part of the work of freedom. Once we grasp the contingency of the present, we confront the work of developing new cultural forms. In his later writings, Foucault spoke of the desirability of developing new "forms of life"—forms of erotic and intimate association that resist the regime of sexuality. If there is a utopian tone to these calls for new forms of life, it is not the utopianism associated with Freudo-

Marxist humanism and its theories of a new man. Foucault did not believe we could escape the present *tout court* and install a new society on the basis of a pre-social human nature—but he did believe that we could effect very specific changes through a practical attitude oriented toward testing the limits of the present. He called this attitude or ethos a philosophical life "in which the critique of what we are is at the same time the historical analysis of the limits that are imposed on us and an experiment with the possibility of going beyond them" (1984b, 50). The goal of such experimental practices is to develop alternative ways of being that empower us without intensifying pernicious disciplinary power relations.

Accordingly, one might argue, our sexual freedom lies not solely in securing the rights to express a sexuality within us but rather in our capacity to invent new experiences, pleasures, and forms of life that expand the realm of human possibility—to experiment with possibilities for self-understanding and embodiment beyond the discourses of desire and sexual identity. This would require that we come to see our freedom not simply as something to be secured but rather as something we must *exercise* in the form of ethical practices of self-constitution. In an interview with the gay press, Foucault remarked: "It is not just a matter of integrating this strange little practice of making love with someone of the same sex into pre-existing cultures; it's a matter of constructing cultural forms" (quoted in Halperin 1995, 80). Hence, the task for gays and lesbians is "to become homosexual," not to persist in acknowledging that we *are*. Perhaps in this way, he thought, we might use our sexual subordination as a springboard for inventing new forms of life.

Although Foucault was not advocating a return to Greek ethics—after all, the genealogist is not advocating a return but rather using the past to highlight features of the present—he did suggest that some of its elements might be useful in our contemporary context. As we have seen, he retrieved the idea of work on the self in hope that it might acquire a new meaning in the present. Moreover, there are other aspects of Greek ethics that might be useful in analyzing gay and lesbian struggles for sexual freedom. Consider for example the fact that the ethical status of the Greek citizen who engaged in same-sex practices was not related to his *being* homosexual, but rather a matter of whether he exhibited self-mastery. Were his sexual urges well governed? Was his soul well balanced? In contrast, in modern times, homosexuals have been defined within juridical and scientific discourses, as well as other cultural representations, as inherently sexually excessive and morally corrupt.[5] Foucault's portrait of Greek sexual ethics brings into relief the possible importance of moving away from understandings of our homosexuality that seem to embrace the reduction of our identities to their sexual aspect and to romanticize our outlaw status—our inherent unfitness for citizenship.[6] Desexualizing our struggles and the dominant cultural representations through which we become visible as gay or lesbian may require that we move away from such one-dimensional self-understandings—and that we highlight other aspects of our queerness as well—new forms of relationship, of erotic and intimate association that we have already created as well as the connections we form with nonhomosexual groups to resist oppression.

&

> I share Michel's distaste for those who consider themselves marginals; the romanticism of madness, perversion and drugs is less and less bearable for me.
> —Gilles Deleuze, *Foucault and His Interlocutors*

If it is ironic, it is certainly not surprising that after his death from AIDS in 1984, Foucault's life did become the object of intense scrutiny and utter fascination. Was it at all probable that the man who once proclaimed the death of the author—the man who described the broad and impersonal forces that constitute and regulate individuals in modern societies—could escape inquiry into the deep significance of his own desires? That he did not is indeed testimony to the power and resiliency of the regime of sexuality that he described. Indeed, some conservative critics seized the opportunity to dismiss the authority of Foucault as that of a depraved, immoral, and perverse man with nihilistic and sadistic tendencies—as if the life were final testimony to the moral and political bankruptcy of the "work." The equation of homosexuality with moral depravity and sexual excess may be less salient than it was in the first half of the twentieth century, but it still has the power to undermine the credibility and authority of homosexual subjects.[7]

Foucault's biographer, James Miller, also succumbs to the temptation to read Foucault's desires and to privilege the role of transgression in them. In his book *The Passions of Michel Foucault*, Miller explores the relationship between Foucault's sexual desires and his work. To be sure, following Foucault's suggestion, Miller treats both the life and the texts as part of the work; but he interprets this work as the expression of deeply rooted and "secret" passions. Miller's central thesis is that throughout this written work and his life, Foucault exhibited an obsession with limit experiences. He sought the possibilities of self-transcendence that might be found in transgressive pleasures associated with sex, drugs, violence, cruelty, and death. This pursuit of limit experiences was a high-minded one, Miller assures us, for its ultimate intention was—here Miller quotes Foucault out of context—"to defeat 'the fascism in us all—the lust for domination, the yearning for rebirth of a violent, dictatorial, even bloody power'" (Miller 1993, 244). The portrait of Foucault that emerges in Miller's text is that of a modern Saint Anthony, a nihilistic and tortured soul, flagellating himself at gay bathhouses and S/M clubs in San Francisco in order to achieve self-transcendence—to get free of himself in the name of antifascism. Although Miller professes to admire what he sees once Foucault has been undressed, he seems to be deceiving himself in thinking that the ultimate effect of the undressing is not tantamount to exposing the emperor.

In at least one respect, David Halperin's *Saint Foucault* provides a refreshing alternative to Miller's account of Foucault's life and work. Halperin offers an apology for Foucault's pleasures that contrasts starkly with Miller's reticent admiration. In an "impertinent" (his adjective) and poignant reversal of what he regards as the likely response of Foucault's opponents to Miller's sensationalist exposé, he makes the case for Foucault's sainthood. Yet, as I will argue, Halperin's account of Foucault's queer politics rests on an account of queerness that privileges self-shattering as a primary vehicle of social transformation—a move that Foucault would have resisted.

Halperin recognizes that "becoming other than what one is" involves not only historical work but also work on the self. The strategic work of self-transformation requires not only the genealogical practice of defamiliarizing the present but also the invention of new forms of discipline. Indeed, Halperin believes many gays and lesbians qualify for sainthood insofar as they are constantly exposed to the condemnations of a homophobic society. Such exposure, he argues, creates the need and the capacity for spiritual exercises, for self-mastery and transformation, akin to that of the ancient Greeks. Halperin appeals to this notion of "spiritual exercise" in order to, in his words, "indicate something of the effort required to produce the social and psychic ruptures that lesbians and gay men must engineer daily in order to detach ourselves from heteronormative society, so as to be able to lead our queer lives without apology or compromise, and to continue to forge new and better ways of being queer" (Halperin 1995, 108). Halperin suggests that the voluntary self-exposure of queer writers and activists, as well as the sexual practices of S/M, be included in the panoply of contemporary forms of work on the self that so fascinated Foucault in his studies of ancient technologies of the self. The need for "social and psychic rupture" plays a central role in Halperin's understanding of queerness, and in his argument that Foucault's work (his writings and his life) be regarded as the quintessential example of a "queer" practice.

Halperin appropriates a particular meaning of the term "queer." "Queer is by definition whatever is at odds with the normal, the legitimate, the dominant. There is nothing in particular to which it refers. It is an identity without an essence" (Halperin 1995, 62). For Halperin, queerness simply denotes opposition to dominant sexual norms. Hence, it is a political concept. It does not refer to any positive facts about a person such as sexual object choice, degree of femininity or masculinity, or genetic makeup. To be queer is to be off-center, eccentric. To cultivate queerness is to cultivate a permanent capacity for self-distancing and social criticism that not only resists normalization but is also dynamic and creative. Halperin regards both Foucault's suggestion that homosexuality is a site of potential transformation of existence and his efforts to resist the forms of sexual subjectivity transmitted through the regime of sexuality as support for his claim that Foucault's understanding of his own sexual identity was a "queer" one. More importantly, he suggests that Foucault understood S/M as a queer practice that could be used to shatter the self, to disarticulate identity, and, thus, to approach the nonidentity (anti-identity) associated with queerness.[8]

How did Foucault understand S/M? Might it be understood as a form of queer practice? Foucault described it as both a subculture organized around an attachment to certain types of practices and a strategy for producing bodily pleasure. He rejected the view that it can be reduced to a mere reproduction of social relationships of domination and subordination. He observed: "[S/M] is an acting out of power structures by a strategic game that is able to give sexual pleasure. . . . it's a process of invention. . . . What is interesting is that in . . . heterosexual life those strategic relations [e.g., pursuit and flight] come before sex. It's a strategic relation in order to obtain sex. And in S/M those strategic relations are inside sex, as a convention of pleasure . . ." (Halperin 1995, 86–87).

To be sure, Foucault also regarded S/M as a process of invention that degenitalizes pleasure. He suggested that insofar as S/M involves an organization of bodily pleasure around other body parts, and refuses an exclusive focus on the genitals, it represents a desexualization of pleasure. Here "sexual" is understood in its narrow sense—as referring to a masculine libidinal economy associated with genital (primarily penile) stimulation to orgasm. Furthermore, he speculated, when two "macho" gays engage in such practices, they are not valorizing dominant norms of masculinity but instead representing a nonvirile, receptive, passive, and vulnerable masculinity in the guise of "men."

Halperin rightly suggests that we might see Foucault's experiments with bodily pleasure as an effort to erect counter-disciplines—in this case a form of work on the self that resists the amalgamation of gender identity and sexual object choice into a distinct type of sexual identity—work that resists conventional psychoanalytic understandings of sex that still permeate our cultural representations of it. But he exceeds Foucault when he describes the aim of such practices as a "shattering of the subject of sexuality." Echoing utopian appeals to the transformative possibilities of polymorphous perversity found in Freudo-Marxism, he claims: "The shattering force of intense bodily pleasure, detached from its exclusive localization in the genitals, and regionalized throughout various zones of the body, decenters the subject and disarticulates the psychic and bodily integrity of the self to which a sexual identity has been attached" (Halperin 1995, 97). Of course, for Halperin, self-shattering is central to queer practice. It purifies the self, and the body, by emptying it of past determinations. It creates a site for future change and "opens up the possibility for the cultivation of a more impersonal self" (Halperin 1995, 97).

Yet to speak, as Foucault did, of the need to "detach oneself from oneself" (*deprendre soi même*) is not necessarily to advocate self-shattering, or the cultivation of nonidentity. Halperin's image of the goal of queer sex as an evacuation of the sexual subject is rhetorically, theoretically, and practically excessive. Although he invokes a panoply of technologies of the self, he sometimes appears to regard the work of social and psychic disintegration as necessary to the process of creating new forms of life. He continues: "Only something . . . bad for the integrated person that the normalized modern . . . [individual] has become can perform the crucial work of rupture . . . that may be necessary in order to permit new forms of life to come into being" (Halperin 1995, 107). In contrast, Foucault was notoriously reluctant to link theory to practice in this way. Halperin denies that he is erecting a theory of the subject, but it is tempting to read the evacuated subject of his queer politics as a queer version of the subject of history.

Despite Halperin's protests to the contrary, his concept of queer practice encourages a romanticized view of erotic marginality and transgression. It tends toward vanguardism in sexual politics. Foucault claimed that the possibilities of resistance might be found anywhere—presumably at the center as well as the margins of the social—assuming that he would have endorsed the language of center and margin at all—which I doubt. Accordingly, there is no reason to assume that the liberal strategy of securing the rights of gays and lesbians to marry is any less likely to produce new forms of subjectivity and new cultural forms than participation in more radical erotic subcultures.[9]

Furthermore, while Foucault did speculate about the transformational potential of S/M, surely his purpose was not to provide yet another theoretical apology for it. After all, as I have argued, a principal aim of his writings on sexuality was to free us from the tendency to attach so much moral and political significance to it—particularly as it has been conceived within the regime of sexuality and the normalizing discourse of psychoanalysis. To be sure, Halperin anticipates this objection. He argues that his is not an apology for S/M but rather an effort to emphasize the *work* that is necessary to bring about the sorts of changes we desire. Moreover, Halperin understands that Foucault's chief contribution to lesbian/gay and queer politics lies in his effort to de-psychologize sex—to treat it as the effect of discursive and political strategies rather than a natural thing to be known. Surely Foucault would have been reluctant to privilege the sex acts associated with S/M as a strategy for inventing new forms of relationship and new forms of subjectivity. To privilege any erotic acts as the royal road to a new economy of bodies and pleasures makes little sense without a psychological account of the connection between the activities and the new subjects that they produce.[10] Yet this is exactly the sort of move that Foucault wanted to bypass.

In his later interviews, Foucault speculated that gay friendship, gay networks, and gay forms of life might be more threatening than sex: "I think what most bothers those who are not gay about gayness is the gay life-style, not sex acts themselves. . . . it is the prospect that gays will create as yet unforeseen kinds of relationships that many people cannot tolerate" (Foucault 1988b, 301). In an interview with the gay press, Foucault continued in this vein: "People can tolerate two homosexuals they see leaving together, but if the next day they're smiling, holding hands, and tenderly embracing one another, then they can't be forgiven. It is not the departure for pleasure that is intolerable, it is waking up happy."[11] This might explain the fact that in San Francisco, gay bathhouses and S/M bars are tolerated and gay marriage is not. I am not suggesting that struggles to secure access to gay marriage are preferable to efforts to deregulate sexual practices, but rather that there is no prima facie reason to assume that it is less likely to produce the sort of cultural innovation and self-making that Foucault endorsed. Foucault was less reluctant to challenge the tendency of male homosexuals to remain caught in the trap of demanding the right to their sexuality. He applauded the fact that feminist movements had "departed from the discourse conducted within the *dispositif de sexualité*"—that they had, in effect, desexualized feminist discourse insofar as they looked for "new forms of community, co-existence, pleasure" (Foucault 1980, 220).

My reference to gay marriage is not arbitrary. The question whether the right to the legal recognition of our queer intimate associations is reactionary has divided queer activists for more than a decade. On the one hand, Foucault might have found it troubling since it involves an appeal to the state to legitimate our relationships. On the other hand, Foucault also recognized the necessity of engaging in political contestation over the state's role in governing our lives. His critique of the liberal discourses of freedom, truth, and rationality need not be read as a rejection of them *tout court.* Indeed, securing the space (both subjective and objective) necessary to experiment on ourselves depends upon a particular instantiation of liberal rights and freedoms. To be sure, as an *intellectual,* Foucault consistently adopted an attitude of suspicion toward government and political structures—toward all efforts to legitimate a particular set of power relations as necessary to freedom. He understood power as both necessary and dangerous. Nonetheless he recognized the necessity for us to make political choices and to adopt political strategies as *citizens* even as he encouraged us not to be satisfied with them.[12] Attention to forms of self-making exhibited in Foucault's discussions of an "art of living" or "aesthetics of existence" might be construed as his antidote to the pernicious effects of "governmentalization," that is, social practices that subjugate individuals within particular relations of power and knowledge. Yet this creative activity must use the materials available in the culture—and, I suggest, may involve struggle over the interpretation of liberal concepts and values as well as struggle over the role that the state might play in governing erotic welfare.

In Halperin's view, Foucault appears as the enemy of liberalism. Consider his remarks in the conclusion to *Saint Foucault:*

> Political resistance to Foucault's interventions has come not from queer activists . . . but from old-style liberal authorities whose power to define the political *on behalf of everyone* is threatened with delegitimation by Foucault's critique of the various forms of expertise to which they customarily appeal in order to ground their claims of authority. But lesbians and gay men, by contrast—we who, far from having been the beneficiaries of liberal, humanist notions of freedom, truth, and rationality, have tended rather to be the targets of a new kind of terror in their name . . . —we who have been denied our *freedom,* our claims to be able to speak the truth about our lives, by having been denied a rational basis on which to speak at all—we have little cause to bewail the passing of those liberal humanist notions, to be threatened by their demolition, or to feel deprived of a politics by Foucault's critique. (Halperin 1995, 123)

Here Halperin throws out the baby with the bathwater. His queer politics threatens to become a politics of despair. In the wake of AIDS, gay and lesbian activists have been painfully reminded of their vulnerability to the authority of experts, to the power of homophobic indifference and condemnation, and to many of the policies and values of a liberal society. Is it surprising that some of the political thinking emerging out of such circumstances would show signs of despair? Is it surprising that such circumstances might tempt us to resurrect the martyr as our emblem of political agency?

And yet, I suspect that despite his own pessimistic tendencies, Foucault would have been as reluctant to put both feet in Halperin's queer politics camp as he was to identify wholly with any other.

Halperin is certainly right to emphasize the effacement and displacement of gays/lesbians and queers in civil society—our inability to speak for and as ourselves with any authority. And there is a compelling aspect to his logic—if our identities are merely traps that operate by denying us a voice as gay citizens within civil society, then perhaps the best antidote to our erasure is erasing ourselves as such. If the operations of power were as total as this logic suggests, then Halperin might be right. Are visibility and identity necessarily traps? Or are they, instead, paramount for those of us denied the right to speak with authority as queer subjects in the public sphere?

What I have found most remarkable about Foucault's work is its capacity to stimulate a wide range of strategies for resisting modern forms of subjection. He was reluctant to identify with any political tradition, or to assume the role of the cosmopolitan intellectual who might adjudicate between competing struggles. This did not prevent others from identifying him with every political position imaginable—as anarchist, leftist, ostentatious, or crypto-Marxist, antiliberal, new liberal, and neoconservative. There is no doubt about it, he was a bit queer. The difficulty associated with assigning a political label to Foucault's work is a source of both its strength and its vulnerability. Perhaps his strength lies in this vulnerability—his openness to a variety of uses. In any case, Foucault claimed to have enjoyed this ambiguous status since his aim was less to bolster particular programs than it was to pose questions and problems for politics as usual across the political spectrum—and, I would add, to serve as a stimulus to a myriad of possible forms of resistance to dominant regimes of power and knowledge.

Having said this, I want to conclude by indicating another direction in which Foucault's work might take those of us struggling to advance the freedom of sexual minorities.

❧

> Greek ethics is quite dead, and Foucault judged it as undesirable as it would be impossible to resuscitate this ethics; but he considered one of its elements, namely the idea of a work of the self on the self, to be capable of reacquiring a contemporary meaning, in the manner of one of those pagan temple columns that one occasionally sees reutilized in more recent structures.
>
> —Paul Veyne, *Foucault and His Interlocutors*

What sort of potential might Foucault's "resuscitation" of an aesthetics of existence, of the self's work on itself, have for the contemporary struggles of gays/lesbians and queer people against sexual normalization? Recognizing, as many of us do, that individuals make themselves under conditions over which they have little control—conditions marked by systematic inequalities of power associated not only with compulsory heterosexuality but also subordination based on class, race, and gender—we have good reason to challenge the adequacy of unexamined appeals to "choice," or individual autonomy, as sufficient guarantors of erotic justice. At the same time, I agree with those who argue that developing our erotic potentials, our potential for connection with others in a myriad of forms, is critical not only for human flourishing but also for social transformation.[13]

While there is no prima facie reason to rule out S/M as a form of work on the self that might produce new forms of self-understanding and relationships with others, it is important not to privilege this arena. Furthermore, the sorts of arguments developed to create and sustain the social conditions that might enable such forms of self-making are also important. As I have indicated, Halperin links S/M with a project aimed at the dissolution or emptying of the self—a project that he understands as anathema to the principles and values associated with liberal humanism. I suggest that rather than jettison liberal values, we might instead contest dominant understandings of them. After all, a plausible reading of Foucault's so-called antihumanism is that it represented just that—a challenge to prevailing interpretations of this concept within specific institutional and historical situations, and an effort to expose and dislodge particular understandings of humanism insofar as they support pernicious relations of power.

Thus, for example, Morris Kaplan offers a bold and substantive conception of gay and lesbian rights that exploits the radical potential of liberalism. In a brilliant appropriation of *Bowers v. Hardwick,* Kaplan moves beyond the usual liberal demands for decriminalization of sexual behaviors and protections of gays and lesbians from discrimination in employment, housing, and public accommodation to insist that modern, democratic liberal states must recognize a plurality of forms of intimate association as integral to the right to privacy. The freedom to choose our own forms of erotic life, family, and community—and the right to have them recognized by the state—are necessary conditions for fostering and supporting the experiments in living and the ethics of self-making that Foucault endorsed in his late work. Kaplan claims that "it is crucial that queer couples and families emerge in relation to a proliferation of social institutions—from student groups to professional associations to AIDS mobilization to bars, bathhouses and sex clubs . . ." (Kaplan 1997, 225). Within a radically democratic liberal framework, erotic or sexual freedom would not be tantamount to the right to express a given sexuality, but rather the capacity to choose and create the forms of experience, forms of life, and the communities within which we constitute ourselves. Such freedom is secured, and assimilation to dominant norms resisted, by ensuring that there be a wide range of spaces in which "self-making" might take place—livable spaces, not spaces in which individuals are so vulnerable that their practices of freedom involve risking or flirting with social or actual death. One such set of spaces would be those established for exploring erotic possibilities in the form of sexual practices. Another might be the spaces of legally recognized domestic partnerships, or civil unions, in which queer families are creating new forms of intimate association and family life.[14]

Feminist social and political theorist Chesire Calhoun has argued that homosexuality, like heterosexuality, is not merely an orientation of desires or sexual practices but, more broadly, "ways of being oriented in the social world . . . a vantage point [from which one might find it reasonable] to prize a picture of, sit next to, dance with, date, have a crush on, or dream of marrying someone of the same sex" (Calhoun 2000, 101). These ways of being oriented might include a range of alternative social events, films, literatures, and styles of dress. Accordingly, she claims, discriminatory policies are aimed not only at maintaining a normative hierarchy of sexual behavior but also at determining which ways of being oriented in the social world are visible and legitimate. Calhoun develops a more desexualized representation of homosexuality—homosexuality as a form of life, not merely a preference for a particular sexual activity or gender—one in which there are a myriad of practices and discourses within already established structures for contesting dominant norms and expanding our sense of what is possible.

It is easy to imagine Halperin raising the following objections: What distinguishes this radically democratic liberal pluralism from a more pernicious form of liberal pluralism that operates by converting politicized identities or forms of life into private interests and relying on disciplinary power to normalize them? Are these countercultural spaces any less likely to bring such norms to bear upon practices of self-making? Must we not first get free of ourselves? How do we combat the pressures toward assimilation, normalization, and depoliticization that we have come to recognize as so pervasive in modern liberal societies? Can we expect our communities to provide support for work on ourselves and simultaneously serve as sites for a radical questioning of who we are? Perhaps. Can we expect the state to support us in this project? It remains to be seen. And yet, it seems to me that these are questions that might be raised about any political strategy that we adopt.

In his final writings, Foucault suggested that to expect our political theories to answer questions about how best to govern our sexual pleasures is at best futile, and at worst dangerous. He ultimately believed that such questions might more productively and safely be answered within an expanded understanding of erotic autonomy. In other words, the only way we might answer such questions is to find ways to keep the emperor from executing the dreamers. Exploiting the possibilities found within liberal institutions and ideals for securing the spaces necessary for practicing our freedom strikes me as preferable to shattering ourselves.

NOTES

1. A point not lost on Marcuse, to be sure. See Marcuse (1955).

2. Foucault remarks, "the fixing of homosexuals to their sexual specificity is much stronger, they reduce everything to the order of sex." See Foucault (1980, 220).

3. In a pseudonymous description of his own work, Foucault described the question of sexuality as a "relatively privileged case." See Foucault (1998, 461).

4. I am indebted to John Rajchman for this analysis. See Rajchman (1991), especially 96–98.

5. See Calhoun (2000) for a compelling account of the modern construction of the homosexual as a deviant citizen who is inherently immoral and sexually excessive.

6. See the chapter entitled "The Gay Outlaw" in Bersani (1995) for an example of this "tendency."

7. Calhoun (2000) claims that gays and lesbians have little authority as gay or lesbian in the public sphere—that we gain such credibility only at the cost of appearing to be heterosexual.

8. For a provocative account of the centrality of self-shattering to the pleasures of S/M, see Bersani (1995, 94).

9. The question whether gay and lesbian activism designed to secure the right to marry amounts to assimilation to dominant social norms has been at the center of debates among queer and lesbian/gay activists for several years now. See, for example, Warner (1999) and Kaplan (2000, 57–77). Of course, there is a long tradition of feminist (including lesbian feminist) critiques of marriage that antedates this current trend. See, for example, Card (1996).

10. Bersani suggests that despite Foucault's hostility to psychoanalysis, his belief that S/M might have some political importance is most satisfactorily justified within a psychoanalytic account of it. See Bersani (1995, 90).

11. Quoted and translated by Bersani (1995, 77–78). Note that like Halperin, and despite these remarks by Foucault, Bersani believes that Foucault accorded a certain primacy to sex acts as a vehicle for inventing new forms of relationship. As will become clear, I'm skeptical about this reading of Foucault—a reading that must work assiduously to dismiss other possible readings of the passage quoted above. For another reading of what Foucault might have meant at the end of volume 1 of *The History of Sexuality,* when he called for a new economy of "bodies and pleasures," see McWhorter (1999).

12. This distinction between Foucault's work as an intellectual and his work as a

citizen might be fruitfully compared with Kant's distinction between the public and the private use of reason. See Dianna Taylor's "Hannah Arendt and Michel Foucault: Toward a Politics of Transformation," Ph.D. dissertation, SUNY-Binghamton (2000), chapter 2, for a fascinating discussion of Foucault's relationship to Kant and his understanding of critique more generally.

13. See Kaplan (1997). Kaplan's "sexual justice" refers not only to a political ideal governing relations between sexual minorities and the state but also to the capacity of an individual to approximate a "right relation to her own desires" (8).

14. For a provocative defense of the centrality of gay and lesbian marriage rights, and the definitional authority to define marriage and family, to the struggle against gay and lesbian subordination, see Calhoun (2000).

WORKS CITED

Bersani, Leo. 1995. *Homos.* Cambridge: Harvard University Press.

Calhoun, Chesire. 2000. *Feminism, the Family, and the Politics of the Closet.* London: Oxford University Press.

Card, Claudia. 1996. "Against Marriage and Motherhood." *Hypatia* 11: 1–23.

Deleuze, Gilles. 1997. "Desire and Pleasure." In *Foucault and His Interlocutors.* Edited by Arnold I. Davidson. 183–92. Chicago: University of Chicago Press.

Foucault, Michel. 1978. *The History of Sexuality.* Volume 1. *An Introduction.* Translated by Robert Hurley. New York: Vintage.

———. 1980. "The Confession of the Flesh." In *Power Knowledge: Selected Interviews and Other Writings, 1972–1977.* Edited by Colin Gordon. 194–228. New York: Pantheon.

———. 1984a. "On the Genealogy of Ethics: Overview of a Work in Progress." In *The Foucault Reader.* Edited by Paul Rabinow. 340–72. New York: Pantheon.

———. 1984b. "What Is Enlightenment?" In *The Foucault Reader.* Edited by Paul Rabinow. 32–50. New York: Pantheon.

———. 1986. "Postscript." In *Death and the Labyrinth: The World of Raymond Roussel.* Translated by Charles Ruas. Introduction by John Ashbery. 169–86. Berkeley: University of California Press.

———. 1988a. "Technologies of the Self." In *Technologies of the Self: A Seminar with Michel Foucault.* Edited by Luther Martin, Huck Gutman, and Patrick Hutton. 16–49. Amherst: University of Massachusetts Press.

———. 1988b. "Sexual Choice, Sexual Act: Foucault and Homosexuality." In *Michel Foucault: Politics, Philosophy, Culture: Interviews and Other Writings, 1977–1984.* Edited by Lawrence D. Kritzman. 286–303. New York: Routledge.

———. 1994. "Sex, Power, and the Politics of Identity." In *Ethics: Subjectivity and Truth.* Edited by Paul Rabinow. 161–73. New York: New Press.

———. 1998. "Foucault." In *Aesthetics, Method, and Epistemology.* Edited by James D. Faubion. 459–63. New York: New Press.

Freud, Sigmund. 1978. *The Interpretation of Dreams.* Translated by A. A. Brill. New York: Modern Library.

Halperin, David. 1995. *Saint Foucault: Toward a Gay Hagiography*. London: Oxford University Press.

Kaplan, Morris. 1997. *Sexual Justice: Democratic Citizenship and the Politics of Desire*. New York: Routledge.

———. 2000. "Constructing Queer Communities: Marriage, Sex, Death, and Other Fantasies." *Constellations* 8 (1): 57–77.

Marcuse, Herbert. 1955. *Eros and Civilization: A Philosophical Inquiry into Freud*. New York: Vintage.

McWhorter, Ladelle. 1999. *Bodies and Pleasures: Foucault and the Politics of Sexual Normalization*. Bloomington: Indiana University Press.

Miller, James. 1993. *The Passions of Michel Foucault*. New York: Simon & Schuster.

Rajchman, John. 1991. *Truth and Eros: Foucault, Lacan, and the Question of Ethics*. New York: Routledge.

Taylor, Dianna. 2000. "Hannah Arendt and Michel Foucault: Toward a Politics of Transformation." Ph.D. diss. SUNY-Binghamton.

Veyne, Paul. 1997. "The Final Foucault and His Ethics." In *Foucault and His Interlocutors*. Edited by Arnold I. Davidson. 225–33. Chicago: University of Chicago Press.

Warner, Michael. 1999. *The Trouble with Normal: Sex, Politics, and the Ethics of Queer Life*. New York: Free Press.

❧ 9

Bodies and Power Revisited

Judith Butler

Foucault's early approach to the question of bodies and power is perhaps best known in his analysis of the body of the prisoner in *Discipline and Punish*. Many of us have read and reread this analysis and tried to understand how power acts upon a body, but also how power comes to craft and form a body. The distinction between the two is vexing, since it seems that to the extent that power acts on a body, the body is anterior to power; and to the extent that power forms a body, the body is in some ways, or to some extent, made by power. One can find it clearly in Foucault's own description. In *Discipline and Punish,* he writes, for instance, that "systems of punishment are to be situated in a certain 'political economy' of the body" (1979, 25). And when he attempts to situate the way the body is "directly involved in a political field," he describes the process this way: "Power relations have an immediate hold upon it; they invest it, mark it, train it, torture it, force it to carry out tasks, to perform ceremonies, to emit signs" (1979, 25).[1] Here the body is described not merely in its docility, but in its vulnerability to coercion. It is "forced" to do certain things, and it does them in accord with the demands made upon it. The force that compels the action does not remain anterior to the action itself. The action itself becomes forceful, and in ways that are not always in accord with the original aims of coercive power. "The body," Foucault writes, "becomes a useful force only if it is both a productive body and a subjected body" ["s'il est à la fois corps productif et corps assujetti"] (1979, 26; 31, French). The power imposed upon a body is to be understood as part of the "political technology of the body," a technology that operates through a "micro-physics" exercised in the form of a "strategy" (1979, 26; 31, French). A strategy is not to be understood as a unilateral imposition of power, but precisely an operation of power that is at once productive, diffuse, various in its forms. In relation to this "strategy," which, he makes clear, is not "appropriated" by an anterior subject, one must discern "a network of relations, constantly in tension, in activity, rather than a privilege that one might possess" (1979, 26).

One can see here, in the description by which power is cast as a strategy that works on and through the body, that it takes place through at least two disclaimers, both of which have to do with the status of the subject. On the one hand, a strategy will not be "appropriated," and so not be that which a subject takes on or takes up. On the other hand, a strategy will be an operation of power that is not "possessed" by a subject. So the subject is left behind as the relation of power to the body emerges. But this abandonment, this negation, forms the necessary background for understanding what power is. We will not understand its distinctiveness if we are constrained by understanding power as what one possesses or as that which one appropriates. It will be neither appropriation nor possession and, whatever it will be, will be distinct from at least these two capacities of a subject. Indeed, Foucault immediately offers an account of the agency of the body which is meant to show how one might, in the context of a theory of power, disjoin the thinking of agency from the presupposition of the subject. The theory of power that presupposes the subject once again introduces the notion of bodily agency he would have us accept, but it introduces it by way of a defining negation: "This power is not exercised simply as an obligation or a prohibition on those who 'do not have it'; it invests them, is transmitted by them and through them; it exerts pressure upon them, just as they themselves, in their struggle against it, resist the grip it has on them" ["prennent appui à leur tour sur les prises qu'il exerce sur eux"] (1979, 27; 31–32, French). So power is neither possessed nor not possessed by a subject, since here, in the moment in which a certain "they" is invoked, the "they" are both invested by power and in a struggle against it. It is apparently not something *in* "them," an inherent feature, an abiding interiority, which is invested or which resists, but a feature of power itself, conceived as strategy. Foucault would have us reconceptualize both investment and resistance as different modalities of "a constant tension" and "activity" ["toujours tendues, toujours en activité"], if not a "perpetual battle ["la bataille perpétuelle"] (1979, 26; 31, French). But who is the "they" who struggle and resist? When we try to trace the referent for this "they"—a pronoun and, hence, a personification—it vacillates between two referents: a set of persons and a set of power relations. On the one hand, it refers to "they" who are said not to have power and who, "in their struggle against it, resist the grip it has on them" (1979, 27). And it refers, within the same set of sentences, to "relations" that "go right down into the depths of society" and that, a bit later, are given personified form: "they are not univocal; they define innumerable points of confrontation, focuses of instability, each of which has its own risks of conflict, of struggles, and of an at least temporary inversion of the power relations" (1979, 27).[2]

The "they" is thus at once a humanized referent—those who, in another vocabulary, are said not to have power—and a set of power relations, which are said to sustain certain risks, to constitute certain sites of confrontation. One conventional criticism of Foucault is that he personifies power and de-personifies or dehumanizes persons by making them into the effects of pow-er. But I think we would be mistaken to draw this conclusion too quickly.[3] The vacillation he performs for us, through his practice of ambiguous ref-erence, is an effort to compel us to think according to a nonconventional grammar, a nonconventional way of conceptualizing the relation of the sub-ject and power. That the discussion centers here on the body, as a political economy and, more specifically, a political technology, is not mere back-ground. If there is a certain activity, tension, even battle, that this concep-tualization of the body in terms of "strategy" implies, then is this very ac-tivity, tension, battle, capacity for inversion, a function of the body or a function of power? We know that it is not understood explicitly as a func-tion of the subject. But note how the body emerges here as a way of taking over the theory of agency previously ascribed to the subject. The body does not, however, assume this agency by virtue of some capacities or functions internal to the body itself. It assumes this agency at the same time that the referent to the subject and to the body becomes ambiguous, so that we can-not discern, even upon a close reading of Foucault's texts, whether "they" refers to persons or to relations of power. Under what conditions do activ-ities of the kind that Foucault here seeks to describe presuppose a certain ambiguity between subjects and power? How are we to understand that am-biguity? Is there a new theory of the subject prefigured by this "they" that emerges after the subject, understood in terms of appropriation and pos-session, has been set aside? If appropriation and possession are no longer the defining activities of the subject, and "activity" itself has been redefined as constant, tense, embattled, transvaluative, is this because the new subject, the one who Foucault is trying to introduce to us, is one whose activity is invariably embodied?

When Foucault writes about the movements against incarceration in the nineteenth century, he reminds us that "they were revolts, at the level of the body, against the very body of the prison" ["Il s'agissait bien d'une ré-volte, au niveau des corps, contre le corps même de la prison"] (1979, 30; 35, French). But by using the word "body" twice, once to refer to people, and another time to refer to the institution, he makes clear that he is deal-ing with a conception of the body that is not restricted to the human sub-ject. When he speaks about revolts against the prison system, he makes clear that "all these movements—and the innumerable discourses that the prison has given rise to since the early nineteenth century—have been about the body and material things" (1979, 30). The body is one such material thing, but so is the prison. But these are not exactly two forms of materiality. On the contrary, the very materiality of the prison has to be understood in terms of its strategic action upon and with the body; it is defined in relation to the body: "[the] very materiality [of the prison environment is] an instrument and vector [*vecteur*] of power; it is this whole technology of power over the body that the technology of the 'soul'—that of the educationalists, psychologists, and psychiatrists—fails either to conceal or to compensate, for the simple reason that it is one of its tools" (1979, 30; 35, French). So it is not just that the movements of the nineteenth century are *about* the body and material things, as if these are two unrelated objects for such movements. It is rather that the very materiality of the prison is activated on the body of the prisoner, and through the technology of the soul. The soul is another matter, and we will return to it another time.[4] But for now, consider that for Foucault, the conception of agency that is being conceptualized beyond the theory of the subject is the activity of a strategy, where that strategy consists of the activation of the materiality of the prison on and through, and in tension with, the materiality of the body. Materiality might be said, then, to diverge from itself, to redouble itself, to be at once institution and body, and to denote the process by which the one passes over into the other (or, indeed, the process by which both "institution" and "body" come into separate existence in and through this prior and conditioning divergence). And the distinction between the two is the site where the one makes a transition into the other. To say it is a "site" is to offer a spatial metaphor for a temporal process, and so to derail the explanation from its point, but it would be equally wrong to eclipse the spatial through recourse to a purely temporal explanation. The disjuncture between institution and body, and the passage between them it provides, are where agency is to be found.

Foucault calls this a moment, a site, a scene, using several words to describe this process, substituting a set of provisional names for a technical definition, conveying perhaps that no noun can capture the moment here. So this nexus provides the condition for power to become redirected, proliferated, altered, transvaluated. The introduction of the "nexus," however, is not simply, or exclusively, a way of thinking about power. It is also a way of redefining the body. For the body is not a substance, a surface, an inert or inherently docile object; nor is it a set of internal drives that qualify it as the locus of rebellion and resistance. Understood as the nodal point, the nexus, this site of the application of power undergoes a redirection and, in this sense, is a certain kind of undergoing. So if the "nexus" redefines power as that which is strategy, meaning activity and dispersion and transvaluation, so the "nexus" redefines the body as that which is also a kind of undergoing, the condition for a redirection, active, tense, embattled.

It would be one alternative to say that the nodal point is where or what the body is and to seek recourse to an account of the body that would establish its capacity for resistance and show why it qualifies as this moment. But I think that would be a mistake (and it would reduce Foucault too quickly perhaps to Deleuze). It seems to me that not only the subject but the body itself is being redefined, such that the body is not a substance, not a thing, not a set of drives, not a cauldron of resistant impulse, but precisely the site of transfer for power itself. Power happens to this body, but this body is also the occasion in which something unpredictable (and, hence, undialectical) happens to power; it is one site of its redirection, profusion, and transvaluation. And it will not do to say it is passive in one respect and active in another. Indeed, to be such a site seems to be part of what Foucault means when he describes the body as "material." To be material is not only to be obdurate and resistant to what works upon it, but to be the vector and instrument of a continued "working." His language, his vacillations, his reformulations, compel us to rethink this relation again and again. So when Foucault says "the body becomes a useful force only if it is both a productive body and a subjected body," it is not that the body happens to be subjected and happens also to be productive, but that subjection and production are given "à la fois," and quite fundamentally (1979, 26). The body in subjection becomes the occasion and condition of its productivity, where the latter is not finally separable from the former. These are not two bodies—one subjected, another productive—for the body is also the movement, the passage, between subjection and productivity. And in this sense, it is the name given to the nexus of a transvaluation understood as an undergoing and also, perhaps ultimately for Foucault, a passion.

We can see in the above that Foucault is trying to understand how power can be thwarted at the site of its application, how a certain possibility of resistance and redirection takes the place of a mechanical effect. In the place of a theory of agency located *in* a subject, we are asked to understand, in different contexts, and through different venues, the way that power is compelled into a redirection by virtue of having the body as its vector and instrument. Indeed, the theory of the subject is backgrounded, if not fully declined, for the conceptual point at issue here is to think agency in the very relation between power and bodies, as the continued activity of power as it changes course, proliferates, becomes more diffuse, through taking material form.

Discipline and Punish was published in France in 1975; in 1981, Foucault offered the important essay "The Subject and Power" to Hubert Dreyfus and Paul Rabinow as the Afterword to their book *Michel Foucault: Beyond Structuralism and Hermeneutics*. So it was six or seven years after the publication of the above analysis that he claimed, "the goal of my work during the last twenty years . . . has not been to analyze the phenomena of power, . . . [but] to create a history of the different modes by which, in our culture, human beings are made subjects" (Foucault 1982a, 208). Now we might wonder if Foucault is telling the truth about what his goal has been for the last twenty years. Or it may be that it only appears to him at the end of twenty years, approximately 1961 to 1981, that this is what his goal has always been and that the Owl of Minerva is flying here at dusk. Of course, to come to believe this and to write this at the end of twenty years is not quite the same as having had that goal for twenty years. But perhaps we can also ask whether the analysis of bodies and power in *Discipline and Punish* is an effort to create a history of some of the modes by which, in our culture, human beings are made into subjects.

Foucault refers to subjection in *Discipline and Punish*, and this word, as it is well known, carries a double meaning: *assujettissement* means both subjection (in the sense of subordination) and becoming a subject. It seems as well to contain the paradox of power as that which both acts upon and activates a body. But if power is not the only mode by which a subject is produced, then perhaps the very notion of production, so central to Foucault's early work, is not appropriate for what he seeks now to describe. When he asks, then, how human beings are "made" into subjects, or how they are "crafted" or, indeed, "craft themselves," he is providing for accounts of construction that are not reducible to power in its productive effect. And if the subject now reenters the scene or can become foregrounded within it, it is because the subject is made in times and places in which it is not conceived as a sovereign agent, a possessor of rights or power, an already constituted appropriating agency of the effects of power.

Discipline and Punish gives us bodies and power and asks us to consider how power acts upon, and enacts, a body. But subsequently, indeed starting as early as 1978, Foucault begins to think again about the subject, and to reconsider the body in its mode as crafted and, indeed, in the service of a certain self-crafting.

In "The Subject and Power," and in the volumes of *The History of Sexuality* that follow the first, Foucault turns away from power as a central theme. Is this because he ceases to think about power or because he begins to think about the problem he has identified as power in a new way, and under a new set of rubrics? How does a certain agency, a forceful action, indeed a revolt, emerge from the midst of constraint? How does the condition of being acted on by power produce an action that exceeds the passivity of the target? In

"The Subject and Power," Foucault makes clear that he thinks that the best way to analyze power is through taking resistance as a point of departure. Is he suggesting that we do not start with how power acts but rather seek to know power by the resistance it compels? This new procedure does not, by the way, seem to be the methodological point of departure in *Discipline and Punish*, a text that has been criticized by some for not taking resistance seriously enough. In any case, Foucault writes that "another way to go further towards a new economy of power relations . . . consists of taking the forms of resistance against different forms of power as a starting point . . . it consists of analyzing power relations through the antagonism of strategies" (1982a, 210–11). He then refers to forms of opposition that are conventionally understood as "anti-authority struggles" and offers, as the ultimate characterization of these struggles, that they pose the question, "who are we?" (1982a, 212). In opposing authoritative forms of power, we become unknowing about who we are. Why should this be the case? There is a recognition that power is involved in the very making of who we are and in constraining the ways in which we might refer to ourselves and ultimately represent ourselves. Foucault makes this clear when he characterizes such movements as opposing "this form of power [that] applies itself to immediate everyday life which categorizes the individual, marks him by his own individuality, attaches him to his own identity, imposes a law of truth on him which he must recognize and which others have to recognize in him" (1982a, 212).

This formulation starts to outline the specific mechanism by which power acts on a subject and transforms a human being into a subject. But note that these are not the same. If power acts on a subject, then it seems as if the subject is there to be acted on prior to the acting of power. But if power produces a subject, then it seems that the production that power performs is the mechanism by which the subject comes into being. And whereas before we were told that power produces as one of its effects a resistance to productive power itself, we now focus on relatively recent historical formations of resistance or opposition—an even stronger word— to ways of producing the subject. So in this discussion the subject is not only produced by power but objects to and counters the way in which it *is* produced by power.

If the word "subjection" (*assujettissement*) has two meanings, to subordinate someone to power and to become a subject, it presupposes the subject in its first meaning and induces the subject in its second. Is there a contradiction here, or is it a paradox—a constitutive paradox—which he already considered in a different light when, in *Discipline and Punish*, he distinguished between the subjected and productive body? Is he now using the one word, "subjection," to denote both sides of that coin? And what has happened to the body? Is it still with us? Is he, then, suggesting that the only way to become a subject is through the process by which we are subordinated to power? Or is he suggesting that through our subordination to power we run the risk of becoming, indeed, something other than what power, as it were, had in mind for us? In particular, the subject objects to the way in which power categorizes the subject and attaches him to his own identity. What does this mean? What does it mean to be subject to power in such a way that power attaches you to your own identity?

I suggested above that we might understand Foucault as implicitly theorizing a kind of undergoing or passion when he queried how the body becomes the nexus for the redirection of power. In this context, it seems, we have another implicit theorization of passion, since the subject is *not* produced in a simply mechanical way, but power "attaches" a subject to its own identity. Subjects appear to require this self-attachment, this process by which one becomes attached to one's own subjecthood. This is not precisely clarified by Foucault, and even the term "attachment" does not receive an independent critical analysis. Indeed, I cannot help but wonder whether such an analysis would have led Foucault to consider Freud on the matter of self-preservation and, consequently, on self-destruction; and whether his refusal to subject the term to critical scrutiny was not, in part, a refusal to follow that path. What does seem to be at work here is perhaps a Spinozistic presumption that every being seeks to persist in its own being, to develop an attachment, or cathexis, to what will further the cause of its own self-preservation and self-enhancement. But for Foucault, it is clear that one attaches to oneself through a norm, and so self-attachment is socially mediated; it is no immediate and transparent relation to the self. It is also contingent: we will become attached to ourselves through mediating norms, norms that give us back a sense of who we are, norms that will cultivate our investment in ourselves. But depending on what these norms are, we will be limited to that degree in how we might persist in who we are. What falls outside the norms will not, strictly speaking, be recognizable. And this does not mean that it is inconsequential; on the contrary, it is precisely that domain of ourselves that we live without recognizing, which we persist in through a sense of disavowal, that for which we have no vocabulary, but which we endure without quite knowing. This can be, clearly, a source of suffering. But it can be as well the sign of a certain distance from regulatory norms, and so also a site for new possibility.

Even though Foucault asks us to look away from a theory of power at this juncture, we can defy him gently and see that the theory of power becomes linked with norms of recognition. Power can act upon a subject only if it imposes norms of recognizability on that subject's existence. Further, the subject must desire recognition, and so find himself or herself fundamentally attached to the categories that guarantee social existence. This desire for recognition constitutes, then, a specific vulnerability, if power imposes a law of truth that the subject is *obliged* to recognize. This means that one's fundamental attachment to oneself, an attachment without which one cannot be, is constrained in advance by social norms, and that the failure to conform to these norms puts at risk that capacity to sustain a sense of one's enduring status as a subject.

It would appear from the above that social norms exercise full and final power here. But is there not a way to intervene upon the working of the law of truth? There appears to be a law of truth, part of the workings of the regime of knowledge, which imposes a truth upon a subject for whom there is no choice but to recognize this law of truth. But why is there no choice? Who is speaking here? Is it Foucault, or is it the "Law" itself? The law of truth imposes a criterion by which recognition becomes possible. The subject is not recognizable without first conforming to the law of truth, and without recognition there is no subject—or so Foucault, in Hegelian fashion, seems to imply.[5] Similarly, others "have" to recognize this law of truth in him, because the law is what established the criterion of subjecthood according to which the subject can be recognized at all. In order to be, we might say, we must become recognizable, but to challenge the norms by which recognition is conferred is, in some ways, to risk one's very being, to become questionable in one's ontology, to risk one's very recognizability as a subject.

It also means something more, however. If one is compelled to attach to oneself through the available norm, this means that to question the norm, to call for new norms, is to detach oneself from oneself, and so not only to cease to become self-identical but to perform a certain operation on one's passionate attachment to oneself. This means, in fact, suspending the narcissistic gratifications that conforming to the norm supplies, a satisfaction that comes from the moment of believing that the one whom one sees framed by the norm is identical to the one who is looking. Jacques Lacan tells us that this form of self-identification is always hallucinatory, and that there is no final approximation of the mirror image, that narcissism is always derailed or, indeed, humiliated in this process. In an analogous way, we might say that conforming to the norm allows one to become, for the moment, fully recognizable, but since the norms at issue are constrained, one sees there, in the conformity, the sign of one's constraint. Indeed, perhaps we can speculate that the moment of resistance, of opposition, emerges precisely when we find ourselves attached to our constraint, and so constrained in our very attachment. To the extent that we question the promise of those norms that constrain our recognizability, we open the way for attachment itself to live in some less constrained way. But for attachment to live in a less constrained way is for it to risk unrecognizability, and the various punishments that await those who do not conform to the social order.

Thus, Foucault, in "What Is Critique," makes clear that the point of view of critique requires risking the suspension of one's own ontological status (1997).[6] He asks, "'What, therefore, am I,' I who belong to this humanity, perhaps to this piece of it, at this point in time, at this instant of humanity which is subjected to the power of truth in general and truths in particular?" (1997, 46). Put another way: "What, given the contemporary order of being, can I be?" And he clearly holds out for a possibility of a desire that exceeds the terms of recognizable identity when he asks, for instance, what one might become. This seems central to his task when he calls for the production of new subjectivities, for becoming something other than what we have been, and so for becoming itself as a way of life.

By 1983, he seems to be even more removed from the analysis of *Discipline and Punish*. He established his distance from the theory of power through a preterition, a rhetorical figure by which one mentions, sometimes emphatically, the very thing that one seeks to minimize:

> I am no theoretician of power. The question of power does not interest me. When I did speak often about this question of power, I did so because the given political analysis of the phenomenon of power could not be properly given justice from the fine and small appearances which I wanted to recall, when I asked about the "dire-vrai" about oneself. If I "tell the truth" about myself, I constitute myself as subject by a certain number of relationships of power, which weigh upon me, and which weigh upon others. . . . I am working on the way the reflexivity of self to self has been established and which discourse of truth is tied to it. (Foucault 1989, 254)

Reflexivity enters, as it does with the later volumes of *The History of Sexuality,* to make the claim that it is the venue through which power creates and informs the subject. And whereas it may seem that the subject was vanquished in *Discipline and Punish* and perhaps more seriously still in the first volume of *The History of Sexuality* only to be resurrected in the early 1980s, it is important to note that this is a very different subject that emerged. Similarly, one might suspect that the body ceases to provide the central way to think about power, but this would be, I believe, a mistaken reading. The subject who emerges here is still no sovereign, is still not one who is free to appropriate or not appropriate the effects of power that come its way, or that can be figured to possess or to lack basic rights or properties. This subject is more deeply constrained and manifests its agency in the midst of this constraint. Moreover, Foucault has also told us, and consistently so, that the very reflexivity through which power works is one of attachment and, hence, one of desire or passion of some kind. Power weighs upon that attachment to myself, and it weighs upon others, and it puts us in a common bind of undergoing that constraint, and of resisting its offer of recognizability and, hence, intelligibility. It also lays out for us the risks that becoming something that challenges recognizability entails. What must I be in order to be recognized, and what criterion holds sway here at the very condition of my own emergence? What is this "I" who can ask about its recognizability? Does it not exceed the very terms it seeks to interrogate?

So whereas power acted upon the body, and the body was said to revolt against that coercion, now it seems that power acts upon the body, specifically, in the very formulation of bodily passion in its self-persistence and knowability the very modes by which we affectively seize upon or release a fundamental sense of identity. The body in some ways becomes passion in this reformulation, a passion for my own being which must pass through what is Other, the condition of my reflexivity in which I undergo those norms over which I have no choice. It is also, however, in that undergoing that I stand a chance of discovering some other way to be.

Although Foucault sometimes spoke as if one might simply opt out of identity and create, as if through a simple transcendence, something new, a new set of subjectivities, some new forms of life, I would suggest that he had another conception of transformation at work. If we understand the norms by which we are obliged to recognize ourselves and others as those that work upon us, to which we must submit, then submission is one part of a social process by which recognizability is achieved. We are, as it were, worked upon, and only through being worked upon do we become a "we." But matters do not need to end there. The conditions for revolt were also occasioned by submission, by the fact that human passion for self-persistence makes us vulnerable to those who promise us our bread. If we had no appetite, we would be free from coercion, but because we are from the start given over to what is outside us, submitting to the terms that give form to our existence, we are in this respect—and irreversibly—vulnerable to exploitation. The question that Foucault opens, though, is how desire might become produced beyond the norms of recognition, even as it makes a new demand for recognition. And here he seems to find the seeds of transformation in the life of a passion that lives and thrives at the borders of recognizability, which still has the limited freedom of not yet being false or true, which establishes a critical distance on the terms that decide our being.

193

NOTES

1. "Mais le corps est aussi directement plongé dans un champ politique; les rapports de pouvoir opèrent sur lui une prise immédiate; ils l'investissent, le marquent, le dressent, le supplicient, l'astreignent à des travaux, l'obligent à des cérémonies, exigent de lui des signes" (1975, 30).

2. "Enfin elles ne sont pas univoques; elles définissent des points innombrables d'affrontement, des foyers d'instabilité dont chacun comporte ses risques de conflit, de luttes, et d'inversion au moins transitoire des rapports de forces" (1975, 32).

3. This represents not only a misunderstanding of power but a failure to understand that the "effect" in Foucault is not the simple and unilateral consequence of a prior cause. "Effects" do not stop being effected: they are incessant activities, in a Spinozistic sense. They do not, in this sense, presuppose power as a "cause"; on the contrary, they recast power as an activity of effectuation with no origin and no end.

4. See my discussion of this passage (1993, 32–35).

5. For Foucault's debt to Hegel, see the appendix in Foucault (1982b), originally published as *L'archéologie du savoir* (Paris: Gallimard, 1969).

6. This essay was originally a lecture given at the French Society of Philosophy on May 27, 1978, subsequently published in *Bulletin de la Société française de philosophie* 84:2 (1990): 35–63.

WORKS CITED

Butler, Judith. 1993. *Bodies that Matter.* New York: Routledge.

Foucault, Michel 1975. *Surveillir et punir: Naissance de la prison.* Paris: Gallimard.

———. 1979. *Discipline and Punish: The Birth of the Prison.* Translated by Alan Sheridan. New York: Vintage.

———. 1982a. "The Subject and Power." In *Michel Foucault: Beyond Structuralism and Hermeneutics.* By Hubert L. Dreyfus and Paul Rabinow. 208–26. Chicago: University of Chicago Press.

———. 1982b. "The Discourse on Language." In *The Archaeology of Knowledge and the Discourse on Language.* Translated by Alan Sheridan Smith. New York: Pantheon.

———. 1989. "How Much Does It Cost for Reason to Tell the Truth?" In *Foucault Live.* Translated by Mia Foret and Marion Martius. 348–62. New York: Semiotext(e).

———. 1997. "What Is Critique?" In *The Politics of Truth.* Edited by Sylvère Lotringer and Lysa Hochroth. 23–82. New York: Semiotext(e).

Part 3:
Feminist Ethos as Politics

Feminist Identity Politics: Transforming the Political

Susan Hekman

Identity politics and the questions it has raised have polarized the feminist community in recent decades. The defenders of identity politics argue that it is a necessary antidote to liberal politics' exclusion and denigration of women and other marginalized identities. Identity politics, they assert, brings these marginalized identities into the political arena, granting them the political agency they have been denied. With regard to the specific case of feminist identity politics, they argue that only by uniting under the banner "women" can feminists achieve their political goals.

The critics of identity politics are just as vehement in their condemnation of the practice. Appealing to the arguments of postmodernism and post-structuralism, these critics argue that identity politics falsely fixes the identity of its participants and is thus a counterproductive political strategy. In her now (in)famous condemnation of identity politics, *Gender Trouble*, Judith Butler argues that we must replace the essentialist subject of modernist discourse with inessential woman, a being constructed by the discourses constituting her world. Butler condemns identity politics because, rather than accomplishing this goal, it merely fixes the identity of "woman" in a new location. The critics of identity politics thus argue that the political practice of identity politics is damaging to the feminist cause in several important respects. By subsuming all women under one category we deny the differences between women, inadvertently privileging one group of women. We also embrace the injured identity that excluded women from politics in the first place (Brown 1995).

In this essay I would like to sidestep the polarities of this debate by arguing that implicit in the theory and practice of identity politics is a fundamental challenge to the grounding assumptions of liberal politics. It is my contention that the feminist debate surrounding identity politics cannot be resolved within the confines of liberal politics because it transforms the basis of that politics. First, identity politics brings identity into the political arena, violating one of the most fundamental tenets of liberalism. Liberalism's universal citizen has no identity; he [sic] is abstract, eschewing the particularity of identity. Identity politics challenges this by bringing the particular into politics. Second, identity politics challenges another fundamental assumption of liberalism: the autonomous, agentic subject. Although the critics of identity politics accuse it of fixing identity, in practice identity politics reveals the social constitution of identities. Identity politics emphasizes that identities are created, not given; it is about challenging the identity we have been assigned and espousing another. It presupposes that we are not the autonomous agents of liberalism but the products of discursive regimes. Third, identity politics reveals that the forces that constitute our identities are everywhere; they transcend the strictly legal/political sphere. It thus forces us to look for the power that creates subjects/identity everywhere in society. Fourth, as a consequence, identity politics demands a new strategy of resistance. If power is everywhere, so must resistance be. Resisting state power is not enough; resistance, like power, must be everywhere.

My argument is that identity politics has the potential to radically alter liberal conceptions of identity, power, and resistance but that this potential has not been realized. The question of identity politics is a question that cannot be answered within liberalism because the elements of that question are defined as illegitimate in liberal politics. My goal in the following is to explore the dimensions of identity politics' transformation of liberalism with the hope that this will begin the process of moving beyond its parameters.

In order to explore these questions, I will employ the work of Michel Foucault. Foucault's work is usually cited by the critics of identity politics to challenge the fixing of identity that it allegedly entails. I am citing his work not to argue for or against identity politics as it exists today but to develop a new perspective on the significance of identity politics in the context of liberalism. Although identity politics has the potential to transform liberalism, that potential has been thwarted by the structure of the liberal polity. Foucault's theory of power is significant in this context because it challenges the juridical conception of power that informs liberalism and, by default, identity politics. His theory of subjectification challenges the autonomous subject that likewise grounds liberal theory and practice. Together these theories offer an understanding of power and resistance that places the practice of identity politics in a different light. Although I will argue that Foucault ultimately fails to fulfill the radical potential of his theories, he nevertheless lays the groundwork for a new conception of politics in general and identity politics in particular.

The principal thesis I will develop with regard to the significance of Foucault's work for identity politics is that the source of women's subordination/subjectification has undergone a significant shift in recent years.

Whereas for most of Western history the control of women's sexuality has been linked to state power, in the last half century the locus of that control has moved beyond the state into civil society. This move is the culmination of a trend that, according to Foucault, began in the sixteenth century. It constitutes a change of historical proportions. In her ambitious book *The Creation of Patriarchy* (1986), Gerda Lerner argues that the subordination of women was institutionalized in the first written legal codes in the Middle East. Previous to the emergence of these codes, roughly 1750 B.C., the source of women's subordination was the patriarchal family. Lerner argues that the enactment of these laws, like all laws, is an indication that the practice it addresses existed and had become problematic (1986, 102). In other words, the control of women by the patriarchal family had become insufficient, and it was necessary for the state to step in and reinforce that control.

One of the significant results of this development was that, from its inception, the archaic state recognized its dependence on the patriarchal family. And, most importantly, the orderly functioning of the patriarchal family was equated with order in the public domain (ibid., 121). Thus the patriarchal family was defined as the basic building block of political order. Specifically, the control of women's sexuality was the responsibility of the state; punishment for deviation from the established code of sexuality was the state's responsibility. The legal classification and regulation of women's sexual activities, Lerner argues, was a historical watershed.

I believe that women in the contemporary United States are at another historical watershed. One of the principal goals of the U.S. women's movement since the 1960s has been to remove the regulation and control of women's sexuality from the purview of the state. This effort has had significant success. Most, if not all, of the legal restrictions on women have been removed. In her analysis of the history of marriage in the United States, *Public Vows*, Nancy Cott (2000) documents this success. After enumerating the myriad ways in which marriage has constrained women throughout U.S. history, Cott then analyzes the series of legal decisions that have removed the majority of those restraints. Her thesis is that the law establishes and maintains an "official morality" that, until recently, has been centrally defined in terms of marriage. In recent decades, however, the Supreme Court has moved toward displacing marriage from the seat of that official morality (Cott 2000, 199). Her conclusion is that "This alteration between marriage and the state might be called 'disestablishment'" (ibid., 212). Although Cott qualifies this conclusion by arguing that this disestablishment does not apply to homosexuals and that marriage remains a privileged status, she nevertheless argues that the political role of marriage has evaporated as "ballast for the form of governance" (ibid., 213).

It does not follow from this that the legal/political sphere is now irrelevant. The second-class citizen status of women is still implicit in many legal definitions. In an era of conservative politics, the reinstitution of legal restrictions on women is a continual threat. What does follow, however, is that we must look beyond the strictly legal/political structure of our society in order to combat the subordination of women. We need a dual strategy that targets both the political and social realms. And, increasingly, our focus must be on the social rather than the political. My argument is that identity politics has the potential to provide such a strategy.

POWER AND THE STATE

Foucault never specifically examines the subordination of women or the source(s) of their subjectification. But if we look at this theory from the perspective of the thesis I have advanced, his work provides an analysis of the emergence and functioning of this new form of power over women. Foucault states clearly that the goal of his work is to trace the evolution of a new form of power in Western society since the sixteenth century. His thesis is that this new form of power demands a form of analysis that is lacking in what he calls the juridical conception of power that dominates political theory. In the course of his analysis, Foucault identifies several new forms of this power rather than one. This in itself is significant. Foucault is not arguing, as did Marx, that power has shifted from one single location to another. Rather, he argues that power has become diffused. Instead of emanating from a single source, it is spread throughout every corner of society, informing the social structure as a whole.

Foucault's effort to trace the genealogy of these new forms of power leads him, first of all, to the Christian church in the Middle Ages. He argues that the practices of the church developed a kind of power that had the individual as its object: "This form of power applies itself to immediate everyday life which categorizes the individual, marks him by his own individuality, attaches him to his own identity, imposes a law of truth on him which he must recognize and which others have to recognize in him" (1983, 212). Foucault asserts that this form of power, what he calls "pastoral power," was integrated into the modern Western state, turning that state into "A modern matrix of individualization, or a new form of pastoral power" (ibid., 215).

Foucault has much to say about pastoral power, but for my purposes the most significant is his claim that non-state institutions, most notably the family, were mobilized to carry out pastoral power (ibid., 215). In other words, as the Western state takes on a radically new function, overseeing the individuality of its subjects, the locus of power is diffused beyond the state to the institutions of civil society. And central among these institutions is the family, the source of most gender socialization and definition.

One of Foucault's means of characterizing the workings of pastoral power is "disciplinary power." The purpose of *Discipline and Punish* (1979) was to present a genealogy of this power, its effects and justifications. But Foucault's study is much more than a history of prisons. Prisons are, after all, state institutions. Foucault's point, however, is that this manifestation of state power changed the nature of power itself. He argues that disciplinary relations "go right down into the depths of society, that they are not localized in relations between the state and its citizens" (ibid., 27). In the seventeenth and eighteenth centuries, disciplinary methods, which had been in existence in various social institutions, became general formulas of domination: "Discipline may be identified neither within an institution nor within an apparatus; it is a type of power, a modality for its exercise, comprising a whole set of instruments, techniques, procedures, levels of application, targets; it is a 'physics' or an 'anatomy' of power, a technology" (ibid., 215).

Central to disciplinary power is the distinction between the normal and the abnormal. Disciplining subjects means channeling their behavior in the "right" direction and defining other activities as abnormal, deviant. This power of normalization is, for Foucault, diffused throughout society. But, significantly, he defines one locus of this power as crucial: the family. The family, he argues, is the "privileged locus" of the emergence of disciplinary power. It is in the family that the essence of disciplinary power, the distinction between the normal and the abnormal, is defined and enforced (ibid., 216).

Two themes dominate Foucault's discussion of disciplinary power. First, it is radically incompatible with relations of sovereignty (1980b, 104). Disciplinary power is not a relationship between sovereign and subject but a network of power relations that permeates society. Second, as a consequence, the rise of disciplinary power forces us to look beyond the state if we want to understand power relations. The emblem of disciplinary power, the Panopticon, was not confined to prisons. It was in barracks, factories, schools, hospitals. The normalization that is the goal of disciplinary society is everywhere; the "judges of normality" pervade every aspect of society.

Pastoral power entailed oversight of the whole individual, encompassing every aspect of his/her life. The disciplinary mechanisms that begin to permeate Western society are one aspect of pastoral power. Another is what Foucault calls "biopower." In the eighteenth century, Foucault claims, the interest in the population extends to "power over life" (ibid., 226). Biopower designates "what brought life and its mechanisms into the realm of explicit calculations and made knowledge-power an agent of transformation of human life" (1980a, 143). Instead of dealing with individuals in terms of their juridical/legal status, governments, through the police, dealt with individuals as living beings—working, trading, living (1988b, 156). "One might say that the ancient right to *take* life or *let* live was replaced by a power to *foster* life or *disallow* it to the point of death" (1980a, 138).

In his study *The Policing of Families,* Jacques Donzelot supplies further evidence of this development. He argues that the aim of state control of the family was to reconcile the interests of families and the state and that this was accomplished through the moralization of behavior within the family. He documents a transition from "a government of families to a government through the family" (Donzelot 1979, 92). Two aspects of this transition are significant. First, one of the keys to this transition was not the government per se but the doctor working in conjunction with the government. It was the doctor who, in Foucault's terms, pronounced on normalcy. Second, the tool of the doctor's power in the family was the mother. Ironically, the mother, as the executor of the doctor's prescriptions, gained influence and, consequently, so did women as a whole.

One of the most innovative aspects of Foucault's thesis is the connection between biopower and the contemporary human sciences. Central to the deployment of biopower was knowledge of the population that was to be controlled. The government had to know everything about its subjects in order to govern their lives in the sense demanded by biopower. Aggregate characteristics of the population had to be available in order to formulate policies to address them. A new discourse—statistics—evolved to meet this need, and this discourse became central to the evolving human sciences. The technology of statistics made it possible for governments to create a reality—the statistical facts of their populations—that they could then control. The population was defined as a reality possessing certain statistically defined characteristics that could then be addressed by government policies (Hunter 1996, 154). Statistics became one of the major mechanisms by which the government defined and maintained the "normal." Thus the rise of the human sciences, the discourses whose object is the individual, are inseparable from the rise of biopower.

It is significant for my thesis that Foucault identifies the most effective and characteristic manifestation of biopower as the control of sexuality. He argues that in the nineteenth century a discourse of sexuality developed; the subject became a scientific question that produced knowledge and truth. Foucault spends a good deal of time analyzing how the discourse of sexuality is deployed. The keys to this power, he argues, are educational and psychiatric institutions and, again, the family (1980a, 46). His central thesis is that the expansion of power over sex was deployed in a way "quite different" from the law. This is a power distinct from the juridical power of sovereign and subject: "never have there existed more centers of power; never more attention manifested and verbalized; never more circular contacts and linkages; never more sites where the intensities of pleasures and the persistency of power catch hold, only to spread elsewhere" (ibid., 49).

Foucault claims that he is not offering a "theory" of power but only a description of a field of analysis (1988a, 38). This claim makes little sense. Foucault offers much more than a description of this new form of power. He develops a sophisticated theoretical understanding of this power and, most importantly, defines a means of resisting its influence. The first step in his project is an understanding of contemporary political theory and the juridical conception of power it espouses. The juridical conception of power is negative—it defines power only in terms of prohibitions. And, most importantly, because it defines power as limited to the state, it misses the myriad deployments of power that exist outside the law (1980a, 82–87). What is needed if we are to understand these new deployments of power is a political theory that is not erected around the problem of sovereignty: "We need to cut off the king's head: in political theory that has still to be done" (1980b, 121). Foucault's aim is to develop a theory of this new kind of power.

The most powerful metaphor that Foucault employs to describe this new kind of power is that of the "capillary": "But in thinking of the mechanisms of power, I am thinking rather of its capillary form of existence, the point where power reaches into the very grain of individuals, touches their bodies and inserts itself into their actions and attitudes, their discourse, learning processes and everyday lives" (ibid., 39). Foucault defines a number of characteristics that distinguish capillary power. First, it is everywhere—it is "'always already there,' that one is never 'outside' it" (ibid., 141). It is coextensive with the social body; there are no spaces it does not encompass. Second, as a consequence of the pervasiveness of power, power relations are hidden from view, indeed, are "perhaps among the best hidden things in the social body" (1988a, 118).

One of the major differences between Foucault's theory of power and that of juridical power is that, for Foucault, power is productive rather than purely negative. Power produces knowledges, subjects, social relations (1980b, 59). Society is inconceivable without power. The juridical theory defined power as restrictive, oppressive, productive of nothing. Thus freedom or liberation was defined as the escape from or absence of power. But if power is everywhere, producing the very elements of social life, then freedom must be defined in different terms. Resistance to power cannot, as in the juridical conception, be escape from the power of the sovereign but, rather, an attempt to reconfigure power.

Rejecting the juridical sovereign also entails redefining power not as a thing but as a relation, a process. Power/domination is not one person dominating another but, rather, a series of relations between and among people that extends through the social body, "a multiplicity of force relations immanent in the sphere in which they operate" (1980a, 92). Once more the capillary metaphor is useful. Capillaries are hard to trace. They are myriad; they lack definable origin. In studying power we should not be looking for an origin—either in the state or in the economy—but for the effects of power, the points of power that are manifest in relations (1980b, 96–97).

Foucault's injunction to cut off the king's head is central to his redefinition of power. But Foucault does not argue, à la Marx, that the state and the apparatuses created by the state do not wield power. Rather, he argues that sovereignty and disciplinary mechanisms "are absolutely integral constituents of the general mechanisms of power in society" (ibid., 108). He is not claiming that no power resides in the state, but that we must go beyond the power of the state to understand modern power. The state, furthermore, occupies a unique place in the pantheon of power in society: it is the form of power that defines all the other forms; it is the reference point for the other forms (1983, 41). Despite this, however, it does not follow that these forms of power are derived from the state (ibid., 224). They have an independent existence that must be addressed in any attempt to understand—or change—that power.

The relationship between power in the state and beyond it is a complex aspect of Foucault's theory. Because state power defines the configuration of power in the rest of society, a different configuration of state power will produce a different configuration of civil society. Liberalism is premised on the dichotomy between the political and the private, government and civil society. Central to this dichotomy is the assumption that civil society is the realm of freedom. These assumptions and these dichotomies are peculiar to liberalism; they are not universal.[1] This is a particularly important point for the analysis of the contemporary situation of women in the United States. We live in a state that permits much latitude in the institutions of civil society. It is also a state that, to a large extent, has relinquished control of women's sexuality. This is a particular historical situation, not a general phenomenon. It dictates a particular, not a general, strategy.

Foucault's understanding of the nature of the relationship between state and non-state power is evident in one of the major subjects of his last works: what he calls "governmentality." Foucault's concern with this topic brings together themes that had occupied him for decades. He defines "governing" in the broadest sense as the effort to "structure the possible field of action of others" (1983, 221). Thus governmentality can encompass everything from the government of oneself to the institutions of the administrative state. Governmentality for Foucault is, like disciplinary society, more an ethos than an event. It describes a way of life in which everything, from the individual to the state, is regimented, disciplined, and controlled (1991). It also entails an understanding of the subject that is distinct from that of the juridical subject. The juridical subject is a bearer of rights, the autonomous, rational individual of the liberal/modernist tradition. The subject of governmentality, in contrast, is a subject in relationship to others, a subject subjected to multiple forms of discipline, both state and non-state (1988c, 20).

Foucault's critique of political theory's concept of power and his development of an alternative theory of power, like many of his theses, forces us to rethink some of our basic assumptions. I have argued that Foucault's theory is particularly relevant to the situation of women in contemporary U.S. society. My thesis is that the control of women's sexuality that had been a pillar of state dominance since the evolution of the state has in the last half century been effectively removed from the state. What this means for the effort to combat the subordination of women is, first, that we must develop an understanding of this non-state-based power and, second, that we must develop a new strategy of resistance in which the focus must shift from the state to the institutions and relations of society. Foucault's work is instrumental in achieving both of these objectives.

One might argue, however, that, as far as the contemporary women's movement is concerned, this admonition is unnecessary. Since its inception the rallying cry of the women's movement has been "the personal is political." Beginning at least with the work of Mary Wollstonecraft, women have realized that the identity "woman" is constituted by social as well as political forces and, thus, that our resistance must target both these forces. In the wake of the political, legal, and economic success of the contemporary women's movement and the rise of feminist identity politics, however, the social side of the dual strategy has been overshadowed by the political. The political success of the women's movement has produced the tendency to seek a political solution to every problem confronting feminism. I think this is a mistake. The political and legal success of the women's movement dictates that our emphasis must shift from the political to the social. For many feminists, this has not been the case.

From the perspective of the discourse of contemporary political theory, what Foucault is exploring is the parameters of "civil society." For political theorists, civil society is the "sphere of social interaction between economy and state, composed above all of the intimate sphere (especially the family), the sphere of associations (especially voluntary associations), social movements and forms of public communication" (Cohen and Arato 1991, ix).

Foucault's exploration of this sphere, furthermore, has been recognized by political theorists as a significant contribution to the area of study. Jean Cohen and Andrew Arato, for example, devote a good deal of attention to Foucault's work, although ultimately they dismiss it because they claim it lacks a normative dimension.

Even though the topic of civil society has achieved a certain prominence in contemporary political theory, it does not follow that contemporary political theory has embraced Foucault's theory of power and cut off the king's head. Political theorists claim that power is wielded in civil society, but few engage in a detailed analysis of how this power operates. If, for example, the subordination of women is constituted primarily in civil society, then we would expect to see political theorists engaged in extended examinations of how this is effected. But such examinations have not been forthcoming.

It is ironic that the analysis of the constitution of subjectivity in social institutions is being done today, but not under the rubric of political theory. Scholars of cultural studies explore how subjectivities are constituted in the myriad practices of civil society. They provide a detailed analysis of how these institutions and practices constitute subjects, regulate behavior, and establish and enforce standards of normalcy. These studies have been particularly significant in analyzing how the subject "woman" is created and maintained. But cultural studies is not a recognized part of political theory and is not taken seriously by most political theorists. If Foucault is right about power, however, this is precisely what political theorists should be studying. If we are to understand and resist power in contemporary society, we must pursue a dual strategy: we must understand the framing mechanisms of state power but, most importantly, analyze the subjectification that occurs primarily in civil society.

To be fair, however, I do not think that even Foucault fully realizes the radical potential of his theory. He claims that power is everywhere, that it has moved beyond the state to the interstices of civil society. But in his actual analyses, he concentrates heavily on the examination of state apparatuses. The prison, the mental institution, his analysis of governmentality, all focus on state or quasi-state apparatuses. Foucault's analysis of sexuality provides the best opportunity to realize the radical potential implicit in his approach. But even here Foucault never engages in a concrete analysis of how sexuality is constituted in civil society, in the practices of the family, the influence of advertising, economic practices, religion. Foucault's theory defines these institutions as central to the practice of power, but he does not follow through by examining them fully.

A NEW POLITICS OF IDENTITY

I have argued here that identity politics has the potential to challenge the fundamental tenets of liberalism. It brings identity into the political arena, challenging the universal citizen of liberalism; it challenges the autonomy of the agentic subject of liberalism by defining identity as socially constructed; it defines power as extending beyond the political sphere, entailing a new strategy of resistance. I also have argued that identity politics has not fulfilled this potential but, rather, has been distorted by the liberal polity.

In order to substantiate this final claim, I will look at the most prominent defense of identity politics in contemporary theory and practice: multiculturalism. Both the theory and practice of multiculturalism appear to meet the challenge posed by identity politics. Unlike liberals, multiculturalists claim to place identity at the center of politics. The whole point of multiculturalism is to bring identities, and particularly previously excluded identities, into the political arena as equal citizens.

I would like to propose another interpretation of multiculturalism. Multiculturalism is parasitic on liberalism in a number of key respects. Multicultural politics does not bring identity per se into the political arena but, rather, the identity of the political "others." Multicultural politics is politics for the "others," not politics for those already in the political arena. In practice, then, multicultural politics reinforces the status of the "other" in liberalism. Multicultural politics fosters political practices that maintain the distinction between the "normal" citizen of liberalism and the "others." The multiculturalists' goal is to gain recognition for these others *as* others. This fails to challenge the fundamental basis of the liberal polity, the universal citizen who lacks an identity.

There is a strange ambiguity at the center of the multicultural position. Multiculturalism is both parasitic on liberalism in that it tries to fit identity into the liberal polity and at the same time incompatible with that polity. This ambiguity is most clearly revealed in the work of Charles Taylor. Taylor asserts that our identity is in part shaped by our need for recognition and that our identities can suffer real damage if this recognition is withheld (Taylor 1992, 25). He further argues that identity is a dialogic process that emerges in relations with others. But Taylor then goes on to claim that because recognition is a basic human need, it should be acknowledged in the liberal polity. This is a futile aspiration. The theoretical universalism of liberalism precludes the recognition of identities in the political sphere. No amount of tinkering with the liberal polity will change that fundamental fact.

It is significant, furthermore, that the most prominent contemporary proponent of multiculturalism, Will Kymlicka, argues for the compatibility of liberalism and multiculturalism. Kymlicka's strategy is to define liberalism in a way that reveals this compatibility. The first element of his argument is his assertion that liberalism does not necessarily entail abstract individualism. He then makes the historical point that minority rights were a prominent part of nineteenth-century liberalism and should be recovered. But the center of Kymlicka's argument is his assertion that "The notion of respect for persons *qua* members of cultures based on the recognition and importance of the primary good of cultural membership is not, therefore, an illiberal one" (Kymlicka 1989, 167). This argument is a bid to subsume his position under Rawlsian liberalism. Kymlicka hopes that by defining cultural membership as one of the primary goods that individuals in a liberal polity would pursue, he can make multiculturalism compatible with John Rawls's theory.

What Kymlicka comes up with, however, is a curious hybrid that is incompatible with liberalism and a cultural perspective that identifies culture as constitutive of identity. The greatest obstacle to Kymlicka's argument is that Rawls makes it very clear that identity characteristics belong in the private sphere. Citizens cannot enter the public sphere *as* cultural identities but only as "universal citizens." All of Kymlicka's attempts to bring cultural identities into the political sphere are defeated by this prohibition. But one of the curious aspects of Kymlicka's theory is that the cultural identity that is the focus of his perspective is an entity in which culture plays a strangely muted role. He states: "Cultural membership affects one's very sense of personal identity and capacity" (ibid., 175). Affecting is not constituting. For Kymlicka we are detached from our cultural membership: "The value of the communal and cultural aspects of our existence depends, to a large degree, on the way that individuals form and revise attachments to projects around those features of social life" (ibid., 253–54). Culture thus becomes only one element of the individual's life plan, an element that can be isolated and examined. This results in a definition of cultural membership that is oddly neutered. In Kymlicka's schema the fact that everyone possesses a cultural identity effectively cancels out the effect of that identity. For Kymlicka we do not enter the public sphere as culturally different citizens but, rather, as equal citizens who all possess an entity, culture, that we all equally value. It follows that our differences do not constitute us as different but, rather, as the same.

In *The Sexual Contract,* Carole Pateman's critique of liberalism from a feminist perspective, she argues that the universal citizen is gendered masculine but that his gender and, hence, his dominance are hidden (veiled) by the claim of universality. Identity politics will not be successful until this claim is exposed and it is acknowledged that all of us possess identities and that these identities are necessarily brought into the political sphere. Multiculturalism fails to meet this challenge. Multiculturalism also fails to meet another significant challenge facing identity politics: the fixing of identity. There is a pervasive assumption in the contemporary liberal polity that fixing identities is the necessary complement of the move to a multicultural polity. This assumption is pernicious. It is also ironic. The emergence of identity politics has served to reveal the constructed nature of identity, exposing apparently essential identities as socially constituted. Yet as it has evolved in the context of the liberal polity, identity politics has had the effect of reestablishing essential identities. This tendency toward fixing identities is the Achilles' heel of identity politics. It has led many feminists, along with Butler, to reject the practice entirely.

The fixing of identities, however, is not endemic to identity politics but is, rather, the result of the structure of the liberal polity. Since that polity both denies and excludes identities in the political sphere, when identities do enter politics the structure of that polity demands that they be fixed as particular "others." Most advocates of multiculturalism buy into this assumption, demanding recognition for fixed categories of excluded others. But this is not the only possible way of understanding the practice of identity politics. The goal of identity politics is to challenge the public identities under which we are subsumed. The participants in identity politics act to construct a different public identity—for example, the liberated woman as opposed to the woman of patriarchy—and enter the political arena under the banner of that new identity. This political action need not be conceived in terms of fixing the private identities of the participants. Although public identities construct and constrain private identities, it is nevertheless the case that identity politics is about public labels, not about private selves. Participating in identity politics is a political action that challenges the hegemonic power that constructs demeaning identities.[2]

If multiculturalism has failed to transform the liberal polity, however, there are other contemporary political/theoretical movements that may offer this possibility. The most notable is critical race theory. Advocates of critical race theory challenge the ahistoricism of the law, expressing skepticism toward dominant legal claims of neutrality, color blindness, and meritocracy (Matsuda et al. 1993, 6). Instead of trying to eliminate racism by insisting on a neutral, objective, standard for all citizens before the law, critical race theorists have argued that we must acknowledge the effect of race in our society and, far from excluding it from legal decisions, bring it into the forefront. In other words, critical race theory tears the veil away from the neutral, universal citizen and reveals a white male establishment that has fostered a history of racism and domination.

Critical race theorists argue that racial identities have profoundly shaped both our society and the legal system that society has created. They insist that we must acknowledge that history and its effects, and, further, bring those particular racial identities into legal discussions. Their principal thesis is that we cannot overcome racial subordination by ignoring that history or the system of domination that created and perpetuated it. As one theorist puts it, "Critical Race Theory can mature toward a significant representation of cultural analysis as it bears on legal values and thereby move to destroy the foundations and structures of racial subordination" (Calmore 1995, 324).

The veiled citizen of the liberal polity finds its purest expression in the law. Challenging the objectivity and neutrality of the law is, thus, the most radical critique of that citizen. Arguing that the law should recognize differences among citizens and make this a central part of adjudication is, from the perspective of liberalism, rank heresy. The strong resistance to critical race theory indicates that the (veiled) universal citizen of liberalism is deeply rooted in our political consciousness. Bringing identity into politics has been defined as a perversion of the public space since the creation of the liberal polity. But it is also an important step in the direction of a new understanding of identity and citizenship.

Identity politics has begun the process of destabilizing liberalism, but this process is far from completed. By simultaneously bringing identity into politics and revealing the veiled identity of the universal citizen, identity politics points to a new set of political understandings based on difference rather than universality. It advocates what Cornell West has called "the new cultural politics of difference." The distinctive features of this politics are "to trash the monolithic and homogeneous in the name of diversity, multiplicity and heterogeneity; to reject the abstract, general and universal in light of the concrete, specific and particular; and to historicize, contextualize and pluralize by highlighting the contingent, provisional, variable, tentative, shifting and changing" (West 1995, 147). That this will not be an easy process should be obvious. Notions of universality and generality are at the very heart of the modernist/liberal tradition and will not be easily dislodged.

Another source for the transformation of liberalism can be found in the tradition of feminist theory itself. Although feminist identity politics and even feminist political theory have, with rare exceptions, not adopted a Foucauldian theory of power as extending beyond the strictly political, other aspects of feminist analysis employ a distinctly Foucauldian definition of power. The emblematic slogan of the movement, "the personal is political," acknowledges that power extends beyond the political sphere and that the forces that define and constrain the identity "woman" are both political and social. From the outset the women's movement as a whole has employed the dual strategy that I am advocating—simultaneously challenging the subordination of women in the political and social spheres.

One of the central thrusts of the women's movement has been to uncover and combat the forces that define "woman" as subordinate. There is by now an extensive literature on the formation of gender consciousness in girls who grow up in this society. Judith Butler's analysis, in *Gender Trouble*, of the formation of gender identity is a case in point. She discusses the extensive forces in society that create this identity; few if any of those forces originate in the state. Likewise, Carol Gilligan argues that what she calls the "sea of Western culture" molds girls into the category "woman" at an early age (Brown and Gilligan 1992). The forces that effect this socialization are myriad; no one influence can be singled out as definitive. The conclusion fostered by these studies is that we need a strategy of resistance that focuses on each of those forces individually. We need to see these forces as on a par with if not more important than strictly political forces. Most importantly, we must integrate these studies into a distinctly feminist political theory.

Such a strategy should not and cannot ignore the state. The state shapes the structure of civil society, defining the parameters in which it operates (Phelan 2000, 432). Furthermore, legal categories that define a "normal" person or citizen are profoundly influential in shaping identities. This point is also central to critical race theory. What I am arguing is that a focus on identity and its formation/degradation forces us to look beyond the state for strategies of resistance. By making the personal political, by deconstructing the public/private distinction that grounds liberalism, identity politics has the potential of also deconstructing the foundation of the liberal polity.

It should be clear from the foregoing discussion of critical race theory and the women's movement why I am arguing that the work of Foucault is so central to the project of redefining power and identity. By deconstructing the fundamental assumptions of the liberal polity, Foucault's theory explains the incompatibility of liberalism and identity politics. If identity politics is to succeed, it must reveal the universal citizen of the liberal polity, the rational, autonomous subject, as an impostor. Identity must be defined as a social construction, not a metaphysical given. And, most importantly, power must be defined as everywhere; the distinction between the personal and the political must be obviated. Foucault's theory accomplishes all of these objectives.

In his work on subjectification and resistance, furthermore, Foucault outlines the political implications of his theory. Since the forces that constitute us as subjects are everywhere, resistance must be everywhere as well. Foucault develops his theory of subjectification and resistance in his early and middle work. It becomes a major theme of his later work in which he traces the constitution of the subject in the West from its inception in Greek and Christian thought. What I am arguing here is that Foucault's theory offers us a new way of understanding the phenomenon of identity politics in the contemporary United States. I am not arguing either for or against identity politics as it is currently practiced but, rather, for a different interpretation of the phenomenon. This interpretation reveals, first, that we need not, as Wendy Brown and Judith Butler argue, reject identity politics out of hand, and, second, that the definition of identity politics advanced by multiculturalism is not the only option open to us. My thesis is that the perspective offered by Foucault's theory reveals why the debate over identity politics cannot be resolved within the liberal polity and why liberalism distorts the impact of identity politics. Identity politics requires a new understanding of the relationship between identity and politics, an understanding that is only beginning to be realized in contemporary politics. It has been my intention here to foster that new understanding.

NOTES

1. For a discussion of these issues, see Burchell (1991).

2. The question of the interface between public and private identities is a complex issue. I explicate this more fully in my forthcoming book, *Private Selves, Public Identities: Reconsidering Identity Politics.*

WORKS CITED

Brown, Lyn, and Carol Gilligan. 1992. *Meeting at the Crossroads: Women's Psychology and Girls' Development.* Cambridge: Harvard University Press.

Brown, Wendy. 1995. *States of Injury: Power and Freedom in Late Modernity.* Princeton: Princeton University Press.

Burchell, Graham. 1991. "Peculiar Interests: Civil Society and Governing 'The System of Natural Liberty.'" In *The Foucault Effect.* Edited by Graham Burchell et al. 119–50. Chicago: University of Chicago Press.

Butler, Judith. 1990. *Gender Trouble.* New York: Routledge.

Calmore, John. 1995. "Critical Race Theory, Archie Shepp, and Fire Music: Securing an Authentic Intellectual Life in a Multicultural World." In *Critical Race Theory.* Edited by Kimberle Crenshaw et al. 315–29. New York: Free Press.

Cohen, Jean, and Andrew Arato. 1992. *Civil Society and Political Theory.* Cambridge: MIT Press.

Cott, Nancy. 2000. *Public Vows: A History of Marriage and the Nation.* Cambridge: Harvard University Press.

Donzelot, Jacques. 1979. *The Policing of Families.* New York: Pantheon.

Foucault, Michel. 1979. *Discipline and Punish.* New York: Pantheon.

———. 1980a. *The History of Sexuality.* New York: Vintage.

———. 1980b. *Power/Knowledge.* New York: Pantheon.

———. 1983. "The Subject and Power." In *Michel Foucault: Beyond Structuralism and Hermeneutics.* By Hubert Dreyfus and Paul Rabinow. 208–26. 2nd ed. Chicago: University of Chicago Press.

———. 1988a. *Politics, Philosophy, Culture: Interviews and Other Writings 1977–1984.* New York: Routledge.

———. 1988b. "The Political Technology of the Individual." In *Technologies of the Self: A Seminar with Michel Foucault.* Edited by Luther Martin et al. 143–62. Amherst: University of Massachusetts Press.

———. 1988c. "Technologies of the Self." In *Technologies of the Self: A Seminar with Michel Foucault.* Edited by Luther Martin et al. 16–49. Amherst: University of Massachusetts Press.

———. 1991. "Governmentality." In *The Foucault Effect.* Edited by Graham Burchell et al. 87–104. Chicago: University of Chicago Press.

Hekman, Susan. Forthcoming. *Private Selves, Public Identities: Reconsidering Identity Politics.* University Park: Pennsylvania University Press.

Hunter, Ian. 1996. "Assembling the School." In *Foucault and Political Reason.* Edited by Andrew Barry et al. 143–66. Chicago: University of Chicago Press.

Kymlicka, Will. 1989. *Liberalism, Community, and Culture.* Oxford: Clarendon Press.

Lerner, Gerda. 1986. *The Creation of Patriarchy.* New York: Oxford University Press.

Matsuda, Mari, et al. 1993. *Words That Wound: Critical Race Theory, Assaultive Speech, and the First Amendment.* Boulder: Westview Press.

Pateman, Carole. 1988. *The Sexual Contract.* Stanford: Stanford University Press.

Phelan, Shane. 2000. "Queer Liberalism?" *American Political Science Review* 94 (2): 431–42.

Taylor, Charles. 1992. *The Ethics of Authenticity.* Cambridge: Harvard University Press.

West, Cornell. 1995. "The New Cultural Politics of Difference." In *The Identity in Question.* Edited by John Rajchman. 147–71. New York: Routledge.

❧ 11

Foucault and Feminism: Power, Resistance, Freedom

Margaret A. McLaren

There is no agreement among feminists about the usefulness of Foucault's work. Many feminists, such as Susan Bordo, Judith Butler, Jana Sawicki, and Ladelle McWhorter, find his work promising and productive for feminist theory. Yet many feminists remain skeptical about engaging with Foucault's work, and some are absolutely vociferous in their condemnation of Foucault.[1] For example, Toril Moi warns, "the price for giving in to his [Foucault's] powerful discourse is nothing less than the depoliticisation of feminism" (Moi 1985, 95). Two of the most significant reasons that feminists are wary of Foucault are his lack of a normative framework and his lack of an adequate theory of the subject.[2] Feminist critics claim that without a theory of norms or a theory of the subject, Foucault's work is of little use for feminist politics.

Foucault has been famously criticized for his lack of a normative framework, and thus his lack of any grounding for an emancipatory or liberatory politics.[3] This apparent lack has been particularly problematic for feminists, who are committed to the emancipatory political project of ending women's oppression.[4] They claim that demands for social justice rely on a normative framework because those demands must appeal to normative notions such as rights, justice, and truth. Subjectivity poses a different but related problem for feminist critics. In fact, feminists lodge two seemingly contradictory complaints about Foucault's notion of the subject. Some argue that Foucault rejects notions of subjectivity, viewing the subject as fictional or hopelessly "de-centered."[5] Other feminist critics claim that Foucault presents us with a subject completely determined by discourses, institutions, and practices. Given that these critics usually focus on Foucault's genealogical work, their claims are in a sense understandable: Foucault's genealogies do chronicle the ways that practices, institutions, and disciplines constitute subjectivity and thus may seem to leave little room for agency and resistance. But Foucault's genealogical work is clearly critical of the normalization that can occur when the categories of the human sciences are imposed on individuals and groups of individuals. For example, in volume 1 of *The History of Sexuality*, he claims that the rise of social control is coincident with new knowledges, such as knowledge about population, reproduction, and genetics. And at the level of the individual subject, he notes that the proliferation of categories of sexual perversion and the normalizing effect of categories contributed to understanding sexuality as an identity.

I argue that Foucault's work can provide valuable resources for feminist politics. In his genealogical work, Foucault employs a skeptical method that questions relationships of domination in contemporary society and reveals the contingency of current institutions and practices. His genealogical work appeals to implicit normative notions, such as critique and freedom, that he makes more explicit in his later work. In this essay, I focus on Foucault's explication of a notion of freedom, specifically his discussions of non-normalizing technologies of the self, life as a work of art, and practices of freedom, in that later work. Doing so, I respond to feminists who, by focusing on Foucault's genealogies, have overlooked the political relevance of his work more generally. Foucault borrows the notion of practices of the self (askesis) from antiquity. However, practices of the self are not limited to antiquity, to which Foucault admits we cannot return. In his later essays, he discusses practices of the self as contemporary practices of freedom. Given the non-normalizing, emancipatory character of practices of the self, I argue for the possibility of a Foucauldian politics and its compatibility with the aims of feminism.[6] In my conclusion, I suggest that Foucault's practices of freedom can be applied to contemporary feminist practices.

RESISTANCE AS SITUATED SOCIAL CRITICISM

As we have seen, feminist critics question the political relevance of Foucault's work given his lack of normative notions that they claim are necessary to justify appeals to rights, equality, and justice. Some even claim that Foucault's stance is downright dangerous to emancipatory social and political movements. Feminist critics charge Foucault with presenting a normative paradox: How can Foucault call for resistance or social change when his own theory undermines the universal norms that would justify such change? While it is clear that Foucault does not endorse universal norms, it is equally clear that he calls for a politics of resistance.

Foucault's suspicion of norms runs throughout his work, but he criticizes at least two very different types of norms. He is critical of universal norms such as truth, justice, and rights. And he is critical of social norms that prescribe particular behaviors or that categorize individuals into groups. There is an implicit critique in his genealogies of the appeal to universal norms. In Foucault's view the universal norms of humanism are a set of themes that have arisen in different social and historical contexts. These themes are always connected to value judgments, and these value judgments are in turn connected to interpretations of man available in religion, science, or politics. Foucault is suspicious of humanistic universals because they have been used to justify and support totalitarian regimes. Often critics confound his rejection of humanism with a rejection of the Enlightenment.[7] Foucault endorses the critical impulse of the Enlightenment while rejecting its emphasis on rationality, its notion of freedom as unencumbered, and its acceptance of universal values. He does not contradict himself in this regard because norms are precisely what one is resisting. And Foucault is rightly suspicious of norms: his genealogical work makes clear their dangers. Social norms, especially those established and perpetuated by social science, have a normalizing effect. The dividing practices that concern Foucault in his genealogical work evaluate, judge, and categorize—they divide the criminal from the noncriminal, the pervert from the nonpervert. Social norms are established within discourses, institutions, and practices that are embedded in normative discourses. For example, the "truth" about the smaller size of the cranium of white women and Black men and women was used to justify the subordination of these groups in the late nineteenth and early twentieth centuries. Normative notions themselves can serve to disempower and exclude some while justifying the status quo. Thus, it is not surprising that Foucault urges us to be suspicious of them.

These normalizing practices are the central concern of Foucault's genealogical work. In volume 1 of *The History of Sexuality*, he demonstrates how the discourse of sexuality created new categories of deviant and pervert, while simultaneously encroaching upon the sphere of private life by exercising control over the family and inserting itself into our psyches by changing our conception of ourselves into sexual subjects. In *Discipline and Punish* he illustrates how practices of punishment, even while they have become more humane (we no longer draw and quarter people), operate in a deeper and more insidious way through constant surveillance. Furthermore, Foucault demonstrates that whereas punishment used to operate on the body alone, for example, through execution, it now operates at the level of the "soul" through self-surveillance and self-monitoring. *Madness and Civilization* provides a third example of the dangers of normalization. In his history of madness, Foucault points out the ways in which madness has been increasingly marginalized. Here again his critical description compels us to look closely at the "progress" of the treatment of the mad. Certainly, extensive mental health networks and appropriate drugs are preferable to the confinement and restraint of the mentally ill that was so prevalent even in the United States less than a century ago. But his long-term historical perspective reveals that what looked like advances in the treatment of the mad—for instance, the medicalization of madness and the practice of performing lobotomies—are now viewed as inadequate and primitive forms of treatment. In fact, his history of madness reveals that what often looked like advances were not. (Most people would rather be exiled from their city than lobotomized.)

By extension, then, Foucault's analysis and critical description should lead one to question current practices. Feminists, for instance, should be especially concerned with the increasing medicalization of mental health. Currently in the United States, women on prescription antidepressants by far outnumber men. While antidepressant medication undeniably has some positive effects, its widespread use and the gender gap between the number of women and the number of men on antidepressants should cause some concern. It raises a number of questions, the most obvious being, "Why are more women diagnosed as depressed than men?" But more significantly, the medical model of mental health may obscure some important issues. Antidepressants individualize and psychologize depression when, in fact, it may be the appropriate response to the current social and political situation for women. Individualizing and psychologizing this problem forestalls the possibility of political action and social change.

Foucault's approach allows him to subject particular norms to scrutiny without having to assume the Enlightenment stance that social critics can somehow stand outside the social. Resistance takes place within power relations. Like power, resistance is local, specific to the configuration of power-knowledge relations that define the situation. One of the reasons critics find Foucault's politics of resistance untenable is that they claim there is "no outside to power." As I shall demonstrate, this is a misinterpretation of Foucault's notion of power. Foucault's own direct rebuttal to this idea of power as inescapable bears repeating here. Foucault himself says, "Should it be said that one is always 'inside' power, [that] there is no 'escaping' it, [that] there is no absolute outside where it is concerned, because one is always subject to the law in any case? . . . *This would be to misunderstand the strictly relational character of power relationships*" (Foucault 1980, 95). For Foucault, power is first and foremost a relationship, and as such it is fluid, flexible, and dynamic. Where there is power, there is freedom: "power relations are possible only insofar as the subjects are free" (Foucault 1997c, 292). For Foucault, resistance and power are co-implicated: "in power relations there is necessarily the possibility of resistance because if there were no possibility of resistance (of violent resistance, flight, deception, strategies capable of reversing the situation), there would be no power relations at all" (Foucault 1997c, 292). So long as there is power, there is freedom.

Foucault's concern with freedom runs throughout his later work. For him power and freedom are co-implicated, and philosophical investigation aims toward freedom. This concern with freedom can be seen in Foucault's middle as well as his later work; it is implicit in his genealogies that criticize practices of domination and normalization. And in *The Use of Pleasure* and *The Care of the Self*, he analyzes the forms of self-constitution that preceded disciplinary society. As I discuss later, his own life as an engaged intellectual testifies to the importance he placed on freedom.

In his later work, Foucault focuses on the constitution of subjectivity. Because subjectivity is constituted through cultural and social institutions and practices, the possibility for new forms of subjectivity that Foucault explores in his later work and the social criticism implicit in his genealogies are intimately connected. Thus, exploring the limits of our self-constitution is an ethical task involving both work on oneself and social criticism. This ethical task both relies on and strives toward freedom, "it is seeking to give new impetus . . . to the undefined work of freedom . . . as work carried out by ourselves upon ourselves as free beings" (Foucault 1984a, 46–47). The undefined work of freedom lurks in the background of Foucault's genealogical texts as an implicit norm. But Foucault's notion of freedom differs from the Enlightenment notion of freedom. Kant's freedom, for example, relies on a noumenal world. For Foucault, freedom has to do with the possibility of new forms of subjectivity that are historically and socially constituted, not in escaping the social and historical altogether. His approach opens up the possibility for critique; it allows him to question the normalizing function of norms from within a situated social and historical context. Resistance, then, is a form of situated social criticism.

POWER, RESISTANCE, FREEDOM

As we have seen, at least part of the reason why Foucault's feminist critics have a problem accepting his ideas as politically useful results from a misunderstanding of his conception of power. There is good reason for this misunderstanding because Foucault himself is not clear about the functioning or limits of power. He provides an "analytics of power," rather than a theory of power.[8] This is consistent with Foucault's general approach because an analytics of power is contextual and historical, yet still generalizable.[9] Foucault is not making universal claims about what power is or the way that power functions. Nonetheless, power is a central concept in his work and arguably one of his most important contributions to contemporary social theory. Given the significance of power and its analysis for feminism, examining the concept of power is indispensable for feminist theory and practice.[10] Thus, examining Foucault's analytics of power is essential for judging whether his work might be useful for feminists.

Foucault urges us to have a more complex understanding of power. He reconceptualizes power, claiming that it can be positive and productive.[11] Foucault characterizes power as relational; it is the "multiplicity of force relations immanent in the sphere in which they constitute their own organization" (Foucault 1980, 92). Because it is relational, it is omnipresent; it is constantly produced among and between persons, institutions, things, and groups of persons. Power is mobile, local, heterogeneous, and unstable. Power comes from everywhere; it is exercised from innumerable points. Foucault emphasizes the ubiquity of power; it comes from below, not solely from above as in the juridico-discursive model of power. And relations of power are immanent in other relationships such as economic relationships, knowledge relationships, and sexual relationships. As Foucault says, "Power is everywhere; not because it embraces everything, but because it comes from everywhere" (Foucault 1980, 93). Power is not possessed. And power relations are both intentional and nonsubjective.

This last claim, that power relations are both intentional and nonsubjective, may seem contradictory. After all, isn't it subjects that have intentions? It may help to explicate this claim. Foucault holds that power is all-pervasive, that it is relational, and that it can be understood through the strategies by which it takes effect. So, in each manifestation of power in the strategies and the relations among individuals, institutions, and things, aims, goals, and objectives are revealed. For example, the "war on masturbation" against children in the nineteenth century had a specific explicit objective—to stop or reduce the activity of masturbation among children. On Foucault's reading it also had other less explicit objectives, for instance, to increase the power of state control over the individual and the family. In the sense that local and specific power relations have aims, goals, and objectives, power is intentional. Yet Foucault also claims that power is nonsubjective.[12] This is consistent with his claim that it is not possessed by anyone (because it is relational, and because it is shifting, mobile, and unstable). Power is nonsubjective in the sense that individuals do not *have* power; rather, they participate in it. Much of that participation is beyond the control of the individual, because she is entangled in a web of relationships and institutions. And even that which is within one's control has unintended consequences and effects (cf. Dreyfus and Rabinow 1982, 187). The local and specific aims, objectives, and goals interact with other local and specific aims, objectives, and goals, resulting in effects and consequences that are not the plan of any one person, or even any group of people. Thus, because there are specific aims, objectives, and goals, power is intentional. Yet because power is neither possessed nor controlled by individuals, it is nonsubjective. A specific example from volume 1 of *The History of Sexuality* may help to illuminate the way that power can be both intentional and nonsubjective. Foucault discusses how in the nineteenth century, science, medicine, and the law worked together to mark some people as sexually deviant. Although these discourses—as well as various others, such as religious discourse, psychiatry, and psychology—functioned together to create categories of perverts and to criminalize those classified as such, this classification, categorization, and criminalization was not the work of any one person, or even any one group of people. And this is precisely Foucault's point—power operates in ways that are beyond our control. Still, we inevitably participate in these power relations, making conscious decisions about what to do and how to do it. Yet the impact and consequences of our actions, particularly with regard to the larger social and cultural scheme of things, are beyond us.[13] Thus, power is nonsubjective, in part because it always supersedes any person or group of persons, but, more importantly, because it is relational, existing only between and among persons, institutions, discourses, practices, and objects.

Some feminists claim that because power runs through all relations, Foucault's notion of power cannot make sense of gender dominance or any consistent asymmetry of power.[14] Foucault speaks directly to this concern in his later work. Although he does reject hierarchical and unilateral models of power, he does not believe that power is distributed or exercised equally. In "The Subject and Power" and "The Ethics of Concern for the Self as a Practice of Freedom," Foucault distinguishes between power and domination. Whereas power is fluid and always subject to reversal, states of domination are static, ossified relations of power. Relations of domination are particular formations of power—"the locking together of power relations with the relations of strategy" (Foucault 1982b, 226). Even states of domination are subject to reversal, but this involves collective action. Relations of domination include the consolidated power of a nation-state over its people, the systemic gender imbalance of patriarchy, and the relations of colonizers over the colonized. Collective actions to change relations of domination include political action, social movements, and cultural revolution. Foucault's analysis of power does not result in the equal distribution of power, as feminist critic Nancy Hartsock claims: "[Foucault's notion of power] carries implications of equality and agency rather than the systematic domination of the many by the few" (Hartsock 1990, 169). Nor does it preclude social and political analyses of gender, racial, or class domination. The relationships among power, domination, freedom, and resistance are complex, but Foucault does attempt to distinguish among them in his later work. Power does not exclude freedom, but implies it: "It would not be possible for power relations to exist without points of insubordination which, by definition, are means of escape" (Foucault 1982b, 225). Nor does domination exclude freedom, although freedom is more limited under states of domination. In response to the question about how freedom is possible if power is everywhere, Foucault answers, "if there are relations of power in every social field, this is because there is freedom everywhere. Of course, states of domination do indeed exist. In a great many cases, power relations are fixed in such a way that they are perpetually asymmetrical and allow an extremely limited margin of freedom" (Foucault 1997c, 292). Even though options are more limited in states of domination, resistance is still possible. Foucault's example of a state of domination—conventional marital structure in the eighteenth and nineteenth centuries—offers some limited options to women short of reversing the gendered power relations: "they could deceive their husbands, pilfer money from them, refuse them sex" (Foucault 1997c, 293).

Feminists may be less than satisfied with deception, stealing, and chastity as forms of women's resistance. Yet two literary examples draw on precisely these strategies to demonstrate the possibility of women's resistance in situations of domination. *Lysistrata* remains a classic example of women's power and determination to change things through their individual actions (of refusing sex) and the collective power that this engenders. Nora in Ibsen's *A Doll's House* deceives her husband and "pilfers" money to save his life. In spite of her fragile and flighty persona, she comes off as a character of remarkable strength and courage, even if a bit manipulative. These examples illustrate a form of resistance to domination in situations where there is a pervasive asymmetry of power. Foucault also allows for situations where women's resistance actually changes the balance of power. The example of the Mothers of the Plaza de Mayo, an Argentinean women's activist group, illustrates one way that a Foucauldian notion of resistance can illuminate real political practices.

The Mothers of the Plaza de Mayo in Argentina used the gender norm of virtuous motherhood to their advantage as a form of resistance. The Mothers of the Plaza de Mayo is a political group composed of women whose children disappeared under the repressive governmental regime in Argentina during the 1970s and 1980s. During this time the military government systematically "disappeared" people numbering in the thousands. The disappeared were abducted, often in the middle of the night, with no warning and no trace of their whereabouts left behind. Although the military government claimed that the disappeared had been arrested as political agitators, many of the disappeared had no political ties, and the disappeared included students, blue-collar workers, writers, scientists, journalists, lawyers, professors, labor leaders, doctors, psychiatrists, and religious leaders. Because Argentine society is still somewhat traditional in terms of gender roles, it was the women of the families who searched for their missing children because the fathers had to go to work. When the mothers of the disappeared inquired about their daughters' or sons' whereabouts, they were shuffled from government agency to government agency or met with staunch denial of the abductions in spite of the fact that there were often eyewitnesses. The mothers of the disappeared began their efforts to find their children individually but began to share their stories in the waiting rooms of various government agencies. Soon they began to meet in each other's homes and churches to coordinate their efforts to find their children and to seek support from international human rights groups, such as Amnesty International. After awhile the mothers decided to meet in front of the government offices at the Plaza de Mayo. They first met there on April 30, 1977, and since that time have held weekly meetings and demonstrations there. The Mothers of the Plaza de Mayo went on to draw international attention to the plight of the disappeared in Argentina and to continue to press for the prosecution of those responsible for the disappearances in Argentina. The mothers' political activism both grew out of and subverted gender norms: "When they began their frantic search for their children, they were primarily homemakers, content with their absorption in family and household and expressing little interest in the world beyond. They had been socialized into these roles by a traditional Argentine society that regards the male as the dominant figure, the sole participant in public life and the undisputed head of the home" (Bouvard 1994, 65). The mothers used the gender norms of traditional Argentine society that honored and valued motherhood even as it excluded women from the public sphere.

Invoking their status as culturally revered mothers helped to protect the women in Argentina who demonstrated on behalf of those who had disappeared.[15] Drawing on their socially and culturally revered status as mothers was a way of using the power of the social, political, and cultural norms that sanctified motherhood and the family. These social and political norms served the dominant power by perpetuating the traditional roles and status of women and thus reinforcing the status quo. Originally a way of keeping women in their place at home and circumscribing their power, this technique of domination failed when women used the same stereotype of virtuous motherhood to call attention to the government's abuse of power. While drawing on traditional gender norms, the mothers also subverted these norms, as they became political activists and public figures. The work of the Mothers of the Plaza de Mayo is an instance of feminist resistance insofar as it demonstrates the collective political power of women. And it is compatible with Foucault's ideas about power and resistance; according to Foucault power operates at least in part through social norms. The Mothers of the Plaza de Mayo drew upon the constraining societal norms of gender roles and motherhood to develop strategies of political resistance. Consequently, they changed the gender norms that they drew upon, for instance, by significantly changing the meaning of motherhood and the scope of public political activity in which Argentinean women engaged.

The example of the Mothers of the Plaza de Mayo helps show what Foucault got right about power and resistance. For Foucault power and resistance are inextricable. Resistance does always take place from within power relations, although at the same time it shifts those relations. Women have been resisting patriarchal power for a long time in various social and cultural contexts. Norms can both dominate and empower, as in the case of the "good mother." Foucault's notion of power can help make clear how nonlegislative action can be political—for instance, demonstrations at the Plaza de Mayo. And maybe even more significantly for feminists, Foucault's ideas can help show how individual actions of resisting norms also can be political and how they can help produce cracks in the seamless wall of patriarchy by empowering women in situations of gender domination. Although we may still have to wait awhile for the total abolition of gender domination, women's activism provides us with myriad examples of successful resistance.

Foucault's accounts of power, resistance, freedom, and domination are interconnected. Some feminist critics seem to cling to the model of power that Foucault rejects, the juridico-discursive model of power that limits and prohibits. Other feminist critics believe that Foucault's new view of power offers feminists ways to articulate and analyze the effects power has on the body but still think his view of power results in domination. However, as I pointed out earlier, domination is consolidated relations of power. And even these consolidated relations of power are susceptible to change. Moreover, there is limited freedom even within states of domination. Freedom for Foucault is never outside power relations but occurs when power relations shift through reversal or collective resistance. Reversal takes place when the balance of power shifts, giving one person or group of people the upper hand. Foucault likens these shifts in the relations of power to playing a board game; there are always power relations in play among the players, with respect to their changing positions on the board, but the balance of power shifts with each move. Resistance, too, involves shifts and changes in power relations. So, both reversal of power and resistance to power can be individual or collective. And shifting power relations can end a situation of domination and increase possibilities for freedom. The fact that resistance is possible even in situations of domination bodes well for social change. And although Foucault explicitly rejects the repressive model of power that views freedom or liberation as the freedom of the individual from power, he does use the term "liberation" specifically with respect to the colonized. He believes that in a situation of domination by one group of people over another, for instance the colonizer over the colonized, liberation is possible. Note that liberation implies the end of domination but not the end of power. Liberation from domination does, however, result in expanded possibilities for freedom. Freedom is not a final state to be realized but occurs only through its exercise as reversal, resistance, and other practices of freedom.

One of the most significant ways that power functions is through creating and maintaining norms. Norms, like power, function ambivalently. New categories are created through norms, group identity can be consolidated through norms, and norms can serve as positive guidelines for behavior. Yet as we have seen, Foucault is suspicious of norms because they codify behavior, and they categorize individuals as either normal or pathological. The fact that power functions through norms, and not simply through laws, is an insight that is especially valuable for feminists. Although gender norms are sometimes enforced through the law (there used to be laws prohibiting cross-dressing, for example), they are primarily enforced through social taboos. These social taboos not only prohibit cross-gender behaviors, but they also dictate proper behavior for each gender. Feminists have discussed the damage that the beauty ideal and the cult of slenderness can inflict on women. Even "positive" norms such as the association of women with virtue, care, and nonviolence can serve to perpetuate the status quo by keeping women "in their place." Yet norms, like power, are everywhere. Norms are constitutive of behavior and communication. We can and do resist norms, even as we create new norms. For Foucault, the task does not appear to be to escape all social norms, which would be impossible, but to create ways of being and interacting that are non-normalizing. One of the ways that Foucault suggests that we resist normalization is through self-creation.

ONE'S LIFE AS A WORK OF ART: THE PERSONAL AS POLITICAL (AND ETHICAL)

Foucault raises the question "How can one define a work amid the millions of traces left by someone after his death?" (Foucault 1984b, 104). Although he raises this issue with regard to general questions about authorship and the unity of an author's work, the question has particular relevance to the interpretation of Foucault's own work. Foucault's untimely death leaves many questions unanswered. In the midst of a multivolume series on the history of sexuality, Foucault's work had come to increasingly focus on ethics and subjectivity. Some scholars contend that this focus on ethics and subjectivity in Foucault's later work constitutes a dramatic break from his earlier work, which they see as lacking an adequate notion of the subject and as apolitical. I have argued that Foucault's middle work focuses on the normalizing practices that constitute subjectivity, and that it is thus centrally concerned with ethics, politics, and subjectivity. Foucault himself states that the theme of subjectivity runs throughout his work, and that therefore his work ought not be seen as discontinuous or inconsistent: "My objective, instead, has been to create a history of the different modes by which, in our culture, human beings are made subjects. My work has dealt with three modes of objectification which transform human beings into subjects. . . . Thus it is not power, but the subject, which is the general theme of my research."[16] Sorting through the question of what defines a work, what ought to be included or excluded from consideration of an author's *oeuvre,* is no easy task.[17] I do not intend to provide a general or definitive answer to this complex question here, but I offer some reasons why in Foucault's case all of his writings, including his essays in the popular press, interviews, and political tracts should be included, as well as his political activism itself.

For Foucault the critical investigation that characterizes a philosophical attitude is an ongoing task that defines a life. In other words, Foucault applies the skepticism, the critique of domination, and the analysis of power apparent in his philosophical writings to actual historical situations with the goal of lessening domination. His historical analyses intersect with his concern for important contemporary social issues. For instance, during the time he researched and wrote *Discipline and Punish,* he was active in prison reform. Foucault's interviews and his articles in the popular press demonstrate his consistent engagement with political issues. Foucault's interviews and articles in the popular press should be included in his *oeuvre* because he considered them important and because they provide an important supplement to understanding his larger theoretical texts.[18] Moreover, Foucault's political activism should also count as evidence that he advocated social change.

Foucault himself proposed an intentional connection between the way one lived one's life and ethics. He advocated an aesthetic paradigm for ethics rather than a scientific paradigm because, as he demonstrates in his genealogical work, the scientific paradigm relies upon a priori notions and universals and he believes it is a mistake to apply universals to human behavior, which is variable and culturally and historically relative. He makes this connection between the aesthetic and the ethical explicit in his later work. He proposes that one's life should be a work of art, and that this entails ethical work on one's self. "From the idea that the self is not given to us, I think there is only one practical consequence: we have to create ourselves as a work of art" (Foucault 1982a, 237). Creating oneself as a work of art is an ethical project. Contrary to critics' charges that Foucault's aesthetics of existence in his later works was individualistic and aestheticized (as opposed to political), his discussions of the self as a work of art, the stylization of the self, and the aesthetics of existence involve ethical self-transformation in a social and political context.[19]

In his later work, especially *The Use of Pleasure*, *The Care for the Self*, and his interviews, Foucault makes the connection between self-creation and ethics. He views self-creation as inextricable from ethics. For Foucault self-transformation takes place through work on the self and involves what he calls techniques of the self. Foucault defines techniques or practices of the self as "techniques that permit individuals to effect by their own means or with the help of others a certain number of operations on their own bodies and souls, thoughts, conduct, and way of being, so as to transform themselves in order to attain a certain state of happiness, purity, wisdom, perfection or immortality" (Foucault 1988a, 18). Practices of the self include writing, truth-telling, and living a balanced life in terms of one's appetites. In his discussions of antiquity, Foucault specifically mentions the notebooks (*hypomnemata*) that the ancients kept and the letters of the early Romans as vehicles for ethical reflection. He notes that the role this "self-writing" played was not only to record one's thoughts and activities, but to seek advice from friends in letters, and to compile wise sayings in the notebooks. Writing as a practice of the self helped to develop ethical subjectivity by connecting one to others and by providing a tool for engaging in ethical reflection.

In volumes 2 and 3 of the *History of Sexuality*, Foucault examines "practices of the self" and "care of the self," respectively. In *The Use of Pleasure*, he details the "practices of the self"—those specific practices that one engages in to live an ethical life. In ancient Greece the task of becoming an ethical subject was achieved not through universalizing principles but through individualized action with respect to one's daily activities. The practices of the self that are discussed in his last two books revolve around the body. Foucault discusses the role that diet, sex, and exercise played in the development of the self for the ancients. He notes that there were many ethical guidelines, such as those in Artemidorus's dream interpretation, but that these guidelines did not function as moral prohibitions. Instead, they served to intensify one's relation to oneself, thus forming the basis for ethical subjectivity. Attention to various aspects of life—one's health, one's diet, the economy of

226

the household, one's spousal relationship, exercise, and sexual activity—were all included in what Foucault calls care of the self. Foucault's interest in describing and analyzing these ancient practices of the self is to explore the connection between moral systems and the specific forms of subjectivity that arise in relation to them. Cultivation of the self was fostered through care of the self and produces the ethical subject. According to Foucault, subjectivity arises within the history of ethics: "a history of 'ethics' [can be] understood as the elaboration of a form of relation to self that enables an individual to fashion himself into a subject of ethical conduct" (Foucault 1985a, 251). The formation of the subject, then, is the formation of an ethical subject formed through practices of the self and care of the self.

This cultivation of the self, however, is not an individual project; it takes place within established social practices, discourses, and institutions. In his later work dealing with ethical subjectivity and the aesthetics of existence, Foucault invokes the Greek notion of the "art of life" [*techne tou biou*], and he explicitly says that in fourth- and fifth-century Greece, the art of life involved taking care of the city and one's companions (Foucault 1982a, 235). As Foucault says, "the subject constitutes himself [*sic*] in an active fashion, by the practices of the self, [but] these practices are nevertheless not something the individual invents" (Foucault 1988a, 11). For Foucault the formation of the subject is a social practice; it relies on communication with others: "Around the care of the self, there developed an entire activity of speaking and writing in which the work of oneself on oneself and communication with others were linked together. Here we touch on one of the most important aspects of this activity devoted to oneself: it constituted, not an exercise in solitude but a true social practice" (Foucault 1986, 51).

Foucault's historical investigations indicate a productive way to think about subjectivity—as embedded in social practices, and cultural and historical traditions, as a process of individuation through self-mastery and discipline, and as a process of socialization through communication with others. His later works invite an expansive notion of subjectivity that includes looking at one's life as a work of art. Foucault's life as an engaged public intellectual participating in public debate through his writing for the popular press and challenging current structures of domination through his political activism suggest that his own "aesthetics of existence" should be seen as part of his attempt to create a new nondisciplinary, non-normalizing ethics.[20]

FOUCAULT, FEMINISM, AND FREEDOM

I have argued, contra Foucault's feminist critics, that his genealogies are a form of critique that does not rely on traditional Enlightenment norms. I have also explicated his notion of power in an attempt to defend his position against widespread misreading. Finally, I have shown how Foucault's later work urges us to think of our very lives as the material for ethical transformation. Foucault's focus on the self is far from individualistic and purely aesthetic, as some critics have claimed. In fact, Foucault's later work echoes the feminist claim that "the personal is political" and that theory and practice are inseparable.

Why should feminists embrace Foucault? One reason is because he provides a compelling account of social norms. He graphically illustrates the damage that norms can do through the process of marginalization and exclusion of those who do not conform to them. Foucault's work illustrates the ways that norms operate at the level of the body itself. Feminists should be sympathetic to the damage that norms can do. Although they masquerade as neutral, all too often norms universalize the perspective and position of the dominant.[21] A first step in resisting norms is to recognize them and to recognize them as potentially damaging. The obvious next step is to somehow resist the norms that are damaging. Like most feminist theorists, Foucault wants to allow that power exists and operates on the interpersonal, micropolitical level as well as on the structural, macropolitical level. His account of power helps to elucidate the ways that gender inflects power relationships. And through his concept of domination, power relations can also account for the asymmetry of power between men and women. Feminists need a multipronged approach in order to achieve gender equality. Feminists have long recognized that power pervades social, institutional, and interpersonal relationships, in addition to operating at the level of the law and the state. The primary way in which power operates on individuals is through norms. Foucault's relationship to norms is complex, but I have argued that this allows him both to question norms and to develop critical social analyses. In his genealogical work, the link between ethics and politics can be found in the link between self-constitution and social norms. To resist normalization is at once both ethical and political. Feminists should be sympathetic to resisting norms as a form of political action. Gender norms have perpetuated women's oppression in myriad ways. For example, feminine stereotypes such as physical weakness and emotional instability have historically restricted women's opportunities in the workplace. Foucault's call for new forms of subjectivity and individualization imply new social and political structures, since for him the process of "subjectification" has always and will always take place in a historically, socially, and culturally specific framework.

Foucault's notion of practices of the self offers a way to link individual action to social change. The feminist principle of not speaking for others (after all, one should be conscious and careful not to usurp power) is consistent with Foucault's own approach of eschewing general, abstract, universal solutions. Foucault's approach points to the specific, the local, the concrete, the particular. While his writings and interviews do not spell out solutions to social and political problems, his life as an activist provides many examples of specific and local resistance. To conclude, I suggest that Foucault's notion of practices of freedom can be applied to feminist consciousness-raising.

Truth telling or *parrhesia* is one of the practices of the self that Foucault discusses in his last lecture courses at Berkeley and at the Collège de France. Foucault discusses the role of truth telling in antiquity; it is both a political and a moral virtue. It is a political virtue because it arises in a democracy and is necessary to maintain democracy. Truth telling requires individual liberty, and those who tell the truth often challenge convention and the status quo. The following questions are relevant with regard to the practice of truth telling: Who is able to tell the truth? About what can she tell the truth? What are the consequences? What are the relations between the activity of truth telling and relations of power? These questions situate the practice of truth telling within specific social and historical conditions. As a moral virtue, truth telling is a necessary part of friendship and necessary for self-examination. Friends need to be truthful to one another in order to help each other learn. Likewise, one must be honest with oneself in order to improve and develop as an ethical person. Foucault likens the role of self-examination to a craftsperson examining her work, rather than a judge pronouncing edicts. Truth telling is a practice of the self that has political and moral dimensions and that involves both self and others in a political context. Like other practices of the self, truth telling can be a practice of freedom insofar as it challenges settled relations of power.

Feminists employed a method of truth telling to help achieve the goals of the Women's Liberation Movement. Consciousness-raising was a crucial organizing tool for feminist groups in the United States in the late 1960s. Consciousness-raising begins from women's experience; it involves weekly small-group meetings where women openly discuss issues in their lives. The process of consciousness-raising proved to be significant for the Women's Liberation Movement because as women shared their experiences, they came to recognize that their individual problems were not personal pathologies but reflected a larger pattern of social and political discrimination. In fact, the explicit goal of consciousness-raising was to link women's personal experiences with political and social structures and to help women to see that rather than individual shortcomings, sexism was the cause of many of the problems they faced. Consciousness-raising as a practice of the self supported women in telling the truth to one another and to speaking out against the male dominant political and social systems. Many consciousness-raising groups included action sessions where women strategized about how to promote social and political change. However, as discussed earlier, change at the political level is important but not sufficient. Because power operates at a multitude of levels, so must change. Consciousness-raising allows women to challenge gender norms. Indeed, the connection between gender roles and norms and social policies and practices that discriminate against women is not incidental. Consciousness-raising assumes a relationship between the personal and the political and connects individual subjectivity to social and institutional structures.

Consciousness-raising exemplifies the type of self-transformation that Foucault refers to in his discussion of practices of the self. One engages in practices of the self to produce self-transformation within a social context. Practices of the self draw upon the rules, methods, and customs of one's culture but are also practices of freedom, that is, they create new non-normalizing modes of existence and relationships. I suggest that consciousness-raising can be thought of as a practice of freedom. Foucault's idea of practices of the self involves work on the self and transformation of the self. Like other practices of the self, consciousness-raising draws on the rules and conventions of the culture and follows specific guidelines, but with the aim of transforming cultural convention. Indeed, its power lies in exposing oppressive, sexist social norms and the ways that they affect individual experience. It is this link between the normalizing practices of subjection and the process of individualization that Foucault makes explicit in his genealogical analyses. Self-transformation, then, implies social transformation because institutional and social practices constitute subjectivity. One of the ways that we resist this normalization is through engaging in practices of freedom that open up new possibilities for being, thinking, doing. Foucault's later work has much to offer feminists; it articulates a connection between self-transformation and social transformation. And practices of freedom open up space for both individual creativity and social innovation, both of which are important for a feminist refashioning of the world.

NOTES

I would like to thank the editors of this volume, Dianna Taylor and Karen Vintges, and the readers for the University of Illinois Press for their helpful suggestions on this essay. Some of the ideas here are more fully articulated in McLaren (2002).

1. Prominent feminist critics of Foucault include Nancy Hartsock, Nancy Fraser, Rosi Braidotti, Linda Alcoff, and Toril Moi. See citations that follow for specific references to their work.

2. Many feminists who engage with Foucault make these criticisms. On the issue of norms, some of the most compelling criticisms are made by Hartsock (1990) and (1996), and Fraser (1981) and (1983). For feminist criticisms regarding subjectivity, see Alcoff (1990), Braidotti (1994, especially chapter 7), and McNay (1991) and (1992).

3. For feminist criticisms, see Fraser (1985) and (1981) and Hartsock (1996) and (1990). For some nonfeminist criticisms, see Taylor (1986), Rorty (1986), and Habermas (1986). See also Habermas (1987, chapters 9 and 10).

4. There are various types of feminists, but a minimal condition for feminism is a commitment to equality between women and men and a commitment to ending women's oppression; see Jaggar and Rothenberg (1993, introduction).

5. I will not pursue this line of argument here. For an argument that Foucault rejects only particular formulations of subjectivity, see McLaren (1997) and (2002).

6. Although Balbus (1988) has claimed that Foucauldian feminism is a contradiction in terms, see Sawicki (1991) for compelling arguments that there can be a Foucauldian feminism, and that in fact Foucault's work can be a valuable resource for feminists, especially as we think through the issue of difference.

7. For instance, Hartsock (1998a) does this.

8. See Dreyfus and Rabinow (1982, 184, 188). Also see McWhorter (1990).

9. For a good discussion of this issue, see Dreyfus and Rabinow (1982, 184).

10. This is because feminism is based on the idea that there is an inequality of power between men and women. See Jaggar and Rothenberg (1993, introduction) for an overview of this issue. See also Allen (1999).

11. For Foucault's most extensive discussions of power, see Foucault (1980, 88–96), (1984c), and (1982b).

12. This claim is frequently cited as one of the reasons that Foucault's theory cannot be used by emancipatory social movements such as feminism: If there is no subject wielding power, then how are we to assign blame and responsibility, or to effect any sort of a change in the balance of power relations? As I will demonstrate, this is a misunderstanding of Foucault's rather complicated notion of power.

13. For a discussion of this, see Dreyfus and Rabinow (1982, 187) where they quote Foucault: "People know what they do; they frequently know why they do what they do; but what they don't know is what what they do does" (personal communication).

14. See, for instance, Allen (1996).

15. However, their status as women and mothers did not completely protect them. The leaders of the Mothers of the Plaza de Mayo were threatened, harassed, and physically assaulted. Some of them were even abducted and killed.

16. Foucault (1982b, 208–9). See also Foucault (1985a, preface).

17. One may well wonder what to make of Foucault's own authorship in light of his "What Is an Author?" In this essay Foucault examines the way that the concept "author" has functioned. He questions how an author's *oeuvre* is determined. Is it only published works? What does that mean for works published posthumously? Using Nietzsche as an example, Foucault includes rough drafts, plans for his aphorisms, deleted passages, and marginal notes as part of his work. But what if one

finds among the aphorisms a laundry list, the notation of a meeting? Foucault says that we lack a theory of the work that would provide an answer to this question— "How can one define a work amid the millions of traces left by someone after his death?" (Foucault 1984b, 104).

18. For a longer argument that justifies such inclusion, in fact demands it, see Cook (1993).

19. This is contrary to some critics who claim that Foucault lapses into aestheticism and individualism in his later work. See, for example, Grimshaw (1993) and Dews (1989). For a more detailed argument against this criticism, see McLaren (1997).

20. This is how Foucault describes his own project; see Foucault (1982a, 236–37).

21. This is by now a fairly commonplace argument; for example, feminists argue that the "neutral" perspective of the Enlightenment subject is, in fact, masculine and white.

WORKS CITED

Alcoff, Linda. 1990. "Feminist Politics and Foucault: The Limits to a Collaboration." In *Crises in Continental Philosophy*. Edited by Arleen Dallery and Charles Scott. Albany: State University of New York Press.

Allen, Amy. 1996. "Foucault on Power: A Theory for Feminists." In *Feminist Interpretations of Michel Foucault*. Edited by Susan Hekman. University Park: Pennsylvania State University Press.

———. 1999. *The Power of Feminist Theory: Domination, Resistance, Solidarity*. Boulder: Westview Press.

Balbus, Isaac. 1988. "Disciplining Women: Michel Foucault and the Power of Feminist Discourse." In *Feminism as Critique*. Edited by Seyla Benhabib and Drucilla Cornell. Minneapolis: University of Minnesota Press.

Benhabib, Seyla, and Drucilla Cornell, eds. 1988. *Feminism as Critique*. Minneapolis: University of Minnesota Press.

Bernauer, James, and David Rasmussen, eds. 1988. *The Final Foucault*. Cambridge: MIT Press.

Bouvard, Marguerite Guzmán. 1994. *Revolutionizing Motherhood: The Mothers of the Plaza de Mayo*. Wilmington, Del.: Scholarly Resources.

Braidotti, Rosi. 1994. *Nomadic Subjects: Embodiment and Sexual Difference in Contemporary Feminist Theory*. New York: Columbia University Press.

Brodribb, Somer. 1992. *Nothing Mat(t)ers: A Feminist Critique of Postmodernism*. North Melbourne: Spinifex Press.

Cook, Deborah. 1993. "Umbrellas, Laundry Bills, and Resistance: The Place of Foucault's Interviews in His Corpus." In *The Subject Finds a Voice: Michel Foucault's Subjective Turn*. 97–106. New York: Peter Lang.

Dews, Peter. 1989. "The Return of the Subject in the Late Foucault." *Radical Philosophy* 51: 37–41.

Dreyfus, Hubert, and Paul Rabinow. 1982. *Michel Foucault: Beyond Structuralism and Hermeneutics*. Chicago: University of Chicago Press.

Foucault, Michel. 1980. *The History of Sexuality.* Volume 1. *An Introduction.* New York: Vintage.

———. 1982a. "On the Genealogy of Ethics: An Overview of Work in Progress." In *Beyond Structuralism and Hermeneutics.* By Hubert Dreyfus and Paul Rabinow. Chicago: University of Chicago Press.

———. 1982b. "The Subject and Power." In *Beyond Structuralism and Hermeneutics.* By Hubert Dreyfus and Paul Rabinow. Chicago: University of Chicago Press.

———. 1984a. "What Is Enlightenment?" In *The Foucault Reader.* Edited by Paul Rabinow. New York: Pantheon.

———. 1984b. "What Is an Author?" In *The Foucault Reader.* Edited by Paul Rabinow. New York: Pantheon.

———. 1984c. "Truth and Power." In *The Foucault Reader.* Edited by Paul Rabinow. New York: Pantheon.

———. 1985a. *The History of Sexuality.* Volume 2. *The Use of Pleasure.* New York: Pantheon.

———. 1985b. "Final Interview." *Raritan* 5, no. 2: 1–13.

———. 1986. *The History of Sexuality.* Volume 3. *The Care of the Self.* New York: Pantheon.

———. 1988a. "The Ethic of Care for the Self as a Practice of Freedom." In *The Final Foucault.* Edited by James Bernauer and David Rasmussen. Cambridge: MIT Press.

———. 1988b. "Technologies of the Self." In *Technologies of the Self: A Seminar with Michel Foucault.* Edited by Luther H. Martin, Huck Gutman, and Patrick Hutton. Amherst: University of Massachusetts Press.

———. 1997a. "Subjectivity and Truth." In *The Essential Works of Foucault.* Volume 1. *Ethics, Subjectivity, and Truth.* Edited by Paul Rabinow. New York: New Press.

———. 1997b. "Self Writing." In *The Essential Works of Foucault.* Volume 1. *Ethics, Subjectivity, and Truth.* Edited by Paul Rabinow. New York: New Press.

———. 1997c. "The Ethics of the Concern for Self as a Practice of Freedom." In *The Essential Works of Foucault.* Volume 1. *Ethics, Subjectivity, and Truth.* Edited by Paul Rabinow. New York: New Press.

Fraser, Nancy. 1981. "Foucault on Modern Power: Empirical Insights and Normative Confusions." *Praxis International* 1, no. 23: 272–87.

———. 1983. "Foucault's Body Language: A Posthumanist Political Rhetoric?" *Salmagundi* 61: 55–73.

———. 1985. "Michel Foucault, A 'Young Conservative?'" *Ethics* 96, no. 1: 165–84.

———. 1989. *Unruly Practices: Power, Discourse, and Gender in Contemporary Social Theory.* Minneapolis: University of Minnesota Press.

Gordon, Colin, ed. 1980. *Power/Knowledge: Selected Interviews and Other Writings 1972–1977.* New York: Pantheon.

Grimshaw, Jean. 1993. "Practices of Freedom." In *Up against Foucault: Explorations of Some Tensions between Foucault and Feminism.* Edited by Caroline Ramazanoglu. New York: Routledge.

Habermas, Jürgen. 1986. "Taking Aim at the Heart of the Present." In *Foucault: A Critical Reader.* Edited by David Couzens Hoy. Oxford: Blackwell.

———. 1987. *The Philosophical Discourse of Modernity.* Cambridge: MIT Press.

Hartsock, Nancy. 1990. "Foucault on Power: A Theory for Women?" In *Feminism/Postmodernism.* Edited by Linda Nicholson. New York: Routledge.

———. 1996. "Postmodernism and Political Change: Issues for Feminist Theory." In *Feminist Interpretations of Michel Foucault.* Edited by Susan Hekman. University Park: Pennsylvania State University Press.

Hekman, Susan, ed. 1996. *Feminist Interpretations of Michel Foucault.* University Park: Pennsylvania State University Press.

Hoy, David Couzens. 1986. *Foucault: A Critical Reader.* Oxford: Blackwell.

Jaggar, Alison, and Paula Rothenberg, eds. 1993. *Feminist Frameworks.* New York: McGraw-Hill.

McLaren, Margaret. 1997. "Foucault and the Subject of Feminism." *Social Theory and Practice* 23, no. 1: 109–28.

———. 2002. *Feminism, Foucault, and Embodied Subjectivity.* Albany: State University of New York Press.

McNay, Lois. 1991. "The Foucauldian Body and the Exclusion of Experience." *Hypatia* 6: 125–37.

———. 1993. *Foucault and Feminism: Power, Gender, and the Self.* Boston: Northeastern University Press.

McWhorter, Ladelle. 1990. "Foucault's Analytics of Power." In *Crises in Continental Philosophy.* Edited by Arleen Dallery and Charles Scott. Albany: State University of New York Press.

———. 1999. *Bodies and Pleasures: Foucault and the Politics of Sexual Normalization.* Bloomington: Indiana University Press.

Moi, Toril. 1985. "Power, Sex, and Subjectivity: Feminist Reflections on Foucault." *Paragraph: Journal of the Modern Critical Theory Group* 5: 95–102.

Nicholson, Linda, ed. 1990. *Feminism/Postmodernism.* New York: Routledge.

Rabinow, Paul, ed. 1997. *The Essential Works of Foucault.* Volume 1. *Ethics, Subjectivity and Truth.* New York: New Press.

Ramazanoglu, Caroline, ed. 1993. *Up against Foucault: Explorations of Some Tensions between Foucault and Feminism.* New York: Routledge.

Rorty, Richard. 1986. "Foucault and Epistemology." In *Foucault: A Critical Reader.* Edited by David Couzens Hoy. Oxford: Blackwell.

Sawicki, Jana. 1991. *Disciplining Foucault: Feminism, Power, and the Body.* New York: Routledge.

———. 1996. "Feminism, Foucault, and 'Subjects' of Power and Freedom." In *Feminist Interpretations of Michel Foucault.* Edited by Susan Hekman. University Park: Pennsylvania State University Press.

Taylor, Charles. 1986. "Foucault on Freedom and Truth." In *Foucault: A Critical Reader.* Edited by David Couzens Hoy. Oxford: Blackwell.

Foucault, Feminism, and the Self:
The Politics of Personal Transformation

Amy Allen

In recent years, the feminist literature on the self has grown considerably.[1] The expansion of this literature might well lead one to wonder why the self has become such a hot topic for feminist theory. Initially, at least, the answer to this question seems obvious: how we conceptualize the self is closely related to our views about reason, critique, autonomy, and agency, all of which are concepts that lie at the heart of law, moral theory, political theory, and social science. As feminists have subjected existing work in these domains to critique and have developed feminist perspectives on legal, moral, political, and social theory, they have had to confront the assumptions about the self that underpin inquiry in these areas. Thus, it makes perfect sense that feminists have been so concerned with critiquing mainstream philosophical conceptions of the self and with offering their own reconceptualizations.

Now, one might wonder, why bring Foucault into this conversation about feminist theory and the self? One reason to attempt this is that there are features of his account of the self that seem quite attractive from a feminist perspective. For example, in his genealogies of power, Foucault envisions the self as embodied, embedded in a social and cultural milieu, constituted by power relations, in short, thoroughly contextualized. This account not only dovetails with feminist critiques of the abstract individualism of mainstream philosophical conceptions of the self, it also offers feminists extremely useful resources for thinking about the role that oppressive socialization plays in the formation of gendered selves.[2] Critics, of course, have complained that the account of the self in Foucault's genealogical works is *too* contextualized; social relations imbued with power that render bodies docile threaten to obliterate the agency and autonomy of the self. In response to this line of criticism, one might look to Foucault's late work (Foucault 1985, 1986, and 1997a), with its account of practices of the self. From these texts, one might argue, a conception of the self that is useful for feminist theory and politics can be reconstructed, according to which the self is embodied and embedded in specific social and cultural relations but still capable of agency.[3]

However, this appeal does not settle the issue, for there has been a lively debate among feminists over just how to interpret Foucault's late work and the account of practices of the self that forms its core. The initial feminist reaction to this account was negative; feminist critics charged Foucault with offering an overly individualistic, decontextualized, even masculine account of the self that is of little relevance to feminist theory and politics. More recently, some Foucauldian feminists have begun to reassess Foucault's late work, arguing that Foucault's critics have overlooked the social dimension of his analysis of practices of the self. Further, it has been suggested that his analysis of these practices is not only useful for feminist and queer politics but may even overlap in a significant way with the relational conception of the self that has figured prominently in feminist moral, social, and political theory. My primary task in what follows will be to adjudicate this debate. To this end, I will be addressing the following questions: is the account of the self offered in Foucault's late work guilty of the sort of decontextualized individualism of which feminists have been so critical? Or, alternatively, is there a relational account of the self to be found in Foucault? If so, what sort of relational account of the self does he endorse? Does it or does it not overlap with the account of the relational self elaborated by feminists? Is it or is it not useful for feminist theory and politics? Although I will argue, in the end, that the account of the self that can be reconstructed from Foucault's late work is rather limited from a feminist perspective, I will also suggest that getting clear on the limitations of this account can be quite helpful for feminists who are rethinking the self.

I shall proceed as follows. In the first section, I shall briefly rehearse arguments on both sides of feminist debate about the late Foucault. In the second section, I will attempt to tease out what I take to be the central insight of feminist conceptions of the relational self—namely, that the self is both created and maintained by social interactions structured by mutuality and reciprocity. In the third section, I shall consider Foucault's late work on practices or technologies of the self in detail. I shall argue that, despite the fact that there are senses in which Foucault conceives the self as having a social dimension, nevertheless, his account of the self and the assumptions about social relations that undergird it differ in important ways from the conception laid out in the second section. Moreover, I shall argue that these differences cause problems for Foucault's account of the self on two levels: first, at the level of his general philosophical project of exploring the formation of the ethical subject; and, second, at the level of his historico-political project of uncovering resources for certain sorts of contemporary projects of personal transformation. I shall conclude by sketching out some desiderata for a feminist account of the self that are made evident by this consideration of the late Foucault.

FOUCAULT'S CONCEPTION OF THE SELF: INDIVIDUALISTIC OR RELATIONAL?

Lois McNay offers one of the earliest and most extensive feminist discussions of Foucault's late work. Although McNay credits Foucault's late work with correcting what she sees as a deficiency in his earlier genealogical works—in particular, the lack of a satisfactory account of subjectivity or agency—she remains highly critical of Foucault's analysis of practices of the self. Her major objection is that Foucault's account "privileges an undialectical and disengaged theory of the self. . . . [T]his privileging of the isolated self in the idea of an aesthetics of existence conflicts with recent feminist attempts to understand more fully the intersubjective dimension of social relations" (McNay 1992, 157).[4] In addition, McNay worries that this undialectical account of the self cannot offer an effective antidote to the normalizing and disciplinary effects of contemporary power/knowledge regimes that Foucault so brilliantly exposed. Thus, McNay questions whether "the idea of the formation of the self as a work of art, predicated on the severance of links between the self and other social structures, is really an adequate strategy with which to resist the government of individualization" (ibid., 165). In the end, McNay concludes that "Foucault's nondialogic conception of the individual leads to a false dichotomy between the individual and the social. The social realm is seen as invariably antipathetic to individual interest, rather than as a realm which both protects and threatens these interests, and, therefore, as a realm of contestation and struggle" (ibid., 190).

Kate Soper echoes some of McNay's concerns. She refers to the account of the self that emerges in Foucault's late work as "individualistic and even narcissistic" (Soper 1993, 35–36). Soper goes beyond McNay, however, in suggesting that this account is not merely in conflict with feminist investigations; it is, in her view, thoroughly masculine. Here, Soper is not so much concerned with the fact that Foucault's late work focuses on ancient Greek and Roman practices that were carried out exclusively by men, and, more specifically, men who were not slaves, though she does note this in passing.[5] Instead, she suggests that it is the abstract and individualistic nature of Foucault's self that makes it characteristically masculine. As she puts it, "by abstracting as much as he can both from the social context of the ethical codes he is charting, and from the dialectic of personal relations, [Foucault] defines the ethical so as to make it appear a very private—and masculine—affair: a matter primarily of self-mastery and authorial creation" (ibid., 41).

Finally, Jean Grimshaw argues that, despite the fact that Foucault claimed—at least in some passages—that his conception of the self was a social one, he does not do more than "pay lip service" to the idea of the social in his analysis of technologies of the self" (Grimshaw 1993, 68).[6] According to Grimshaw, Foucault's late work is concerned with "the relation to self of a few elite males; and it is noteworthy that those with whom they have relationships seem to be thought of as instruments through which they fashion their own freedom" (ibid.). Grimshaw points out that much work in feminist ethics has gone beyond the narrow and impoverished conception of sociality that seems implicit in Foucault's late work; whereas for Foucault, social relations seem to be conceived exclusively in terms of instrumental or strategic relations with others, for many feminist ethicists, social relations are also structured by mutuality, cooperation, and collectivity (see ibid.). (I shall discuss this issue in much more detail below.)

Recently, however, Foucauldian feminists have begun to respond to this line of criticism by suggesting a more sympathetic reading of Foucault's late work. For example, Ladelle McWhorter defends Foucault's notion of the care of the self as offering the basis for an appropriate ethics for those who are interested in challenging the current regime of sexual normalization. In the context of this defense, McWhorter points out the social dimensions of the practice of care of the self that feminist critics of Foucault's late work had tended to overlook or underemphasize. As she puts it: "care of the self need not be antisocial. It is even possible that putting care for one's self above all else might mean developing the competence and self-confidence that make true generosity possible, the peace of mind that makes real sharing possible, and the desire for community that makes honesty, patience, and cooperation paramount. Putting care for one's self above all else could be the founding moment of an intensely ethical life" (McWhorter 1999, 196). In other words, an ethics of care for the self need not amount to nothing more than an embrace of narcissistic individualism and of using others as means to one's own end of individual self-fashioning, as Foucault's feminist critics have alleged. But saying that care of the self *need not be* antisocial is obviously not the same as saying that it *is* not antisocial. Does care of the self necessarily lead to an intensely ethical life? Again, McWhorter defends Foucault's account, noting that "no one engages in any sort of ethical practice—no one establishes routines, values, systems of meaning—alone. . . . [E]ven though my ethical work must be my own, I need the work of other people. So I'll be inclined to pay some attention to others and to care about and even foster at least some of their work" (ibid., 197). Here,

McWhorter echoes a comment that Foucault made in a late interview on the topic of care of the self: "I would say that if now I am interested in fact in the way the subject constitutes himself in an active fashion, by the practices of the self, these practices are nevertheless not something the individual invents. They are models that he finds in his culture and are proposed, suggested, imposed upon him by his culture, his society, and his social group" (Foucault 1997b, 291). From this passage, it is clear that the care of the self is a social practice in the sense that the practices used by individuals to care for themselves are derived from the broader social and cultural context in which they find themselves; thus, there is *in some sense* a social or relational dimension to Foucault's account of the self. However, it is worth noting that McWhorter still conceives of this dimension in instrumental terms: because I need others in order to care for myself, I shall be inclined to care for them and foster their own work on themselves, at least to the extent that it fosters my own in return. Interestingly enough, Foucault himself does not explicitly draw the same instrumentalist conclusion that McWhorter does; however, inasmuch as her defense of Foucault seems to turn on this instrumentalist understanding of social relations, it does not adequately address the concerns of the critics discussed above.

Margaret McLaren agrees with McWhorter that care for the self "takes place within established social practices, discourses, and institutions" (McLaren 1997, 118). However, she also goes further than McWhorter, arguing that Foucault's late work offers an account of a "fundamentally social self," one that "bears a resemblance to care ethics' relational self" (ibid., 112). In order to make her case, she argues that "care of the self and the attendant intensification of the relation of self to self relied on communication with others" (ibid.).[7] Thus, she contends, "care of the self did not result in individualism, but on the contrary was a social practice" (ibid., 119).

Although McWhorter and McLaren do succeed, I think, in establishing the point that there is an often overlooked social dimension to his account of practices of the self, it remains unclear how exactly Foucault conceived this social dimension. Foucault's contention that practices of the self are always drawn from a broader social context seems to boil down to the no doubt indisputable but also quite minimal claim that no one invents their practices out of thin air. McLaren makes a stronger, but also much more controversial, claim that care of the self relies on communicative relations with others; I shall return to discuss this issue in more detail in the third section. At the very least, these defenses of Foucault should lead us to wonder: In what sense are practices of the self social practices? Assuming that the conception of the self that can be reconstructed from Foucault's late work is social or relational, is it so in the same sense that characterizes fem-

inist conceptions of the relational self? What assumptions about social relations underlie feminist accounts of the relational self? What assumptions
underlie Foucault's account? Are these assumptions compatible? These are
the sorts of questions that need to be addressed before we can adjudicate
the disagreement among feminists over how to assess the final Foucault.

FEMINISM AND THE RELATIONAL SELF

In order to begin to answer these questions, more needs to be said both
about how feminists have conceived the self and about the assumptions
about social relations that underlie such conceptions. In this section, I will
consider feminist accounts of the relational self. Let me note at the outset
that I am using the term "relational self" in much the same way that Catriona Mackenzie and Natalie Stoljar use the term "relational autonomy" in
the introduction to their recent anthology on that topic, namely, as an "umbrella term, designating a range of related perspectives" (Mackenzie and
Stoljar 2000, 4). It is not my intention to suggest that there is a single, unified,
feminist conception of the self in general, or of the relational self in particular. However, I do believe that one can discern a shared insight of these related feminist perspectives on the relational self: namely, that mutual, reciprocal, communicative social interactions are necessary for the formation,
sustenance, and repair of the self.

Perhaps the most influential feminist model of the relational self was initially elaborated by Nancy Chodorow and later extended by Carol Gilligan.[8]
In Chodorow's view, both male and female infants depend for the development of their identity on their primary identification and subsequent
separation from their primary caregiver, usually, in our culture, their mother
(or another female mother-substitute). For girls, the fact that they and their
mothers are the same gender means that the development of their own
(feminine) identity can be based on an identification with their mother and
that this identification translates into women defining themselves relationally. As Chodorow puts it: "As a result of having been parented by a woman,
women are more likely than men to seek to be mothers, that is, to relocate
themselves in a primary mother-child relationship, to get gratification from
the mothering relationship, and to have psychological and relational capacities for mothering. . . . [W]omen's sense of self is continuous with others. . . . [W]omen define and experience themselves relationally" (Chodorow 1978, 206–7). For boys, the fact that their gender is different from that
of their primary caregiver means that their primary identification with the
mother is something that must be repudiated in order for them to develop
their (masculine) identity. This leads boys to repress and curtail their rela-

tional capacities: "Men . . . do not define themselves in relationship and have come to suppress relational capacities and repress relational needs. This prepares them to participate in the affect-denying world of alienated work, but not to fulfill women's needs for intimacy and primary relationships" (ibid., 207). The upshot of this view of the self is that although all selves are relational in some sense, inasmuch as they are all formed through our early childhood relations with others, the institution of female parenting creates girls and women who have relational selves in some additional sense (that is, women view relations with others as a fundamental part of who they are) and boys and men who do not (that is, men view detachment from others and independence as definitive of who they are).

Gilligan famously extended Chodorow's views to the realm of ethics, arguing that Chodorow's model of infant development could help to explain the emergence in women of a care perspective on moral reasoning, distinct from the masculine justice perspective with its attendant focus on rights, equality, and abstract moral rules.[9] As Gilligan puts it, the care perspective "is grounded in the assumption that self and other are interdependent, an assumption reflected in a view of action as responsive and, therefore, as arising in relationship. . . . [T]he self is by definition connected to others. . . . Within this framework, detachment, whether from self or from others, is morally problematic, since it breeds moral blindness or indifference—a failure to discern or respond to need" (Gilligan 1995, 36). Although Gilligan was always careful to note that her different voice was "characterized not by gender but by theme" and that she did not intend to offer generalizations about either men or women, the care perspective is clearly associated with femininity and the justice perspective with masculinity, at the very least at the level of cultural images and representations of these two paradigms (Gilligan 1982, 2).[10]

As influential as these feminist models of the relational self have been, they have also been subjected to a good deal of feminist criticism.[11] More recently, feminist models of the relational self have emerged that rely neither on Chodorow's ahistorical and acultural story about the development of gender identity nor on Gilligan's questionable revaluation of feminine relationality. Instead, these models delineate both the ways in which everyone's sense of self is formed relationally through attachments to and relationships with others and the importance of such relational models of the self for feminist theory. For instance, Johanna Meehan argues that an intersubjective model of the self, such as the one offered by Jürgen Habermas, is necessary for an adequate feminist analysis of the way that gender is "psychically invented and socially elaborated" (Meehan 2000, 40). Drawing on the work of social psychologist George Herbert Mead, Habermas argues that selves are formed "on the path from without to within," through their so-cial and, thus, linguistically saturated relations with others (Habermas 1992, 177). Meehan argues for a feminist extension of this account, based on the observation that, in cultures such as our own, both social competence and linguistic competence depend on understanding gender difference and per-forming a stable gender identity. Thus, for us, "getting gender right" and becoming a self go hand in hand (Meehan 2000, 41). Meehan argues that this sort of intersubjective account of the self is necessary for feminists who are struggling to understand "the stubbornness of identity and its persist-ence despite feminist interventions" (ibid., 40). In short, Meehan argues that Habermas's account offers feminists a view of the self that can help us to explain "how we could be gendered all the way down" (ibid.).[12]

Although Meehan draws on Habermas's account of individuation through (linguistic) socialization, she also argues that this account must be supple-mented with an account of the emotional, psychic, and affective attachments to others that play crucial roles in the formation of (gender) identity. If we really want to understand the recalcitrance of gender identity even in the face of feminist critique, we need to understand not only how children take on gender identities as they take up roles in language, but also how they be-come emotionally and psychically attached to their gender identity, an at-tachment that tends to blunt the force of intellectual critique. According to Meehan, this means supplementing Habermas's analysis of the commu-nicative dimensions of subjectivity with more attention to the affective and psychic dimensions of our relations with others and the role that these di-mensions play in the formation of the self.

Susan Brison develops a similar account of the self as fundamentally re-lational from a very different perspective. In her analysis of trauma and its aftermath, Brison argues that human-inflicted traumas such as rape, war, torture, and concentration camps reduce their victims to mere objects. Thus, "[the victims'] subjectivity is rendered useless and viewed as worth-less. . . . Without [the belief that one can *be oneself* in relation to others, which is destroyed by trauma] . . . one can no longer *be oneself* even to one-self, since the self exists fundamentally in relation to others" (Brison 2002, 40). In order to survive trauma, one must "remake" oneself after having one's sense of self virtually obliterated. Brison argues that this heroic feat can be accomplished only in the context of the right sorts of relations with others. For example, the experience of trauma reduces the victim to silence, or, worse, turns her into the instrument of someone else's speech. After this experience, the only way for a survivor to regain her voice is for her to tell her story to others; as Brison puts it, "fortunately, just as one can be re-duced to an object through torture, one can become a human subject again through telling one's narrative to caring others who are able to listen" (ibid., 57). Communicative relationships with caring others thus form, for Brison, a kind of scaffolding that a survivor of trauma can use to rebuild her sense of self.

I would not pretend that the foregoing sketch offers a comprehensive overview of feminist work on the relational self, but such is not my aim.[13] Instead, I present these feminist accounts in order to bring out what I see as their shared insight: namely, that the self itself is thoroughly relational inasmuch as it can only be created, sustained, and remade in the face of threats to its coherence in and through certain sorts (communicative, reciprocal, mutual) of relations with others. This, in turn, entails an assumption about social relations: namely, that communicative, reciprocal, mutual relations with others are both possible and crucial for how we think about the self. This is not to suggest that feminists interested in the relational self would be so naive as to argue that all social relations are structured by reciprocity and mutuality; Meehan and Brison would no doubt agree that many social interactions are characterized by strategic imperatives, if not by domination or outright violence. However, it seems clear that the possibility of mutuality, reciprocity, and communication as features of social interaction is a central feature of these feminist accounts of the self.[14] Having delineated this feminist conception of the relational self and isolated its central insight, we are now in a position to return to some of our earlier questions about the conception of the self implicit in the late Foucault, in particular: Is the conception of the self found in the late Foucault social or relational in the same sense that these feminists have analyzed the social or relational self? Do his assumptions about social relations square with the insight that communicative, mutual, and reciprocal social interactions are crucial for the formation, maintenance, and repair of the self?

TECHNOLOGIES OF THE SELF

In order to answer these questions, we need to look closely at Foucault's analysis of practices or technologies of the self. The first thing to note is that often when Foucault talks about technologies of the self, he says nothing at all about their social dimension. For instance, when he introduces the idea of the technologies of the self, he defines them as "techniques that permit individuals to effect, by their own means, a certain number of operations on their own bodies, their own souls, their own thoughts, their own conduct, and this in a manner so as to transform themselves, modify themselves, and to attain a certain state of perfection, happiness, purity, and supernatural power" (Foucault 1997e, 177). This passage and others like

243

it provide grist for the mill of Foucault's feminist critics. As McLaren and McWhorter rightly point out, however, there are times when Foucault explicitly recognizes a social dimension of practices of the self.[15] Nevertheless, I shall argue that when we look closely at how Foucault conceives of this social dimension, his conception differs substantially from the feminist conception of the relational self discussed above.

One way that Foucault conceptualizes the social dimension of practices of the self is evident in his discussion in *The Use of Pleasure* of the link between mastery of the self and mastery of others. This link figures prominently in his account of the marital relationship in classical Greece. For example, regarding the Greeks' attitude toward extramarital sex, Foucault notes that the wife was expected to remain faithful to her husband simply by virtue of his authority over her. "In the man's case," on the other hand, "it was *because he exercised authority and because he was expected to exhibit self-mastery in the use of his authority,* that he needed to limit his sexual options. For the wife, having sexual relations only with her husband was a consequence of the fact that she was under his control. For the husband, having sexual relations only with his wife was the most elegant way of exercising his control" (Foucault 1985, 151; emphasis added). According to Foucault, the assumption that mastery of oneself was a necessary component of or perhaps even a precondition for the mastery of others was not limited to the marital relationship but was extended by Nicocles to his account of the proper exercise of political power as well. As Foucault puts it, Nicocles argues that "the prince's moderation . . . serves as the basis of a sort of compact between the ruler and the ruled: the latter can obey him, seeing that he is master of himself . . ." (ibid., 174). Thus, for both the husband and the prince, striving to live a beautiful life meant practicing what Foucault calls "an ethics of self-delimiting domination" (ibid., 184). Moreover, it was because the classical Greeks viewed such an ethics as a requirement for a beautiful life that erotic relationships between men and boys were problematized. Foucault argues that the Greeks associated being the object of love, and, thus, being the submissive partner in an erotic relationship with being submissive or dominated more generally; thus, with respect to love of boys, "one had to keep in mind that the day would come when he would have to be a man, to exercise power and responsibilities, so that obviously he could then no longer be an object of pleasure—but then, to what extent could he have been such an object? . . . The relationship that he was expected to establish with himself in order to become a free man, master of himself and capable of prevailing over others, was at variance with a relationship in which he would be an object of pleasure for another" (ibid., 220–21). In these passages and others like them, Foucault clearly recognizes a social dimension to practices of the self, but there are two things to note about his account of this dimension. First, the move-ment is from an already formed self seeking to refine his existence so that it has the most beautiful form possible outward to others, not, as in the femi-nist models that I considered above, from certain sorts of social relations that serve as necessary preconditions for attaining and maintaining a sense of self at all toward the formation of the self. Second, the sort of relation that does the work of linking self and other in this case is one of domination, mastery, and control, not, as in the feminist models of the relational self, communi-cation, reciprocity, mutuality.

A different sense in which there is a social dimension to ancient practices of the self is evident in Foucault's discussion of the care of the self in vol-ume 3 of *The History of Sexuality.* There, Foucault argues that as the prac-tices of the self intensified in the first centuries of the common era, "there developed [around the care of the self] an entire activity of speaking and writing in which the work of oneself on oneself and communication with others were linked together. Here we touch on one of the most important aspects of this activity devoted to oneself: it constituted, not an exercise in solitude, but a true social practice" (Foucault 1986, 51). Elsewhere, Foucault notes that "care of the self . . . implies a relationship with the other insofar as proper care of the self requires listening to the lessons of a master. One needs a guide, a counselor, a friend, someone who will be truthful with you" (Foucault 1997b, 287). These passages do suggest a relational dimension of the self of some sort. However, once we consider the ways of relating with others that Foucault has in mind here, we will see that his conception of this relational dimension is quite different from the feminist accounts discussed above.

In the essay "Self-Writing," for example, Foucault specifies what he has in mind when he speaks of relying on a friend or guide in one's own care for oneself. He discusses two particular practices: the *hypomnemata* and correspondence. The *hypomnemata* were notebooks in which one wrote down quotes, reflections, reasonings, excerpts from books that one found especially meaningful, events that one had witnessed, and so forth. They were not personal journals; rather, they were "books for life," whose pur-pose was "to capture the already said, to collect what one has managed to hear or read, and for a purpose that is nothing less than the shaping of the self" (Foucault 1997d, 211). While it is true that Foucault says, in the con-text of his discussion of these notebooks, that "the help of others is neces-sary" for their creation "for one could not draw everything from one's own stock or arm oneself by oneself with the principles of reason that are in-dispensable for self-conduct," this remark occurs in the context of a dis-cussion of the importance of *reading* for the creation of the *hypomnemata* (ibid.). In his discussion of correspondence, Foucault suggests that correspondence is a practice of the self inasmuch as it "constitutes a certain way of manifesting oneself to oneself and to others. . . . To write is thus to 'show oneself,' to project oneself into view, to make one's own face appear in the other's presence" (ibid., 216). In both cases, Foucault seems to be assuming an already formed self who either uses the writings of others as a guide to his own self-practices or who manifests himself to others via correspondence. Neither of these examples evinces a recognition that one needs particular relationships with concrete others in order to attain one's sense of self in the first place or to maintain it once it has been achieved.[16]

Indeed, Foucault underlines this difference when he says: "The care of the self is ethically prior [to care for others] in that *the relationship with oneself is ontologically prior*" (Foucault 1997b, 287; emphasis added). For the feminist theorists discussed above, precisely the opposite would seem to be the case: relationships with others are ontologically prior to the relationship with oneself, inasmuch as acquiring and maintaining a sense of self is possible only when the right sorts of relations with others are in place. Reciprocal and communicative relations with others are a necessary (though not a sufficient) condition for being a self or having a sense of self at all.

Not only does Foucault's late account of the self seem to overlook the importance of mutuality and reciprocity for the creation and maintenance of the self, one can even discern in his discussions of care of the self a lingering anxiety about reciprocity. In *The Care of the Self*, reciprocity is discussed explicitly in several passages. However, what is notable about these passages is that they all deal with the shift that took place between classical Greece and late antiquity with respect to the sexual relationship that was taken to be paradigmatic: for the classical Greeks, that relationship was the love of boys; by late antiquity, the emphasis had shifted to the marital relationship. As a result of this shift, Foucault writes,

> Henceforth one was in a world where . . . the relation of superiority exercised in the household and over the wife had to be associated with certain forms of reciprocity and equality. As for the agonistic game by which one sought to manifest and ensure one's superiority over others, it had to be integrated into a far more extensive and complex field of power relations. Consequently, the principle of superiority over the self as the ethical core, the general form of "heautocraticism," needed to be restructured. Not that it disappeared; but it had to make room for a certain balance between inequality and reciprocity in married life. (Foucault 1986, 95)

In late antiquity, according to Foucault, there is an injunction upon the individual who cares for himself to marry and a further requirement that his married life should take "a deliberate form and a particular style. This style, with the moderation it requires, is not defined by self-mastery alone and by the principle that one must govern oneself in order to be able to rule others. It is also defined by the elaboration of a certain form of reciprocity" (ibid., 163). Foucault also says that this shift led to a "crisis of subjectivation" (ibid., 95). Thus, Foucault suggests that the more reciprocity became a part of the picture for the ancients, the more problematic subjectivation became. Although it could be that Foucault is, in these passages, merely reporting an anxiety that the Greeks and Romans themselves felt about the emerging norms of egalitarian reciprocity that governed the marital relationship in late antiquity, there is also reason to think that these passages are indicative of Foucault's own anxiety. As is made clear by the general trajectory of the argument in volumes 2 and 3 of *The History of Sexuality*, the supplanting of the love of boys by love within marriage as the most privileged erotic relationship paves the way for the later confining of legitimate sexuality to marriage that was part and parcel of the emergence of modern heteronormativity and the mechanisms of sexual normalization it employs. Given that the only explicit discussions of reciprocity in these texts occur in the context of discussions of this shift, it seems unlikely that Foucault is entirely sanguine about the emergence of reciprocity as a norm for sexual relationships.

Taken together, these three ways of conceiving of the link between practices of the self and relations with others—the link in *The Use of Pleasure* between self-mastery and the mastery of others, the sorts of relations with others that Foucault offers as examples of the social dimension of the care of the self, and the anxiety about reciprocity expressed in his account of the marital relationship in late antiquity—should be sufficient to establish that Foucault's account of the self is significantly different from the feminist models of the relational self discussed above, with their emphasis on mutuality, communication, and reciprocity.

Up to now, I have been considering only the account of the self to be found in Foucault's late work. One might argue that my reconstruction of Foucault's conception of the self is thus incomplete. After all, Foucault himself claims that his account of "technologies of the self" needs to be integrated with his earlier account of "technologies of domination" (Foucault 1997e, 177). Indeed, he suggests that the reason he is interested in ancient technologies of the self is that the genealogical exploration of them might yield some insight into both how the current regime of normalization developed and how it might be possible to carve out a space of freedom within it. Greek and Roman practices of the self were, according to Foucault, relatively independent of the kinds of structures of normalization to which our own contemporary technologies of the self are bound.[17] Thus, although he is clear that he does not think we can or should even try to "go Greek," he does suggest that there are certain elements of ancient practices of the self that might be useful for us to recover, that might even allow us to challenge and/or resist the normalizing and disciplinary power/knowledge regimes that he discusses in his genealogies. As he puts it: "Among the cultural inventions of mankind there is a treasury of devices, techniques, ideas, procedures, and so on, that cannot exactly be reactivated, but at least constitute, or help to constitute, a certain point of view which can be very useful as a tool for analyzing what's going on now—and to change it" (Foucault 1997c, 261). Foucault's teacher and mentor Georges Canguilhem puts it more succinctly: "In the face of normalization and against it, *Le Souci de Soi*" (Canguilhem 1997, 32).

If we follow Foucault's lead here and consider these two aspects of his account of the self together, one might suggest, we would see a truly social or relational self emerge.[18] On this integrated Foucauldian account, the self is constituted from without by disciplinary, normalizing power relations and then (potentially, at least) constitutes itself through practices of self-discipline that (again, potentially) allow it to transform itself from a normalized individual into a living work of art. However, even assuming, as I think we should, that these two aspects of Foucault's work fit together in a coherent way,[19] it still seems to me that the account of the self as social or relational that results would have significant limitations. What remains unsatisfactory about this sort of account of the self is the lack of attention paid to the role that relations of mutuality, reciprocity, and recognition play in the creation and sustaining of the self. In his genealogies of power, the social relations that constitute the self are normalizing and disciplinary and, as such, not structured by reciprocity and mutuality.[20] And, as I have argued above, in his account of ethics, the self constitutes itself via practices that are drawn from the social world around him and in some cases relies on relations with others in order to do so, but once again there is no account of the role that reciprocal relations with others necessarily play in the formation of the self, and there is even a lingering anxiety about reciprocity evident in Foucault's account of care of the self.

However, this leaves open the question of whether some sort of an account of the role that communicative, mutual, reciprocal relations with others play in the formation of the self *could* be integrated into Foucault's analysis of technologies of the self without generating massive contradictions. It seems to me that the answer to this question is not obvious; there is textual support on either side. On the one hand, Foucault is fairly consistent right up to the end on his view that social relations always involve power and that power, for him, is always strategic. He makes this clear more than once when he is pressed by interviewers to defend his claims that there is no outside to power, that power is coextensive with the social realm. In response to one such interviewer, Foucault says: "when I speak of relations of power . . . I mean that in human relationships, whether they involve verbal communications such as we are engaged in at this moment, or amorous, institutional, or economic relationships, power is always present: I mean a relationship in which one person tries to control the conduct of the other" (Foucault 1997b, 292). Later in the same interview, he notes, "power relations are not something that is bad in itself, that we have to break free of. . . . [P]ower is not evil. Power is games of strategy" (ibid., 298). Moreover, Foucault explicitly links these assumptions about power with his account of practices of the self. For example, in the conclusion to *The Use of Pleasure*, Foucault notes that, for the Greeks, "reflection on sexual behavior as a moral domain was . . . a means of developing—for the smallest minority of the population, made up of free, adult males—an aesthetics of existence, the purposeful art of a freedom perceived as a power game" (Foucault 1985, 252–53). Similarly, in late interviews, Foucault talks at length about the intimate interconnections between power and freedom, noting that "liberation paves the way for new power relationships, which must be controlled by practices of freedom" and "power relations are possible only insofar as the subjects are free" (Foucault 1997b, 283–84, 292). Thus, for Foucault, power and freedom are interconnected in (minimally) two ways: first, power operates only where individuals are free; second, self-constituting practices of freedom involve strategically reworking the power relations to which individuals find themselves subjected. The point here is that all social relations, including the ones that play an important role in practices of the self, involve power. Inasmuch as Foucault defines power relations as strategic games in which one person tries to conduct or control the other, it follows that, in his view, all social relations have this strategic dimension. This line of thought suggests that Foucault would be unwilling to go along with the assumptions about social relations that underlie the feminist accounts of the relational self discussed above, inasmuch as these accounts tend to assume the possibility of nonstrategic, mutual, reciprocal, cooperative, communicative interactions with others and to stress the importance of such relations for developing and maintaining a sense of self.

On the other hand, Foucault indicates that he does not view his own strategic model of power as necessarily incompatible with more collectivist or communicative understandings of power. In a late interview, Foucault notes that his analyses of power are analyses of specific sorts of power relations and "can in no way . . . be equated with a general analytics of every possible power relation" (Foucault 1984, 380). He explicitly leaves open the possibility that other ways of conceiving of power and social relations more generally, including conceiving of them as consensual or collective, may be compatible with his analysis (ibid., 380).

Setting this thorny interpretive issue aside, it nonetheless seems clear that the account of social relations that underlies the conception of the self in the late Foucault differs significantly from the assumptions about sociality that figure in the works of the feminists discussed above. However, my main concern is not just to establish that there is a difference here, though I do think it important to make this clear. I also want to push the point that where the Foucauldian and feminist accounts of the self diverge, it is Foucault's account that suffers. As I see it, two limitations of the Foucauldian conception of the self have emerged from this discussion. The first is a general philosophical limitation. The philosophical account of the self that can be reconstructed from Foucault's late work is incomplete and thus inadequate inasmuch as it ignores the necessary role that communicative, reciprocal, mutual interactions play in the formation of a self that is capable of recognizing, shaping, and beautifying itself via the sorts of aesthetic practices that Foucault discusses in such detail.[21]

The second limitation is one that I will label, in a Foucauldian spirit, historico-political. As I discussed above, Foucault suggests that his investigation of Greek and Roman practices of the self is linked, however tentatively, to contemporary political concerns. Thus, Foucault indicates that he is hopeful that his historical investigations might uncover resources for contemporary projects of personal transformation. However, the details of Foucault's account of the self lead him into a rather thorny problem with respect to this historico-political aim. As Jean Grimshaw notes, Foucault avoids "the crucial question of when forms of self-discipline or self-surveillance can with any justification be seen as exercises of autonomy or self-creation, or when they should be seen, rather, as forms of discipline to which the self is subjected, and by which autonomy is constrained" (Grimshaw 1993, 66). With respect to practices that are gendered, for instance, Grimshaw wonders "when should we see a concern for one's body, a programme of monitoring of one's fitness or concern for one's appearance, as an exercise of creative self-mastery rather than as a result of the internalisation of norms of bodily appearance which serve to undermine other norms of autonomy?" (ibid., 67). Does Foucault offer us the resources for distinguishing these sorts of disciplinary practices from one another? It seems to me that he does not, and his rather impoverished account of the self and the assumptions about social relations that underpin it are at least partly to blame. Restricted as it is to a strategic-game model, his account of social relations does little to illuminate the kind of collective or communicative power that emerges out of social movements.[22] Via the exercise of this collective power or solidarity, such movements are able to generate the conceptual and normative resources on which individuals draw in their own efforts to transform normalization into liberation.[23]

In other words, a broader view of social relations—one that envisions social relations as not just strategic but also as (potentially) reciprocal, communicative, and/or mutual—would be needed in order to articulate what Foucault himself and Foucauldian feminists are struggling to get clear on: how can selves who have been constituted by disciplinary and normalizing relations of power start from where they are and yet still take up a self-constituting relation to themselves that is empowering and transformative? In short, how can personal transformation be accomplished in a context of subjection? To the extent that feminists accept something like Foucault's analysis of power as a compelling conceptual tool for analyzing relations of dominance and subordination, this becomes a crucial question for feminists to answer as well.[24] My argument is that Foucault's account of practices of the self does not help us to answer this question because it pays insufficient attention to the reciprocal, mutual, and communicative dimensions of social relations, dimensions that are crucial for understanding the attainment and maintenance of one's sense of self and, as such, are also crucial for understanding the possibility of autonomy, agency, resistance, and self-transformation. Feminists need an account of the self that illuminates these contradictory elements of gendered selves.[25]

CONCLUSION

What insights into feminist theorizing about the self can be gleaned from this discussion of Foucault? In conclusion, I would like to highlight three points. First, this discussion suggests that there is some need for clarification of the terms "relational self" and "social self" in the literature on feminism, Foucault, and the self. As I have argued, there are very different ways of specifying the notion of the social or relational self, depending upon what sort of assumptions are made about the nature of social relations; for example, relations of dominance and subordination threaten, while relations of reciprocity and mutuality enable the formation of agency and autonomy. Thus, even if we all agree that the self is social or relational, our work has just begun. Feminists should be careful to distinguish different modes of relationality and the differential impact that they have on the formation of gendered selves.

Second, once we have distinguished these ways of conceiving of the self relationally, we need to reintegrate them into an account of the self that allows us to see selves as constituted by relations of power but also capable of being self-constituting. On the one hand, accounts of the self that do not acknowledge the impact of widespread, systematic relations of domination and subordination on the capacity for critical reflection and autonomous self-determination of subordinated individuals will have difficulty explaining the recalcitrance of oppressive gender norms. On the other hand, conceptions of the self that fail to account for the possibility of some measure of critical reflection and autonomy, however limited, will be unable to make sense of transformation on either an individual or a collective level. What is needed is an account that integrates these two dimensions of the self. Although Foucault offers a powerful account of the former dimension, his attempt to analyze the latter founders because his narrow account of social relations is unable to explain how individuals acquire the capacity to be self-constituting in the first place—namely, as a result of their reciprocal, communicative, mutual relations with others.

Finally, clarifying these points about how to conceptualize the self can help us understand what sorts of conditions have to be in place for effective personal transformation along feminist lines. Personal transformation of any sort can be accomplished only if reciprocal affective and communicative relations with others are in place such that a coherent self can be formed. More specifically, personal transformation in the context of and as a response to oppression can be accomplished only if there are conceptual and normative resources for individuals to draw upon in naming, understanding, criticizing, and ultimately overcoming assumptions, norms, practices, ideals, and experiences that reinforce oppression. These resources are generated collectively (and the collective action that generates them relies, in turn, on the actions of a group of individuals) in social movements and coalitions.

In the end, although my contention is that the account of the self that can be reconstructed from Foucault's late work has some serious limitations from a feminist perspective, I would nonetheless argue that getting clear on these limitations is extremely productive, inasmuch as doing so helps to illuminate what is at stake in feminist work on the self.

NOTES

Many thanks to Dianna Taylor, Karen Vintges, Susan Brison, Johanna Meehan, and audiences at the University of New Hampshire, the Eastern Division of the Society for Women in Philosophy, and the Foucault Circle for their helpful comments and questions on earlier versions of this chapter.

I borrow the phrase "the politics of personal transformation" from Bartky (1991).

1. The entry on feminist theory and the self in the online *Stanford Encyclopedia of Philosophy* provides an excellent overview of the current literature as well as an extensive bibliography. See Meyers (2001).

2. For a classic feminist critique of abstract individualism, see Jaggar (1983, 29). For helpful feminist discussions of oppressive socialization, see Benson (1991) and Stoljar (2000). Bartky (1991) shows brilliantly how Foucault's account of power can be used for a feminist analysis of oppressive socialization.

3. This is not to say that Foucault intends in his late work to offer a fully elaborated theory of the self. Rather, his late work had the less abstract aim of uncovering ancient practices of the self that might be useful for the contemporary project of countering the regime of sexual normalization that had been exposed in volume 1 of *The History of Sexuality*. Nevertheless, a more general account of the self is implicit in Foucault's late work, and it is this account that I shall discuss. I am grateful to Dianna Taylor for pushing me to clarify this point.

4. McNay mentions in particular the work of Benhabib and Young. See Benhabib (1987) and Young (1987).

5. On this point, see also Grimshaw (1993). Foucault acknowledges that the practices of the self under consideration were practiced solely by men who were not slaves, and he expresses his disgust for this fact. See Foucault (1997c).

6. Grimshaw (1993) refers to Foucault's remarks in his "Ethics of Concern for the Self."

7. McLaren quotes the following passage from *The Care of the Self*: "Around the care of the self, there developed an entire activity of speaking and writing in which the work of oneself on oneself and communication with others were linked together. Here we touch on one of the most important aspects of this activity devoted to oneself: it constituted, not an exercise in solitude, but a true social practice" (Foucault 1986, 51). I shall discuss this passage and Foucault's account of communication with others in more detail below.

8. It may well be the case that other feminist conceptions of the relational self are more compatible with the conception of selfhood implicit in Foucault's work and less open to the kinds of criticisms that have been made of Chodorow and Gilligan, some of which I will discuss briefly below. However, I choose to focus initially on Chodorow and Gilligan for two reasons: first, their conception of the relational self has been the most influential, at least among Anglo-American feminists; and, second, it is their conception of the relational self, or something like it, that McLaren claims bears striking similarity to Foucault's account of the self. Thus, it seems reasonable to begin my discussion of the feminist relational self with a consideration of their work.

9. Gilligan is critical, however, of Chodorow's reliance on object-relations theory, which she sees as problematic inasmuch as it "sustains a series of oppositions that have been central in Western thought and moral theory, including the opposition between thought and feelings, self and relationship, reason and compassion, justice and love" (Gilligan 1995, 41).

10. For a very helpful discussion of this point, see Friedman (1995).

11. For instance, critics of Chodorow and her followers have argued that her view tends to obscure rather than illuminate historical, cultural, racial, ethnic, and class-specific variations in the practice of mothering and also has the potential for un-wittingly reinforcing heterosexist norms. See, for example, Sawicki (1991, chapter 3). Chodorow defends herself against a version of this criticism (Chodorow 1978, Afterword). Feminist critics have also taken Gilligan and other ethic-of-care the-orists to task for revaluing the care perspective without taking into account the fact that relegating concern for relationships to women helps to reinforce women's sub-ordinate status. For some examples of this criticism, see Card (1995), MacKinnon (1987), and Tronto (1995).

12. Of course, Foucault's work arguably offers feminists such an account as well. Meehan acknowledges this but prefers Habermas's approach because it allows us to view the rules that enforce gender construction and enactment as "norms that coordinate action and speech, as well as functioning to maintain a gender system" rather than as "instances of power" (Meehan 2000, 41).

13. For more comprehensive overviews of recent feminist work on the self, see Mackenzie and Stoljar (2000), Meyers (1997), and Meyers (2001).

14. Although Meehan and Brison do not make any claims about women's unique capacities for relationality, they are *feminist* accounts of the self in the sense that they offer powerful tools for the analysis of, on the one hand, the recalcitrance of gender identity in the face of the ongoing critique of it and, on the other hand, the possibility of remaking selfhood in the wake of sexual violence. I am grateful to Charlotte Witt and Ruth Sample for pushing me to clarify this point.

15. For example, he later modifies his definition of technologies of the self, stat-ing that they are techniques "which permit individuals to effect by their own means, *or with the help of others,* a certain number of operations on their own bodies and souls, thoughts, conduct, and way of being, so as to transform themselves . . ." (Foucault 1997f, 225; emphasis added).

16. On concrete (vs. generalized) others, see Benhabib (1987).

17. On this point, see Foucault (1997c, 254).

18. On this point, see McLaren (1997, 117).

19. McWhorter (1999) offers an excellent argument in favor of this claim.

20. Of course, there is a sense in which Foucault views power relations as recip-rocal. As he is fond of pointing out, power is not a thing that can be possessed by one person and withheld from another but is itself a relation between two (or more) people. See, for example, Foucault (1978, 92–97). By definition, however, power relations are structured by a kind of asymmetrical or unegalitarian reci-procity, whereas the feminist accounts discussed above seem to presuppose a sym-metrical or egalitarian form of reciprocity. Foucault himself seems to understand the term "reciprocity" in this way in *The Care of the Self;* see the passage quoted above.

21. Of course, I would not want to suggest that these relations take the same spe-cific form across all cultural, social, and historical contexts. It would be very in-teresting, for example, to compare classical Greek, Hellenic, and contemporary in-

fant care and young child-rearing practices. Would that such a comparison had been part of Foucault's account of practices of the self.

22. For such an account of collective power, see Arendt (1958, chapter 5). I discuss Arendt's conception of power as it relates to feminist solidarity in Allen (1999a).

23. For a discussion of conceptual and normative resources generated by the feminist movement, see Mansbridge (1993).

24. I defend the usefulness of Foucault's conception of power for feminist theorizing in Allen (1999b).

25. McWhorter (1999) attempts to blunt the force of this sort of criticism by arguing that Foucault's work is enormously useful as a kind of handbook for personal transformation. She cites her own life and political involvements, which drew inspiration from her reading of Foucault, as evidence for this claim. Although I do not take issue with the substance of McWhorter's claim here, I think it is largely beside the point. However useful Foucault's work might be for practical projects of personal transformation, it does not offer a satisfactory way of *conceptualizing* such transformation, inasmuch as it does not have the necessary theoretical resources for clarifying the ways in which selves are created, maintained, and transformed via the kinds of social relations that provide the conceptual and normative resources for individual agency, resistance, and transformation. This means that insofar as feminists, for example, are interested in developing a theoretically informed but historically specific analysis of how feminist work on the self is possible, that is, what sorts of conditions have to be in place in order for people to transform their lives individually and collectively in light of the feminist critique of society, then we will have to go beyond Foucault.

WORKS CITED

Allen, Amy. 1999a. "Solidarity after Identity Politics: Hannah Arendt and the Power of Feminist Theory." *Philosophy and Social Criticism* 25, no. 1: 97–118.

———. 1999b. *The Power of Feminist Theory: Domination, Resistance, Solidarity.* Boulder: Westview Press.

Arendt, Hannah. 1958. *The Human Condition.* Chicago: University of Chicago Press.

———. 1969. *On Violence.* New York: Harcourt, Brace.

Bartky, Sandra. 1991. *Femininity and Domination.* New York: Routledge.

Benhabib, Seyla. 1987. "The Generalized and the Concrete Other." In *Feminism as Critique.* Edited by Seyla Benhabib and Drucilla Cornell. 77–95. Minneapolis: University of Minnesota Press.

Benson, Paul. 1991. "Autonomy and Oppressive Socialization." *Social Theory and Practice* 17, no. 3: 385–405.

Brison, Susan. 2002. *Aftermath: Violence and the Remaking of a Self.* Princeton: Princeton University Press.

Canguilhem, Georges. 1997. "On *Histoire de la folie* as an Event." In *Foucault and His Interlocutors.* Edited by Arnold Davidson. 28–32. Chicago: University of Chicago Press.

Card, Claudia. 1995. "Gender and Moral Luck." In *Justice and Care: Essential Readings in Feminist Ethics.* Edited by Virginia Held. 79–98. Boulder: Westview Press.

Chodorow, Nancy. 1978. *The Reproduction of Mothering: Psychoanalysis and the Sociology of Gender.* Berkeley: University of California Press.

Foucault, Michel. 1978. *The History of Sexuality.* Volume 1. *An Introduction.* Translated by Robert Hurley. New York: Vintage.

———. 1984. "Politics and Ethics: An Interview." In *The Foucault Reader.* Edited by Paul Rabinow. 373–80. New York: Pantheon.

———. 1985. *The Use of Pleasure: The History of Sexuality.* Volume 2. Translated by Robert Hurley. New York: Vintage.

———. 1986. *The Care of the Self: The History of Sexuality.* Volume 3. Translated by Robert Hurley. New York: Vintage.

———. 1997a. *Ethics, Subjectivity, and Truth: Essential Works of Michel Foucault.* Volume 1. Edited by Paul Rabinow. New York: New Press.

———. 1997b. "Ethics of Concern for the Self as a Practice of Freedom." In *Ethics, Subjectivity, and Truth.* Edited by Paul Rabinow. 281–301. New York: New Press.

———. 1997c. "On the Genealogy of Ethics: An Overview of a Work in Progress." In *Ethics, Subjectivity, and Truth.* Edited by Paul Rabinow. 253–80. New York: New Press.

———. 1997d. "Self-Writing." In *Ethics, Subjectivity, and Truth.* Edited by Paul Rabinow. 207–22. New York: New Press.

———. 1997e. "Sexuality and Solitude." In *Ethics, Subjectivity, and Truth.* Edited by Paul Rabinow. 175–84. New York: New Press.

———. 1997f. "Technologies of the Self." In *Ethics, Subjectivity, and Truth.* Edited by Paul Rabinow. 223–51. New York: New Press.

Friedman, Marilyn. 1995. "Beyond Caring: The De-Moralization of Gender." In *Justice and Care.* Edited by Virginia Held. 61–77. Boulder: Westview Press.

Gilligan, Carol. 1982. *In a Different Voice: Psychological Theory and Women's Development.* Cambridge: Harvard University Press.

———. 1995. "Moral Orientation and Moral Development." In *Justice and Care.* Edited by Virginia Held. 31–46. Boulder: Westview Press.

Grimshaw, Jean. 1993. "Practices of Freedom." In *Up against Foucault: Explorations of Some Tensions between Foucault and Feminism.* Edited by Caroline Ramazanoglu. 51–72. New York: Routledge.

Habermas, Jürgen. 1992. "Individuation through Socialization: On George Herbert Mead's Theory of Subjectivity." In *Postmetaphysical Thinking: Philosophical Essays.* Translated by William Mark Hohengarten. 149–204. Cambridge: MIT Press.

Jaggar, Alison. 1983. *Feminist Politics and Human Nature.* Totowa, N.J.: Rowman and Allanheld.

Mackenzie, Catriona, and Natalie Stoljar, eds. 2000. *Relational Autonomy: Feminist Perspectives on Autonomy, Agency, and the Social Self.* New York: Oxford University Press.

MacKinnon, Catharine. 1987. "Difference and Dominance: On Sex Discrimination." In *Feminism Unmodified: Discourses on Life and Law.* 32–45. Cambridge: Harvard University Press.

Mansbridge, Jane. 1993. "The Role of Discourse in the Feminist Movement." Paper presented at the annual American Political Science Association Meeting, Washington, D.C.

McLaren, Margaret. 1997. "Foucault and the Subject of Feminism." *Social Theory and Practice* 23, no. 1: 109–28.

McNay, Lois. 1992. *Foucault and Feminism: Power, Gender, and the Self.* Cambridge: Polity Press.

McWhorter, Ladelle. 1999. *Bodies and Pleasures: Foucault and the Politics of Sexual Normalization.* Bloomington: Indiana University Press.

Meehan, Johanna. 2000. "Feminism and Habermas's Discourse Ethics." *Philosophy and Social Criticism* 26, no. 3: 39–52.

Meyers, Diana T., ed. 1997. *Feminists Rethink the Self.* Boulder: Westview Press.

———. 2001. "Feminist Perspectives on the Self." In *The Stanford Encyclopedia of Philosophy.* Edited by Edward N. Zalta. <http://plato.stanford.edu/archives/fall2001/entries/feminism-self>

Sawicki, Jana. 1991. *Disciplining Foucault: Feminism, Power, and the Body.* New York: Routledge.

Soper, Kate. 1993. "Productive Contradictions." In *Up against Foucault.* Edited by Caroline Ramazanoglu. 29–50. New York: Routledge.

Stoljar, Natalie. 2000. "Autonomy and the Feminist Intuition." In *Relational Autonomy: Feminist Perspectives on Autonomy, Agency, and the Social Self.* Edited by Catriona Mackenzie and Natalie Stoljar. 94–111. New York: Oxford University Press.

Tronto, Joan. 1995. "Women and Caring: What Can Feminists Learn about Morality from Caring?" In *Justice and Care.* Edited by Virginia Held. 101–15. Boulder: Westview Press.

Young, Iris Marion. 1987. "Impartiality and the Civic Public: Some Implications of Feminist Critiques of Moral and Political Theory." In *Feminism as Critique.* Edited by Seyla Benhabib and Drucilla Cornell. 57–76. Minneapolis: University of Minnesota Press.

❧ 13

Foucault's Ethos:
Guide(post) for Change

Dianna Taylor

> Whoever cannot be mobilized when freedom is threatened will not
> be mobilized at all.
> —Hannah Arendt, "On the Nature of Totalitarianism: An Essay in
> Understanding"

> The critical ontology of ourselves has to be considered not, cer-
> tainly, as a theory, a doctrine, nor even as a permanent body of
> knowledge that is accumulating; it has to be conceived as an atti-
> tude, an ethos, a philosophical life in which the critique of what we
> are is at one and the same time the historical analysis of the limits
> that are imposed on us and an experiment with the possibility of
> going beyond them.
> —Michel Foucault, "What Is Enlightenment?"

Many European intellectuals who lived through the Second World War, including Theodor Adorno, Hannah Arendt, Albert Camus, Simone de Beauvoir, Max Horkheimer, and Jean-Paul Sartre, perceived something about
their situation during and particularly after the war to be unique. The social, political, and economic conditions from which totalitarianism sprang;
the terror that it wrought; and the moral, metaphysical, and political effects that it produced were, to use Arendt's term, "unprecedented." From
the perspective of these thinkers, the relevance of existing concepts and
principles upon which persons had traditionally drawn in order to make
sense of the world was called into question by the "terrible newness" of totalitarianism (Arendt). Continuing to rely upon traditional concepts and
principles was therefore potentially destructive, insofar as these had been
used in the service of totalitarian domination. By leaving persons without
apparent ways of making sense of the world, totalitarianism produced an
overall "crisis in meaning."[1]

Such a crisis is deeply disconcerting, and Arendt recognizes that in the face
of it persons may disengage from rather than face reality. Yet she believes that
responding in this way simply deepens the crisis and thus reproduces the

conditions for the possibility of terror and domination. In order to understand and make positive changes within the world, she argues, persons must
engage reality in both a critical (so that potentially destructive developments
may be identified and resisted) and creative (so that the conditions for the
possibility of meaning-making may be sustained, and new, potentially emancipatory ways of thinking and acting may be developed) manner. Making
sense of the post-totalitarian world, as well as of totalitarianism itself, does
not involve establishing a new set of definitive, absolute meaning-making
tools, and, therefore, a totalizing worldview. Rather, from Arendt's perspective, when persons lack recourse to existing modes of meaning-making they
can turn to the lives and work of those who have themselves practiced thinking without the aid of tradition for insight regarding how to proceed (Arendt
1977). To be clear: Arendt is not endorsing uncritical or blind emulation of
such individuals or their work. Rather, she argues that these individuals and
their work can function as "guideposts": "they do not [offer] prescriptions
on what to think or which truths to hold," but their examples can prevent
us from becoming totally lost as we engage in the practice of thinking and
acting for ourselves within the particularities of our own situations (1977, 14).

The September 11, 2001, attacks on the World Trade Center and Pentagon
and downing of United Airlines Flight 93 are clearly different from the phenomenon of totalitarian domination. Nonetheless, I argue that the attacks
created an analogous situation within the United States in the sense of producing a crisis in meaning. As I shall discuss, the attacks were unprecedented
and, as such, are incomprehensible in terms of traditional political, moral,
and legal concepts and principles. General (but particularly official) failure
to recognize this unprecedentedness has resulted in responses to the attacks
that, at best, do not aid in making sense of them and, at worst, are oppressive. Whereas Arendt believed that thinkers such as Kierkegaard, Marx, and
Nietzsche could function as guideposts in the wake of totalitarianism, in
this essay I offer Michel Foucault's later work, specifically his notion of an
ethos characterized by practices of the self, as one possible guidepost to
which persons trying to think and act in emancipatory ways within a post–
September 11 context may turn. Foucault conceives of self-practices as a way
of furthering freedom within contexts where social, political, and ethical
norms possess "normalizing" or oppressive potential and cannot, therefore,
be uncritically invoked, contexts where, to put it another way, uncritical acceptance of and adherence to convention may result in domination. This
normalizing function of norms as Foucault conceives of it is analogous to
the problematization or destruction of traditional forms of meaning-
making that occurs within a crisis in meaning: within both contexts, the
efficacy of traditional modes of thinking and acting is compromised. Hence,

emancipatory political responses to both normalization and a crisis in meaning must be critical (emancipatory responses must facilitate the identification and problematization of conventional modes of existence that function in oppressive ways), creative (emancipatory responses must facilitate the development of new, non-normalizing modes of existence), and public (the non-normalizing modes of existence that are developed must facilitate connection among and between political participants).[2]

Foucault's later work is frequently construed as apolitical or even antipolitical, primarily because self-practices are construed as something akin to "self-discovery," a purely idiosyncratic process that is significant only to the person who undertakes it and therefore lacks the power to generate social criticism. Through elucidating the critical, creative, and public character of Foucault's notion of self-practices, however, I make a case for its current political relevance. Once the political significance of a Foucauldian ethos characterized by practices of the self is made apparent, its compatibility with the aims of feminism becomes clear. I therefore suggest that a renewed conversation between feminism and "the final Foucault" might prove politically expedient for feminists. Before initiating my analysis of Foucault's work, I discuss the analogous relationship between the crises in meaning precipitated by totalitarianism and the events of September 11.

Arendt argues that, given the stressful and disorienting nature of a crisis in meaning (particularly one produced by terrifying events), persons are likely to seek a quick resolution in order to reestablish a sense of normalcy to their lives. They may attempt to orient themselves by locating something familiar or, if that is not possible, by reducing their situation to known experiences. Doing so, they adopt the attitude that their current situation is really no different than others that exist or have existed in the world. Subsuming the new and terrible under the known and familiar can provide persons with a sense of comfort: they know what they are dealing with, they possess or are able to access the tools necessary to negotiate their situation, and they can therefore carry on more or less in the ways that they have always carried on.[3]

Yet Arendt believes that humanity pays a high price when it seeks to achieve, or convinces itself that it has achieved, certainty in the face of contingency. In disengaging from a horrible reality, persons reject not only horror but also reality itself, and this rejection of reality paves the way for its replacement with ideology, or the reinforcement of existing ideology. The assertion of an ideological account of the world compromises public space because a shared arena in which persons may present and deliberate multiple and conflicting interpretations of reality is no longer needed. In disengaging from reality, therefore, persons also disengage from one another.[4] Arendt sees the substitution of ideology for reality and the destruction of the public realm as conditions for the possibility of totalitarian domination. Seeking to "free" oneself from an unprecedented, terrible, and disconcerting reality by denying or disavowing it, while understandable, is therefore ultimately not emancipatory; in fact, such a response may reproduce the very oppressive circumstances from which persons are seeking emancipation. Persons who wish to promote freedom within a crisis in meaning must therefore engage reality. Doing so, they take on the task of identifying current practices that have become oppressive, analyzing their oppressive function, and developing new, nonoppressive modes of interacting with the world and with each other.

The political climate after September 11, 2001, in the United States, I believe, signals a need to revisit the challenges and potential dangers of political engagement within a context of contingency. This is not to say that the September 11 attacks are somehow "the same" as the events of the Second World War in Europe.[5] The two phenomena can be understood as analogous, however, in that the attacks were unprecedented events within the United States, which, as I see it, initiated the same kind of crisis in meaning that has been identified with postwar Europe. The attacks were terrifying, and they evoked reactions of horror, whether persons experienced them directly or indirectly. Moreover, the attacks rendered problematic the means by which sense might be made of them. People have struggled with how to categorize the attacks (Were they an act of war, an act of terrorism, or both?) and the victims (Were they "civilian casualties of war"? Should their numbers be included in the violent crime statistics of New York and Washington? What about those who perished aboard the aircraft?). Difficulties in meaning-making are exacerbated by the conflation of the concepts of "war" and "terrorism" that has emerged within official post–September 11 rhetoric. If neither concept in and of itself sufficiently makes sense of the events that occurred, combining them in order to create what David Luban refers to as a "hybrid war-law approach" to dealing with the events of September 11 is no more enlightening and has in fact resulted in decidedly oppressive effects (Luban 2002, 9). Treating the attacks as an act of war frees the U.S. government from traditional legal constraints, while treating them as terrorist and therefore criminal activity effectively applies those same constraints to persons who might oppose and therefore want to protest against action being taken by the U.S. government. Thus, as Luban argues, "selectively combining elements of the war model and the law model" allows the government to "maximize its own ability to mobilize lethal force against terrorists while eliminating most traditional rights of a military adversary, as well as the rights of innocent bystanders caught in the crossfire" (2002, 10).[6]

Responses to the crisis in meaning brought about by the attacks also reflect the impulse toward disengagement with reality that Arendt finds so problematic. Initial reactions of shock and horror, along with the accompanying sense that nothing quite like these events had ever occurred within the United States—reactions that might prompt critical engagement with reality—were almost immediately eclipsed by efforts to resolve the crisis. The day of the attacks, government officials and major network news broadcasts most frequently likened them to Japan's December 1941 attack on Pearl Harbor. This comparison both stemmed from and in turn facilitated an interpretation of the attacks as an act of war that required a swift and decisive military response. One can see in this interpretation precisely what Arendt cautions against: uncritically subsuming new phenomena under existing categories that may not adequately or accurately aid in the process of trying to understand them. A frightening, complex reality is replaced by an ideology that renders the situation no worse than an event with which U.S. citizens are all familiar and which, coincidentally, was eventually (and "successfully") resolved through military action. Individual citizens need not offer alternative interpretations of the situation; indeed they are actively discouraged from or punished for doing so. (Deploying the rhetoric of "patriotism" as a means of achieving conformity with the official interpretation of events is particularly instructive on this point.) Public space and, subsequently, civil liberties are curtailed.

I do not mean to suggest that the United States is on the road to becoming a totalitarian state. Nor am I suggesting that a U.S. response, even a military one, to the attacks is *inherently* unfounded or unjust. Rather, I have tried to identify some troubling political implications of current U.S. responses to the events of September 11 in order to show that the complexities and dangers of political engagement within the context of a crisis in meaning, while specific, are not limited to a particular historical era or to cultures and individuals that the United States might deem "stupid . . . wicked, or . . . ill-informed" (Arendt 1994a, 358). Given the continued relevance of these complexities and dangers, how might the current crisis in meaning be productively negotiated?

Foucault's later work on practices of the self proves instructive on this point. Foucault develops his notion of self-practices through analyzing ancient Greek, Greco-Roman, and early Christian cultures.[7] Such practices, he argues, "permit individuals to effect by their own means, or with the help of others, a certain number of operations on their own bodies and souls, thoughts, conduct, and way of being, so as to transform themselves in order to attain a certain state of happiness, purity, wisdom, perfection, or immortality" (Foucault 1997a, 225). Foucault provides numerous examples of such practices within the various cultures that he studies, including diet and exercise for the ancient Greeks, and self-writing (letters, diaries) for the Stoics and early Christians.[8] Practices or, as he also refers to them, "technologies" of the self function in conjunction with other "technologies," or the means (the "techniques") by which human beings produce knowledge about and come to understand themselves (1997a, 224). In addition to technologies of the self, Foucault identifies technologies of production ("which permit us to produce, transform, or manipulate things"), technologies of sign systems ("which permit us to use signs, meanings, symbols, or signification"), and technologies of power ("which determine the conduct of individuals and submit them to certain ends or domination, an objectivizing of the subject") (1997a, 225). Each technology, Foucault states, "is associated with a certain type of domination," which he defines as the "training and modification of individuals" through acquisition of both skills and attitudes (1997a, 225). Foucault's primary concern is with domination as it occurs within technologies of power and the self. He analyzes ways in which modern subjects, through producing knowledge about themselves, are constituted (technologies of power) and constitute ourselves (technologies of the self) as both subject and object. As I shall discuss shortly, in his "middle" or genealogical works, Foucault shows how the "training and modification of individuals" takes on a normalizing or "disciplinary" function within modern societies. Foucault relates that he has perhaps occupied himself "too much" with analyzing technologies of power; hence his emphasis in later work on self-discipline, "the mode of action that an individual exercises upon himself," and its emancipatory possibilities (1997a, 225).

Foucault's association of self-practices with both domination and freedom seems contradictory and cannot be understood without a proper conception of his account of the workings of modern power. Foucault always conceives of power in terms of "power relations." Power relations are perhaps most easily understood as a particular way in which actions influence or "modify" other actions within an overall matrix or "field" (Foucault 1983, 219). Taking the field of possible actions as a particular sociohistorical context, different actions are open to each individual subject within that context and, thus, individual subjects will be differently constituted and constrained based upon the ways in which their actions affect and are affected by the actions of others. In the classroom, for example, I as professor have courses of action available to me that my students do not. (I can speak without raising my hand, for instance.) Within this particular context, my actions are backed with the weight of authority and may therefore strongly influence the actions of my students. When I leave the classroom and go to a department meeting, however, my actions as a junior, female faculty member lose that authority and the capacity of my actions to influence those of others is diminished: I have fewer (depending upon the individual department, perhaps very few) courses of action available to me.

Foucault's genealogical analyses in *Discipline and Punish* and volume 1 of *The History of Sexuality* exemplify what he refers to as power's "normalizing" or "disciplinary" function. "The chief function of disciplinary power," Foucault argues, "is to 'train,' rather than to select or levy" (Foucault 1979, 170). Disciplinary power "makes individuals," not by imposing "majestic rituals of sovereignty or the great apparatuses of the state" but rather through "humble" and "minor," yet pervasive and "calculated" modalities, including "hierarchical observation," "normalizing judgment," and "examination" (1979, 170). It is social norms and convention, not sovereign power, that function as a "determining" or constraining mechanism within modern societies. Disciplinary power circulates throughout society by way of convention and norms that persons internalize and come to accept simply as "the way things are and have always been"; to conform to these norms is simply to behave "naturally." Once a particular mode of existence becomes accepted as normal, natural, and necessary, modes that do not conform to the norm come to be seen as deviant; their censor, punishment, or (forcible) alteration therefore seems justifiable or even required: criminals are deemed "animals" or "monsters" whose execution is needed for the good of society; beating and killing homosexuals is justified because they are considered "immoral." Hence Foucault's claim that norms have the capacity to function in (highly) oppressive ways.

Normalizing power is not, however, only externally directed. One of the most important things to understand about modern power is that individuals subject themselves to it. When I internalize norms, in other words, I subject myself to the same kinds of examination, judgment, and observation to which other people and institutions subject me. Modern subjects are self-regulating in the sense that they constitute themselves as subjects via the very norms that subjugate them. The same norms through which I constitute myself as a faculty member with professorial authority dictate that I must conduct myself in a "professional" manner and, accordingly, I regulate my behavior or "discipline myself" within the classroom, the department meeting, and the academic conference. It is not the case, then, that some norms are inherently "good" or non-normalizing whereas some are inherently "bad" or oppressive. Rather, norms function in varying ways across different social and historical contexts. Once we understand this, the significance of Foucault's remark "it is not that everything is bad but rather that everything is dangerous" becomes clear: persons must work to distinguish, within their particular sociohistorical context, "pernicious forms of normalization" from "non-pernicious norms" (Sawicki 2002).[9]

It is indeed the case, as some critics of Foucault argue, that from his perspective one cannot extricate oneself from social norms and, therefore, from power relations. But it is also the case, as Foucault makes clear in his later work, that one need not do so in order to resist normalization or practice freedom. To return to previous examples, one may be inclined to say that within the context of my classroom I am free, whereas within the context of the department meeting I am not (or at least that I am less free). But from a Foucauldian perspective, I am free in both contexts: "Power is exercised only over free subjects and only insofar as they are free" (1983, 221). While my actions are more obviously constrained in the department meeting, I do not lack the capacity to act within that context. (I can vote on departmental issues, for instance.) In the classroom and in the meeting (and indeed, for Foucault, within the context of all power relations), some "determining factors" exist; but in neither context do they "saturate the whole" (221). With respect to technologies of power, such "saturation" is what constitutes domination, a situation in which one party is in control such that another party completely lacks the capacity to act. (Foucault uses the example of slavery to illustrate a state of domination.) Foucault makes quite clear that it is domination, not power, that marks an absence of freedom: "At the very heart of the power relationship, and constantly provoking it, are the recalcitrance of the will and the intransigence of freedom" (222). From a Foucauldian perspective, power is not opposed to but is in fact a condition for the possibility of freedom. Power, by virtue of its "agonistic" nature, produces a kind of "permanent provocation" (222).

That the field of power relations is constantly changing is a double-edged sword. On the one hand, we want to keep power mobile because power is a condition for the possibility of freedom: if I find myself in an unjust situation, I want to be able to resist and change it. On the other hand, the means by which I change my situation in one context may not help me in my efforts to resist in another—in fact they may function in an oppressive manner. Given the intricacies of modern power, Foucault sees persons being presented with a twofold "task": First, they must keep power relations mobile in order to sustain conditions under which freedom is possible. Second, they need to expand the overall field of possible actions, such that new and potentially non-normalizing ways of thinking and acting become possible. This task is analogous to that which Arendt and thinkers of her time perceived for themselves: identify norms that function in oppressive ways within one's current context; acknowledge their contingency; work to understand their oppressive function; and strive to develop new, non-normalizing modes of existence.

Foucault posits practices of the self as a way of fulfilling the task with which modern forms of power present us. The "work that we do on our-selves as free subjects" is, as I have shown, disciplinary in nature: it entails both "training" and "modification" (1984, 47). The point is to begin to engage in self-discipline in such a way that not only are power relations kept mobile, but new modes of existence are also made possible. As Ladelle Mc-Whorter argues, "Normalizing disciplinary practices may enhance a person's ability to perform certain kinds of functions or accomplish certain kinds of tasks, but they decrease the number of different ways in which a person might be able to respond in a given situation; they narrow our options. With normalizing discipline, we end up with a highly efficient and productive, yet simultaneously meek and conformist (docile) subject" (Mc-Whorter 1999, 180). We need to modify existing practices in ways that "mitigate against standard outcomes" (1999, 181). Within a context of normalization, this "modification" constitutes the work of freedom.

Despite the fact that Foucault connects self-practices with freedom, such practices are generally perceived to be lacking in political import. According to critics, insofar as the emancipatory potential of such practices is limited to the individual, it cannot possibly generate meaningful social critique. How, then, are practices of the self to inform political thought and action? Feminists have been particularly critical of Foucault on this point. Jean Grimshaw characterizes practices of the self as "formalistic" and "subject-centered" and argues that they are anathema to any feminist politics (Grimshaw 1993). Likewise, Lois McNay argues that Foucault portrays "the ethics of the self" as a "solitary process, rather than as socially integrated activity" (McNay 1992, 177). From her perspective, therefore, "it is unclear how such an ethics translates into a politics of difference that could initiate deep-seated social change" (1992, 177). In what follows, I problematize these criticisms by elucidating the public and critically creative character of self-practices and arguing for their emancipatory political potential.

That practices of the self constitute a relationship of the self to itself seems to suggest that one "works on oneself" completely independent of others. But Foucault's descriptions and analyses of self-creation consistently illustrate its social character: from their inception, practices of the self implicate both other people and social institutions. Foucault argues that the idea of a practice of "caring" (examining the soul in order to achieve the proper "alignment" of its parts, self-knowledge producing correct action) for the self emerges within Plato's *Alcibiades*. His analysis of this text links proper care of the self to pedagogy, the student/mentor relationship, and politics. Care of the self must be grounded in a proper education. Alcibiades' "defective" education hinders his efforts to gain influence within the city; he has learned to value the wrong things in life and is therefore ill-equipped for self-examination and correct action (Foucault 1997a). Proper care of the self is also facilitated by way of one's relationship to one's mentor (1997a). Those engaged in self-practices are guided through the process, as Socrates guides Alcibiades (1997a). Moreover, proper care of the self is itself a requirement for participating in the life of the polis as well as for engaging in relations with other people: it is only through correctly caring for oneself that one is able to "occupy his rightful position in the city, the community, or interpersonal relationships" (Foucault 1997b, 287).

Clearly, practices of the self are social: they are shaped by social norms and occur within particular sociocultural contexts. Having established this, it is now possible to proceed to the question of political relevance: Are practices of the self political in the specific sense of fostering non-normalizing relationships among persons? That is, do such practices have the potential to facilitate modes of relating that differ from and may in fact challenge institutionally recognized, normalizing relationships such as student/teacher, wife/husband, prisoner/correctional officer? Foucault's association of self-practices with a "way of life" or ethos suggests that these practices do possess such potential. A way of life as Foucault conceives of it involves engaging in self-practices in ways that facilitate new (not yet conceptualized and non-normalizing) forms of relating both to oneself and to others. "A way of life," Foucault asserts, "can be shared among individuals of different age, status, and social activity. It can resemble intense relations not resembling those that are institutionalized. It seems to me that a way of life can yield a culture and an ethics" (Foucault 1997c, 138). A way of life does not somehow replace (and thereby release subjects from) the normalizing, "institutionalized" relations that characterize a disciplinary society. But neither does it involve accepting existing modes of relating and simply trying to arrange them in new ways. Rather, one utilizes existing disciplinary practices in such a way that differences ("age, status, and social activity") among individuals become primary in relationships. One adopts a critical stance toward "socially acceptable" relationships, adjusts the manner in which one relates to others, and comes together with those with whom one ostensibly has nothing in common. A way of life begins from a position of critical resistance, not acceptance, and from that position attempts to create something new and thus expand the field of possible courses of action: it is produced by and in turn fosters critical and creative capacities among and between subjects. Foucault's notion of a way of life constitutes a positive response to the failure of traditional relational forms; that is, he offers an initial formulation of non-normalizing relations among persons.

As the above discussion suggests, practices of the self are critical, but not in a merely negative sense. Rather, critique of existing modes of existence may facilitate both individual and social transformation. The critically creative character of self-practices may therefore be understood in terms of Foucault's notion of transgression. In its most general sense, transgression for Foucault means challenging predetermined or existing limits (Foucault 1977). His conception of the relationship between power and freedom makes clear, however, that challenging limits is not the same as extricating oneself from them. Limits and their transgression, Foucault argues, mutually define one other; they are involved in a kind of "instantaneous play" through which transgression comes to accomplish not "victory over limits" but the "nonpositive" affirmation of "limited being" (Foucault 1977, 35). The idea of "play" between transgression and limit suggests that their relationship is dynamic rather than fixed. And, as with power relations, this mobility is a condition for the possibility of freedom. Transgressing limits can be said to "clarify" them. Clarification in this context can be understood in terms of explication and delineation (making overt what has been taken for granted) which is intended to yield insight into function and, thus, facilitate creative negotiation: we cannot hope to make a productive intervention in the world if we are not actively engaged in assessing what is going on around us or if we uncritically accept crucial aspects of our situation as mere background. Thus freedom should not be equated with absence of limits but rather with the clarifying work that takes place in the space between limits and their transgression. The point is to sustain the condition of mobility between limit and transgression, to keep limits from coalescing and modes of challenging them from becoming rote.

The above discussion highlights several politically relevant aspects of practices of the self. First, practices of the self characterize a "way of life" or ethos. Foucault is not concerned with social transformation in a merely abstract sense. Clearly, he conceives of an ethos characterized by self-practices as a response to the present. As I have shown, Foucault's concern with technologies of the self derives from his understanding of the workings of modern power; to be viable, self-practices and the ethos that they comprise must withstand the "test of contemporary reality" (Foucault 1984, 46). Moreover, self-practices are not esoteric but, rather, the practical stuff of daily life. Foucault's primary concern in his analysis of technologies of the self is with "what [people] do and the way they do it" (1984, 48). Second, Foucault ties the public, critically creative character of self-practices to freedom. Practices of the self entail a particular kind of "work," "done at the limits of ourselves," that persons perform "upon ourselves as free beings" (47). This work does not extricate persons from their current limits, but it does enable them to clarify those limits and in doing so to "separate out, from the contingency that has made us what we are, the possibility of no longer being, doing, or thinking what we are, do, or think" (46). Practices of the self challenge given limits in creative, productive ways; their aim, as Foucault puts it, is to "grasp the points where change is possible and desirable, and to determine the precise form this change should take" (46). The "clarifying," "separating," and "grasping" that Foucault describes is, from his perspective, the practice of freedom. It is no accident, then, that Foucault refers to freedom not as an end state to be achieved but specifically in terms of work. The point of the way of life he describes is to, in effect, (re)create conditions under which more of this kind of work can be done. Hence Foucault's remark that when adopting such an ethos, persons are "always in the position of beginning again" (50). Foucault offers no guarantee of freedom; to dictate what freedom must look like within a context where norms possess normalizing potential would be oppressive. His ethos is inherently risky, yet it is precisely within this risk that possibilities for freedom emerge. A Foucauldian ethos characterized by practices of the self is thus perhaps best conceived in terms of "commitment without Truth": collective engagement undertaken by persons that not only sustains their existing differences but produces a proliferation of new and unpredictable differences in the name of freedom (Vintges 2003).[10]

Despite the fact that Foucault overtly connects risk and freedom, the riskiness of his ethos is a prime target of feminist criticisms. As I have presented it here, Foucault's ethos seems highly compatible with general feminist aims: it promotes difference in the cultivation of relationships among political participants, it points to the oppressive function of convention and inspires social critique, and it functions in the service of emancipatory social transformation through expanding the various ways in which people are able to relate to themselves and to one another. Still, feminist wariness and overt rejection of Foucault's work continues, at least in part, because of misperceptions regarding his conceptualization of power. Many feminists focus on Foucault's genealogical works, which, by his own admission, are concerned almost exclusively with analyzing technologies of power. Even though Foucault overtly states in volume 1 of *The History of Sexuality*, for example, that power and resistance mutually condition one another ("where there is power there is resistance"), because the middle texts expound the normalizing, objectifying function of power, focusing on them at the exclusion of his later work presents a distorted picture not only of power, but of subjectivity and freedom as well. Nancy Hartsock, for example, articulates a common feminist protest: "Why is it that just at the moment when so many of us who have been silenced begin to demand the right . . . to act as subjects rather than objects of history, that just then the concept of subjecthood becomes problematic?" (Hartsock 1990, 163). According to Hartsock, through his critique of humanism Foucault effectively dismantles subjectivity to the point where "things" rather than "people" possess agency (1990). In the face of his apparent failure to provide a compelling account of subjectivity, some feminists argue that Foucault cannot possibly articulate a meaningful notion of freedom. Both Hartsock and Monique Deveaux believe that Foucault's account of power as a condition for the possibility of freedom does not reflect the reality of "women's experiences" and thus must be approached with caution (Deveaux 1996) or rejected (Hartsock 1990). Yet Foucault neither dismantles subjectivity nor destroys freedom's efficacy. As I have argued, he does not abandon these concepts but rather reconceptualizes them in ways that resist normalization.

Even if Foucault does not completely jettison notions of freedom and subjectivity, some feminists still find his problematization of norms politically lacking or even dangerous. How, Nancy Fraser asks, can Foucault hope to articulate a coherent politics if his work cannot provide the normative foundations that political endeavors require? (Fraser 1994). In response to such criticism, it is important to note that challenging the normalizing function of norms does not oppose but rather promotes feminists aims. Exposing and undermining the oppressive effects of normative gender roles, for example, is a common feminist practice. Moreover, feminists of color have revealed as oppressive and critiqued the assertion within feminist discourse of white middle-class women's experiences and perspectives as representative of all women. Still, despite their recognition that particular norms such as gender roles and racial categories may function in oppressive ways, many feminists share Fraser's view that the norm of normativity itself is foundation and, therefore, beyond critique and deliberation. From a Foucauldian perspective, however, calling into question and critically interrogating the *current* definition, foundational status, and function of the concept of normativity within feminist discourse (and philosophical discourse more generally) need not entail the destruction or abandonment of the concept. Rather, such questioning and interrogation of the norm of normativity's status as a privileged mode of legitimation may clarify it, in the sense of providing insight into its definition and function, facilitating the identification of normalizing and therefore oppressive effects associated with this definition and function and, therefore, paving the way for its positive reconceptualization. But it is up to feminists to determine how this critical work ought to be done, and to do so in the absence of guarantees about its "success"; from a Foucauldian perspective, efforts to vouchsafe freedom may function in the service of domination. Karen Vintges's point that feminism aims to "make women free in the sense that they can create new situations, new cultural meanings, and new ways of experiencing what life as a woman can be" is therefore apt (Vintges 2003).[11] Struggling against women's oppression opens up opportunities and presents feminists with the "task" of creating new modes of existence or ways of life.

Understood in these terms, feminism seems compatible with the kind of critically creative work that characterizes a Foucauldian ethos as I have described it. Foucault's ethos offers a vision of an emancipatory, practical politics that is able to function, even thrive, within a context where traditional foundations for action and thought are no longer reliable; it does not celebrate the absence of foundations but rather posits a pragmatic approach to living without absolute foundations and certainty.[12] Insofar as it shows that prevailing modes of existence are not necessary modes, a Foucauldian ethos characterized by self-practices makes clear that the end of the uncritical deployment of accepted political strategies does not mark the end of politics. A critically creative approach to politics provides for a way of both rejecting normalizing political forms and transforming society by (continually) developing and experimenting with new, potentially emancipatory forms.

I have argued that a Foucauldian ethos characterized by practices of the self possesses emancipatory potential within a context of normalization as well as within a crisis in meaning such as the one the United States is currently experiencing. Given this potential, I have further argued that Foucault's ethos can function as a guidepost for persons, such as feminists, who wish to promote freedom in these kinds of contexts and crises. My use of Arendt's notion of a "guidepost" is significant given the criticisms of Foucault that I have addressed here. A guidepost is not a map. I can use a guidepost to get my bearings, but it is ultimately up to me to make my own way, to figure out where I am going and how I am going to get there. Foucault himself described his work in terms of "tools"; he said that his books were like "little toolboxes." Again, as with Arendt's notion of the guidepost, tools can help us in our work, but they do not spell out for us what that work is or ought to be. Moreover, we can use tools in ways other than those for which they are intended; we can experiment and innovate.

The notions of the guidepost and the toolbox thus help to make sense of Foucault's overt refusal to provide maps or "blueprints for change." Foucault did not make it his business to tell others what to do and how to do it, I submit, not because his work lacks political commitments, or because he simply wanted to duck questions about the validity of his work, but rather because "he was well-acquainted with the 'futility and dangers'" of prescription in the face of contingent, normalizing reality (Gandal 1986, 124). Foucault's work reflects an understanding of Arendt's point that in the face of disorientation and confusion there will always be individuals who are more than willing to step up and dictate to persons what they ought to do and think. That Foucault insists upon difficult work without guarantee of desired results suggests that he took seriously the arguments of Arendt and thinkers of her time that the effects of allowing others to think for us are less than desirable and potentially lethal. Foucault's work thus reasserts a question that is particularly pressing within the current sociopolitical context of the United States: What lies behind the highly antipolitical impulse to shun responsibility?

Thus far the official U.S. response to the events of September 11 has functioned to reduce a complex geopolitical landscape to a simplistic matter of "good versus evil," where these concepts are defined in absolute, universal, and mutually exclusive terms.[13] If any nation or individual who questions U.S. strategy is by default "with the terrorists," critical analysis of, for example, the Bush administration's policy of "preemption" approaches an act of sedition.[14] As the struggle continues over how to make sense of and respond to the political, moral, and metaphysical effects of unprecedented events within the United States and the world, from the perspective of Foucault and Arendt we would all be wise to participate in and perpetuate that struggle. For, as both thinkers make clear, it is only within the struggle over and at the limits of ourselves that freedom, or something like it, "perhaps . . . eventually will appear" (Arendt 1977, 14).

NOTES

1. Arendt argues that totalitarianism "has destroyed our categories of thought and standards of judgment." Given this destruction, "How can we measure length if we do not have a yardstick, how could we count things without the notion of numbers?" See Arendt (1994b).

2. My formulation of the concept of publicity and hence my understanding of the workings of politics are informed by Arendt's work. That is, from my perspective, politics entails persons coming together for the purposes of action and speech in ways that distinguish them as "unique, distinct" individuals. See Arendt (1958), particularly her analysis of action, for an account of politics and the public realm.

3. As Arendt puts it, "We . . . console ourselves that nothing worse or less familiar will take place than general human sinfulness." See Arendt (1994b, 312).

4. For a detailed analysis of the process that I briefly outline here, see Arendt (1994a) and (1973).

5. The claim of uniqueness or unprecedentedness here, as with respect to totalitarianism, does not imply that the attacks were more heinous than acts of violence and terror occurring in other parts of the world today.

6. The detainment of the prisoners at Guantanamo Bay is instructive on this point. For an insightful analysis, see Judith Butler (2002).

7. It is important to understand the way in which Foucault conceives of "the self" in his work on self-practices. He problematized the idea that "there exists a human nature or base that, as a consequence of certain historical, economic, and social processes, has been concealed, alienated, or imprisoned in and by mechanisms of repression." "The self" is therefore not prior to but rather comes into existence through self-practices. Moreover, these practices allow subjects to become something other than their socially prescribed, conventional, "institutionalized" role. For an astute discussion of these points, see David Halperin (1995).

8. Foucault provides in-depth analysis of self-practices in volumes 2 and 3 of *The History of Sexuality*. See Foucault (1990) and (1988).

9. I am grateful to Jana Sawicki for her helpful comments on this point.

10. I am grateful to Karen Vintges for encouraging me to think about Foucault's ethos in these terms.

11. I am grateful to Karen Vintges for her helpful comments on this point.

12. Again, I am grateful to Jana Sawicki for her helpful comments on this point.

13. President Bush's remark "You are either with us or you are with the terrorists" provides a case in point.

14. For an insightful analysis of recent developments in the Bush administration's foreign policy, see Richard Falk (2002).

WORKS CITED

Arendt, Hannah. 1958. *The Human Condition*. Chicago: University of Chicago Press.

———. 1973. "Ideology and Terror: A Novel Form of Government." In *The Origins of Totalitarianism*. 460–79. New York: Harcourt Brace.

———. 1977. *Between Past and Future: Eight Exercises in Political Thought*. New York: Penguin.

———. 1994a. "On the Nature of Totalitarianism: An Essay in Understanding." In *Essays in Understanding: 1930–1954*. Edited by Jerome Kohn. 328–62. New York: Harcourt Brace.

———. 1994b. "Understanding and Politics." In *Essays in Understanding: 1930–1954*. Edited by Jerome Kohn. 307–27. New York: Harcourt Brace.

Butler, Judith. 2002. "Guantanamo Limbo." *The Nation* (April 1): 20–24.

Deveaux, Monique. 1996. "Feminism and Empowerment: A Critical Reading of Foucault." In *Feminist Interpretations of Michel Foucault*. Edited by Susan Hekman. 211–38. University Park: Pennsylvania State University Press.

Falk, Richard. 2002. "The New Bush Doctrine." *The Nation* (July 15): 9–11.

Foucault, Michel. 1977. "A Preface to Transgression." In *Language, Counter-Memory, Practice*. Edited by Donald F. Brouchard. 29–52. Ithaca: Cornell University Press.

———. 1979. *Discipline and Punish*. New York: Vintage.

———. 1983. "The Subject and Power." In *Michel Foucault: Beyond Structuralism and Hermeneutics*. By Hubert Dreyfus and Paul Rabinow. 208–26. Chicago: University of Chicago Press.

———. 1984. "What Is Enlightenment?" In *The Foucault Reader*. Edited by Paul Rabinow. 32–50. New York: Pantheon.

———. 1988. *The History of Sexuality*. Volume 3. *The Care of the Self*. Translated by Robert Hurley. New York: Vintage.

———. 1990. *The History of Sexuality*. Volume 2. *The Use of Pleasure*. Translated by Robert Hurley. New York: Vintage.

———. 1997a. "Technologies of the Self." In *The Essential Works of Foucault*. Volume 1. *Ethics: Subjectivity and Truth*. Edited by Paul Rabinow. 223–51. New York: New Press.

———. 1997b. "The Ethics of Care for the Self as the Practice of Freedom." In *The Essential Works of Foucault*. Volume 1. *Ethics: Subjectivity and Truth*. Edited by Paul Rabinow. 281–301. New York: New Press.

———. 1997c. "Friendship as a Way of Life." In *The Essential Works of Foucault*. Volume 1. *Ethics: Subjectivity and Truth*. Edited by Paul Rabinow. 135–40. New York: New Press.

Fraser, Nancy. 1994. "Michel Foucault: A 'Young Conservative?'" In *Critique and Power: Recasting the Foucault/Habermas Debate*. Edited by Michael Kelly. 185–210. Cambridge: MIT Press.

Gandal, Keith. 1986. "Michel Foucault: Intellectual Work and Politics." *Telos* 67: 121–34.

Grimshaw, Jean. 1993. "Practices of Freedom." In *Up against Foucault: Explorations of Some Tensions between Foucault and Feminism*. Edited by Caroline Ramazanoglu. 51–72. New York: Routledge.

Halperin, David. 1995. "The Queer Politics of Michel Foucault." In *Saint Foucault*. 15–125. New York: Oxford University Press.

Hartsock, Nancy. 1990. "Foucault on Power: A Theory for Women?" In *Feminism/Postmodernism*. Edited by Linda J. Nicholson. 157–75. New York: Routledge.

Luban, David. 2002. "The War on Terrorism and the End of Human Rights." *Philosophy and Public Policy Quarterly* 22, no. 3: 9–14.

McNay, Lois. 1992. *Foucault and Feminism*. Boston: Northeastern University Press.

McWhorter, Ladelle. 1999. *Bodies and Pleasures: Foucault and the Politics of Sexual Normalization*. Bloomington: Indiana University Press.

Sawicki, Jana. 2002. Personal communication.

Vintges, Karen. 2003. Personal communication.

❧ 14

Endorsing Practices of Freedom: Feminism in a Global Perspective

Karen Vintges

Much as I sympathize with postmodernism as a philosophical point of view, I cannot but conclude that the postmodern perspective has been devastating for the theory and practice of contemporary feminism. In the last two decades, postmodern "deconstructionism," namely, the postmodern attack on all kinds of universals and universalizing languages, has heavily influenced feminism. Contemporary postmodernist thinkers such as Jacques Derrida, Jean-François Lyotard, Gilles Deleuze, Julia Kristeva, Sarah Kofman, and Michel Foucault unmasked all universalizing "grand narratives" as a will to mastery. Reason, truth, man, and all other supposed universals do not exist outside language, history, and power relations. Moreover, the narratives that are based on them are "discursive" power practices that suppress otherness on the individual and the collective level. The grand narratives of Western modernity, the ideas and perspectives that originated in the Enlightenment, and political liberalism, are postmodernism's target par excellence. Western modernity's claim of human progress through reason is criticized as imprisoning people in a restrictive identity and as the will to dominate all kinds of "irrational" others—the abnormal, the senseless, the "stranger."

In line with the postmodern approach, since the mid-1980s, feminist thinkers have attacked the category "woman" as a universal that represses otherness on the individual and the collective level. Instead of taking "woman" as an essential feminine subject that has to be liberated, we should unravel and deconstruct fixed meanings of femininity, so that an open space is created that permits the shaping of new ways of thinking and living.[1] Universal similarities between women are no longer taken for granted: postmodern feminism, with its suspicion of any fixed subject "woman," stresses the differences between women rather than their common identity. The acknowledgment of differences expresses the political mood of the feminist movement in the past decades. The influence of postmodernism has created a climate in which one can no longer speak on behalf of neutral standards. Since feminism is generally seen as presupposing the values of Western Enlightenment and liberalism, feminists are mindful not to impose their own Western standards on women from other cultural backgrounds. However, this lack of a universal normative perspective has had paralyzing effects. What began as academic feminism has spread throughout feminist practice, disorienting many former activists who no longer seem to know what to do.[2] Simone de Beauvoir, in the Introduction of *The Second Sex,* states:

> Proletarians say "We"; Blacks also. Regarding themselves as subjects, they transform the bourgeois, the whites, into "others." But women do not say "We." . . . [W]omen lack concrete means for organizing themselves into a unit. . . . They have no past, no history, no religion of their own: and they have no such solidarity of work and interests as that of the proletariat. They are not even promiscuously herded together in the way that creates community feeling among the American blacks, the ghetto Jews, the workers of Saint-Denis or the factory hands of Renault. They live dispersed among the males, attached through residence, housework, economic condition, and social standing to certain men—fathers or husbands—more firmly than they are to other women. If they belong to the bourgeoisie, they feel solidarity with men of that class, not with proletarian women; if they are white, their allegiance is to white men, not to black women. . . . The bond that unites her to her oppressors is not comparable to any other. (Beauvoir 1974, 19)[3]

Since women lack the concrete means for organizing themselves into a unit, I think it is about time to conclude that a purely postmodern perspective does not work for feminism: women at the minimum need—in the words of Beauvoir—the "concrete means" of a unifying ethical-political language.

Suzan Moller Okin complains that the global movement for women's human rights in the past years has missed the intellectual and political support from almost all Western feminists, who were "bending over backward out of 'respect for cultural diversity'" (Okin 1998, 46). In the Netherlands the lack of univocality has resulted in disorientation and almost total withdrawal by feminists from the public sphere. The pronoun "we" no longer encompasses Western women who live as individuals coping with "their own" problems; it certainly does not include or refer to women from non-Western, mostly Islamic, cultural backgrounds in the Netherlands.

In her famous essay *Is Multiculturalism Bad for Women?* Okin argues that feminists should no longer hesitate to accept Western liberalism's "fundamentals" as *the* universal norm of a cross-cultural feminism. She attacks the point of view of multiculturalism that minority cultures should be protected by special rights: such a politics is bad for women. Polygamy, forced marriage, female genital mutilation, punishing women for being raped, differential access for men and women to health care and education, unequal rights of ownership, assembly and political participation, and unequal vulnerability to violence are practices and conditions that are not unusual in many parts of the world, while the norm of gender equality is endorsed, at least formally, by Western liberal states (Okin 1999).

While Okin advocates a close connection between feminism and Western liberal values, Seyla Benhabib aims to ground a global feminism in a cross-cultural dialogue. Benhabib is after the articulation of "a pluralistically enlightened ethical universalism on a global scale" (Benhabib 2002, 36) and interestingly tries to combine the postmodern perspective of difference with an ethical universalism. She distinguishes four meanings of the term "universalism": (1) the philosophical belief that there is a fundamental human nature or human essence; (2) the assumption that philosophical reason is an "impartial," "objective," and "neutral" judge; (3) the principle that all human beings are morally equal and should be treated as equally entitled to moral respect; and (4) the principle that all human beings are entitled to certain legal rights (ibid., 26–27). Benhabib is convinced that it is impossible to defend the third principle without the second. The cross-cultural open dialogue she advocates is one of normative "reasoning." Benhabib takes her conception of normative reasoning from the German philosopher Jürgen Habermas.[4] Like Habermas, she privileges rational decision making and defends the internal relationship between Western modernity and rationality. She therefore situates her cross-cultural dialogue within the limits of the democratic liberal state and ultimately sides with Okin's view that feminism ought to be closely linked to Western liberalism.

I strongly agree with Benhabib that we need a "pluralistically enlightened ethical universalism" as a basis for feminism, but the model she proposes does not seem to be sufficiently cross-cultural. To be pluralistically informed, we need a more inclusive normative viewpoint than the Western Enlightenment's claim of human progress through reason, which postmodernism, in my view, rightly unmasked as inherently exclusionary.

In this chapter I will try to formulate an ethical universalism that builds on postmodern insights. In other words, I will sketch a post-postmodern conception of ethical universalism. For this task I think the work of the later Foucault can be of great help. In fact, I consider his later work partly a response to the question of how to conceive of a post-postmodern ethics and politics. In the next two sections, I will explore the final Foucault's thinking on these matters, and I will argue that his notion of the ethical-spiritual life was an attempt to rethink politics and ethics. In the third section, I will argue that he suggests an ethical universalism when he endorses access to the ethical-spiritual life for everybody. In the fourth section, I will try to show that this ethical universalism is a "pluralistically enlightened" one by applying it specifically to Islamic religion. In the fifth and final section, I will deal with the issue of feminism and multiculturalism, and I will propose an ethical universalism for a feminism that wants to be truly global.

THE MODERN ATTITUDE

Notoriously, *the* issue in the debate around Foucault's work is its lack of an ethics.[5] Foucault is heavily criticized for not offering any normative criteria. Habermas characterizes Foucault as a "cryptonormativist" (Habermas 1987). Nancy Fraser criticizes Foucault for being a moral nihilist after all (Fraser 1994). Lois McNay, who unlike most critics takes into account Foucault's later work, also concludes that his theoretical framework is unacceptable given that political movements such as feminism require a normative viewpoint (McNay 1992; 1994). Even though I agree with McNay on this latter point, I disagree with her reading of the later Foucault's work, which, in my view, so far has been highly under-theorized. Foucault's last two volumes on the history of sexuality, *The Use of Pleasure* and *The Care of the Self,* and the short texts, lectures, and interviews from the period 1976 until his death in 1984 contain a specific type of ethics that reflects and builds on the normative impact of his earlier work.[6]

In the works of the 1970s, Foucault analyzed the "biopolitics" of Western societies: the political rationality that is applied to people's bodies on a collective as well as a personal level. In *Discipline and Punish,* he describes these power processes as the other side of the Enlightenment: "'The Enlightenment,' which discovered the liberties, also invented the disciplines" (Foucault 1979, 222). Since around 1800, these disciplines, panoptic, controlling "discursive" practices such as prisons, schools, medical and welfare institutions, installed an "inner self" in people. The surveying power techniques that are applied to their bodies generate rational self-control. In this way an inner space is installed: the subject is born. Normal man from now on is a "deep self," a source of meaning, sense, thinking, and action, in other words, an "original" subject. In volume 1 of *The History of Sexuality,* Foucault claims to find an interior subject posited at an even deeper level. This subject is an effect of the so-called scientia sexualis: discourses such as psychology, psychiatry, pedagogy, and medicine that force people to talk about their supposedly hidden, "sexual" feelings and allocate a sexual identity to each of them. We are nailed according to the middle Foucault by this so-called authentic deep self. It is our own prison house that we cannot escape and in which we are trapped, locked and secluded from others.

The historian Jean Pierre Vernant, referring to three *literary* genres—the biography, the autobiography, and the diary—proposes to make a distinction between the following three corresponding levels: "the individual," the "subject," and "the ego."[7] Vernant maintains that the history of the individual concerns his place and role in his group or groups: "the value accorded him; the margin of movement left to him; his relative autonomy with respect to his institutional framework." The subject according to Vernant is the person that speaks in his own name, enunciates certain features that make him a unique being. The ego, finally, is the unique being with an authentic nature residing entirely in the secrecy of his interior life, "at the very heart of an intimacy to which no one except him can have access because it is defined as self-consciousness" (Vernant 1991, 321; quoted in Davidson 1994, 73–74). I believe that Foucault's middle works can be viewed as criticisms of all three categories. He attacks the first two categories in *Discipline and Punish*. The third is the target of the first volume on sexuality, which deals with the production of the ego on a mass scale in Western societies. The middle Foucault was of the opinion that we are controlled and held in check through the three types of subjectivity, which he saw as extensions of each other. In interviews he refers to them under the single label "the subject," or the "deep self," which he rejects as the "ordre interieur" of a dominating and continually inhibiting social order. Marshall Berman, in my view, rightly characterizes this perspective as an echo of Max Weber's theme of "the iron cage": "the modern inexorable order, capitalistic, legalistic and bureaucratic, which determines the lives of all individuals who are born into this mechanism, shaping their souls to fit the bars" (Berman 1982, 27, 34).

The middle Foucault showed that in the production of normal man as "subject," many people are simultaneously constructed as deviating from this norm, which itself is constituted by pinpointing the abnormal. The disciplines function as a funnel of rationality, so to speak, in Western societies.[8] At the bottom, this funnel has two exits, one for the normal and one for the abnormal: the perverse, the sick, the criminal, the madman—and, we can add endlessly: for the not clever, the "stranger," the hyperactive child, and so forth. In sum, it has a separate exit for all those people who do not live up to the standard that is imposed on them, that is, the standard of the "original" subject or "deep self." Western Enlightenment's promise of harmony and justice for each individual via the path of reason is unmasked by Foucault as producing something else in fact: the cost of this social project is the production of the abnormal, the ones who stand for dissonance, for non-reason, for what does not fit in the quest for harmony and unity. What is at stake here is compassion for those who are labeled "abnormal." This is postmodernism's "responsibility to otherness," as Stephen White pointedly phrased it (White 1996). But for the normal, there is compassion too. It is obvious that Foucault would much rather have them leading another life than the one of the "original subject" or "deep self," the soul of modernity's iron cage. These concerns clearly show that Foucault's middle works are normatively engaged all along.

From 1976 onward, however, Foucault started to articulate the normative dimension of his work by conceptualizing a specific type of ethics. When he began to study antiquity's discourses on sexuality, to complete his series on the history of the sexuality, he came across a type of ethics which from that time until his death became his main topic and source of inspiration. In the first chapter of *The Use of Pleasure,* Foucault sketches the contours of his new project. He begins by making a distinction between ethics and moral rules, or "moral codes." Today we think of the former only in terms of the latter: we think of ethics only in terms of prescriptive rules of how to behave. But in antiquity ethics to a large extent consisted of vocabularies that were intended as guides for the concrete shaping of one's own existence. These vocabularies constituted an ethical relationship of the self to itself, a so-called ethos. They enabled individuals "to question their own conduct, to watch over and give shape to it, and shape themselves as ethical subject" (1986a, 12–13). Foucault then distinguishes four aspects of the ethos: the ethical substance, the mode of subjection, the self-technologies, and the telos or goal. These are a set of analytical tools to study and chart the ethos side of moral systems in history. According to him, all moral systems in principle do have an ethos side, but the autonomy of the ethos varies: sometimes it is totally dominated by the moral code; sometimes it is more autonomous; and sometimes it can develop in relative *autonomy* (ibid., 26–32). The types of ethos that we find in antiquity belong to the latter category. Foucault characterizes them as "aesthetics of existence" and "care of the self." He also paraphrases them as "practices of freedom." A freedom to create oneself was offered through vocabularies that provided the tools and techniques to acquire an ethos (1997b). In his two books on antiquity's ethics, Foucault demonstrates how extensive these "practices of freedom" were—which is not to say they were meant for everybody: they were not aimed at women and slaves, but only at the free men who were members of the polis. He details the various techniques they had intricately worked out to style their behavior, everything from little self-tests and keeping daily inventories of their actions to letter writing and so-called *hypomnemata:* personal notebooks designed for recording insights and ideas to guide future actions.

The practices of the self are "not something invented by the individual himself. They are models that he finds in his culture and are proposed, suggested, imposed upon him by his culture, his society, and his social group" (ibid., 291). Thus, for Foucault freedom is a situated thing. It exists within the social discourses and vocabularies that give us the tools for a care of the self. The concept of freedom practices does not reinstall the "original" subject or "deep self" that was deconstructed in his earlier work. Freedom for Foucault is neither absolute nor pure but the effect of discursive self-technologies.

When asked whether we should update the ethics of ancient Greeks and Romans to confront contemporary life and circumstances, Foucault responds, "absolutely." But he then quickly adds that contact with antiquity's ethics in the present context will produce "something new." He is eager to avoid any analogy with Heidegger's thinking in terms of a *Seinsvergessenheit* (forgottenness of being): "such forms of analysis, . . . (that) claim that philosophy has from the outset been a forgetting . . . neither of these approaches is particularly interesting or useful" (ibid., 294–95). But he certainly advocates the reintroduction of the freedom practices of the care of the self: in a comparable manner to ancient ethics, we should develop an ethos ourselves, instead of submitting to conventional moral rules.

Western culture still contains freedom practices aimed at the concrete shaping of one's own existence. However, they have become disregarded since nowadays they often are appropriated by panoptic institutions and practices that transform people into disciplined subjects. The freedom practices in fact have never disappeared but need a reaffirmation of their autonomy. "What is at stake, then, is this: how can the growth of capabilities [capacités] be disconnected from the intensification of power relations?" (1997d, 317). In his article on Kant, Foucault links his concept of freedom practices to the French writer and poet Charles Baudelaire's concept of modernity. "Modern man for Baudelaire . . . is the man who tries to invent himself" (ibid., 311). Being modern implies an awareness of the contingency of reality, including the contingency of one's self-understanding. Foucault then points out that this "modern attitude" is connected with a philosophical attitude or ethos that already can be found in Kant's essay "What Is Enlightenment?" In this essay Kant shows an awareness of the contingency of the Enlightenment as a social and historical event. Here we have a modern philosophical attitude that, according to Foucault, comes down to a "work carried out by ourselves upon ourselves as free beings" and "a patient labor giving form to our impatience for liberty" (ibid., 316, 319). Foucault concludes his article by calling himself a modernist in this sense. If modernity is a certain attitude that we should practice—an awareness of self-creation—Foucault's studies on antiquity suggest that here as well we can find the modern attitude, since there was room for a relatively autonomous ethos. Thus, modernity in terms of Foucault can be found in several moments and places in history. And according to this definition, Western culture is still not sufficiently modern because freedom practices ought to get more space than they have had thus far and replace and reform the Truth regime of the disciplines.

COMMITMENT WITHOUT TRUTH

But what exactly did Foucault have in mind in arguing for freedom practices, namely, the modern attitude? Was he after a modernist and aestheticist type of self-creation, comparable to a Baudelairean dandyism? As Pierre Hadot phrases it, Foucault's final work contains "a tacit attempt to offer contemporary mankind a model of life" (Hadot 1995, 208). Paul Veyne wrote in a similar vein, "Greek ethics is quite dead and Foucault judged it as undesirable as it would be impossible to resuscitate this ethics; but he considered one of its elements, namely, the idea of a work of the self on the self, to be capable of reacquiring a contemporary meaning, in the manner of those pagan temple columns that one occasionally sees reutilized in more recent structures" (Veyne 1993, 7; quoted in Davidson 1994, 67).

But which recent structures did Foucault have in mind? To really understand his concerns, we have to situate his final works within the context of the French intellectual climate of his contemporaries. Thus, we have to take into account not only the work of Foucault's French fellow postmodernists but also the work of the French leading "classicists" Veyne and Hadot. Foucault mentions both of them in his Introduction to *The Use of Pleasure* as colleagues he regularly consulted for his studies on antiquity. He was a careful reader of Hadot's major essay on ancient spiritual exercises, originally published in 1977 and reprinted as the first chapter of his *Philosophy as a Way of Life*. Foucault refers to this article in the preface of *The Use of Pleasure* and in one of the chapters of *The Care of the Self*. His research on antiquity's ethics to a great extent is framed in terms of Hadot's approach to ancient philosophy as spiritual exercises or askesis (see Davidson 1990; 1994; 1995).

According to Hadot, "it is philosophy itself that the ancients thought of as spiritual exercise" (Hadot 1995, 126). He explains: "Exercise corresponds to the Greek terms *askesis* or *melete*. . . . For ancient philosophers, the word *askesis* designated exclusively the spiritual exercises" (ibid., 128). These exercises, such as meditation, dialogue with oneself, examination of conscience, exercises of the imagination and of the styling of daily behavior, were about transforming one's *mode of being*, not just one's thought. Ancient philosophy was a *way of life* that engaged the whole of existence.[9] Hadot considers the term "spiritual" the most appropriate one. He says,

"The expression is a bit disconcerting for the contemporary reader. In the first place, it is no longer quite fashionable these days to use the word 'spiritual.' It is nevertheless necessary to use this term, I believe, because none of the other adjectives we could use—'psychic,' 'moral,' 'ethical,' 'intellectual,' 'of thought,' 'of the soul'—covers all the aspects of the reality we want to describe. . . . the word 'thought' does not indicate clearly enough that imagination and sensibility play a very important role in these exercises" (ibid., 81–82).[10] Hadot then goes into the metaphysical dimension of the spiritual exercises. By means of them, "the individual raises himself up to the life of the objective Spirit; that is to say, he re-places himself within the perspective of the Whole" (ibid., 82). Thus, Hadot encourages us to conceive of ancient philosophy as spiritual exercise that engages the whole of existence and is at the same time a going beyond oneself because one becomes a part of the cosmic order of universal reason (ibid., 211).

As I have already noted, Foucault also focuses on the practical exercises of ancient philosophy, which he refers to as "self-technologies." He too uses the term *askesis:* "taking ascetism in a very general sense—in other words, not in the sense of a morality of renunciation but as an exercise of the self on the self by which one attempts to develop and transform oneself, and to attain to a certain mode of being" (1997b, 282). He likewise uses the term "spirituality": "By spirituality I mean—but I'm not sure that this definition can hold for very long—the subject's attainment of a certain mode of being and the transformation that the subject must carry out on itself to attain this mode of being. I believe that spirituality and philosophy were identical or nearly identical in ancient spirituality" (ibid., 294). It is clear that Foucault to a large extent was guided by Hadot's approach of ancient philosophy as spiritual exercises.

In a special chapter of *Philosophy as a Way of Life,* Hadot goes into the similarities between his own work and Foucault's studies on ancient ethics. He states that what Foucault calls "practices of the self" do indeed correspond to a movement of conversion toward the self. "One seeks to be one's own master, to possess oneself, and find one's happiness in freedom and inner independence. I concur on all these points. I do think however, that this movement of interiorization is inseparably linked to . . . a new way of being-in-the-world, which consists in becoming aware of oneself as a part of nature, and a portion of universal reason" (Hadot 1995, 211). Hadot argues that since Foucault focuses too narrowly on the culture of the self, the care of the self, and conversion toward the self, his interpretation is too aesthetic.[11] Martha Nussbaum makes a similar kind of criticism, arguing that Foucault fails to confront antiquity's fundamental commitment to universal reason (Nussbaum 1994, 5, 353).[12] Arnold Davidson concludes that Foucault's approach to ancient philosophy is too narrow since he limits the care of the self *to ethics alone.* "Foucault was not able to see the full scope of spiritual exercises, that physics (and logic) as much as ethics, aimed at self-transformation." Davidson illustrates this by pointing to a conversation between Foucault and Veyne, which the latter reported as follows: "One day when I asked Foucault: 'The care of the self, that is very nice, but what do you do with logic, what do you do with physics?' he responded: 'Oh, these are enormous excrescences!'" (Davidson 1995, 24–25).

Whether Foucault is right on this is beyond the scope of this chapter. Here I want to focus on the fact *that he concentrates on ethics from the perspective of spiritual exercises,* the concept he borrows from Hadot. Spiritual exercises are aimed at the transformation of one's whole mode of existence, including body, heart, and soul. They involve the whole of one's daily life. Foucault approaches antiquity's ethics in these terms and thus comes up with *the ethical-spiritual way of life:* ethics for him involves the whole person and the whole of daily life. The ethos according to him is "a way of being and of behavior. It was a mode of being for the subject, along with a certain way of acting, a way visible to others" (1997b, 286). The ethos certainly is a way of life, in other words, a *lived* ethics.

Foucault's awareness of the metaphysical dimension of ancient philosophy is clear from many passages in his work. Commenting on Plato's text on Alcibiades, which he considers as the first text on the care of the self, he states, "The soul cannot know itself except by looking at itself in a similar element, a mirror. Thus, it must contemplate the divine element. . . . Alcibiades will be a good politician insofar as he contemplates his soul in the divine element" (1997a, 231). Elsewhere he formulates, "This elaboration of one's own life as a personal work of art, *even if it obeyed certain collective canons* was at the centre, it seems to me, of moral experience, of the will to morality in Antiquity . . ." (1988, 49; my emphasis). However, the most important characteristic of ancient philosophy in his view is the fact that it did not impose metaphysical truths on people by means of moral codes that should be obeyed, but that to a large degree it consisted of vocabularies that offered tools to create oneself as an ethical subject—thus containing an ethics relatively autonomous in relation to the metaphysical truth. Foucault wants to focus on what he considers to be the most prominent aspect of ancient philosophy, namely, ethical self-creation. He puts forward this mode(l) of life as an alternative to the predominant subjugated ones in contemporary Western culture. But in this way he is also aiming to fill in the ethical-political gap of postmodernist thinking: the type of ethics he puts forward builds on the postmodern insight that universal truths are repressive and can be characterized as a "lived ethics without Truth."

Foucault's postmodern interpreters mostly read his later work as the continuation of his criticism of the subject and as arguing for a life beyond any identity and beyond any subject form. But they seem to miss the final Foucault's real concerns. It seems to me that, to begin with, we have to realize that his argument for an ethics as "care of the self" is in fact a plea for a certain ethical coherence of the self. Care of the self requires *work on* the self, organizing the fragments. The final Foucault's subject is not the nomadic self that goes beyond any identity; in fact, we can conclude the opposite. The theme of identity is reintroduced by Foucault in the following way: "*Self . . .* has two meanings. *Auto* means 'the same,' but it also conveys the notion of identity. The latter meaning shifts the question from 'What is this self?' to 'Departing from what ground shall I find my identity?'" (1997a, 230). Thus, the care of the self is about identity. Where shall I find it? Foucault goes on: "Alcibiades tries to find the self in a dialectical movement. When you take care of the body, you do not take care of the self. The self is not clothing, tools or possessions; it is to be found in the principle that uses these tools, a principle not of the body but of the soul. You have to worry about your soul— that is the principal activity of caring for yourself." Then Foucault immediately adds that it is not the soul-as-substance that is at stake here but the soul as activity (ibid., 230–31). A personal identity is not to be found inside. It is not a substance but exists in acting. To create a personal identity is a matter of making our ethical acts coherent by applying askesis, that is, technologies of the self. In this way we "make the self appear, which happily one never attains" (1997e, 137), since the ethos is a process of self-creation that is open to the future.

By emphasizing the creation of an ethical self, in acting, Foucault in fact argues for taking personal responsibility for a set of values, in other words, for a *commitment without Truth*—something most Foucauldian thinkers seem to have overlooked thus far. Jon Simons comes close when he interprets Foucault's concept of ethos as a plea for a balance between "unbearable lightness" (freedom beyond all limits) and "unbearable heaviness" (living within the safety of inescapable limits). We should not "be tempted to seek life without limits, a subjectivity without any identity" (Simons 1995, 124). But in the end, Simons mainly emphasizes one of these opposing poles of Foucault's concept of ethos, namely, openness to the future. Simons's last lines are, "Take care of yourself; know 'yourself' by transgressing your limits; practise liberty" (ibid., 125). Like most Foucauldians, he concentrates on transgression, the openness of the ethos, and the work of transforming ourselves in the later Foucault.

However, besides openness to the future, the ethos has another side, namely, commitment to values. The term "commitment" here is all the more adequate since for Foucault the ethical subject is always already a political subject. "Being occupied with oneself and political activities are linked" (1997a, 231); and "freedom is thus inherently political" (1997b, 286). Foucault's concept of ethos is political through and through. A concern for who you want to be in life and how you want to act is a political concern. At the same time, it is a concern about acting in the polis—making politics, in the stricter sense of the word; one cannot be a good citizen if one does not take good care of oneself, and the care of the self spells itself out in a polis. In his article on Kant, Foucault criticizes Baudelaire on the grounds that he cannot imagine that the ascetic elaboration of the self has a "place in society or in the body politic" (1997d, 312). Foucault's concern is not the aestheticist mode of life, but one of acting in the world.[13]

By way of his new concepts—"ethos," "freedom practices," and "care of the self"—the later Foucault also finalizes his critique on the modern Western subject. We can conclude that he does not reject the individual, or the subject that can speak for itself in the first person as such, but merely their total subjection to Western modernity's political rationality that transforms them into the "deep self" and the "ego." Vernant points out that in antiquity we do find some forms of biographies and autobiographies, the genres to which he himself refers in outlining his concepts of the individual and the subject respectively. However, we do not find confessions and diaries in antiquity, the genres that go with the "deep" psychological ego. "The characterization of the individual in Greek autobiography allows 'no intimacy of the self'" (Vernant 1991, 190; quoted in Davidson 1994, 74). In line with his orientation to antiquity, the later Foucault puts forward the free individual ethical-spiritual way of life as an alternative to the disciplined life of "the deep self" and the "ego" that Western modernity imposes on people in the name of Truth.

FREEDOM PRACTICES FOR ALL

I now come to my main thesis that Foucault in his later work hints to an ethical universalism. First of all he rejects a type of power he calls "domination," which he describes as follows: "When an individual or social group succeeds in blocking a field of power relations, immobilizing them and preventing any reversibility of movement by economic, political, or military means, one is faced with what may be called a state of domination. In such a state, it is certain that practices of freedom do not exist or exist only unilaterally or are extremely constrained and limited. . . . liberation is sometimes the political or historical condition for a practice of freedom" (1997b, 283). Elsewhere he explicitly advocates not only to enlarge the domain of freedom practices but to democratize these practices as well. He is concerned with the reintroduction of the ancient form of ethics but distances himself from its content, linked as it is to "a virile society, to dissymmetry, exclusion of the other. . . . All that is quite disgusting!" (1997c, 258). Instead, "couldn't everyone's life become a work of art?" (1997a, 261). Clearly, Foucault wants everyone to have access to the domain of freedom practices. Here we find him hinting to a universalist normative perspective that demands access to the ethical-spiritual life for all people—an ethical universalism that I would like to coin as "freedom practices for all," the status of which, as the previous section has clarified, is one of a commitment without Truth.

William Connolly argues that Foucault's emphasis on the contingency of any self-understanding implies an "ethical sensibility," a respect for the (self-understanding of) others. He concludes that because agonistic respect is central to Foucault's thinking on politics, this must extend even to respect for every sort of fundamentalist (Connolly 1998). I think, however, that the opposite is the case. The normative perspective of "freedom practices for all" opposes any imposition of absolute truths, in other words, any fundamentalism. It implies on the contrary that life should not be under the control of Truth regimes, be they of religious or secular origin. It also involves calling into question domination "at every level and in every form in which it exists, whether political, economic, sexual, institutional, or what have you" (1997b, 300–301). Since freedom practices encompass the whole of daily life and involve its free ethical shaping, the normative perspective of "freedom practices for all" implies the demand of social freedom for all. The concept of freedom practices not only refers to the ethical-spiritual dimension as such but implies the social level, since it focuses on the ethical-spiritual *way of life,* that is, on the free shaping of one's daily life.

Now that we have articulated Foucault's ethical universalism without Truth, that is, the normative perspective of "freedom practices for all," we can ask ourselves how this perspective relates to non-Western cultures. Do we really deal here with a cross-cultural, universal normative perspective? Foucault rejected the modern norm of "the deep self" and the "ego," but are not the subject that speaks in the first person and the individual as such, the concepts that go with his "freedom practices," Western norms as well? In what follows I will concentrate on Islamic religion and argue that it is also possible to make sense of the concept of freedom practices in this context.

To demonstrate this, I first want to turn to the final Foucault again, more specifically, to the way he uses the term "spirituality." We have seen that his use of the concept parallels the way Hadot uses the term to indicate the philosophical way of life that involves body, heart, and soul. Jeremy Carrette interestingly argues that there is a spiritual dimension in this sense in all of

Foucault's work, which he characterizes as "corporeal spirituality" and a "political spirituality of the self" (Carrette 2000). But here I want to focus on the way Foucault himself uses the term "spirituality." He states, "By spirituality I mean—but I'm not sure that this definition can hold for very long—the subject's attainment of a certain mode of being and the transformation that the subject must carry out on itself to attain this mode of being" (1997b, 294). Unlike Hadot he does not go into the metaphysical side of ancient philosophy but concentrates on ethics and more specifically on those vocabularies that offer the tools for ethical self-creation. His use of the term "spirituality" parallels his definition of ethics as a "mode of being." Carrette also emphasizes that spirituality for Foucault involves an ethical transformation of the subject. He signals in the later Foucault "an overlapping and merging of ethics, politics and spirituality as each pertains to a 'mode of self-formation' or a 'mode of being'" (Carrette 2000, 136, 138).

According to Carrette, Foucault uses the term "spirituality" in a similar fashion to refer to religion as such. By focusing on religious practices instead of religious belief, Foucault is said to want to "strategically disrupt traditional religious meaning" (ibid., 6), so as to render religion "into the more inclusive realm of our common humanity" (ibid., 154). Carrette, on the one hand, seems to approve of this because he talks about a clearer understanding of religion, which makes it possible for religion to assume "a far greater cultural significance than has otherwise been acknowledged in academic studies" (ibid., 152). But on the other hand, he speaks in terms of "the poverty of Foucault's underdeveloped 'religious question'" and of his "expunging" of any metaphysical reference from spirituality (ibid., 114, 180).

Carrette does not seem aware of the fact that for Foucault spirituality and religion are not the same. The concept "spirituality" in the later Foucault does not refer to religion as such, as Carrette presumes, but when used in the context of religion, it refers to *freedom practices within religion*. Foucault does not want to expunge anything from religion but wants to make visible its dimension of freedom practices. This is clear from the fact that Foucault started to apply his concepts in a non-Western context, namely, the 1979 Iranian revolution. In an article on this subject, Foucault talks about Shi'ism as a form of Islam that differentiates between "external obedience to a code and the deeply spiritual life."[14] In revolutionary Iran at that time, identification with the Islamic tradition combined with the renewal of spiritual experiences.[15] In the same way, when Foucault talks about a "political spirituality," it is this dimension of freedom practices opposing Truth regimes that he has in mind, and he is not suggesting that all religion is a politics of the self, as Carrette implies (Carrette 2000).[16]

We also find Foucault mentioning the presence of freedom practices within religion in another context, namely, when he speaks of certain ascetic practices within Christianity: "(I)n Christianity, with the religion of the text, the idea of God's will and the principle of obedience, morality took much more the form of a code of rules. Only certain ascetic practices of Christianity were more closely linked to the exercise of a personal liberty" (1989, 311). Elsewhere he writes, "What is interesting is that during the Renaissance you see a whole series of religious groups (whose existence is, moreover already attested to in the Middle Ages) that resist this pastoral power and claim the right to make their own statutes for themselves. According to these groups, the individual should take care of his own salvation independently of the ecclesiastical institution and of the ecclesiastical pastorate. We can see, therefore, a reappearance, up to a certain point, not of the culture of the self, which had never disappeared, but a reaffirmation of its autonomy" (1997c, 278). According to Foucault, the concept of freedom practices has a place within religious context.

FREEDOM PRACTICES IN ISLAM

In what follows I will elaborate on Foucault's first application of his concepts to Islam religion. I will concentrate on his concept of ethical freedom practices for which Hadot's notion of spiritual exercises provides an important interpretive framework. I will focus on those religious practices in Islam that cannot be reduced to obedience to a code of rules, but whose aim is the ethical-spiritual way of life. I will then articulate what a "pluralistically enlightened ethical universalism," in line with the thinking of the final Foucault, could look like.

Being a great religion with a long history, Islam contains much diversity. This, in combination with the fact that I am an outsider to this tradition, makes it impossible for me to deal adequately with the subject "freedom practices in Islam." I will only tentatively try, on a very modest scale, to elaborate what, in my view, could be the application of Foucault's concepts to Islam.

In terms of the later Foucault, we could first of all state that the moral code of Islam is always paired with an ethos side, since every moral system implies an ethical relation to itself. Second, we can detect whether the relation between the code and the ethos varies in history. The Koran explicitly states that there can be no compulsion in religion. The core teaching of Islam is loyalty only to Allah and not to any authority that interprets the Koran. Each Muslim, male or female, has his or her freedom of conscience. From this spiritual base, it is not surprising that we do find freedom practices in the history of Islam, where the ethos is relatively autonomous in relation to the moral codes and where there are traditions of spiritual exercises aimed at the ethical-spiritual *way of life*. If we want to concentrate on this ethos side in the sense of the free ethical-spiritual way of life, the best way is to focus on Islam mysticism, that is, Sufism.

This spiritual form of Islam aims at union with the divine through deep meditation and contemplation. It goes back to the eighth century, is widely known, and has been followed ever since. Until the twentieth century, Sufism was a big moving force in the Middle East at all levels of society (Lindholm 1996). Today it continues to play an important part in the lives of many Muslims at a more personal level. For example, many believers read Sufi literature and visit graves of Sufi saints for personal inspiration. Sufism offers them schemes to cultivate their spirituality often in reaction to the formalist rule following of the more conventional forms of Islam. Annemarie Schimmel points out that the main target of original Sufi criticism was philosophy, influenced by Greek thought: "The whole 'Universal Reason' is nothing in the presence of a single divine order" (Schimmel 1975, 18, 19). But when we distance ourselves from the differing transcendental goals, we see a similarity between the emphasis on ethical-spiritual exercises in both Western antiquity and Sufism.

Reynold Nicholson states that ascetic exercises in Sufism were "regarded not as having their end in future salvation or perdition but rather as a means of purifying the soul so that it may know and love God and attain to union with Him" (Nicholson 1923, 8). Although Sufism is on the verge of pantheism, "the ultimate goal is not death to self (faná) but life in God (baqá)," a state "in which the mystic, having become endowed with Divine attributes, displays the Divine truths to mankind and fulfills the Divine Law in the world" (ibid., 14). In Islamic mysticism "it is prayer that supplies the best evidence of personality—not the ritual prayer (salat) but the free prayer (du'á) and in particular the long converse with God (munáját) when the mystic speaks out of the depths of his heart" (ibid., 36). Unlike the system of Muslim theology, Sufism not only leaves room for personal religion but contains an idea of personality as well. By means of exercises, such as long prayer, the Sufi mystics sought to unite with God, without, however, vanishing but with the hope of manifesting God's virtues in their lives. "One not only manifests the Divine attributes and actions in himself to others, but maintains a personal relation to God with whom he is one and who nevertheless transcends him" (ibid., 20). Sufism thus is not only oriented to the spiritual life on the level of the mind but also to the shaping of an ethical self on a practical daily level. It is here that we find the concept of the free ethical-spiritual way of life for the individual, in other words, of freedom practices as Foucault conceptualized them.

Moreover, in Sufism these freedom practices are aimed at women as well as at men. In fact, the founder of Sufism is generally thought to be Rabi'a al-Adawiyya, a woman mystic who lived in the eighth century and whose life is the subject of many legends. Margaret Smith points out that the biographies of the Muslim saints are full of references to her and other women Sufis and their saintly lives. These women were so influential that Muslim theologians who opposed the Sufi movement denounced not only Sufi men but also these women saints and the worship given to them (Smith 1928, 3). Sufism does not consider women as women or men as men but counts only the devotional exercise of the believers. "The title of saint was bestowed upon women equally with men, and since Islam has no order of priesthood and no priest caste, there was nothing to prevent a woman from reaching the highest religious rank in the hierarchy of Muslim saints" (ibid., 2).

Leila Ahmed has pointed out that many women truly feel themselves taken seriously by Islam in the realm of spirituality. Women do not feel themselves oppressed in Islam because of the Koran's explicit statement that men and women are equal in the eyes of God and its explicit appeal to women to get educated. However, Muslim women are often oppressed by the Islamic moral codes, especially in the form of family law. Ahmed thus puts forward Islam's ambiguity with respect to the role of women (Ahmed 1992, 66).[17]

But if we approach Islam's spiritual traditions from the perspective of freedom practices, that is, from the concept of ethical-spiritual exercises aimed at the ethical way of life, then we see another tradition in Islam that is not ambiguous with respect to women. Sufi spiritualism then comes forward not as a limited otherworldly kind of experience but as a tradition in which we find the combination of the spiritual life with the free social life for women. According to Ahmed, Rabi'a *did* live a free life, retaining "full control and legal autonomy with respect to herself in that she is neither wife, nor slave, nor under any male authority."[18] Sufism also "cherished and projected as ideal the example of a woman leader, a woman in free and open interchange with other men and women . . . and cherished and projected as ideal individuals, women and men, not as embodiments of biological urges but as creatures needing resourcefully and thoughtfully to balance, as Rabi'a does, spiritual, biological and social dimensions" (Ahmed 1989, 149).

This demonstrates that feminism does not necessarily have to take the route of secular Western liberalism to defend the possibility for women to lead free lives as individuals, outside the control of men.[19] This is not to say, of course, that to be a Muslim feminist one should lead the life of a female mystic. It suggests that the concept of the free individual woman appears in Islamic tradition and history and is not a Western product per se.

A number of authors have pointed out that supposedly "Western liberal" values are in fact to be found in many forms in many non-Western cultures (see, for instance, the work of Aziz Al Azmeh for the Islamic world, and the writings of Amartya Sen for the Asian world). Here we can add that in the heart of Islam itself we find freedom practices containing the concept of the free individual life for men *and women.*

FEMINISM AND MULTICULTURALISM

I have argued in the foregoing section that in a non-Western context, namely, in the context of Islam religion, we find practices that can be considered as freedom practices and that are also aimed at both men and women. Once we recognize that freedom practices exist within the framework of religion, it makes sense to presume that freedom practices are to be found in many other cultures.[20] In this sense Carrette is right in claiming that the work of Foucault can help us in rediscovering religion "outside the superstitions, misconceptions and illusions through which 'secular' academics have so far dismissed the subject" (Carrette 2000, 152). Chinese culture and philosophy are too rich and complex to be presumed to be without a tradition of freedom practices in terms of the ethical-spiritual way of life. Joel Kupperman states, "In many Asian traditions, how it is that one becomes the kind of person who leads a good life is regarded as the central problem of ethics. . . . The formation of self is considered as an ethical problem" (Kupperman 1999, 3). Kupperman points out how the Confucian philosopher Mencius (fourth century B.C.E.), unlike Confucius, endorses personal freedom and "existential moments": we find in Mencius's work the image of men and women as "divided selves that can be led to create their own unity by means of an appropriate focus" (ibid., 108).

Inoue Tatsuo states that especially the seventeenth-century Neo-Confucian movement has a tendency to emphasize "the worth of individual self-development and the importance of an independent, critical, and creative attitude toward the Confucian texts and their authoritative exegeses." This critical tendency competes with an authoritarian tendency that originated from Confucianism, but it has been present all along and has cultivated a "critical spirit toward political power and the courage to resist persecution, which indicates the moral autonomy and independent political agency of one who has internalized moral principles as the basis of identity" (Tatsuo 1999, 51).

There is more room for women in Taoism than there is in Neo-Confucianism because Taoism emphasizes the individual spiritual life. In the history of Taoism, women have been present and active all along. They could live their own lives as, for instance, writers and teachers (see Despeux 2000). In Buddhism the individualist tendency can be found perhaps even more vividly. According to Tatsuo, in Buddhism we find a "spiritual individualism" as well. Foucault, during his visit to Japan in 1978, showed great interest in the practice of Zen Buddhism. He took lessons and afterward said to his teacher, "I'd like to ask you just one question. It's about the universality of Zen. Is it possible to separate the practice of Zen from the totality of the religion and the practice of Buddhism?" He also remarks that whereas Zen and Christian mysticism are two things you cannot compare, the *technique* of Christian spirituality and that of Zen are comparable. We can understand Foucault's question and remark against the background of his emphasis on self-techniques as a universal dimension.[21]

In the same conversation, when asked about the state of Western philosophy, Foucault alluded to a new ethical universalism: "European thought finds itself at a turning point . . . (which) is nothing other than the end of imperialism. The crisis of Western thought is identical to the end of imperialism. . . . There is no philosopher who marks out this period. For it is the end of the era of Western philosophy. Thus, if philosophy of the future exists, it must be born outside of Europe, or equally born in consequence of meetings and impacts between Europe and non-Europe" (Foucault in Carrette 1999, 113).

In my view Foucault himself can count as the philosopher who marks out our times in that he delivered the crucial elements for a new universal normative perspective. Using Greek ethics, he came up with a *new type* of universalist ethics. Foucault's ethics is new because it is focused on the ethical-spiritual way of life, which is relatively autonomous in relation to moral codes and metaphysics; and it is new since it is democratic, contrary to the elitism of Greek ethics. The universal normative perspective of "the ethical-spiritual way of life for all people" translates into a cross-cultural ethical universalism that endorses freedom practices for all people throughout cultures, including the Western ones.

A cross-cultural feminism from this perspective can be coined as a shared ethos—or commitment without Truth—that wants to endorse and foster freedom practices for all women in all cultures, including the Western ones. It comes down to the universal(izing) normative demand for access to the ethical-spiritual life for all women. This is not to say that feminism deals only with spiritual matters. The ethical-spiritual way of life is about the shaping of one's whole life. Endorsing and enlarging freedom practices therefore implies calling into question "domination at every level and in every form in which it exists, whether political, economic, social, institutional or what have you" (1997b, 300–301).

Following the lead of Leila Ahmed and Nancy Cott, when I speak of "women," I refer to those who, by virtue of being defined as women by their societies, are subjected to oppressive cultural and legal rules, who, in other words, "can't avoid being women whatever they do" (Ahmed 1992, 7; Cott 1987, 5); and I also refer to those who, if less affected by the broad discourses on gender within their societies, commit themselves by way of an ethos to this identity.

I have tried thus far to formulate a universal norm for a feminism that wants to be truly global and does not seek to impose the standards of Western secular liberalism. In my view the concept of freedom practices is to be preferred much above the triumphant liberal view of Western modernity, which denies its own permanent production of deviancy and its own "subterranean fundamentalism" (Connolly 1998, 125).

Many essays in this volume elaborate what a feminism that orients itself to freedom practices would amount to for Western societies. Paraphrasing Foucault, we can state that it amounts to an ethos that wants to disentangle modernity's growth of capabilities from the dominant, disciplining power in the field of gender.[22] It entails opposing domination of women in any field and creating alternative ways of living to that which is deemed the life of "normal woman" by the predominate culture. The normative perspective of "freedom practices for all" is a cross-cultural one and on a practical political level comes down to a cross-cultural *coalition* of all those who in their cultures oppose Truth regimes that impose moral codes. Depending on the context, it remains to be seen whether human rights can or cannot be used as a *tool* in these struggles for freedom practices.[23] A feminism that wants to be truly global is best served by an alliance with the latter concept.

NOTES

I am indebted to Mohammad Seifikar for his excellent editing of the English text. Many thanks go to my students and former students in the Department of Philosophy of the Universiteit van Amsterdam, and to my colleagues in the same department.

1. See especially Butler (1990).

2. For a similar conclusion about Western human rights activism, see Ignatieff (2001, 62).

3. I translated "les noirs" and "femmes noirs" as "blacks" and "black women," respectively, instead of "Negroes" and "Negro women," as translator H. M. Parshley does.

4. According to Habermas, we should stick to the internal relationship between modernity and rationality. See Habermas (1987, 2, 4–5). Based on his idea of mo-

dernity as an unfinished project of rationalization, he argues that norms as well as facts should become the topic of open debates, the outcomes of which can count as "rational" in the degree in which the procedure of the debate was free of coercion and only arguments were decisive. Benhabib likewise advocates such a "procedural ethics," as the necessary foundation for an ethical universalism. But she amends Habermas's model by focusing attention on the "situated self." In the dialogue we should not deal with each other as abstract persons, but as concrete others, embedded in culture and history. See Benhabib (2002).

5. For an overview of this debate, see Kelly (1995).

6. Collected in Foucault (2001).

7. Note that he refers to genres of literature and not to psychological matrixes.

8. Here I am making use of a metaphor that Harry Kunneman put forward to characterize Habermas's critique of the current direction of Western culture, namely, as a "funnel of Truth." Habermas upholds communicative rationality as the norm of Western cultures instead. See Kunneman (1986).

9. See Davidson (1995, 21). According to Hadot, who himself was influenced by French existentialism, remainders of this concept of philosophy as a way of life can be found in the works of, among others, Descartes, Spinoza, Nietzsche, Schopenhauer, Marx, and even Husserl, and last but not least in "the movement of thought inaugurated by Heidegger and carried on by existentialism [that] seeks—in theory and in principle—to engage man's freedom and action in the philosophical process" (Hadot 1995, 272).

10. Elsewhere he states that it is adequate to use the term "spiritual" because the goal of ancient philosophy's exercises is "the transformation of our vision of the world, and the metamorphosis of our being. They therefore have not merely a moral, but also an existential value. We are not just dealing here with a code of good moral conduct, but with a *way of being,* in the strongest sense of the term. In the last analysis, then, the term 'spiritual exercises' is the best one, because it leaves no doubt that we are dealing with exercises which engage the totality of the spirit" (Hadot 1995, 127).

11. Hadot discusses, along with other aspects of Foucault's work, his interpretation of Seneca's "Disce gaudere, learn how to feel joy." Seneca holds that gladness will never fail you if you "look toward the true good, and rejoice only in that which comes from your own store [de tuo]. But what do I mean by 'your own store'? I mean your very self and the best part of you." Foucault interpreted Seneca as pleading for a cultivation of the self, but Foucault missed the phrase "the best part of you." "Seneca does not want us to find joy in the self *per se,* but in that 'best part of the self' that Seneca identifies with perfect reason and ultimately with divine reason." Seneca thus finds his joy by transcending Seneca. It is the *sage* in himself that he is after (Davidson 1994, 68, 75).

12. In a similar vein, Maria Antonaccio criticizes Foucault for focusing too much on "the practice of self-formation over its content, the manner of self-cultivation over its substance" and for conceiving askesis primarily as an "aesthetics" or "stylistics" of existence (Antonaccio 1998, 79).

13. Foucault, in my view, can be characterized as a postexistentialist, or neoexistentialist, reconciling individual freedom with a radical historical approach, and presenting a new type of political commitment. See Vintges (2003). Part of my argument can be found in Vintges (2001).

14. "Ce qui est la simple obéissance externe au code et ce qui est la vie spirituelle profonde" (Foucault 2001, 749).

15. Foucault also states: "Il y avait autre chose que la volonté d'obéir plus fidèlement à la loi, il y avait la volonté de renouveler leur existence tout entière en renouant avec une expérience spirituelle qu'ils pensent trouver au cœur même de l'Islam chiite" (Foucault 2001, 749).

16. In the last lines of his "What are the Iranians dreaming of?" he puts forward "the possibility of which we others have forgotten since the Renaissance and the grand crises of Christianity: a *political spirituality*. I can already hear some Frenchmen laughing, but I know they are wrong" (Foucault 2001, 694; translated in Leezenberg 1999). Foucault responds to the violence that marked the postrevolutionary power struggle in Iran by putting forward, in journalistic articles, published in April and May 1979, the rights of the individual against the "bloodthirsty government of a fundamentalist clergy" (Foucault 2001, 793). Michiel Leezenberg questions "on what *philosophical basis* Foucault can make such an appeal, given his earlier attempts to cast doubt on the universalist aspirations of reason since the Enlightenment" (Leezenberg 1999, 78). Foucault articulated this philosophical basis in the years to come, elaborating his universalist ethics of freedom practices for all.

17. "The unmistakable presence of an ethical egalitarianism explains why Muslim women frequently insist, often inexplicable to non-Muslims, that Islam is not sexist. They hear and read in its sacred text, justly and legitimately a different message from that heard by the makers and enforcers of orthodox, androcentric Islam" (Ahmed 1992, 66).

18. For a discussion of the free ethical-spiritual life of a religious woman in Western culture, see Jeannette Bloem's essay in this volume on the life and work of Anna Maria van Schurman.

19. In an article on the internet, Leonard Hudson argues in a similar vein. See Hudson (1996).

20. Gyekey (1995) argues that traditional African thought encompasses a philosophy, although not a written one, that stands in need of elaboration, clarification, and interpretation. "African philosophical thought is expressed both in the oral literature and actions of the people. Thus, a great deal of philosophical material is embedded in the proverbs, myths and folktales, folk songs, rituals, beliefs, customs, and traditions of the people, in their art symbols and in their sociopolitical institutions and practices" (Gyekey 1995, 13). In succeeding chapters, Gyekey (1995) deals with the concept of the person, free will and responsibility, morality, ethics, and character.

21. "Techniques of the self, I believe, can be found in all cultures in different forms" (Foucault 1997c, 277). This is in line with his idea that all moral systems in

principle do have an ethos side. For a relative autonomous ethos self-techniques have to offer the tools for ethical self-creation, i.e., the modern attitude.

22. See Dianna Taylor's essay in this volume.

23. For instance, the prohibition of child labor can have disastrous effects on children and their families. Offering meals in schools has turned out to be far more effective, because it is then in the parents' interest to send their children to school. Ignatieff (2001) argues for a "thin," minimalist concept of human rights, which can be endorsed by many moral comprehensive views. But his phrasing of this concept in terms of "the negative freedom of private agency" hardly seems helpful. Ignatieff considers human rights as implying the Western norm of liberal individualism. However, it is about time that individual rights are conceived much more "thickly" than they have been considered thus far and that the concepts of individual rights and democracy are enriched so as to include voices other than the Western ones. See Tatsuo (1999, 59).

WORKS CITED

Ahmed, Leila. 1989. "Feminism and Cross-Cultural Inquiry: The Terms of the Discourse in Islam." In *Coming to Terms*. Edited by E. Weed. New York: Routledge.

———. 1992. *Women and Gender in Islam*. New Haven: Yale University Press.

Al Azmeh, Aziz. 1993. *Islams and Modernities*. London: Verso.

Antonaccio, Maria. 1998. "Contemporary Forms of Askesis and the Return of Spiritual Exercises." *The Annual of the Society of Christian Ethics*. 69–92. Baltimore: Georgetown University Press.

Beauvoir, Simone de. 1974. *The Second Sex*. Translated by H. M. Parshley. Harmondsworth: Penguin.

Benhabib, Seyla. 2002. *The Claims of Culture*. Princeton: Princeton University Press.

Berman, Marshall. 1982. *All That Is Solid Melts into Air*. New York: Simon and Schuster.

Butler, Judith. 1990. *Gender Trouble*. New York: Routledge.

Carrette, Jeremy. 1999. *Religion and Culture by Michel Foucault*. Manchester: Manchester University Press.

———. 2000. *Foucault and Religion: Spiritual Corporality and Political Spirituality*. London: Routledge.

Connolly, William. 1998. "Beyond Good and Evil: The Ethical Sensibility of Michel Foucault." In *The Later Foucault: Politics and Philosophy*. Edited by J. Moss. London: Sage.

Cott, Nancy. 1987. *The Grounding of Modern Feminism*. New Haven: Yale University Press.

Davidson, Arnold. 1990. "Spiritual Exercises and Ancient Philosophy: An Introduction to Pierre Hadot." *Critical Inquiry* 16 (Spring): 475–82.

———. 1994. "Ethics as Ascetics: Foucault, the History of Ethics, and Ancient Thought." In *Foucault and the Writing Of History*. Edited by J. Goldstein. 63–80. Oxford: Blackwell.

————. 1995. "Introduction: Pierre Hadot and the Spiritual Phenomenon of Ancient Philosophy." In *Philosophy as a Way of Life.* By Pierre Hadot. Oxford: Blackwell.

Despeux, Catherine. 2000. "Women in Daoism." In *Daoism Handbook.* Edited by
L. Kohn. Leiden: Brill.

Foucault, Michel. 1979. *Discipline and Punish.* New York/Toronto: Vintage Books.

————. 1981. *The History of Sexuality.* Volume 1. Harmondsworth: Pelican.

————. 1986a. *The Use of Pleasure.* Harmondsworth: Penguin.

————. 1986b. *The Care of the Self.* Harmondsworth: Penguin.

————. 1988. "An Aesthetics of Existence." In *Politics, Philosophy, Culture: Interviews and Other Writings, 1977–1984.* Edited by Lawrence D. Kritzman. New York:
Routledge.

————. 1997a. "Technologies of the Self." In *Ethics: Subjectivity and Truth.* Edited
by Paul Rabinow. 223–51. New York: New Press.

————. 1997b. "The Ethics of the Concern for Self as Practice of Freedom." In
Ethics: Subjectivity and Truth. Edited by Paul Rabinow. 281–301. New York: New
Press.

————. 1997c. "On the Genealogy of Ethics: An Overview of Work in Progress."
In *Ethics: Subjectivity and Truth.* Edited by Paul Rabinow. 253–80. New York: New
Press.

————. 1997d. "What Is Enlightenment?" In *Ethics: Subjectivity and Truth.* Edited
by Paul Rabinow. 303–19. New York: New Press.

————. 1997e. "Sex, Power, and the Politics of Identity." In *Ethics: Subjectivity and
Truth.* Edited by Paul Rabinow. 163–73. New York: New Press.

————. 2001. *Dits et Ecrits. 1954–1988.* Paris: Gallimard.

Fraser, Nancy. 1994. "Michel Foucault: 'A Young Conservative?'" In *Critique and
Power: Recasting the Foucault/Habermas Debate.* Edited by M. Kelly. Cambridge:
MIT Press.

Gyekey, Kwame. 1995. *An Essay on African Philosophical Thought.* Cambridge: Cambridge University Press.

Habermas, Jürgen. 1987. *The Philosophical Discourse on Modernity.* Cambridge:
Polity Press in association with Basil Blackwell.

Hadot, Pierre. 1995. *Philosophy as a Way of Life: Spiritual Exercises from Socrates to
Foucault.* Edited and with an introduction by Arnold I. Davidson. Oxford:
Blackwell.

Hudson, Leonard. 1996. "Islamic Mysticism and Gender Identity." <http://www.ilstu
.edu/mtavakol/hudson.html>

Ignatieff, Michael. 2001. *Human Rights as Politics and Idolatry.* Princeton: Princeton University Press.

Kelly, Michael. 1995. *Critique and Power.* Cambridge: MIT Press.

Kunneman, Harry. 1986. *De waarheidstrechter.* Meppel: Boom.

Kupperman, Joel. 1999. *Learning from Asian Philosophy.* New York: Oxford University Press.

Leezenberg, Michiel. 1999. "Power and Political Spirituality: Michel Foucault on the Islamic Revolution in Iran." In *Cultural History after Foucault*. Edited by J. Neubauer. Hawthorne, N.Y.: Aldine De Gruyter.

Lindholm, Charles. 1996. *The Islamic Middle East*. Oxford: Blackwell.

McNay, Lois. 1992. *Foucault and Feminism: Power, Gender, and the Self*. Cambridge: Polity Press.

———. 1994. *Foucault: A Critical Introduction*. Cambridge: Polity Press.

Nicholson, Reynold. 1923. *The Idea of Personality in Sufism*. Cambridge: Cambridge University Press.

Nussbaum, Martha. 1994. *The Therapy of Desire: Theory and Practice in Hellenistic Ethics*. Princeton: Princeton University Press.

Okin, Suzan Moller. 1998. "Feminism, Women's Human Rights, and Cultural Differences." *Hypatia* 13, no. 2: 32–52.

———. 1999. *Is Multiculturalism Bad for Women?* Princeton: Princeton University Press.

Rabinow, Paul, ed. 1997. *Ethics: Subjectivity and Truth. Essential Works of Foucault 1954–1984*. Volume 1. New York: New Press.

Schimmel, Annemarie. 1975. *Mystical Dimensions of Islam*. Chapel Hill: University of North Carolina Press.

Simons, Jon. 1995. *Foucault and the Political*. London: Routledge.

Smith, Margaret. 1928. *Rabi'a the Mystic and Her Fellow-Saints in Islam*. Cambridge: Cambridge University Press.

Tatsuo, Inoue. 1999. "Liberal Democracy and Asian Orientalism." In *The East Asian Challenge for Human Rights*. Edited by J. Bauer and D. Bell. Cambridge: Cambridge University Press.

Vernant, Jean Pierre. 1991. *Mortals and Immortals: Collected Essays*. Edited by Froma I. Zeitlin. Princeton: Princeton University Press.

Veyne, Paul. 1993. "The Final Foucault and His Ethics." *Critical Inquiry* 20, no. 1.

Vintges, Karen. 2001. "'Must We Burn Foucault?' Ethics as Art of Living: Simone de Beauvoir and Michel Foucault." *Continental Philosophy Review* 34, no. 2: 165–81.

———. 2003. *De terugkeer van het engagement* [The Return of Commitment]. Amsterdam: Boom.

White, Stephen. 1996. *Political Theory and Postmodernism*. Cambridge: Cambridge University Press.

❧ CONTRIBUTORS

AMY ALLEN is an assistant professor of philosophy and women's and gender studies at Dartmouth College. She is the author of *The Power of Feminist Theory: Domination, Resistance, Solidarity* and is currently working on a book entitled *The Politics of Ourselves: Power, Autonomy, and Gender in Contemporary Critical Theory*.

STEPHEN M. BARBER is an associate professor of English at the University of Rhode Island. He is the coeditor of *Regarding Sedgwick: Essays on Queer Culture and Critical Theory* and is currently working on a book to be entitled *Virginia Woolf, Here and Now: Encounters with Gilles Deleuze and Michel Foucault*, which concerns the ethical projects that each of these thinkers evolved during the final decade of their work as they investigated previously unproblematized forms of power.

JEANNETTE BLOEM has a master's degree in philosophy from the University of Amsterdam. She currently lives in Amsterdam where she works as a designer.

JUDITH BUTLER is Maxine Elliot Professor in the Departments of Rhetoric and Comparative Literature at the University of California, Berkeley. Her works include *Antigone's Claim: Kinship between Life and Death; Hegemony, Contingency, Universality* (with Ernesto Laclau and Slavoj Zizek); *Subjects of Desire: Hegelian Reflections in Twentieth-Century France; Gender Trouble: Feminism and the Subversion of Identity;* and numerous articles on philosophy and feminist and queer theory.

KATHY E. FERGUSON teaches political science and women's studies and also chairs the women's studies program at the University of Hawai'i at Manoa. She is currently writing a book on Emma Goldman as a political thinker. She and Phyllis Turnbull wrote *Oh, Say, Can You See? The Semiotics of the Military in Hawai'i* and are currently writing articles about global militarism.

SUSAN HEKMAN is a professor of political science and the director of graduate humanities at the University of Texas at Arlington. Her most recent books are *The Future of Differences: Truth and Method in Feminist Theory* and *Private Selves, Public Identities: Toward a Theory of Identity Politics.*

MARGARET A. MCLAREN teaches philosophy and women's studies at Rollins College. She is the author of *Feminism, Foucault, and Embodied Subjectivity,* as well as articles on Foucault and feminism and on feminist ethics. Her current research addresses the intersection of gender, cultural tradition, and human rights.

LADELLE MCWHORTER is a professor of philosophy and women's studies at the University of Richmond, Virginia. She is the author of *Bodies and Pleasures: Foucault and the Politics of Sexual Normalization* and is currently working on a book on Foucault and racism.

HELEN O'GRADY completed her Ph.D. in 2001 at Flinders University of South Australia. While writing her doctorate, she also worked as a counselor in the women's health sector. In 2002–3, she undertook a postdoctoral fellowship at Leeds University and completed a manuscript on women's practices of self-surveillance, narrative therapy, and Foucauldian thought.

SYLVIA PRITSCH, M.A. in German language and literature/cultural anthropology, has published in the fields of feminist theory, cultural studies, and text theory. She wrote her dissertation on feminist self-representations as cultural critique at the University of Bremen/Germany and is currently teaching at the University of Bremen and the International Women's University in Hannover.

JANA SAWICKI, a professor of philosophy and women's studies at Williams College, is the author of *Disciplining Foucault: Feminism, Power, and the Body* and articles on Foucault and feminism. She is currently working on a manuscript on Foucault and queer theory that explores the use of Foucault by queer theorists, his relationship to psychoanalytic theory, and understandings of "sexual freedom" that underpin radical theories of sexuality.

DIANNA TAYLOR is an assistant professor of philosophy at John Carroll University. Her research focuses on twentieth-century French and German philosophy. She has written articles on Michel Foucault and Hannah Arendt and is currently completing an article on Arendt and responsibility and working on a book about Kant's Foucauldian legacy.

MARIANA VALVERDE teaches theory at the Centre of Criminology, University of Toronto. Her current research interest is the deployment of low-level administrative and lay knowledges of vice, sex, and race in various legal complexes. She won the Law and Society Association's Herbert Jacob Book Prize in 2000 for her book *Diseases of the Will: Alcohol and the Dilemmas of Freedom*. Her most recent book is *Law's Dream of a Common Knowledge*.

KAREN VINTGES is a senior lecturer in political and social philosophy in the Department of Philosophy at the University of Amsterdam. She has published *Philosophy as Passion: The Thinking of Simone de Beauvoir* and articles on Beauvoir, feminism, and the work of Foucault.

❦ INDEX

Adorno, Theodor, 258
Ahmed, Leila, 291, 294, 296n17
Alcibiades, 29, 30, 32, 284
Alcoff, Linda, 230n1, 231n2
Allen, Amy, 231n10, 231n14, 232
Althusser, Louis, 120, 125, 127, 130, 137, 139n6
Antigone, 89n7
Antonaccio, Maria, 295n12, 297
Arendt, Hannah, 1, 11, 255n22, 258, 259, 260, 262, 265, 271, 272n2, 273
Aristotle, 24, 78, 88n4
Augustine, 15, 18
Azmeh, Aziz al, 292

Baar, Mirjam de, 15, 16, 17, 18, 19, 22, 25n1, 25n7, 25n13, 26, 26n14
Badinter, Elizabeth, 156
Bakhtin, Mikhail, 88n2
Barry, Kathleen, 151, 155, 159n7, 161
Bartky, Sandra Lee, 94, 95, 96, 97, 114, 253n2
Bataille, Georges, 80
Baudelaire, Charles, 103, 281, 282, 286
Baudrillard, Jean, 71, 88n3, 89
Beauvoir, Simone de, 135, 146, 149, 159n6, 161, 258, 276, 297, 299
Benhabib, Seyla, 69, 88n1, 89, 253n4, 254n16, 277, 295n4, 297
Benjamin, Walter, 74, 89n5
Berkman, Alexander, 28, 30, 32, 33–40
Berman, Marshall, 279, 297
Bernauer, James, 43, 57, 63
Birch, Una, 26, 26n19
Blanchot, Maurice, 80
Bordo, Susan, 214
Bourignon, Antoinette, 15, 25n1
Braidotti, Rosi, 230n1, 231n2, 232

Brown, Peter, 78, 159n1
Brown, Wendy, 197, 212
Butler, Judith, 69, 70, 89, 100, 102, 114, 126, 160n14, 161, 197, 209, 211, 212, 214, 273n6, 294n1, 297

Camus, Albert, 1, 11, 258
Canguilhem, George, 248, 255
Carrette, Jeremy, 25n12, 26, 26n18, 287, 288, 292, 293, 297
Cartesian. *See* Descartes, René
Cassian, John, 36
Castel, Robert, 89, 89n6
Cavendish, Margaret, 15
Chodorow, Nancy, 240, 241, 253nn8–9, 254n11, 256
Cixous, Hélène, 62n5, 63
Connolly, William, 35, 40, 287, 294, 297
Cook, Deborah, 232, 232n18
Cornell, Drucilla, 69, 89
Cott, Nancy, 199, 213, 294, 297

Daly, Mary, 151, 159n7, 161
Deleuze, Gilles, 44, 46, 47, 48, 52, 56, 57, 58, 59, 60, 61n3, 63, 71, 72, 78, 132, 133, 141, 187, 275
Derrida, Jacques, 69, 70, 73, 74, 79, 88n2, 88n4, 89, 89n5, 275
Descartes, René, 25n5, 147, 295n9
Deveaux, Monique, 270, 273
Dews, Peter, 232, 232n19
Doeuff, Michèle le, 139n9
Donzelot, Jacques, 202, 213
Dreyfus, Hubert, 30, 123, 141, 231nn8–9, 231n13

Eckstein, Emmy, 32
Epictetus, 144

Epicurus, 30, 71
Eribon, Didier, 47, 61n3, 63

Flynn, Thomas, 62n10, 63
Fraser, Nancy, 69, 89, 230n1, 231nn2–3, 233, 270, 274, 278, 298
Freud, Sigmund, 163, 164, 169, 170, 174, 181

Gadamer, Hans-Georg, 104
Galen, 71, 78, 85, 86
Gilligan, Carol, 240, 241, 253nn8–9, 254n11, 256
Goldman, Emma, 28–40
Gordon, Linda, 88n1, 90
Grahn, Judy, 149, 150, 151, 155, 158, 161
Greenblatt, Stephen, 15, 18, 27
Griffin, Susan, 147
Grimshaw, Jean, 95, 115, 232n19, 233, 238, 250, 253nn5–6, 256, 266, 274
Guattari, Félix, 46, 47, 52, 63
Gyekey, Kwame, 296n20, 298

Habermas, Jürgen, 81, 231n3, 234, 241, 242, 254n12, 256, 257, 277, 278, 294–95n4, 295n8, 298
Hadot, Pierre, 78, 90, 143, 144, 159n1, 161, 282, 283, 284, 287, 289, 295nn9–11, 297, 298
Halperin, David, 63, 170, 172, 173, 174, 175, 176, 177, 178, 179, 180n11, 182, 273n7
Hamlet, 89n5
Haraway, Donna, 118, 119, 120, 125, 128, 129, 130, 131, 133, 134, 135, 136, 137, 138, 139, 140nn10–12, 140n16, 141
Hartsock, Nancy, 220, 230n1, 231n3, 234, 269, 270, 274
Hebel, Kirsten, 122, 139n1, 141
Hegel, Georg Wilhelm Friedrich, 87, 191, 194n5
Heidegger, Martin, 79, 281
Hekman, Susan, 119, 123, 141
hooks, bell, 103, 104, 113nn11–12, 115
Horkheimer, Max, 258
Hoy, David, 114n17, 115
Huizinga, Johan, 104
Husserl, Edmund, 295n9

Ibsen, Henri, 221
Ignatieff, Michael, 294n2, 297, 298

Jaggar, Alison, 231n4, 231n10, 234, 253n2
James, Henry, 81, 90
James, William, 77

Kant, Immanuel, 121, 133, 169, 218, 281, 286
Kaplan, Morris, 178, 180n9, 181n13, 182
Klee, Paul, 73, 74, 89n5
Kofman, Sarah, 275
Kristeva, Julia, 140n17, 142, 275
Kymlicka, Will, 208, 213

Lacan, Jacques, 68, 69, 191, 139n7, 142
Laqueur, Thomas, 157
Lauretis, Teresa de, 118, 119, 120, 125, 126, 127, 128, 130, 131, 132, 133, 135, 136, 137, 138, 139n6, 139n8, 142
Leavis, Queenie, 41
Lerner, Gerda, 199, 213
Lloyd, Moya, 114n16, 115
Luban, David, 261, 274
Lugones, Maria, 104, 113n12, 114n19, 115
Lyotard, Jan-Francois, 71, 140n18, 275

MacKinnon, Catharine, 106, 112n10, 116, 254n11, 256
Marcuse, Herbert, 164, 180n1, 182
Marx, Karl, 81, 164, 177, 200, 202, 295n9
McNay, Lois, 92, 93, 99, 101, 102, 103, 105, 107, 110, 112n5, 114n16, 116, 119, 120, 123, 137, 139n5, 142, 231n2, 237, 253n4, 257, 266, 274, 278, 299
McWhorter, Ladelle, 160n11, 214, 231n8, 234, 238, 239, 244, 254n19, 255, 257, 266, 274
Mead, George Herbert, 241, 256
Mencius, 292
Miller, James, 171, 172, 182
Moi, Toril, 214, 230n1, 234
Montaigne, Michel, 88n4

Nehamas, Alexander, 78, 81, 90
Nettlau, Max, 34
Nicocles, 244
Nicolson, Nigel, 53, 63, 64
Nietzsche, Friedrich, 35, 44, 56, 59, 73, 77, 78, 80, 88, 90, 160n12, 167, 168, 231n7, 295n9
Nietzschean. See Nietzsche, Friedrich
Nussbaum, Martha, 70, 90, 283, 299

Okin, Suzan Moller, 276, 277, 299

Pateman, Carole, 208, 213
Plato, 24, 29, 30, 32, 39n2, 78, 90, 163, 266, 284
Plutarchus, 84, 85, 86, 144, 148
Probyn, Elspeth, 118, 119, 120, 125, 127, 128, 130, 131, 132, 133, 135, 137, 138, 139n9, 142

Rabi'a al-Adawiyya, 291, 299
Rabinow, Paul, 123, 141, 231nn8–9, 231n13
Rajchman, John, 165, 180n4, 182
Rawls, John, 208
Rorty, Richard, 231n3, 234
Rose, Nikolas, 76, 90
Rousseau, Jean-Jacques, 70, 71, 72, 73
Roussel, Raymond, 166, 181

Sartre, Jean-Paul, 2, 258
Sawicki, Jana, 93, 94, 107, 112n5, 116, 214,
    231n6, 234, 264, 273n9
Schimmel, Annemarie, 290, 299
Schopenhauer, Arthur, 295n9
Schurman, Anna Maria van, 15–27,
    296n18
Scott, Evelyn, 34
Scott, Joan, 88n1, 90
Sedgwick, Eve Kosofsky, 59, 64
Sen, Armartya, 292
Seneca, 71, 78, 144, 295n11
Serenus, 71
Simons, Jon, 285, 299
Smith, Margaret, 291, 299

Smyth, Ethel, 58
Socrates, 28, 29, 30, 31, 32
Soper, Kate, 237, 257
Spinoza, 20, 25n9, 56, 59, 190, 295n9
Spivak, Gayatri, 54, 62n8, 64

Taylor, Charles, 81, 207, 213, 231n3, 234
Taylor, Dianna, 25, 27, 111, 297
Tronto, Joan, 254n11, 257
Turner, Kay, 150, 151, 162

Vernant, Jean Pierre, 279, 286, 299
Veyne, Paul, 78, 282, 284, 299
Vintges, Karen, 25n11, 26n18, 114n16, 269,
    271, 273nn10–11
Voetius, Gisbertus, 17, 22, 25n5

Weber, Max, 26n14, 82
West, Cornell, 210, 213
White, Stephen, 279, 299
Winfrey, Oprah, 71
Wolf, Naomi, 113n14, 117
Wollstonecraft, Mary, 205
Woolf, Virginia, 41–64

The University of Illinois Press
is a founding member of the
Association of American University Presses.

———————————————————————

Composed in 10.5/13 Adobe Minion
with Minion & Woodtype Ornaments display
by Type One, LLC
for the University of Illinois Press
Designed by Dennis Roberts
Manufactured by Thomson-Shore, Inc.

University of Illinois Press
1325 South Oak Street
Champaign, IL 61820-6903
www.press.uillinois.edu